CW00923226

Slaying Dragons II

The Rise of the Occult

What Exorcists and Former Occultists Want You to Know

by
Charles D. Fraune

The Rise of the Occult

Charles D. Fraune

2023

www.SlayingDragonsPress.com
2023

Dedication

To Our Lady of Sorrows,
and to the glorious and triumphant Archangel,
Saint Michael.

For this purpose, the Son of God appeared, that He might destroy the works of the devil.

1 John 3:8

St. Michael the Archangel,
defend us in battle.
Be our protection
against the wickedness and snares of the devil.
May God rebuke him, we humbly pray,
and do thou,
O Prince of the heavenly hosts,
by the power of God,
cast into hell Satan, and all the evil spirits,
who prowl about the world
seeking the ruin of souls.
Amen.

Table of Contents

The Rise of the Occult

In Gratitude

A special note of thanks is given to those who willingly shared their stories for the purpose of bringing to light the active dangers of the occult as it is in our world today. Please remember them in your prayers as you read this work. A special note of thanks also goes to those priests and exorcists and laymen who shared their insights and experiences for the sake of furthering our understanding of how the devil is working within the occult and the ways in which God can liberate souls from the devil's grasp. Please offer a prayer for their continued fidelity to Our Lord. A final thanks goes to all of those who helped review this book and who offered their insights and suggestions. May God reward them for their generosity.

Author's Note

In *The Rise of the Occult*, the testimonies of those who have experienced the evil of the occult often include experiences of curses. Curses come from rituals intended to cause harm to another by some form of spiritual agency which, in reality, can only be demonic. Though these experiences, for many occultists and many exorcists, appear quite real, the Church has no teaching that curses have an actual power over man. Though the devil can indeed act against man, he has no power to infuse rites and rituals with the ability to communicate evil effects. The rituals of the occult are tools of deception by which he ensnares gullible souls into occult practice and by which he strikes fear in those ignorant of the power of Christ. Further, the reality of grace is that upon which Christians must principally focus. In Christ, we are "new creatures"[1] who have been made "partakers" of Christ's divine nature.[2] Bound to Christ, we share in the triumphant victory He achieved through His Cross, in which he "despoiled the principalities and powers,"[3] that is, the fallen angels. As such, curses are not something that faithful Christians should fear. Any evil that Satan is capable of doing is only that which is permitted within God's Providence and extraordinary examples, such as curses, are rare and impact only those who rebel against God and place themselves outside His protection. Christianity is the divine shelter in which pagans have long found the sought-after freedom from crippling fear and debilitating superstition. As long as Christians stay protected by the whole armor of God,[4] they will not only avoid the strikes of the fiery serpents who prowl about this world,[5] but they will be made fearsome in the battle. As St. John Chrysostom said, "The Eucharist is a fire which inflames us, that, like lions breathing fire, we may retire from the altar being made terrible to the devil."[6]

---

[1] 2 Cor 5:17
[2] 2 Peter 1:4
[3] Col 2:15
[4] Eph 6:11
[5] Num 21:6
[6] St. Alphonsus Liguori, *Preparation for Death.* Ascetical Works, Vol. I, Grimm Ed., (Brooklyn: Redemptorist Fathers, 1926), 358.

Preface

When I first took the leap of faith to start the *Slaying Dragons Apostolate* as a full-time work, leaving a long-held teaching position, and trusting in an inspiration that God would provide for the success of what the world would label as an unsustainable path, I was not sure what would be the focus of the next book. However, as Divine Providence works, the seeds were already planted for the emergence of a book focused on the experiences of real people who entered the occult and escaped, as well as exorcists who have helped people like them.

As the full-time work continued, I found myself focusing my research on the issue of the occult, a *dark world* for sure, often labeled just that by exorcists. Delving into the beliefs of this dark world is not the most invigorating endeavor! Nevertheless, God willing, the fruit of the research which is contained in this book makes it worth the effort.

As Divine Providence would have it, my research, and the connections that were made in the process of writing and publicizing *Slaying Dragons*, led me into the acquaintance of many who were converts from the occult. Many of these were fans of *Slaying Dragons*, and it was this connection that brought us together. Parish priests and exorcists introduced me to many other former occultists and vouched for their experiences.

From there, my research "mushroomed," growing exponentially. My database, which at first boasted the testimonies of just a few former occultists, quickly grew to forty people, including sixteen former occultists, eight exorcists, seven parish priests, six families, and a host of anecdotes shared by real Catholics who have had run-ins with the occult in recent years. With this impressive number of testimonies, my understanding of just how ubiquitous the occult truly is began to grow to an uncomfortable degree.

Following the trails of breadcrumbs that the occult has left throughout the culture led me down a number of "rabbit holes," dark and often obscure, but often far too real, examples of how the occult is pulling far too many strings in the world and, yes, even in the Church. Keeping my original focus on the stories of former occultists and exorcists, I had to shut down many intellectual pursuits which, otherwise, would simply have pushed the completion of this project indefinitely into the future.

The current happenings in the world did not cease to suggest something else, nearly every day, which merited a place in this book. I had to "shut the gates" even to new testimonies from former occultists, lest the book become too large even for a multi-volume set, which would, also, likely never be completed. As a result, and at the risk of being entirely unoriginal, "there is so much more to say, but I haven't the time or space."

Presenting on the reality of the occult is like reporting from the trenches of spiritual warfare. So many people in the world are hiding in the bunkers, spiritually weak or confused, unable to lift their heads to acknowledge the truth of the war that rages around them, some for fear and some for ignorance. This, though, is not to their fault – we are all living in this age of confusion and error. However, there is a battle plan we can follow, but we must first acknowledge the battle *as it really is.*[1]

The Stories of Exorcists and Former Occultists

This book relies upon the perspectives of both former occultists and of experienced exorcists in order to develop an understanding of the spiritual situation in which we find ourselves. Among these former occultists are parishioners of exorcists, friends of priests, RCIA candidates, and those recommended to me by pastors. Their stories are real and provide critical insights into the nature of this pseudo-religion which is seducing a nation and a world greatly deprived of God and His Truth. Some people reading this book might be tempted to dismiss the importance of their accounts, but their experiences are not only authentic and in harmony with each other but are also backed up by the teachings of exorcists, of pastors,

---

[1] In addition to *Slaying Dragons* and this book, *Slaying Dragons – Prepare for Battle* is designed to lead individuals into a deeper analysis of their own spiritual warfare.

of Catholic theology, as well as by the experiences of the faithful who have suffered the effects of the occult.

The exorcists I have interviewed each typically have a decade or more of experience in this ministry. They were more than happy to share their insights when they heard about this project. The other priests I interviewed were experienced pastors who have dealt with the occult in the course of their ministries. Some have seen it extensively while others have witnessed it popping up in their parishes just in the last few years.

All of the former occultists to whom I was able to speak said they appreciated the opportunity to share what they know. Many of them consider this to be a form of atonement for the many grievous sins they committed in the occult. For them, preventing just one person from going down this path is worth it. Many of them also said they feel very much alone as a result of having seen the reality of the occult. They have no one to talk to about it because people think they are crazy. It is as if no one believes all this is happening. Even many priests don't understand it. As one former occultist told me, if priests don't take them seriously, how could anyone else in the Church? People with a past in the occult have a different perspective after leaving it, and those without that background often don't understand them.

For a few of them, I was the first person they have had the opportunity to speak to about it, and they indicated that the mere exercise of thinking over it and answering my many questions helped them better process their experiences. It was often a cathartic event for them. Leaving the occult caused many of them to lose all their friends, often bitterly. Some people I spoke to even said they feared retaliation from the groups they used to belong to and hesitated to go into all the details.

While writing this book, I decided to make all contributors anonymous, giving each of them a pseudonym. This was done for what should be obvious reasons. When I was reaching out to priests I knew, asking if they knew anyone who would be willing to share their stories, several priests said they did but that the individuals were not comfortable speaking about it. As one exorcist said, it is such a sensitive issue for some people that they simply cannot talk about it. For others, however, the opportunity is a gift from God. For former occultists and exorcists and parish priests alike, the anonymity provides them the opportunity to speak more candidly about their perspectives, without the fear of reprisals from occultic groups or from members of the Church hierarchy. As the reader will see, the occult is so widespread that it has even infiltrated sections of the hierarchy to a certain, and disturbing, degree. At the end of this Introduction, there will be a short description of each contributor, to which the reader can refer as a reminder when their perspectives are shared in the book.

When I first spoke to Adelaide over Zoom, and I mentioned that I was thankful that she was willing to tell her story, she said, "I don't *want* to; it's making me kinda nauseous, but it's good atonement." By the end of our conversation, she was very much at peace with having shared it with me, and she made it a point to state that.

Philomena said her husband did not know about her background in the occult when they first got married. A sense of shame kept her from telling him. Now, she realized it was very important to speak up about it. Everyone needs to be taught about these issues when they are younger, she said. "Generations have been duped! They are taught that everything is 'happy-go-lucky, hunky-dory.' They have no understanding that there is spiritual warfare."

When I spoke to John, he said it was the first time he had had a chance to talk about his experiences in the depth he was doing with me here, or to have a person willing to listen to him. He said it was difficult to find a priest willing to listen and most laymen would not likely be interested, or even able to handle the information.

Therese thought her involvement in the occult would all be a secret part of her past, but she sees it as God's will to bring this up in my interviews with her. Sharing her experiences can help others, so she was willing and saw that she *has* to do it. She said she has so much to atone for. She stated that she has learned clearly that anything outside of God's will will harm you, and the world will cheer you on as you do it. The plan of the occult is to keep you away from God with the promise of happiness; whereas the truth is that only in God, and according to His will, can you be happy.

When I finished my interviews with many of the exorcists, they mentioned how important it is for people to gain an understanding of the reality of the occult in our culture. Fr. Alphonsus said, "It's just so important because people often don't have the proper resources and could end up in the occult through lack of knowledge, even priests." Fr. Dominic agreed, saying, "More and more information [is needed], getting the word out there. People in the parish being able to talk about the occult beyond just, 'oh, that's naughty,' is a *must*." Likewise, Fr. Anselm said, "We need more priests, laypeople, and good catechists working on this." Dr. Luke said, "These are serious topics but people get afraid of what they don't understand." One exorcist is the pastor of a parish where *Slaying Dragons* has become well-known. He noted that, as a result of that book, there has been a greater awareness of the evil and the danger of the occult, and he has seen this reflected in the things mentioned in Confession. Prior to this, people thought there was no problem with Freemasonry, Yoga, fortune tellers, or playing with a Ouija board. They often think these things are a game and then wonder why they start to witness strange things happening.

It is my hope that *The Rise of the Occult* will further illuminate the minds of Christians today, building on what was presented in *Slaying Dragons*, and show, not just the presence and danger within this new religious movement, but the beauty and glory of the Church of Jesus Christ, which truly fulfills all the longings of the human soul.

The Contributors

Below is a list and brief description of all the people interviewed for this book.[2] In addition to these, the book includes many who are public figures or whose testimony is publicly available.

Former occultists:
-   **Adelaide:** raised by a father who was a lapsed Catholic turned atheist who later converted, and a mother who was Protestant. A hatred toward God led her toward the occult. She began with "angel magic" and then Wicca and magic, which she practiced for over ten years. She experienced

---

[2] NB: when these individuals are quoted in the book, their names will be mentioned but there will be no footnote since it comes from my personal interviews with them.

strong and long-lasting diabolical retaliations after her initial weak[3] conversion to the Church.

- **Christopher:** his parents left the Faith and divorced when he was young, which pushed him toward a hatred toward God in his teenage years. A superstitious form of Charismatic Protestantism led him into "Christian occultism" and occultism in general. He endured immediate diabolical attacks upon returning to the Faith, but they were short-lived.
- **Gabriel:** grew up as a lukewarm Baptist and strayed into an agnostic mindset. This led him toward New Age beliefs which pulled him in and dominated his life. He endured clear diabolical retaliations as he was converting, which vanished after his entrance into the Church.
- **Camilla:** brought up Catholic but strayed into the occult while seeking healing. After witnessing the manifestation of a demon in one of her New Age instructors, she sought the Church's aid in leaving the occult. She was eventually led through a deliverance process with a priest.
- **Andrew:** raised in a non-denominational Protestant home. He left this and entered a phase as an atheist. A curiosity about the paranormal emerged and became strong, leading him into the occult. He practiced Wicca and then became a devout Thelemite for about four years before his conversion, which was followed by several months of diabolical retaliation.
- **John:** a life-long occultist, raised initially with training in Buddhist meditation. This led to a strong and early interest in the occult. He practiced many forms of the occult for over thirty years before his conversion. He has endured diabolical retaliation for several years, ever since his conversion.
- **Therese:** brought up as a Baptist when young and showed an extraordinary understanding of that faith at her young age. She became curious about the occult in her early teens and embraced Wicca and many forms of the occult before settling into witchcraft, Yoga, and Satanism, among others, for about twenty years. She endured diabolical attacks all through her

---

[3] She explains in the book that her first conversion, through a parish RCIA program, was without proper catechesis. For example, in her first many months as a Catholic, she rarely went to Mass on Sunday, ignorant of the obligation to do so weekly.

occult practice. These continue today, though with much less frequency and intensity.

- **Philomena:** raised in a lukewarm Catholic home in which her parents were seldom around. She began practicing the New Age and earth magic in her late teens, eventually marrying a Satanist. She dropped her occultic practices after almost a decade and made a soft return to Christianity, eventually entering the Church. She endured diabolical attacks throughout her practice and occasionally since her conversion.

- **Lucy:** raised as an Anglican by her parents who were otherwise lukewarm in their religious beliefs. Anger at God emerged in her late teens after her father's sudden death, fueling an emerging interest in the occult. A deep immersion into the New Age led her to a mental breakdown, which prompted a semi-miraculous conversion experience. She endured strong diabolical attacks in the process of converting, but they ceased once she entered the Church.

- **Helena:** raised Presbyterian but her father was non-practicing. When she was introduced to the occult at age twenty, she was immediately drawn to it. For twenty-five years, she went from witchcraft to Dianic Wicca, back to witchcraft, and then to the New Age. Though she suffered in various ways from her time in the occult, she had little diabolical retaliation after converting.

- **Anna:** raised in the Church but began to dabble in the occult when very young. Her cultural environment inclined her toward occultic curiosities and the embrace of superstitions. By the time she received the Sacrament of Confirmation, after four years of dabbling, she stopped her occult activities. She experienced several negative events during those years, but nothing afterward.

- **Edith:** raised by a mother who was a Catholic who dabbled in the New Age and a father who was hostile to the Faith. Being introduced to the New Age as a young girl brought confusion and occultic curiosities, in which she experimented for several years. After returning to the Faith, she endured many months of infrequent nightly diabolical retaliation.

- **Timothy:** raised by a Protestant father and a Native American pagan mother. He was not raised in either tradition but gravitated toward the pagan religion. As he began his own family, the immorality of the pagan groups he affiliated with disillusioned him and he eventually entered the Church.
- **Barbara:** raised in a nominal Catholic home and both of her parents embraced a New Age religion. She was also raised in these occultic practices. She eventually embraced them fully and experienced numerous diabolical retaliations, particularly in the last years before she converted.
- **Alex Frank:** former devout practitioner of the form of Yoga known as Kashmiri Shaivism who converted to the Catholic Faith in 2019. He practiced for five years and had one of the best Yoga spiritual directors in the U.S. He is also a former U.S. Army Ranger and a graduate of Yale Law School. He is now a speaker on the dangers of Yoga.

The following priests are pastors and exorcists, many with additional diocesan responsibilities. They are given the pseudonyms listed below:

Exorcists:
- **Fr. Alphonsus**
- **Fr. Athanasius**
- **Fr. Cyprian**
- **Fr. Ambrose**
- **Fr. Blaise**
- **Fr. Sebastian**
- **Fr. Anselm**
- **Fr. Matthew**

Pastors:
- **Fr. Gregory**
- **Fr. Maximilian**
- **Fr. Dominic**
- **Fr. Louis**
- **Fr. Theodore**
- **Fr. Stephen**

Preface

- **Fr. Augustine**
- **Fr. Bartholomew**

In addition to the above, I interviewed numerous laymen who are not former occultists. Many only appear once, so their names are not listed here. The following individuals are referenced more than once in the book, and provided here for ease of reference as to their background:

- **Felicity:** a "seer"[4] who, due to her Church-approved spiritual gifts, works with priests and exorcists in her diocese.
- **Margaret:** a devout Catholic mother of many children. Due to marrying an inactive Catholic husband, who had an affair and abandoned the family, she struggled raising her children. Each of them subsequently left the Faith and fell into various forms of immoral and occultic lifestyles.
- **Dr. Luke:** a licensed clinical mental health counselor. He works with young people and is used by exorcists to help evaluate their cases. He is referred to as "Dr." for ease of association to his work.
- **Elizabeth:** from a devout Catholic family and has remained a devout Catholic herself. Through various circumstances, she became trapped in a relationship with an abusive Satanist named **Damien**, in which she suffered for close to a year before escaping. She has worked with an exorcist for deliverance issues for many years.
- **Clare:** raised by two Catholic parents but her father was actively engaged in many forms of the occult. From a young age, she experienced diabolical attacks, which endured for decades, even into her own marriage and family. Her husband's name is **Lawrence**.
- **Marianne:** a devout Catholic mother.
- **Francesca:** a devout Catholic mother.
- **Rachel Mastrogiacomo:** a devout Catholic mother who, prior to her marriage, suffered at the hands of a priest who

---

[4] A seer, in this case, is a layman who has been recognized by the local Church to have a spiritual gift. These gifts vary as St. Paul describes in I Corinthians 12.

had associated himself with the occult and manipulated her as part of his effort to draw her into his Satanic coven.[5]

In addition to these, numerous witchcraft websites were referenced to gather data on the beliefs of practicing witches in order to compare them to the statements of former witches. These sites are often not referenced in the footnotes, lest this publication generate unwanted attention for, or curiosity about, them, which is not the intention of the book.

---

[5] This is her real name. Her story will mainly be told in *Slaying Dragons III*.

Introduction

Our times are uncomfortably similar to those of the early Church. This is the perspective of those currently escaping the grip of the occult,[1] as well as of the exorcists and of pastors who assist them. An analysis of the times supports their perspective. Since the Fall of Adam and Eve, our world has lived under the shroud of Satan's dominion, beneath the tyranny of both the temptations from the devil and the disorder of our fallen flesh. Our age is no different. Further, our world today bears all the marks of an age that will be particularly noted by history for its indulgence in the occult. Both the Enemy's temptations and the disorder of our fallen nature, a *double tyranny*, are inflamed by the absence of a strong presence of Christianity in the world together with a heightened celebration of the ways of the flesh. With this has come a fascination with "alternative" forms of spirituality.

This double tyranny which oppresses mankind, wounds him, and drives him away from God, was conquered at Christ's victorious first coming, which brought a reprieve to a weary world, releasing from the shackles of sin and death those who would look upon Him, the Incarnate and Crucified Lord. It was a *reprieve* and not a full liberation because, while their souls were set free from captivity to sin and made members of His Mystical Body, the world in which these Christians lived continues to groan under the weight of the consequences of sin, ever susceptible to the viciousness of concupiscence and still subject to the malice of the demons who sought to keep them from returning to God.

The early Church, sanctified as it was, saw the battle between the Kingdom of Satan and the Kingdom of God playing out in an extraordinary way. Faith, the living out of the call to fidelity to Christ, was the complete and all-absorbing mindset for those first

---

[1] See below for an explanation of what is grouped together under the term "occult" in this book.

1

followers. They followed after the *King of Kings* and the *Lord of Lords*, Who had revealed His power and universal dominion to the diabolical agents who had oppressed mankind since the Fall. Satan's kingdom was crashing down in the presence of those who heard the Son of God speak, who saw Him cast out demon after demon, and who beheld His power working through His Church.

> If it is by the Spirit of God that I cast out demons, then the kingdom of God has come upon you. Or how can one enter a strong man's house and plunder his goods, unless he first binds the strong man? Then indeed he may plunder his house.[2]

Our Lord declared, as St. Thomas wrote, that He had come to break into Satan's kingdom with power and authority, and to plunder the "goods" Satan had taken to himself, namely, the souls of men whom the devil had ensnared. St. John the Apostle affirmed this, stating clearly, "The reason the Son of God appeared was to destroy the works of the devil."[3] Our Lord "appeared" in order to conquer the works of Satan, but His first appearance was not at the moment of His exorcisms, nor His preaching and healing, nor His crucifixion and Resurrection. Our Lord's first appearance was at His Incarnation and Birth. This, too, is where the parallel of our own time with that of the early Church is essential to contemplate.

His birth was announced by the beautiful and supernatural event known as the Star of Bethlehem. Was the Star of Bethlehem, though, just for *these* three wise men, pagans from afar, who came to behold the King whose birth was foretold to them by this stupendous apparition? Would God have created, just for them, that supernatural light which led these pagan men to travel to a distant land which God Himself would make His dwelling place? In one sense, yes, most assuredly. God would suffer and die on the Cross to save just one man if that were all who dwelt on the earth. He would also send a supernatural light to that same one man if that were what he needed in order to come home to God his Creator.

---

[2] Matt 12:28–29
[3] I John 3:8b

Introduction

God, though, did not call these wise men through the Star to save their three souls alone. God established this brilliant Star in the history of His work of salvation to show all mankind of all ages that the Birth of Jesus Christ will bring with it, to all who embrace Him, the same joy and wonder which these wise men felt in their hearts on that journey. It will be accompanied by the same transformative power of grace which sent these wise men home "by another way."[4] It will bring with it the same supernatural invigoration which was operating within the souls of His disciples who cried out, "Did not our hearts burn within us while He talked to us on the road, while He opened to us the Scriptures?"[5]

As in the early Church, when pagans fled from their false religions to Christ in His Holy Church, renouncing their occultic practices and false gods, and were delivered from diabolical holds and attachments, so today, under the scourge of the occult, which has struck the hearts and minds of more and more souls, the Church needs to be prepared to receive and minister to those seeking to be liberated from beneath its burden.

The truth of the situation is that those souls trapped in the occult are looking for that Star to enlighten them, to captivate them, to heal them, and to bring them home to the God who loves them. More and more souls who have no knowledge of the Truth have turned to occult practices in order to find the spiritual fulfillment that they can only get from Christ Whom they cannot find. It is upon us, as members of the Mystical Body of Christ, upon whom He has willed to depend for His work of salvation, that the role and responsibility has been laid to help the Scriptures become open before these souls and to help the Star of grace be welcomed into their hearts, that they may then go forward along another way, with the joy and excitement of having encountered, and become one with, the Living God.

The Aim of this Book

The Rise of the Occult will present what former occultists believe the Church needs to know about the current spiritual crises and the

---

[4] Matt 2:12
[5] Luke 24:32

dark realities of the many prevalent occult spiritualities. The book will show how these spiritualities are captivating to the imaginations of souls in a culture which has drifted away from its anchor in Christ. It is based on the testimonies of former occultists, exorcists, parish priests, the experiences of the Catholic faithful, and the current events of the world pertaining to this topic.

The topics will include: the reality of the occult in the culture; how the occult has infiltrated both society and the Church, in many of her members and even the hierarchy; the many reasons why people go into the occult; the darkness into which a soul plunges who enters the occult; the danger and destruction that the occult presents; the diabolical presence within all aspects of the occult; the malice against the Church which is held by many expressions of the occult; the battle involved in extracting oneself from the occult; the role and the power of the Church and her priests in liberating souls from the occult; and, among others, how the Church alone fulfills the spiritual craving that occultists truly possess.

This book seeks to present the stark reality that, without the former widespread Christian influence that once inspired this land, this new religion which has emerged is now beginning to take up a solid identity. To this religion we can safely affix the label *occult*.[6] It includes, among other things, witchcraft,[7] Satanism,[8] Wicca,[9] astrology,[10] the New Age,[11] *manifesting*,[12] Yoga,[13] Reiki,[14]

---

[6] The occult is a conglomerate of subjectivistic religious systems of disparate practices of both modern and ancient origin in which man seeks, by some sort of communing with natural energies, deities, or demons, or by the sheer force of his will, to influence his world and the world around him, find answers and enlightenment, and obtain powers and divinization. The practice of the occult is typically ritualistic, to a greater or lesser degree depending on the specific craft being utilized.

[7] Those who cast spells and curses and work with spirits and deities.

[8] Those who either worship Satan or call upon his name as a model of rebellion, in order to attain power and/or destabilize society from its current form.

[9] Similar to witchcraft, a modern neo-pagan religion which, though extremely diverse and without unity, often believes in a god and goddess figure, magic and rituals.

[10] The study and observance of the arrangement of the stars and heavenly bodies and the impact that these have on mankind. It is used to diagnose why a person is the way he is, giving answers to many questions, often serving as a gateway to deeper occultic practices.

[11] The *New Age* is an amalgamation of occultic practices, modern superstitions, and recycled Eastern religious concepts, presented in a way that makes the practitioner think he is simply tapping into the mysteries of the *Universe* and steering clear of anything occultic or religious.

spiritualism,[15] and a whole host of other superstitious and pagan practices. This will be presented with the necessary details that go well beyond the initial presentation of this topic in the final chapter of *Slaying Dragons*, a great primary read before diving into this book.

As a refresher, to illustrate briefly how the occult is *rising*: Wicca is outpacing Presbyterianism in membership; Satanism is proudly on the scene and spreading, with social and political acceptance; and *manifesting* and witchcraft are the new and "hip" lifestyle choices of the young and old, dominating most social media platforms. The occult is widespread, popular, growing, and trending. It is also dangerous, irrational, illogical, and evil.

The Danger of the Occult

Christians today need to know about the occult because it is becoming a formidable opponent on the spiritual landscape of our country and beyond. It has become such an insidious influence that it now wields a formative power over the minds of the youth in particular though not exclusively. It is weaving its way into the common parlance and practice of our society such that many Christians are clueless when they stand in its presence, and when they themselves blindly take up what are actually occult practices. Further, the occult presents a mockery of the One True Faith, a counterfeit that resembles, in some external respects, the real religion given to us by Our Lord Jesus Christ Himself. Thus, for those who are not actively practicing the Faith, but are seeking meaning in our chaotic world, the occult will begin to stand out as an enticing option.

Further, the occult has appeal to a post-Christian society of spiritual seekers, such as our own, because it presents the "wonderful world of magic" as a reality that anyone can tap into. In this is a powerful danger: the occult *can* produce effects which appear to be magical or supernatural. When a wayward youth investigates the

---

[12] *Manifesting* is when a person seeks to cause a change in the world by a method of *willing* it to happen, by various practices including repeating a statement containing the desired outcome. The person's will is seen as the cause of the change *manifesting* in the world.

[13] The Hindu practice of ritualistic stretching postures and breathing routines to enter an altered state for the purpose of the worship of, and union with, the Hindu deities.

[14] Those who work with *energy* within the body and the Universe to attempt to heal others.

[15] Practice of summoning spirits through various media like Ouija boards and séances.

occult, he will find a plenitude of testimonies, how-tos, explanations, videos, books, and other celebrations of the wonder and amazement of occult practices such as those found in witchcraft, Wicca, and the New Age. He will be told that "magic is real" and he may, therefore, be tempted to try it out for himself, especially given the fact that it is simple and can be done in the privacy of the home.[16]

However, what he will *not* be told is this: while the occult seems to bring a quick response to the "prayers" that Christians appear to have to wait years to have answered, these responses are brought by an *entirely different agency* than the Christian God who listens attentively to His children. The "energy"[17] behind the occult, which brings about the responses to spells and rituals, is none other than the Kingdom of Satan and the activity of the diabolical. Behold the counterfeit! The devil perverts the revealed worship of the One True God, incorporating many natural elements of the world God created, but presenting a mockery of them in the rituals of the occult, in which the practitioner will see and hear and smell, in the candles and chants and incense, a mockery of what God wants to give mankind Himself. The rituals of the occult then orient the practitioner inward toward himself, promising to increase his own power and happiness, devoid of any connection to the God Who made and loves him. All the while, it secretly binds the occultist to mankind's ancient enemy, from whose servitude many do not escape.

The occult is charming in its external presentation, adamant that it is here to help us find our "true selves," obtain happiness, manifest peace, find the right path, obtain inner harmony, and connect with friendly spirits. Many public faces of occult practice give the impression that these are all truly attainable.

Herein lies the point of this book.

If individuals simply look more closely at the reality of the occult, they will see the signature of the Prince of Darkness – but

---

[16] Alternatively, he may also be told that his preferred occult practice, such as Satanism, is all "psychodrama" devoid of anything spiritual, a lie that will bait him into a malevolent self-worship and openness to "dark forces."

[17] "Energy" is a common, almost ubiquitous, term in the occult for the power that can be manipulated through rituals and spells and other manifestations willed by the practitioner.

most do not look. It is here that we see the great value in the testimonies of those who have been in the occult, who have sought from it this same peace and happiness and fulfillment – but did not find it. Instead, they eventually came face to face with the one whose hand signed the checks and wrapped the gifts that the occult offered, and they fled, coming soon thereafter, thankfully, into the embrace of Christ and His Holy Church.

Within the Church, the sure harbor of salvation, these former occultists clearly see the emptiness and vanity and perversion of their occult practices, and they behold the life and beauty and goodness of the right worship of the One True God. Not only can an analysis of the occult's presence in our culture help us understand its appeal and danger, but it can also help us see how beautiful and good and loving Our Lord is in the way He reaches out to us and nourishes us with Truth and Heavenly blessings.

Throughout history, as it will be at the end of time, magic and the occult has plagued and will continue to plague mankind. As Our Lord said in the Gospel of Matthew,

> If anyone says to you then, 'Lo, here is the Christ!' or 'There he is!' do not believe it. For false Christs and false prophets will arise and *show great signs and wonders*, so as to lead astray, if possible, even the elect. Behold, I have told it to you, beforehand.[18]

Likewise, the Book of Revelation states,

> [The second beast] *works great signs*, even making fire come down from heaven to earth in the sight of men; and *by the signs* which it is allowed to work in the presence of the beast, *it deceives* those who dwell on earth.[19]

But this should not make us despair, because we know that throughout time and, perhaps, especially at the end of time, Our

---

[18] Matt 24:23-25. *Emphasis* mine.
[19] Revelation 13:13-14; see also Rev. 16:14. *Emphasis* mine.

Lord has raised up great Saints to face the greatest threats to salvation, and to set mankind back on its course to God.

Former occultists have stated that this is a great time to be a Christian. They offered these comments when reflecting on the fact that occultists are waking up and leaving that dark realm, and that the Church has the power to truly rescue them from the grip of Satan. John said, "There is so much redemption and grace now, and the triumph of Christ over the darkness!" Therese also expressed this hopeful outlook. She said, "With everything so *in your face* right now, it is a wonderful time to become Saints and to be Catholic. It is very edifying and strikes against the idea that nothing positive is happening in the world."

As they were in the early Church, pagans today are still drawn to the Truth. The Magi sought the Truth and followed what they discerned, interested less in their pagan practices than they were in finding the true meaning to life. Today, there are, likewise, pagans looking for the Truth, who are asking, "Where is this great God of the Christians, that we too may worship Him?" Sadly, in this age, which has been called "Satanic" by some exorcists and oppressed by a "great apostasy" by prominent Cardinals, the treasury of the Church's Truth is very much hidden from many, particularly from the youth. These treasures would provide for them the spiritual enrichment which they crave. However, this craving is leading them, in the practical absence of this Treasury, into the embrace of Satan's occultic parody. The occult seems easy and the truth takes work, but the latter is what will give them true Life. As exorcists and those who work with them have seen, the occult is seeking to fill this void of truth since people, even after rejecting Christianity, never stop seeking spiritual experiences.

Chapter One

The Occult is a Reality

Many people are blind to it but the occult is a reality in our culture and in the world as a whole. In one sense, this is not new but, in another, it should be seen as a bright red flag flapping in the winds of the spirit of the age. Christianity's influence is slowly being phased out by cultural shifts, political movements, lackadaisical Christians, and compromised leadership within the Church herself. As has been the custom of mankind back to Adam and Eve, when God is removed from man's life, his religious inclination latches on to something else. Today, it is the occult.

The occult has been on the earth's landscape since the Fall of Adam and Eve. It is, essentially, the devil's religion, first concocted by him when tempting Adam and Eve to go against God as he himself had first done. Original Sin was, for Adam and Eve, the personal sin of seeking secret knowledge and "to be like God" by eating a forbidden fruit and directly breaking a Commandment God had given them. Fr. Ermatinger has said that this act is "the mother of all superstitions,"[1] using the definition of superstition as "*to expect divine effects from less than divine causes*."[2] Here, Adam and Eve sought to obtain divine wisdom and glory through the mere act of eating a fruit which God had forbidden. Speaking specifically about this, in the context of witchcraft, he said, "Witchcraft, as a concept, has a meaning that goes beyond magical practice. The uniting of rubrics,

---

[1] Fr. Cliff Ermatinger, *The Trouble with Magic*, (Padre Pio Press, 2021), IV.

[2] Ermatinger, *The Trouble with Magic*, 4. Superstition, therefore, is to believe that a human cause or action can bring about a divine effect or action. It also includes irreverent worship of God or giving to a creature the reverence due to God alone. Further, it includes the belief that unless certain external practices are performed, contrary to the revealed will of God, God will not respond. It can also appear in the belief that God *must* respond if certain, and often excessive, external practices are performed. Thus, superstition is not simply an overtly occultic practice but also includes corrupted forms of right worship.

rituals, words, evil invocations, amounts to an *anti-religion*; the antithesis of Revelation; the fulfillment of the devil's intention in the Fall of our First Parents."[3] This anti-religion is this religion of the devil, appearing in many forms under the umbrella of the occult. This anti-religion was Satan's intention in his conversation with Eve: draw her within herself, let her crave power and knowledge for herself, turn her away from God, and incite her to sin, thus attaching herself to a mindset of superstition, magic, and the occult.

The devil, all too ready to answer any superstitious ritual that mankind concocts, will turn us toward every sort of superstition and magic and disordered worship. Our ancient enemy uses these various forms to get a foothold in our lives. To incline us to being open to these suggestions, he must first get us to turn away from God. This is how the occult has become such a dangerous reality today: the general spiritual state of the world has created a welcoming environment for a decline into paganism and superstition. The state of the world is like Eve in the Garden, whose ears had already become inclined to consider the serpent's offer.

A Society Declines First

For the occult to find its footing in a culture, there must be an absence of the presence of God and the worship of God, a substantial moral depravity, and a loss of the use of right reason among the citizens. The U.S., a land once partially evangelized, has, to a large extent, achieved these three negative objectives.

The reality of the decline of the worship of God, already on the radar for decades, has been noted by priests and exorcists observing the effect of the closing of Churches during the Covid era, and the subsequent removal of the Sunday obligation throughout the country. The National Catholic Register stated in 2022 that dioceses in the US have experienced an average of a thirty percent drop in Mass attendance since 2019.[4] According to the Catholic News Agency (CNA), the statistics on Catholic prayer in the U.S., as of December of 2021, indicated a continued downward trend in

---

[3] Ermatinger, *The Trouble with Magic*, 126.
[4] *National Catholic Register*, December 1, 2022, "The Catholic Church Battles to Fill the Pews"

devotion. Only half of Catholics stated that they pray every day. Only a quarter of Catholics attend Mass at least weekly. Further, they said 65 percent of Catholics attend Mass a few times a year or less, with 14 percent stating they never attend, and 20 percent of Catholics neither praying nor seeing religion as important. CNA's research indicated an upward trend in the category of "nones," or those who profess no religion: 30 percent of the general population are "nones," up from 19 percent in 2011. Only 63 percent of the population is Christian. For comparison, since 2014, the number of Americans who pray is down 10 percent, the number of Catholics who pray every day is down 8 percent, and the number of Catholics for whom religion is very important is down 10 percent.[5]

The situation in Europe is no better. Further, it seems to be on the exact same trajectory as the U.S. For example, in what was called a "landmark shift toward secularism," England and Wales no longer have a majority Christian population. Shifting from the situation as recorded ten years prior in the 2011 census, in 2021 only 46.2 percent of citizens identified as Christian, down 13.1 points. At the same time, taking second place to Christians as the largest group, "no religion" rose to 37.2 percent, an increase of 12 points.[6]

These are just the current statistics. These trends are accelerating. Given that the spiritual decline has been occurring for close to a century in the U.S., more and more people are being raised either with only the veneer of Christianity, or with no Christian religious background at all. Dr. Gallagher warned about the danger of the latter when he wrote, "In my experience, people with no real religious background who turned to occult practices are among the most frequently attacked by spirits."[7]

Alongside this continual decrease in Christian faith and practice is the rollout of a massive diabolical agenda, hitting the world on nearly all fronts, from politics to religion to entertainment to pastimes to celebrity-worship and even to fitness. The agenda can be seen in the following ways: the rabid desire for abortion up until (or beyond) birth has only increased in the wake of the end of *Roe v Wade*; woke companies are offering to fly their employees anywhere

---

[5] *Catholic News Agency*, December 16, 2021, "Pew survey: Half of U.S. Catholics pray every day, and the number is dropping."

[6] *France24.com*, November 29, 2022, "Christians Now a Minority in England and Wakes."

[7] Dr. Richard Gallagher, *Demonic Foes*, (New York, Harper One, 2020), 166.

in the country so they can murder their babies and get back to work; drag queen story hours[8] continue to spread and transgender mutilation surgeries abound despite the insanity they manifest; Satanic after-school clubs[9] spread to more and more states; pornographic books are approved and defended by counties and school boards despite strong parent protest; schools allow children to use the bathrooms of the opposite sex; Yoga[10] has insinuated itself into nearly all aspects of physical fitness; Disney (and others) are becoming increasingly more obvious and grotesque in the perversion of their storytelling and their promotion of a neo-pagan society; occult stores are opening everywhere, even in *your own small town*; occultists have been outed in the hierarchy of the Church, yet without just anger and reparation being offered in response; the number of "atheistic Satanists" is growing who, despite that modifier, engage in real occultic rituals; and the growing public presence of Satanism which, while parading itself around as a mere publicity stunt, all the while encourages and eggs on the many debaucheries mentioned above.

This moral collapse, and the embrace of every imaginable form of immorality, has further exacerbated the problem. The enumeration of pervasive societal evils in the previous paragraph presents what amounts to a long list of mortal sins. Mortal sins pave the way for all sorts of diabolical manifestations in a person's life, from an intense form of ordinary temptation to all the various extraordinary manifestations. At the heart of this moral depravity is the scourge of pornography, a widespread, addictive, and destructive past-time of a society that has moved on from an orientation toward God.

The ubiquity of pornography has led to a general disordering of human behavior. Among these, it has also caused a perplexing phenomenon which one Catholic family informed me about, and which it is important to hear. Having for decades observed both Catholic and secular schools as parents, the Monroes shared that there is a current of self-identified lesbians who are actually *not*

---

[8] The odd and evil phenomenon of cross-dressing men reading stories to children at libraries.

[9] Sponsored by the Satanic Temple but permitted as a result of religious liberty laws.

[10] For a good examination of the nature of Yoga, read "Should Catholics Practice Yoga?" by Alex Frank, Catholic.com, September 30 2022.

practicing that lifestyle. This form of homosexual identification is directly tied to pornography, for these young women "are just trying to keep the boys away because the boys are all looking at porn," said Mrs. Monroe. "The boys have it in their minds that what they see in the porn is how the girls are and will be." The girls want to stay away from all the boys because of the effect that porn has on them. "It's not [considered] normal if you're not doing it," she added. "The girls know that if they go on a date, they are expected to behave that way, so if the girls present themselves as lesbian or bi-sexual, then they get out of that." On the other hand, "the girls that want the boys' attention have to do all the weird pouty lips and things on Instagram." Thus, normal human relations are being disrupted on a wider scale than imagined by many. Young men, so disordered by pornography, are pushing women into pretended homosexuality, the latter pretense intended to keep the young men away. Women, too, struggle with pornography, but at a lower rate, averaging at approximately one-third of the same statistical numbers for men.[11] The damage which this poses to individual lives and to the stability of the society as a whole cannot be understated.

No Longer in Hiding

While the culture has declined morally and religiously, the occult has arisen from the shadows where it typically resides, likely a result of the spiritual response to it. English borrowed the word "occult" from the Latin *occultus*, which means "hidden, concealed, secret." In English, the word has taken on diabolical overtones, pointing to "hidden" realities and powers, to "secret" rites and societies, to organizations that operate in the shadows of society and, very often, in the dark of night. However, the occult today is, in its activity, abandoning hiddenness and secrecy. According to Fr. Dominic, "Most of the ways that Satan and the demons attack us are the same old ways, and always very personalized, but the difference is we have a culture right now that has largely embraced a lot of this

---

[11] On September 13, 2022, the Recovery Village posted statistics such as "20% of men and 13% of women admit to accessing porn while at work," "1 of 3 visitors of all adult websites is a woman," and "up to 65% of young adult men and 18% of young women report watching pornography at least once a week, among other similar statistics which demonstrate this one-third approximation.

and even celebrated the blatant sins. But as for the deeper, darker side of the occult, I've noticed tons of this in my priestly ministry." Msgr. Rossetti has written, "The number of people practicing witchcraft in our country is rising exponentially. The number of priests is dropping. There are spiritually difficult times ahead. But, in the final analysis, all the witches in the world are powerless in the presence of Christ."[12]

The statistics for the rise of the occult, especially considering those featuring the decline of Christian faith, show the real danger of the situation. The following is just a sampling of what is known but, despite the limitations of the breadth of the data collected, it clearly paints a dire picture. According to *USA Today*, a 2017 Pew Research Center Survey found that about 62% of Americans say they hold "New Age" beliefs, which included a belief in astrology, psychics, reincarnation, and the presence of a *spiritual energy* in inanimate objects.[13] Wicca, an official religion in the U.S. as of 1986, had close to 1.5 million adherents in 2018. In 2021, one researcher on the topic estimated the number of Wiccans (or pagans) to already be close to 2 million.[14]

For comparison, the statistics in Europe are just as alarming as in the U.S. In 2016, Fr. Amorth observed, "Today in Italy there are a few hundred satanic sects; generally, each one has a few members. It is difficult to do a precise charting of them, because they always act in the shadows."[15] He added that a dear friend of his, a scholar who died in 2005, claimed that in Italy there were more than 13 million Italians, about a quarter of the population, who patronized sorcerers.[16] An article titled, "Revival of the Occult," published by *France24* in May, 2021, said that "nearly 70 percent of French youth ages 18-24 believe in parasciences (including astrology, numerology, palm reading, clairvoyance and cartomancy), a trend that has been on the rise for the past 20 years, according to an IFOP poll published last December. Four out of ten French people now

---

[12] St. Michael Center for Spiritual Renewal blog, June 26, 2022, Diary #196

[13] *USA Today*, October 28, 2021, "'We're in the middle of a witch moment': Hip witchcraft is on the rise in the US."

[14] *USA Today*, October 28, 2021, "'We're in the middle of a witch moment': Hip witchcraft is on the rise in the US."

[15] Fr. Gabriele Amorth. *An Exorcist Explains the Demonic* (Manchester: Sophia Institute Press, 2016), 33.

[16] Amorth, *An Exorcist Explains*, 40.

believe in astrology, compared to three out of 10 Americans – an increase of 10 points since 2000, the poll found."[17]

As Allure.com reported, "in the United Kingdom, Google searches for 'birth chart' actually doubled between November 2013 and November 2018, and sales of spiritual books rose 13 percent."[18] The Washington Post reported that the "youth-oriented" TikTok hashtag #witchtok had 19.4 billion views as of October 2021.[19] Msgr. Rossetti, in a post on Oct. 30, 2021, pointed out that there is an online witch who has over 400,000 followers on her platform. As part of my research, I observed and noted aspects of the beliefs of a practicing witch who has close to 200,000 very engaged followers on YouTube. Dr. Gallagher noted that there was a well-attended conference for students of witchcraft hosted in 2019 by New York University for students of witchcraft.[20] Interesting to note, one witch, who was part of the conference, has a prominent online following and a book with an almost identical number of five-star reviews to *Slaying Dragons*, published around the same time in 2019.

The number of adherents and of those taking interest in the occult is not the only statistic pointing to an increased devotion to this new spirituality. According to the Ontario Consultants on Religious Tolerance,[21] in 2008, there were 326 books published on Wicca but, by 2016, there were 1512. This number rose slowly each year from 2008 to 2014, increasing by about one hundred books per year, but it jumped by 300 in 2015 and again by 500 in 2016. The statistics on this website stopped in 2016, unfortunately. Currently on the website of the *Book Depository*, a leading international book retailer, there are 14,384 results under the listing "All Witchcraft and Wicca."[22] The Washington Post reported that book sales on the topic of witchcraft increased forty-three percent last year (2021) from 2020, according to NPD BookScan, an organization which

---

[17] *France24.com*, May 5, 2021, "'Revival of the occult': French youth turn to tarot, astrology during Covid-19."

[18] *Allure.com*, December 26, 2018, "In 2018, Astrology Offered Comfort in a Chaotic World." Article refers to "mind, body, spirit" books.

[19] *The Washington Post*, October 28, 2021, "From spellcasting to podcasting: Inside the life of a teenage witch." The U.S. is the biggest user of TikTok, with 136 million users as of April 2022, while the UK has one-sixth of this, at 23 million; both of these represent approximately one-third of the population of the respective country.

[20] Gallagher, *Demonic Foes*, 178.

[21] ReligiousTolerance.org, "How Many Wiccans are There?" Part Seven

[22] Number captured October 2022.

tracks the publication of books. The NPD said that this growth is "dramatically outpacing" the entire non-fiction print market.[23]

The number of resources available for people to learn how to become a witch is astounding. According to her statements on YouTube, Lola, a practicing witch, in 2022 said that on YouTube there are hundreds of practitioners that you can learn from. Amazon is also a "fantastic resource," with tens of thousands of occult books. "The Witchcraft section in Amazon is huge and is growing every single month," she said, "with hundreds, thousands, tens of thousands of books that cover everything from traditional European witchcraft to shamanism, etc. Everything you can think of...they have it."

Normalizing Witchcraft

The data presented above makes it clear that the occult has become mainstream in our culture. As Fr. Ambrose noted, there is a "tremendous problem" today; we are "normalizing everything sinful including occult practices. People think the occult is all 'fun and games' and have become obsessed with it. From horror movies and watching devil movies to even naming children 'Lucifer'." Exposure to these evils, he added, "has an impact on the person but the culture does not know that, [or else] thinks it's fine." Adam Blai said that books about occultism targeting the youth are conditioning kids to see witchcraft and Satanism as palatable and familiar. This criticism would also apply to movies and TV shows. "Maybe not a big deal when you are 10," Blai said, "but when you're 20 and you're in the dorms and somebody's playing with the Ouija board, you're more likely to engage in it because you've been familiarized to it. It's become normalized to you, it's softening you up to go down that road later."[24] As a pastor and exorcist, Fr. Blaise noted that there has been a significant rise in the occult in the last twenty years, with people calling him specifically about these issues.

A very telling example, in step with my research, comes from a 2019 BBC interview of three witches. In their report, BBC stated

[23] *The Washington Post*, October 28, 2021, "From spellcasting to podcasting: Inside the life of a teenage witch"

[24] *EWTN.* "EWTN on Location - 2019-10-26 - Allure and Truth About Wicca and Witchcraft (The)" *YouTube*, 26 October 2019, youtube.com/watch?v=FCf7JJ4w0dc

that the three witches they interviewed were "among thousands bringing witchcraft to social media." "It will become something that is completely normal, hopefully," one witch stated, sharing the aspirations of a growing number of people. While it used to be "hush, hush," one said, "Now, with social media, it's massive, it's huge." As of this writing, the hashtag #witch has been used seven million times on Instagram. "People," as a result of this abundance, "are more accepting of it, this generation especially," the video stated, adding, "People are really 'out and proud' in terms of their witchiness." In the video, it was said, "These witches hope witchcraft will be more mainstream in the future." This statement was actually quite prophetic, as this interview was posted just *before* the Covid global lockdown, which poured gas on the flames beneath the cauldrons of the modern witchcraft movement. One of the witches added, "In this kind of world, where everything is so stressful, I think it's something for people to turn to, and the fact that it's something you can just practice at home; the ease of it is really what's made it boom. Witchcraft is going to be a practice that's going to be really accessible to a lot of people."[25] This perspective fits with the trajectory of the culture in the direction of greater isolation from each other and from the past, leaving newer generations vulnerable to the spirit of the age, since the wisdom of the past is no longer handed down to them and the older generation is, to a large extent, not fully capable of spiritually supporting them.

The diabolical irony of our situation is that, while the occult is no longer hidden, the publicly revealed Truth of Christianity is. The further irony is that while many Church leaders, nearly as a whole, fear to preach the Truth publicly, Satanists are emboldened to proclaim their wickedness. The message is becoming that Satan and the occult are real and powerful while Jesus and the Church are weak and withering.

Girded with Truth

Given the state of the world, we must know and understand "this present darkness"[26] in which we find ourselves. If we remain

---

[25] *BBC News.* "The Three Witches of Instagram – BBC News." *YoutTube*, 10 February 2019, youtube.com/watch?v=XuX6yxOP7xY

[26] Eph 6:12

ignorant or pretend the rise of the occult is not real, we will eventually acquiesce to the slow manipulations of the Enemy which we pretend are not happening. The knowledge we need is not of the deep dark practices in which occultists are engaged, but an understanding of the lies they are told, the false promises they are made, the evils into which they are lured, the damage their rituals and beliefs bring about, the bondage they endure with demons, the addiction to the power which they suffer, the corruption of their intellects and wills, and the dangers which the fruit of their occult practices pose to themselves and to the world around them.

Jesus Christ conquered evil but there are still battles to be fought. He has recruited us to join Him in the battle and it is through us that He continues His work to save souls. Satan was not erased from the earth two thousand years ago, though he suffered a mortal wound which will one day see him chained eternally. In the meantime, the victory over evil which Christ accomplished plays out in our lives, as members of His Body, through whom He brings about this victory. If we do not participate, He cannot work through us, and evil will have its day. As those whom Christ has united to Himself and to His work of Redemption, we are not to be passivists but participants in the work of salvation.[27] As the Church Militant, we have evils to fight, and we have crowns to merit in eternal life. Christianity is the only religion capable of eradicating the occult, by captivating the souls of those attracted to the occult and showing them the Truth which, in turn, their souls will long to embrace. The history of Christianity in this fallen world consists of this captivation of souls; it is also what my research has demonstrated still to be the case in our world today.

Speaking from his experience, Andrew said the fight is critical because the occult is everywhere, even in politics, entertainment, media, and the big corporations. Therefore, Catholics need to know how to identify occult symbols and themes. Catholics also need to take precautions by living the Catholic Faith to its traditional fullness. "We need to trust God and accept that He is in charge no matter how things look in the world," he said. "We are soldiers in a war. Soldiers need to be able to identify their enemies in battle, in order that they may fight more effectively."

---

[27] Pope Ven. Pius XII, *Mystici Corporis Christi*, #12, 44, 106

Chapter Two

Most People are Blind to the Occult in Their Midst

When I first began this research, I had no real idea of how widespread the occult had become in our culture. I was one of those wearing the blinders, placed there either by naïveté, busyness, or simple ignorance. From my previous research for other books, I knew the occult was out there and, as a high school theology teacher, I had warned my students about it. However, it was only after conducting research on a wide breadth of related topics that I was finally able to see the situation for what it was.

This eye-opening is what former occultists, exorcists, and experienced parish priests want Catholics today to experience. The blinders need to come off all of our eyes. The result is not that we will see the devil under every rock but that we will simply see him where he is – extensively present throughout the culture through his minions and his influence. The occultic mindset has spread throughout the culture to such an extent that even well-meaning people have come to tolerate, and even embrace, superstitious and magical thinking at best, and full occultic practices at worst. An occultic mindset has impacted many Christians, including Protestant denominations, laymen and clergy in the Church, as well as politics and entertainment. It coats the tongues of smooth-talking politicians and "ear scratching" clergymen,[1] whose minds have been infected first by Modernism[2] and then, after that subtle destruction of faith, by occultism. Eventually, after being "slowly boiled" in the decadence and decay of the modern world, we have become so used

---

[1] "For the time is coming when people will not endure sound teaching, but having itching ears they will accumulate for themselves teachers to suit their own likings, and will turn away from listening to the truth and wander into myths." (2 Tim 4:3).

[2] A subtle and widespread movement of heresy which, as Pope St. Pius X said, embraces all heresy. It became so pervasive in the early 20th century that, as the same Pope warned, it made even some priests into open enemies of the Church.

to the modern way of thinking and speaking that it has actually become comfortable to us.

Exorcist Fr. Athanasius commented on our culture, saying, "There is a campaign of desensitizing people to the occult and then a promotion of it." Though he does not use social media, he has been told that there are very many witches and sorcerers on YouTube, Twitter, and other platforms. He is correct on that point. "The occult has entered into the mainstream," he added. "You can find occult books at the airport and at any bookstore." Yoga, for example, is in both Catholic schools and public schools. "Everyone talks about the separation of Church and State," he said, "but they're willing to settle for Yoga, a pagan religion. There are over five thousand demons associated with Hinduism!"

In a clear and startling statement, Camilla, as part of her commentary on the culture at large, said, "We are *living* in the New Age. It is a culture of instant gratification, filled with mechanical things, energy, magnets, technology. We are in love with technology and anything to do with magic and the spiritual world. The culture is in love with books and movies that have anything to do with the occult." John agreed, adding that, in modern story lines, the "hero" characters are now anti-heroes, broken heroes, or, essentially, non-hero heroes. The line between hero and villain is becoming blurred, muddying the clear lines of evil and good, black and white, into the relativistic lines of grey. Dr. Luke agreed, adding that, today, all the superheroes are either woke or flawed. The superhero that kids don't like is Captain America: he is a normal man with good morals and no flaws. Stories no longer pit true good versus evil, but a flawed, unexpected, less-evil hero against the more-evil bad guys. With this embrace of subjective morality, or even an aversion to morality in general, comes an openness to the occult, which, contrary to Christianity, embraces a renunciation of all moral distinctions.

Helena points to many signs indicating that the culture is positioned to tolerate or embrace the occult as a new religious movement. For example, many elements of the New Age and the occult are so prevalent in the culture that, while acknowledged as occultic or from a false religion, they are nonetheless looked at as harmless. "Many, many people embrace these practices as they don't look at them as *occult*," she said. Further, the culture has, in the majority, welcomed and embraced an amorality[3] based on the belief that there are no objective truths. The reign and power and prominence of homosexual and transgender agendas point not only to a diabolical agency at work but also indicate a culture deep in decay. Even more concerning is the fact that, as Helena said, *"These [moral depravities] are things embraced by the occult* and being involved with them can be an indirect way to have you embrace the occult, even without it being a conscious decision."

Accompanying this situation is what Fr. Maximilian called a "spirit of gullibility." This gullibility has obsessed our culture for many decades now. It is seen in many ways but, impacting families, it is visible in a tendency to give blind trust to mainstream news, educational systems, and television.[4] We seem to trust in everything and anything, always assuming the best intentions.[5] Parents seem to think, "Of course we can leave the TV on and trust nothing bad will be shown to us or to our children."[6] As the culture has gradually descended into godless hedonism, this spirit of gullibility has fueled the "slow boil" that many critics of the culture have spoken about. This weakness is leveraged against us in many ways, both by the normal course of diabolical temptation as well as through the efforts of the media, entertainment industry, political powers, and public-school systems to bring about a new culture no longer founded on a Christian vision of man and his purpose and destiny.

What Former Occultists See That We Do Not

The experiences of former occultists are not enviable. They wandered into a realm of darkness and have suffered for it. However, having been in the Enemy's camp, they can warn us about the dangers and true evils of the occult, the ways the Enemy pulls people

---

[3] The belief that there are no objective moral truths and, as a result, there is no such thing as *morality*, in the sense that man is bound, intrinsically, to some sort of moral code.

[4] Leading to such things as allowing children to worship the gods of the Aztecs in the California school system (see p.40) and attend occultic sage smudging ceremonies while on Catholic school field trips in Australia (in *Slaying Dragons III*).

[5] The mother of Satanic murderer, Pete Roland, said the same. She assumed everything was fine, and anything a store would sell (heavy metal albums) must be okay, yet her son was declining into homicidal Satanism partly as a result of his obsession with that music.

[6] Yet many parents are learning the hard way that so-called "children's programming" is rife with sexual deviancy and perversion.

into it, the lies and deceits, and the damage and ongoing harassment that fraternizing with the diabolical in the occult will bring. Their experiences have opened their eyes to an evil more present and active than most people can see for themselves.

For those who have been in the occult and escaped, "the radar for occult things is turned way up," as Philomena explained it. She believes that the Church and Catholic parents need to know what former occultists have to say, "so we can all see what the former occultists see and avoid the pitfalls" that led them into the occult and other forms of diabolical entanglements. "These terrible things happen – they are real," she added. Andrew said, "If more people just knew what to look for, they could avoid, or at least mitigate, the influence that those perpetrating this [hyper exposure to the occult in the culture] are trying to exercise over them. In a best-case scenario," he added, "maybe they can at least fight against it more effectively if they can just identify where it's coming at them from."

Helena said that many people who wander into the occult end up with significant diabolical issues even though they did not set out to open doors to these malevolent entities. From her perspective, the ignorance we may have about the danger of the occult does not prevent us from being harmed. "Even if they don't realize it," she explained, "we have invited these attacks into our lives, whether by things we think are harmless, like a Ouija board, or a desire for power, or emotions such as hate, among others."

Philomena said that, when you come out of the occult, you notice things differently, little things happening, demonic influences lingering around you. She once lived in a house that her middle son hated to be in; he would hear someone walking in the house when she and her husband were sleeping. She knew what this was. She also picked up on times when attitudes and moods were being mysteriously impacted.[7]

A big issue for Andrew is that, now, he cannot help but see the occult everywhere in the culture, from movies, to TV shows, to music videos, and even the politics of our country. The presence of the occult in the culture is subversive and insidious, he said. He considers this awareness to be "damage" that he suffers from his time

---

[7] Though it is possible that mysterious disturbances could be a soul from Purgatory, the characteristics of the disturbances that she noticed point toward the diabolical.

in the occult because it is a disheartening burden to carry, particularly when most people don't believe you and think you are crazy when you bring it up.

"People Think We're Crazy"

Dr. Luke, who works with youth and assists exorcists when assessing cases, said, "People are living in a malaise, a spiritual blindness, and they think that anyone who highlights the moral and spiritual problems that are present today are crazy. Everything has been turned into myth and fantasy, or into psychology and pharmaceuticals. The medical world won't try prayer or anything like it anymore because the doctors are now the gods." Lucy agreed, saying, "You are deemed a bit of an 'extremist' if you believe that occult practices are anything other than 'being about love' or at least 'just a bit of fun'." When Andrew mentions to people that some music videos are cursed,[8] he said, "Of course, many also believe that my saying that is a sign that I'm some sort of crackpot conspiracy theorist, so take that for what you will!" Gabriel expressed the same feelings, saying, "It makes you feel like you look crazy because you are pointing out all these things and they don't see it!"

Gabriel explained this situation further, in the context of a cultural occultic phenomenon involving a rapper named Lil Nas X. Gabriel said, "And this is the thing: it makes you feel like you look crazy, because you're talking about all these things, and people are like, 'What? Nah.' But it's quite clear when you really think about it." He then mentioned Lil Nas X and how he got his start in the music world with the popular song, "Old Town Road." This song was very popular, especially with kids. You can find the official music video online, but there are also lots of videos of him performing this song before children, who are both elated to see him and know the song by heart. The evil, the inversion, is that, just two years after this addictively popular song possessed the minds of children and others, Lil Nas X released his *literally* Satanic song and video, "(Montero) Call Me By Your Name."[9] He received a lot of criticism for that move

---

[8] While many exorcists believe that curses are possible, there are many others who believe they are not. The Church's tradition speaks more of the power of Christ to abolish the influence of the evil one than it does of the evil one's power.

[9] "Satanic" not by the admission of Lil Nas X but by the nature of the song and video.

from parents, but he responded by pointing out that "Old Town Road" sang about drugs and adultery, so the parents are to blame for letting their kids listen to *that* one to begin with.[10] In the end, due to the mega-publicity caused by "Old Town Road," he had gathered an immense following of impressionable youth who then celebrated as he, unsuspectingly to them, gave himself over to Satan in that next video.[11]

The corruption of a Hollywood idol with a large young following is not a new thing for the Prince of this world, but Lil Nas X, at the dawning of what has become a more Satanic age, is showing that this corruption has become perhaps more extreme and swifter. This evil was also on display at the infamous *Astroworld* concert by Travis Scott, in November of 2021, in which ten people died. This concert had the look and feel of an occultic ritual. Former occultists and concertgoers alike highlighted the demonic and hellish look and feel of many aspects of the event.[12]

John said that the longer you are in the occult, *if you successfully get out,* you can see the bigger picture in a way that other people cannot. He said he feels like he has a Cassandra complex: like a prophet saying, "don't do these things!" but everyone ignores you.[13] Once you see the occult, you cannot unsee it. He said it is similar to those who see an exorcism or witness something along those lines: they begin to say less about it after seeing the reality because no one will understand. I remember hearing an exorcist say that, during a Q&A after one of his presentations, someone stated that they simply could not believe what the exorcist was saying. The exorcist then responded, as I paraphrase, "I don't have the luxury of that ignorance. I have seen the reality."

---

[10] *Popbuzz.com,* March 30, 2021, "Lil Nas X shuts down Montero backlash by reminding parents what Old Town Road is about"

[11] In the music video, he descends into Hell and spends intimate homosexual time with the devil, graphically depicted.

[12] The now infamous rap concert by Travis Scott on November 5, 2021, which presented itself as a portal to another world and was filled with numerous occultic images. During the concert, eight people were crushed and killed, and two died later in the hospital. Panic oppressed concertgoers, who later went to social media to describe the event as feeling "like being in Hell."

[13] Cassandra, in Greek mythology, was the daughter of Priam, the King of Troy, and was cursed by Apollo to have the gift of prophecy but the inability of convincing anyone that she was correct in what she understood.

For Philomena, not knowing how to explain it to her husband, it took a year or two before she told him about her past in the occult, even after going to Church together all that time. At that point, it made sense to him, because she had a perspective on TV shows and music that he did not fully understand. As she saw it, "Those things can influence you, they are in your home – that has an impact."

The Occult in Our Midst

Many aspects of our culture are actually infused with or reflective of an occultic mindset or spirituality. They are very prevalent and have been slowly joining the mainstream cultural attitudes and practices in the last few decades, the more recent years in particular. Attitudes focused on "self-love" and emphasizing "self-help," openness to new ideas at the expense of traditional beliefs, and a desire for immediate answers and instant gratification flow out of and also into occultic philosophies.

"Self-help" and "self-love" have become ubiquitous labels within both occultic spiritualities and the secular world at large. They fit well within the occult because the occult is characterized by a Luciferian independence and self-worship. The "I" is the epicenter of all things in the occult, just as it was with Satan himself. The practitioner is in pursuit of self-deification because that is what he has been deceived to believe will bring him peace and the power to overcome all obstacles in his life. Self-help is especially prominent in the New Age movement, about which Gabriel had very strong feelings. "It is everywhere," he said, "Everywhere. Probably, almost every young person at least knows what astrology is.[14] Especially my generation, the way social media is; it's really sad." Something that really solidified it for him was the realization of how dedicated to "self-love" his generation has become. Sacred Scripture, in the words of St. Paul, as Gabriel noted, lists self-love as one of many elements of evil that will plague the world:

> But understand this, that in the last days there will come
> times of stress. For men will be lovers of self, lovers of
> money, proud, arrogant, abusive, disobedient to their

---

[14] A specifically "New Age" occult practice. See below for definition.

parents, ungrateful, unholy, inhuman, implacable, slanderers, profligates, fierce, haters of good, treacherous, reckless, swollen with conceit, lovers of pleasure rather than lovers of God, holding the form of religion but denying the power of it. Avoid such people.[15]

"Charles," Gabriel said to me, regarding this verse from St. Paul, "when I tell you...this is all that goes on. When you talk to a lot of people my age, they talk about self-love and you need to love yourself, and there's this love of money. That whole New Age kind of idea is spread among a lot of people my age, and younger. It's subtle and you might not know it, but it builds up to that."

Lucy agreed that the occult is often marketed under this "self-help" mentality. In this sense, she said, self-help guides that are disconnected from God will easily be absorbed into this occultic self-empowerment trend. The evil of the occult, at least the mainstream New Age trends, is marketed as the means to acquire, for yourself, *love, goodness, and light.* So-called "angels" are often invoked, particularly as a gateway into deeper occultic practices, and what these "angels" bring is the opposite of what was advertised. Witchcraft itself is often marketed as "self-help" which makes perfect sense, given the fact that every witch, and Wiccan, is answerable only to themselves. In these religions, the "self" is the guide and rule, and not in service or obedience to any higher being.[16] The occult perverts the good concept of taking care of yourself and flips it into making yourself a god.

An article in the Washington Post, about a teenage witch, spoke about what witchcraft often looks like to the youth today, emphasizing this element of self-help. "Young witch language," it stated, "can sound like a cross between self-help, prayer and therapy. Witchcraft has 'made me grow as a person, taught me to deal with difficulties and to have a growth mind-set,' Bennett says." The article continued, saying that the other teens who practice witchcraft and who were interviewed for this story also tended to emphasize self-

---

[15] 2 Tim 3:1-5

[16] Wicca and witchcraft, while often meeting in covens, are ultimately solitary practices, where each witch/Wiccan determines their own preferences, beliefs, and morals for their practice, answerable to no one except "the Universe" and pseudo-karmic moral concepts.

empowerment as a benefit of witchcraft. "Witchcraft," it said, "can be a powerful way to focus one's intention, they say, using elements from the natural world to create a feeling of a connection between one's own energy and something much bigger."[17]

Astrology

While the New Age is a very diverse system, it could be said that at the base of New Age thinking is what is known as "astrology," a system of discerning the meaning and purpose to your life, *why you are the way you are*, based on reading the signs of the heavens, including something called a "birth chart," which is the alignment of the stars at the moment of your birth. Astrology claims to be able to predict, and explain, the meaning and direction of your life based on some sort of control which the heavens wield over you. For the practitioner of astrology, this is often the first taste of esotericism[18] and secret knowledge, the first glimpse into secret forces at work in your life, and the first feeling that there is more "good" spirituality out there besides Christianity. Astrology is often the first step people take into the occult, serving as the widest and most outer ring at the top of the occultic "funnel," the diabolical marketing system designed to subtly lure people into the darker practices of magic. The standard and general belief among many youths today is that astrology is a real and valid source of knowledge and wisdom. It is easily accepted by people and has become quite widespread.

After astrology, Gabriel explained from his experience, would naturally come Eastern meditation, Yoga, chakras, crystals and other things, all part of the occult and all more widely accepted today. Alongside astrology, "manifestation" and the belief in the "power of positive thinking"[19] would also be in that outer ring of those first superstitious temptations. "The one that the general public is getting more into is 'positive thinking'," Gabriel said. Even people in his

---

[17] *Washington Post*, October 28, 2021, "From spellcasting to podcasting: Inside the life of a teenage witch."
[18] A philosophy that believes certain powerful truths are secret and attainable only by a select few or by those trained in understanding them.
[19] Some forms of positive thinking are good. See Chapter Seventeen > Seeking Peace.

parents' age group are into that form of the occult, talking about the power of positive thinking and "'manifesting' your reality."

"The occult is everywhere, because people don't recognize it for what it is," Adelaide said. After moving to a new area one time, during an otherwise normal conversation, she heard someone use occult language as if it were commonplace. Explaining that she moved because, among other reasons, she had broken up with someone, the person responded, "Oh, you lost your fiancé? *What sign was he?*" She said she heard that from more than one person, clarifying, "People think horoscopes are just fun and are not the occult; [but] it is divination."

Manifesting

It would seem that "manifesting"[20] is the most widespread form of the specific occultic practice of using the *personal will* to bring about change in the world. Manifesting has become a hip and trendy thing to do but, in truth, it is the same thing that fuels the rituals of "atheistic Satanism," the branch of Satanism which denies the existence of supernatural or preternatural[21] powers and entities. It is the *will* which is believed to have the *power* to effect changes within the person and in the world itself.

"Manifesting" is a new fixture in the occult world which, due to its popularity, needs to be on people's radar. As of August 2022, there were 17 billion views on TikTok #*manifestations* hashtag. One video, from Alex Tripod, who is one of thousands of "manifestation" coaches on TikTok, has 2.3 million views. "Manifestation" is based on another idea, known as the "Law of Attraction,"[22] which is based on "New Thought" from the 19th Century "mesmerist" Phineas Quimby. Rhonda Byrne's book, "The Secret," from 2006, introduced New Thought to unsuspecting millennials. These manifestation coaches are also teaching a technique called "3, 6, 9," in which the

---

[20] See Introduction for definition.

[21] Whereas *supernatural* has to do with God's activity, *preternatural* refers to the activity of angels and demons. Demons operate by the power of their fallen angelic natures, but use these powers to work against God.

[22] Many who are in the occult refer to manifesting as the "Law of Attraction." This is the idea that your thoughts have an energy, and that positive thoughts create positive things in your life, while negative thoughts do the opposite.

practitioner writes down his desire three times in the morning, six times in the afternoon, and nine times in the evening, not as a psychological technique but to "conspire with the Universe" to bring these desires into being. The intent of the practitioner is to cause these desires to *manifest* in reality through these superstitious techniques. They believe there is some sort of "energy" being generated by the practitioner which is then matched by "the Universe," which then sends good energy back to you, in the form you had initially desired.[23]

Embracing Indigenous Spiritualities

Throughout the culture, people tend to embrace certain spiritual elements that formed part of the religion indigenous to their land or from their family backgrounds. In the U.S. two forms of Native American spiritualities, among others, have become commonplace, despite their dangers and their intrinsically superstitious quality: sage smudging and dream catchers.

Philomena explained that sage smudging is a very common form of witchcraft or superstition. Philomena's husband refers to it as "soccer mom witchcraft." She lamented how many times she has seen sage-smudging in the Church. As she said, "[Smudging] is a superstition – and you don't know how that [sage bundle] is put together – there are spells involved!" She said that the fact that it is very common should not cause us to forget that these smudge sticks are put together *by someone* and this process involves real spell work. Despite that, these smudge sticks are available in stores ranging from New Age shops to Amazon and even popular bookstores like Books-a-Million.[24]

Fr. Cyprian pointed out that many indigenous cultural practices are being promoted under the banner of "openness," "inclusivity," and "diversity." This includes dream catchers, which he said are a big problem, creating a *portal* in the home that is dangerous even for those in a state of grace. These are often brought into the home by kids studying the Native American culture in schools. The society

---

[23] *The Federalist*, August 10th, 2022, "How TikTok is Teaching Anxious Gen Z Teens to Manifest Reality through Vibrations."

[24] The issue of sage as an occult practice will be covered more thoroughly in *Slaying Dragons III*.

pressures everyone, especially now children, to "celebrate" these cultures with the threat of being "cancelled" if they don't. The intent of the dream catcher is to filter out bad dreams. This is done through the agency of the pagan gods of the Native Americans which, as St. Paul teaches, are not gods but demons.[25] While sleep loss has a variety of natural causes, people who use dream catchers can suffer from *unexplained* insomnia and nonmedical sleep issues, disturbing things in their dreams, night terrors, and talking in their sleep, among other things.[26] He recommended destroying the thing and then having a priest bless and exorcise the room, the bed, and the pillows.

Sounding the Alarm and Waking Up

Christians need to see the occult's prominence as an infiltration of the culture by an enemy. The infiltration needs to be addressed on many levels, but it first needs to be acknowledged as a reality. John said, "The country is under a state of oppression – I absolutely agree. People are being slowly boiled into the occult by the moral compromises and the oppression, and that is tied in with the rise of the occult." "People are jumping out of the 'slow boil' and calling out that this has gotten worse than we knew!" Philomena added. Many people have gone from oblivious to hyper-aware. "We need a 'red-pill' moment on the issue of the occult. Former smokers and former alcoholics can detect a smoker or a drinker 'a mile away.' Similarly, ex-occultists can pick up on these evil issues before anyone else," she said.

However, when people are told about the occult's presence, many won't listen or are incredulous. Therese said, "When an ex-occultist points all this out to people, they don't understand, or they say it is hopeless, but God is always in control." Despite the difficulty of reaching people about the issue, the challenge, she said, only makes the victory more triumphant. Therese explained further, saying, "Today, with all the traditional penances being optional in

---

[25] I Cor 10:20. Psalm 106:36-37 equates the "idols" of the nations with "demons." This is repeated in Deut 32:17.

[26] There are a lot of sleep issues that have natural causes, so prudent discernment must take place before assuming the cause of the sleep issue is diabolical. Sleep paralysis and night terrors, for example, can have natural causes.

the Church, it is a great time for people to become Saints: the will is more required."[27]

Christian parents in particular have a grave obligation. They are entrusted with their children as gifts, as "talents committed to [their] charge by God...to be *restored to God with interest*."[28] The children of parents are God's children. Parents, therefore, must be fully informed of the intrusion of the occult into their children's lives. Further, they must protect them with their own parental prayers and solicitude and the building up of the child's soul as a strong temple of the Holy Spirit. They are called, commanded even, to present their children to Our Lord on the day of Judgment as holy citizens of Heaven, whose hands are filled with the many merits of good deeds.

"Waking up" also includes a deliberate effort of following St. Paul's advice: "Be not conformed to this world; but be reformed in the newness of your mind, that you may prove what is the good, and the acceptable, and the perfect will of God."[29] It means learning what the true will of God is for us and making that the way of life we embrace. Too many Christians today have merged with the world instead of enlivening it with the fire of the Holy Spirit active within them. Christians must embrace a continual conversion, a continual study of the Way, and a continual inquiry into the Church's traditional teachings on faith and morals. By doing so, they will detect the presence of the occultic perversions of the Truth and be able to counter it with the Church's teaching, which will bring light and peace to those who follow it. They will know that "self-help" is only found by self-denial and reliance on the grace of God for all things. They will know that supernatural assistance does not come from within, or from an object, or from the sheer force of a person's will to receive such things, but as a gift from Almighty God through the agents and causes that He Himself has established. We turn not to the superstitions and spiritualities of false religions, but to the immense Treasury of grace and heavenly helpers that Our Lord Jesus Christ has provided for us: His Church, the Sacraments, the sacramentals, the Angels, the Saints, and, in particular, the perpetual

---

[27] Here is an example of the distinction between the occultic use of the term "will" and the non-religious usage. Here, "the will" simply refers to the act of choosing. This is a natural act, the operation of the soul in making a choice between various options.

[28] Pius XI, *Casti Connubii*, 15.

[29] Rom 12:2 DR

and maternal intercession of our heavenly Mother, the Most Blessed Virgin Mary. For Christians who are truly steeped in the richness of the Faith, all the superstitious occultic practices that may emerge in our path in this world will immediately appear pale and vapid in comparison to the richness of Christ which we already possess.

Chapter Three

The Occult Has Infiltrated the World

The collapse of faith in modern times has blocked out much of the Light intended to shine clearly into the hearts of men through the earthly presence of the Church founded by Jesus Christ. Just as the mystical Star illuminated the path of the pagans from the East, directing them to the Christ Child in the manger, so the Church was created by God to be a living declaration of the beauty brought to earth by the God made man. In the cold absence of this Light, for men to warm their hearts, many have turned to the fires that burn on different altars. Just as when faith diminished in the hearts of the ancient Israelites and, by their sins, they pushed away God's protection, exposing themselves to violent enemies, so too, today, as men's hearts grow cold toward Christ, He cannot[1] block man's mortal enemy from walking through the now open gates of the city.

A Dark Encounter Looming

The internal presence of man's mortal enemy can be seen today through a host of manifestations. All these together, collectively forming some sort of dark spiritual awakening, sound the alarm for exorcists and former occultists. John said, "We are on the verge of a serious occultic world; sides are aligning." The truth of the matter is that, willingly or unwillingly, witches, just like Reiki masters, just like Satanists, just like New Agers, whether they know it or not, all enter into a contract with a demon. While they may have set off in this direction in pursuit of Truth and enlightenment, taking the devil's bait as did Eve, they have entered, instead, into a relationship with Satan.

---

[1] God can block the devil and desires to do so but, when we love what is evil and hate what is good, God respects our choice and we merit the consequences.

This is a clear and present danger to individuals and to the culture at large since the culture has already *jumped on the bandwagon* of the occult and made it its own. The fact that the occult has hit the mainstream and is being promoted means that naïve and curious people, more than likely uncatechized and spiritually blind, are being enticed by the devil's best weapon against souls, which he has perfected over many millennia: a religion that promises instant gratification, without moral restraints, allowing the practitioner to become god-like with little effort and maximum enjoyment. The fact that this is a self-destructive system that never delivers what it promises is only told later, and only by those who manage to escape the delusion.

The Promotion of the Occult

It must be remembered that the devil once held a great control over all mankind, working, though, as he does, in the shadows. From the Fall of Adam to the Birth of Christ, Satan enjoyed relatively unrivaled power over mankind. This was the consequence of mankind's preference, in Adam and Eve, to choose themselves, and the philosophy and teachings of the serpent, over that of their Creator. Originally possessing "dominion over the earth,"[2] man handed that over to Satan when he fell from grace in the Original Sin. This gave Satan a crushing hammer, wielded over millennia through various methods: political oppression, the fomenting of vices, the instigation of the disordered passions of the now-fallen human nature, and diabolical manipulation for the encouragement of superstition and magical arts.[3]

Thus, the occult was promoted unchecked for over four thousand years. The coming of Christ revealed the first authoritative upending of this diabolical spirituality. In Christ, the Eternal Word, the proper orientation of man was Personally re-established. Through Baptism and incorporation into the Church, *all* mankind was then offered participation in true worship and filial obedience to God. Satan, aware of the emergence of the King and Messiah, did everything in his power to take advantage of His mortal existence to

---

[2] Gen 1:26
[3] See Pope Leo XIII, *Humanum Genus* 20, for example.

bring about His death and rid the world of this disturbance to his own kingdom. However, that did not work. As the Book of Revelation teaches, after Christ definitively established His Kingdom on the earth after rising from the dead, Christ Himself presented a crushing hammer to mankind, for us to wield *against* the Kingdom of Satan.

The Book of Revelation says that Satan, knowing his time is now short, and the final end of his oppression of mankind is soon to come, is now lashing out in a great fury.[4] Further, it reveals that, to finally sway man away from Christ and His Holy Church, Satan will stir up great "signs and wonders."[5] These he will use to seduce man into apostasy from the Truth and back into captivity. Thus, the appearance of the occult within our culture must come as no surprise, as it has been a recurrent temptation throughout the history of the world, rearing its ugly head too many times, and causing much destruction and loss of souls. Today is no different, though the scale on which the occult has spread is truly of great concern.

Fr. Ambrose made a disturbing observation about the present infusion of the occult into the culture. He said that, when society mainstreamed homosexuality in the last decade, and it went into all entertainment programming and the media, those who were adults were able to observe the society change, and simply felt like they could not do anything about it. Kids, however, were growing up with the change already in place, and began to see it as normal and, as a result, embraced the ideology. The same thing is happening with the occult, such as Yoga, Reiki, and going to psychics and mediums. Psychics, for example, are in all the programming on TV, and talk shows often bring them on, presenting it as safe and claiming that "everything is fine." The media, he lamented rhetorically, "is run by the devil."

Exorcists and former occultists attest that, as a result of the infiltration by the occult, and its embrace by the culture at large, the number of occultic practitioners is on the rise, and the chance of encountering it as we go about our lives is also increasing. Lucy, for example, sees the occult everywhere in the culture, describing it in these terms: psychics masked as prophets; burning sage in a house to

---

[4] Rev 12:12
[5] Rev 13:13-14,16:14; Matt 24:23-25

cleanse it; reading star signs; the embrace of 'mindfulness'; the proliferation of Yoga; the practice of trying to 'manifest' things through our own 'powers'; the enshrinement of abortion; euthanasia; idolizing public figures; various crystal jewelry, each kind with specific occultic uses (i.e. *rose* quartz is *supposed* to help with love); 'energetic' healing; offering or asking for people to 'send love and light' or 'good vibes'; inclusivism of all behaviors and beliefs, among others. Helena also sees a whole host of occult practices normalized and embraced by the culture. She pointed out Tarot cards, palm reading, belief in past lives, astral projection,[6] Eastern meditation, the Law of Attraction, psychic readings, angel readings,[7] numerology, channeled readings, astrology, "A Course in Miracles," mediumship, and spirit guides. The variety of the manifestations of the occult is truly mind-bending and adds to the difficulty of pinning it down definitively.

The Sources of the Modern Promotion

The culture at large is influenced by organizations with both popular appeal and a widespread reach. While the Church today is relatively good at influencing local areas, the *culture* is being influenced by entities which have a national appeal: online and print magazines, the entertainment industry, government-controlled educational systems (public schools), mainstream media and news outlets, popularized irregular medical practices, and the online social media universe. Many of these directly promote the occult while many others simply parrot its language and further hand it on to the individual citizen.

Magazines

Popular modern magazines often feature aspects of occult practice for their readers. In 2017, *Vogue*, which boasts of twenty-two million monthly readers, published an article titled, "How to Awaken Your Inner Witch," which included a spell to assist in doing so. *Teen*

---

[6] The practice, through drugs or occultic meditation, of attempting to leave the body behind and travel in the "astral planes" or observe the physical universe.

[7] Similar to, but simpler than, tarot card readings, in which the person supposedly communicates with the "angels" that are around him.

Vogue, with twelve million users and fourteen million followers on social media, has stories about witches, psychics, mediums, spells, astrology, and magic, in addition to an entire section called "Practical Magic." As demonstrated in an article in October 2021, titled "10 Signs Your Home may be Haunted," *Teen Vogue* went on to present a list of signs of a ghost's presence which actually intermingled clear signs of the demonic alongside those of a friendly soul from Purgatory. Witches, though, often do not distinguish between ghosts and demons, just between good spirits and bad spirits, so perhaps this is the issue. Nevertheless, the list indicated that an individual could conclude that certain signs, which in truth are typical of a *demon's* presence, actually indicate the presence of a *friendly ghost*, thus setting up the person for untold diabolical harassment. Similar to *Vogue* is Allure.com. *Allure*, which has lots of articles promoting the occult, has close to six hundred thousand followers on Twitter, one and a half million followers on Facebook, and one million followers on Instagram. Further, for example, they have over one thousand articles on "astrology."

Entertainment

There is no question that the entertainment industry is hooked on preternatural and occult themes. This is not necessarily new but it has surely reached a point of infatuation that did not characterize prior decades of moviemaking. It is astounding how many former and current witches and occultists reference the fact that watching popular occult-themed shows served as a gateway to the occult for them. Shows like *Sabrina, Buffy, Supernatural, Charmed, Angel, Ghost Whisperer,* and *Twilight,* among others, have filled this role. Though it did not come up in my research as much, this highlights the related danger of books, such as *Harry Potter,* and their ability to also play on occultic curiosities and encourage someone toward the practice.

While Hollywood's promotion of the occult in film is not as surprising, given its reputation and the worldliness of its stars, there is a very shocking example in Disney. Formerly hailed as a kid-friendly source of television programming and movies, Disney has begun to feature stories and morals that are clearly occultic. "Owl's House" and "Little Demon" are just two examples. "Owl's House" tells the story of a young girl on a journey to become a witch. It was also the first show in which two homosexual characters were depicted showing affection in a Disney Channel series. "Little Demon," a more recent and more grotesque show, depicts a pagan woman, whose child is the spawn of Satan. The show is filled with interplay between demons, pagan rituals, blood and gore, nudity and vulgar language…and is playing on *Disney plus* for all the kiddos to enjoy.

Disney hasn't stopped at occultic shows, though. It is also promoting tools of witchcraft to those who love its products. This can be seen, among countless other examples, in the "Official Disney Nightmare Before Christmas Tarot Card deck." They promote this as "the perfect gift for Tim Burton's The Nightmare Before Christmas fan or tarot enthusiast in your life." This product description comes from the listing for the product on Books-a-Million's website, which is apparently happy to help disseminate this evil.

Education

In a story that made headlines for a while, though perhaps not for long enough, California launched an educational agenda that included coaching children to offer prayers to Aztec gods.

CatholicVote, in January 2022, reported on the successful lawsuit stopping the State of California from including pagan chants in a new Ethics Studies Model Curriculum. As the lawsuit pointed out, the curriculum did not simply teach the children about the chants, as being poetry or history, but presented them as prayers *to be said by the children,* thereby directly invoking these deities. The prayers were intended "for emotional nourishment" and these incantations were intended to be used as true prayers. The co-chair of this program taught that Christianity had committed "theocide" when it converted the pagan Aztecs, and that these prayers would aid in the effort to "regenerate indigenous spiritual traditions." The article also quoted an education reformer named Christopher Rufo:

> Rufo wrote that the incantation's inclusion in public school curricula 'would have forced students to chant to the Aztec god of human sacrifice in order to become

'warriors' for 'social justice'.' 'I grew up in California and we recited the Pledge of Allegiance every morning,' Rufo added. 'It's truly mind-boggling that, one generation later, they're trying to make kids chant to the Aztec god of human sacrifice. But that's what happens when you let neo-Marxists take over the institutions.[8]

The fact that these prayers were to a god of human sacrifice must be noted. The rise in the occult is openly connected to abortion, the modern-day equivalent of ritual sacrifice to many of the pagan gods of old.

The general structure of public schools today, with some exceptions, is setting kids up for interest in the occult. Once they have been worn down with the anti-Christian, woke ideology, all the while searching for a spiritual answer to their souls' longings, kids will be open to the "new religion" popping up around them. Fr. Anselm pointed out that one way young people are falling into occult practices is through the influence of classmates' parents who are doing it. These classmates then bring it into the school and introduce other kids to it. There are videos everywhere on the internet teaching kids how to curse people and cast all sorts of spells. Once the curiosity has been piqued, the internet takes care of the rest.

In one example of the corrupting power of modern schools, Margaret told me of her agonizing decision to end homeschooling and enroll her children in the local public school system. Remembering that good schools did exist and could be helpful, Margaret eventually made the decision. In her area, there appeared to be good options, so she decided to try, and enrolled her two oldest into public middle and high school. The immediate experience was one of vicious teasing. This crushed the spirits of one of her children, "who had a spirit of naïveté and blind trust," Margaret said, adding, "which was broken by the kids." As a result of the hurt from the cruel teasing, the daughter, too, became mean and vicious. Soon, the kids were bringing home pot and cocaine from school, and the older

---

[8] *CatholicVote*, January 17, 2022, "California Removes Pagan Incantation from Schools after Parents Sue."

kids began teaching the youngest, not yet in a public middle school, how to use them. So, as Margaret put it, "They got into drugs." With all of these disordered interests emerging, and the Faith dying inside of them, they also began wandering down the street to the local witch store.

Popular Irregular Medical Practices

In the modern medical world, acupuncture, Eastern meditation, and Yoga, among others, have been incorporated into patient treatments for decades. Reiki,[9] for example, an explicitly occultic practice, has seen a tremendous growth in popularity within hospitals in the last decade or two.[10] The number of hospitals offering Reiki, in 2014, was already at sixty, while Reiki education was being offered at the time to eight hundred hospitals. Further, thirty thousand nurses in 2014 were using Reiki in hospitals in the U.S.[11] In 2020, though Reiki had been offered in hospitals for over six years, many medical providers, as the Atlantic reported, still thought it was "quackery." While Yoga had already become a "popular complement to conventional medicine," having "been the subject of rigorous scientific studies that have established and explained [its] effectiveness,"[12] Reiki "is particularly vexing to naysayers because Reiki delivers demonstrable salutary effects without a proven cause." While studies have demonstrated that Reiki helps alter the experience of pain, regulate the nervous system, and bring better outcomes to surgery, "No conclusive, peer-reviewed study has explained its mechanisms much less confirmed the

---

[9] An occult practice originating in Japan purporting to bring about physical healing by manipulating energies in the body and "the Universe." Those initiated into the practice at the lower level are not told this but the "power" is flowing from a *familiar spirit*, i.e. a demon.

[10] In addition to these, Catholics need to be wary of many other occultic things that have snuck into, or are an essential part of, many "alternative" health procedures today. These include homeopathy, certain chiropractic elements, and associations of medical treatments with abortion. The latter have varying associations with the New Age which Catholics need to prudently analyze.

[11] *Religion News Service*, May 16, 2014, "Reiki goes mainstream: Spiritual touch practice now commonplace in hospitals."

[12] The existence of many studies "explaining" how Yoga works does not, therefore, mean it is "natural" or "medical" or "safe" or devoid of superstitious or dangerous spiritual elements.

existence of a healing energy that passes between bodies on command."[13] Many popular hospitals offer Reiki today and report signs of a more-than-placebo mechanism at work.[14] The embrace of Reiki comes despite the fact that no one knows *why* it is working, that it is clearly an occultic practice, and that it can boast of being one of the few modern occultic practices to receive an explicit condemnation by the United States Bishops.[15]

Music

While not all music is evil, the pop culture of today, with which many kids are truly obsessed, is the offspring of a long and successive lineage of musicians who have dedicated their music to licentiousness, rebellion, sin, Satan, the occult, promiscuity, impurity, anger, violence, and other sorts of disordered and deviant behavior. Many of these "artists" are publicly known to be influenced by the occult in some fashion.[16] Today, even among so-called Catholic youth, the music they are hooked on is shocking in its perversion but, to them, it's just the way music is. Many accept it and go about their day. The shock itself, for many, is simply another form of entertainment.

The inability of parents to regulate the music their children are exposed to is one of the major curses our culture is under. We live in a music-saturated society and, with all things being digital, and earbuds being out of sight, it is almost impossible for busy parents to know what is on their child's playlist. The addictive property of this music, combined with the fact that the youth imbibe in this form of entertainment for hours upon hours every day, makes it tantamount to a form of brainwashing. It should not be a surprise, but rather expected, when those who listen to this music begin to demonstrate that they have truly been formed by it.

Margaret, in raising her children, said that in her house the music was very regulated, but she learned that her children were all

---

[13] *The Atlantic,* April 2020, "Reiki Can't Possibly Work. So Why Does It?"

[14] Johns Hopkins, NY-Presbyterian, California Pacific Medical Center, Dana-Farber/Harvard Center, among many others. (via ReikiInMedicine.org > Reiki in Hospitals)

[15] *USCCB.org,* March 25, 2009, "Guidelines for Evaluating Reiki as an Alternative Therapy."

[16] The documentary *Hells Bells II* is very thorough at presenting this disturbing reality.

going after the horrible music of the culture when away from the house. She mentioned *Suicide Boys*, other heavy metal groups, and other bands she regarded as disgusting. She has seen a strong negative influence on her children as a result of music.

Though there are many examples of perverted music, such as that of Lil Nas X and Travis Scott, another one comes from Dove Cameron, a former Disney star. On the heels of her popular song, "Boyfriend," which amounted to a creepy homosexual rant, Dove Cameron released "Breakfast," a similarly aggressive feminist presentation which calls to mind the image of the Hindu deity, Kali the Destroyer. "Breakfast" has also been a big hit with witches, which is how it appeared in my research, since it is focused on the embrace of a threatening feminine power with the potential to be destructive. The connection between homosexuality, with which Cameron now publicly identifies, and witchcraft is to be noted, as are the self-destructive tendencies of embracing both philosophies.[17] In May of 2022, Cameron shared on her Instagram, as reported by People magazine, that she is "struggling more than half the time" with her identity, her concept of self, gender norms, and sexuality. Mentioning dysphoria in passing, she also stated, "More days than not, I feel pulled towards no identity at all, I feel most natural as something imperceivable to myself, an energy and a presence."[18] Witches, and anyone else infatuated with this sort of music, will similarly feel the negative consequences of the beliefs it celebrates.

People who have been around Hollywood, including those who would become priests, have told the stories of bands dedicating albums to Satan, and witches placing curses on the music as it is recorded or otherwise created. The truth of this reality is not the easiest to discover, but there is much which makes people wonder if it has really reached that level. On this issue, Lucy said, "I believe that music is used to curse people with the words which are sung, the costumes which are worn, possibly the frequency at which the music

---

[17] Fr. Cyprian added that homosexuality, as an inversion of the divine order, is almost always driven by demons. Exorcists have noted the numerous specific demons who encourage the various forms of homosexual attraction. One of these demons also encourages child sacrifice, both in the literal sense and in preventing it from happening in the first place.

[18] *People.com*, May 19, 2022, "Dove Cameron Shares Emotional Post About 'Identity': 'I'm Struggling More Than Half of the Time'"

is played, the symbolism in the clips, and the actual sounds themselves. Listening to and watching negative and evil words and actions, damages minds and souls."[19]

A good example of music's ability to be used for evil is in the statements of then-Satanist Nikolas Schreck.[20] In his 1989 interview with Bob Larson, he discussed his creation of music intended to be used for Satanic rituals. He was clear about its direct connection to this purpose, stating, "Even by the act of listening to it, you are participating in a Satanic ritual. It is stirring, emotionally charged; you can't listen and say you don't feel something because you do." He has one song, called Incubus, about which he says, "It's designed for sexual arousal, of course." The term "Incubus" is given to a demon associated with sexual encounters with people. Further, youth such as Pete Roland, who committed murders in the name of Satan, spoke in interviews of their obsession with heavy metal music and the impact it had on them. Highlighting the bombardment of anger and violence in the lyrics and sound of the music, often combined with elements of Satanism, which he listened to three or four hours a day, every day for months and years, he said, plainly, "It can get to you."[21]

Lucy pointed out that, as is the case in Hollywood, when good actors are forced to go elsewhere because they won't "join the team" and forfeit their morals in order to get ahead, such is also the case with good musicians. Good musicians are often sidelined either because they won't go along and don't get promoted, or they refuse to be affiliated with the big business of music and thus are never heard by the culture. As a result, most of the music that is blasted on the airwaves or streamed online is the sort approved by the woke and wicked cultural powers.

The Occult and Technology

While great blame is placed on the internet and social media for providing the means for the youth and adults to seek out every curious interest, disordered and occultic, it is not just the internet

---

[19] Here, the "curse" could also be an enticement toward evil by means of the elements of the music.

[20] The former husband of Zeena (formerly LaVey) Schreck. In Larson video #1.

[21] Pete Roland interview, by Geraldo Rivera, documentary on Satanism, 1988.

but other modes of technology which are contributing to the spread of the occult.

Gabriel told me that he once had an app on his phone that would allow him to "talk to spirits" by translating the wavelengths in the room, or by some similar technique. Through the app, he said, you could summon a spirit to you and then have a conversation with it. He was doing this early on in his New Age explorations. One time, he spoke through the app and said, "Is there anybody here in the room?" In response, he got a word or two through the app, which led him to react, "Woah, somebody's here!" Speaking about how deceptive the whole thing was, he added, "You don't think it's dark but you think it's a good spirit you're talking to, and that you simply have to be careful to avoid dark spirits, because, as I told myself, 'It's the Satanists and the witches that are doing the dark stuff, not me'." He would also tell himself, "I'm not going to get into the dark stuff," but, as he readily admitted in our conversation, "I already was."

Dabbling with occult things on the phone or computer poses a hidden danger that exorcists are discovering through work with spiritually burdened and afflicted people. Exorcist Fr. Alphonsus shared a story about a man who was in the hospital with various problems. The man's brother came to speak to Father about his concerns. The brother said he had looked at the man's phone and noticed that the man had been visiting websites containing diabolical stuff and he was concerned that the problems the man was having were diabolical. Father was not convinced at first but he took the phone to a seer[22] who helps the diocesan exorcism team. When the seer saw the phone, she nearly dropped it. "There were so many demons present," he said, explaining, "She can see them in pictures and on screens when they appear." Father also showed her a picture of the man in the hospital and she saw demons all over him as well. As it turned out, the man was actually possessed and soon came under the care of Fr. Alphonsus and his deliverance team.

---

[22] A seer, in this case, is a layman who has been recognized by the local Church to have a spiritual gift. They may also be referred to as a "gifted person." These gifts vary, as St. Paul describes in I Corinthians 12. They have no official function in the Church but are individually evaluated by competent priests and deemed authentic, thereby permitted to assist the Church in the manner that their gifts enable.

In the Military

The military has not escaped the impact of the infusion of the occult into society. Fr. Dominic, who served as a pastor near a military base, noted that Nordic paganism, and a lot of the other sorts of occult practices, were growing in popularity there. He said the popularity of Norse pagan religions in popular entertainment (television and movies) has led to its appeal among members of the military. The Norse religion is depicted as "a warlike, earthy, pre-Christian alternative to the Christian ethos, depicting Christianity as soft and ethereal and out-of-touch," he said, adding, "Many want to connect to their heritage or have a sense of their historical identity, and a warrior religion is appealing." These soldiers take up a more or less serious practice of the religion, he said. Some adopt little superstitious rituals or a simple prayer to some Norse god, whereas others will invest thousands of dollars in books and practice rituals on a daily basis. The Norse paganism, Father added, offers something very similar to Satanism, something on which many who adopt the practice likely have not reflected. The principles of both religions are the same, he said, explaining it as, "Don't bend the knee, stand up proud, and grab what you want for yourself. What these people unfortunately figure out – though thankfully many do – is that they're bending their knee to a preternatural and malicious intelligence."

Christopher, who was in the military at one point said he had a lot of friends who engaged in occult practices. He also saw the presence and appeal of the Norse paganism, in particular the belief in Valhalla.[23] "It is ridiculously appealing for warriors to have a place in Heaven just for warriors," Christopher added. He also said there is an increasing number of active Satanists. "They would wear a ring with a Baphomet skull," Christopher said, "just like I would wear a Sacred Heart ring."[24] In one meeting he attended, in an event that is very difficult to understand, the military presented a slideshow on the Covid jab to servicemen to convince them to take the injection. In the slideshow, they decided to present the seven tenets of the Satanic Temple (TST), including an image of Satan resembling

---

[23] A majestic hall where many of those who died in war are permitted to enter. It is overseen by the god Odin.

[24] The Baphomet is the modern patron demon of many Satanists.

TST's demon Baphomet. "In the past," he said, "this would not have been tolerated. A platoon sergeant, for example, would have gotten his whole crew out of there immediately and filed a complaint." Though this incident did make the news, such as with Tucker Carlson, it was much more passively endured than it would have been decades ago.[25]

In his 1988 documentary, Geraldo Rivera asked a captain in the United States Army, who was sitting in the front row of the audience, looking at Michael Aquino[26] on the stage, "What is your feeling, sir, on the fact that a serving officer in the United States Army [Michael Aquino] is also a professed Satanist, a high-ranking person?" The father responded, "Well, I think, in this election year, we've heard a lot about values, Geraldo. We've heard a lot that our little children should be saying the pledge of allegiance to the flag. Mr. Aquino has identified himself as an antichrist. He preaches that as the leader of the Temple of Set. I don't think I'm misquoting him. I find it inconceivable that we can have candidates talking about 'one nation under God,' and having our children say that, yet by the same token we can have somebody in our army, as a colonel, leading our troops in battle, who is opposed to the very concept of God and whose whole purpose it is to fight against God."

The Diabolical and the Occult

With occultic practices come the ones who ride in on the occult: the demons. The real problem with the occult is that it is a vehicle of the diabolical and a powerful means by which demons will infiltrate and gain a hold on a culture. Exorcist Msgr. Rossetti, wrote, "An increasing exposure to the demonic brings with it a darkness,

---

[25] When discussing the military vaccine mandate, Carlson presented a power point presentation that the army was using to help justify, to the military members, why the vaccine was made mandatory for the military. For some reason, it included these seven tenets of Satanism. After he reached out to the military, they admitted it was authentic, but stated it had not been *approved*, "whatever that means," as Carlson said. Sept. 20, 2021.

[26] Michael Aquino is the founder of the Temple of Set, an organization very similar to the Church of Satan, though the Temple of Set differs by declaring a belief in a literal entity known as Set, which is essentially the same entity as Satan.

heaviness, and a depressive effect."[27] This is an all too accurate description of our culture's woes. Msgr. Rossetti then went a step further and described a rising concern regarding the presence of diabolically influenced thinking in the lives of individuals in our country. He recounted a time when a person, who had been offered to evil spirits as a child, by parents who were involved in witchcraft and other forms of the occult, came to him for help. During the consultation with the priest, a demon started speaking through her mouth. People, he said, especially the possessed, when demons have entered their heads, "start thinking like demons." He added, "I'll bet there are more than a few people we meet during the day whose minds are filled with demons. Listen to what comes out of people's mouths. Is it a rational human being speaking or an angry, God-hating, arrogant demon?"[28]

Demons are also infiltrating areas of cities where the occult is practiced. Fr. Alphonsus mentioned, as an example, that more and more tattoo artists are into the occult, cursing needles and the ink they use, and putting cursed tattoos on people.[29] He then told the story of a time when he was attacked by a demon while driving past one of those locations. Father said, "I remember getting diabolically attacked going by a local tattoo parlor at my old parish. As soon as I went by, I suddenly felt a massive oppression. Certainly, the demons were aware of *my* presence! So, I had to go and pray prayers over myself, deliverance prayers, 'In the Name of Jesus Christ...please Lord send them to the foot of Your Cross.' After that, it lifted very quickly." Father said we all need to know this and be prudent about what areas of cities we visit.

Msgr. Rossetti observed that it is now more important than ever that people bless their food and everything they consume. He told the story about a gifted individual on his deliverance team, with the ability to see demons, who was eating with the exorcist one time and suddenly hesitated to eat, requesting that Father bless the food. The manner of her asking made him pause. He asked if there were demons on the food, and she confirmed that there were. After the

---

[27] Fr. Stephen Rossetti, *Diary of an American Exorcist*, (Manchester: Sophia Institute Press, 2021), 151.

[28] Rossetti, *Diary*, 89

[29] Cursing, while not prevalent in the New Age, truly is an aspect of many forms of witchcraft and Satanism.

standard meal blessing, the demons departed. Msgr. Rossetti then advised, "This might seem odd, but I have found out that there are more people cursing things and engaged in occultic practices than I would have expected."[30]

The Resistance

The infiltration of the culture by a hostile spiritual power is not a comforting thing of which to become aware. However, it is important to live with a true understanding of our surroundings and of the prevailing philosophies in our midst. This is the bridge by which we will meet the pagans of our day in the moments of evangelization which will be provided by the Holy Spirit. When St. Paul entered Athens, his spirit was "stirred within him" when he saw "the city wholly given to idolatry."[31] Despite this, he forcefully convinced the Athenians to listen to his presentation of the One True Faith. By the conviction of his words, though some mocked, and some merely wanted to hear him again, many also believed. By his determination and his conviction that Christ had conquered and will definitively conquer all false gods and liberate the hearts of all men who will receive Him, in Athens and elsewhere St. Paul brought a great many into the Church.

As we come to terms with the fact that our culture truly is surrounded by idols, we must begin to let our spirits be *stirred within us* as well and, like St. Paul, increase our reliance on the presence of Christ in our souls. By doing so, living in the fullness of the Truth and embracing the complete sacramental life provided by the Church, we can maintain our own faith in this troubled world and, God willing, bring this occultic world back to its senses and into the Church.

---

[30] Rossetti, *Diary*, 51. Fr. Cyprian, noticing the rise in occultic names for beers, advises that we be certain to bless anything that we consume.
[31] Acts 17:16 DR

Chapter Four

The World and the Occult Have Infiltrated the Church

The infiltration of the occult into human affairs really knows no limits in this age. Sadly, this expansion of evil even includes breaching the doors to the household of the Faith.[1] This breach, while a great scandal to behold, should not shake our faith in Christ or in the truth, beauty, and power of His Holy Catholic Church. Our Lord predicted things like this would come, both in His words and in the Death, instigated by one of His own Apostles, to which He would ultimately submit. At the end of His earthly ministry, He permitted Judas to betray Him unto crucifixion. However, well before that, Our Lord had already warned, in His parable of the wheat and tares, that the enemy of man (Satan) would sow his evil seed, "the children of the wicked one," into the world, and that Our Lord would not uproot them but allow them to grow alongside "the children of the Kingdom" until the end of time.[2] This includes the possibility of corruption inside the Church, against which the Church has ever had to be vigilant.[3]

The fact that priests, religious, and laity have, throughout time, succumbed to the temptation toward worldly morals and the occult, does not indicate that the Catholic Church is *not* truly the Bride of Christ who, remaining ever spotless and faithful to her Divine Spouse, will always steer mankind safely to the gates of Paradise. Instead, it indicates the power of evil to operate against, and within, our fallen human nature *even if* we have been brought into

---

[1] Gal 6:10

[2] Matt 13:38 DR

[3] We must also remember that this battle is intrinsic to the Christian life just as it was to Christ Himself who, as He stated numerous times, eagerly desired to fulfill His mission and offer Himself on the Cross. Cf Luke 12:49-50, "I came to cast fire upon the earth; and would that it were already kindled! I have a baptism to be baptized with; and how I am constrained until it is accomplished!"

communion with Christ through Baptism. Recalling the Fall of Adam and Eve, we see this reality present from the beginning: man, on earth, in this time of testing and proving our fidelity to Christ, can still, no matter how firmly bound he may be to Our Lord, fall away from the Faith and turn to the counsel of the serpent.

As a result, we must all be on our guard against this potential for evil. The devil tempts children, youth, parents, laity, deacons, priests, and Bishops. No one, inside or outside of the Church, is free from diabolical interference until their souls depart from this world at death and are bound eternally to God. Further, it is a clear truth that the devil seeks to take down those who seek to take up their Cross and follow Jesus unto the end. In particular, this concerns those who enter the religious life and, especially, the hierarchy of the Church. *Corruptio optimi pessima*: the corruption of the best is the worst of all. So, when the truth is revealed that *the best*, i.e., the leaders of the Church, have become corrupted by evil, it is not against them that we should open our anger but against the tempter who has deceived them. We are all brethren on a journey through a valley of tears and thorns; there are none against whom we are permitted to spiritually "turn our backs." That being said, when a man aligns himself with evil, he does become our enemy, and we must prudently resist him and stand on guard, lest his malice be permitted to harm us or those we love. All the while, we pray for his soul.

A Diabolical Era of Weakness

While the Church is tasked with drawing mankind away from *the world*[4] and toward eternal life with God, the state of the world is mirrored today in the state of the Church, which sees a decline in fidelity and holiness even among her own members and leaders. The presence of this evil within the Church could not come at a worse time. This scenario places us in a situation that resembles Israel in the time of the Judges, when the Scriptures famously stated, "In those days, there was no king in Israel; every man did what was

---

[4] "The world" is the biblical term used to refer to the fallen state of mankind in this passing realm under the influence of demons.

right in his own eyes."[5] In August 2022, Cardinal Burke echoed this reality:

> The poison of worldly thinking infects the life of the Church, drawing hearts away from Christ, from respect for the truth of Christian doctrine and discipline, and from the worship of God in spirit and in truth. An advancing apostasy is painfully evident in the lives of those who claim to be devout Catholics while at the same time they disregard the apostolic tradition by which the Faith, and divine grace, are handed on to us, at every time and every place. In such times, sincere hearts struggle to understand the permissive will of God, while Satan tempts them to doubt and to discouragement and to the abandonment of the daily battle against the forces of evil.[6]

This apostasy and abandonment of the truths of our Faith leaves the world without a steady anchor in the Truth nor a bright beacon to draw man in the right direction. This leads mankind into absurd behaviors and beliefs and the paganism that is rampant in our world today. The Second Vatican Council warned of the consequences of this decline when it said, "When God is forgotten, however, the creature itself grows unintelligible."[7] Cardinal Robert Sarah, observing this very thing happening, spoke similarly when he said, "If our first concern is not God, then everything else collapses."[8] The world at large has truly forgotten God and, as is on display in the news on a daily basis, mankind is no longer intelligible to itself.[9] Thus, man appears lost, yet he still seeks the answers to the ultimate questions. Since God is shunned from man's life, and not permitted to provide these answers, the demons, whom all the while we

---

[5] Jud 21:25
[6] Institute of Christ the King, Wausau, August 8th, 2022. Institute-christ-king.org/uploads/wausau/sermons/2022-08-08.mp3
[7] Gaudium et Spes, 36.
[8] *National Catholic Register*, September 23, 2019, "Cardinal Sarah's Cri de Coeur: The Catholic Church Has Lost Its Sense of the Sacred"
[9] As seen in the effort to normalize aberrations such as homosexual marriage and transgenderism, as well as the desire the mutilate the body through surgeries (for gender dysphoria) and excessive tattoos, piercings, and other bodily and moral disfigurements.

entertain, will gladly fill the void and give their own. Cardinal Sarah gave an interview with Edward Pentin on September 13, 2019. In that interview, His Eminence addressed this, saying:

> I have tried to show in this book [*The Day is Now Far Spent*] that the common root of all current crises is found in this fluid atheism, which, without denying God, lives in practice as if he did not exist. In the conclusion of my book, I speak of this poison of which we are all victims: liquid atheism. It infiltrates everything, *even our speeches as clergymen.* It consists in admitting, alongside faith, radically pagan and worldly ways of thinking or living. And we satisfy ourselves with this unnatural cohabitation![10]

On July 10, 2021, Cardinal Burke gave an address on the 25th Anniversary of the CREDO of the Catholic Laity. In that address, speaking on the same theme as Card. Sarah above, His Eminence said, "There is no question that we are experiencing an unprecedented crisis in the life of the Church."[11] Acknowledging that crises have emerged before, such as when the Arian crisis led many priests and faithful to deny Christ's Divinity, he added, "Rome, however, even if at times suffering from weakness, always, in the end, held to the truths of the faith and morals. In the present moment in the Church, the See of Peter itself seems confused and unwilling to correct open violations of faith and morals."[12] This alarming enough, but Card. Burke shows how the gravity of the situation is still greater, adding, "In a diabolical way, the crisis which has rendered the Church exceedingly weak comes precisely at a time when the secular culture, which has abandoned not only the Christian faith but reason herself, most needs the Church to teach clearly and strongly the truth written upon the human heart and in

---

[10] *National Catholic Register*, September 23, 2019, "Cardinal Sarah's Cri de Coeur: The Catholic Church Has Lost Its Sense of the Sacred." *Emphasis* mine.
[11] CardinalBurke.com > Media > Presentations. "CREDO of the Catholic Laity" is a group founded in Missouri seeking to correct the waywardness of the Church in that area.
[12] Such as, among many other situations, the silence of Rome when Cardinal Pell called on the Vatican to publicly correct the heretical statements on morality from Cardinal Hollerich and Bishop Bätzing.

nature itself, from the Creation, and revealed in its fullness through the Redemptive Incarnation. We are living in most troubled times in the world and also in the Church."[13]

Though the full presentation of the rich traditions of the Church, in her traditional liturgy and her traditional teachings, are absent from the public presentation of the Faith today, people of the world are indeed craving these sacred treasures, as if sensing that, despite the great silence about them, they truly do exist. My interviews with former occultists revealed this quite clearly. Cardinal Burke, in his address on the 25th Anniversary of the CREDO of the Catholic Laity, obviously sensed this as well. He said, "The world has never needed more the solid teaching and direction which Our Lord, in His immeasurable and unceasing love of man, wishes to give to the world through His Church and especially through her pastors: the Roman Pontiff, the Bishops in communion with the See of Peter, and their principal co-workers, the priests."[14] The terror of the present crisis cannot be understated, and His Eminence is not afraid to associate this crisis with the work of Satan himself. He continued, "But, in a diabolical way, the confusion and error which has led human culture in the way of death and destruction has also entered into the Church, so that she draws near to the culture without seeming to know her own identity and mission, without seeming to have the clarity and the courage to announce the Gospel of Life and Divine Love to the radically secularized culture."[15]

This state of bewilderment from which it appears the Church is reeling is an opportunity for the evil one to strike at the faithful whose feet, owing to wayward shepherds, as St. Peter Damian said, are practically snared "in the bonds of [the wayward Bishop's] own ruin." [16] In an interview with the National Catholic Register in February, 2022, Cardinal Muller said we are living in a time of "tribulation and psychological terror" in which Catholics are persecuted by members of the Church's hierarchy. He described this as a "new situation." In Germany, the hierarchy, with the support of

---

[13] CardinalBurke.com > Media > Presentations

[14] Ibid

[15] Ibid

[16] St. Peter Damian, *Book of Gomorrah: An Eleventh Century Treatise Against Clerical Homosexual Practices*, Pierre J. Payer, trans. (Waterloo, Ont., Wilfrid Laurier University Press, 1982), 72.

several Cardinals, has moved in the direction of revising the teaching on homosexuality, blessing same-sex unions, and ordaining women. "They relativize the Catholic faith, but remain with their titles: Cardinals, Bishops, theology professors," he said. They believe in "pseudo-sciences," not Revelation, and support an "idiotic" agenda embracing the LGBT movement, a "Neo-Gnostic mythology that is absolutely against human nature," both in a biological and a philosophical sense.[17]

These are not the sentiments of just one Cardinal. In his 2019 book, *The Day is Now Far Spent*, Cardinal Sarah said,

> Every day I meet in Rome with priests who are discouraged and wounded. The Church is experiencing the dark night of the soul. The mystery of iniquity is enveloping and blinding her. Every day, the most terrifying news reports reach us. Not a week goes by without the revelation of a case of sexual abuse. Each one of these revelations comes to rend our hearts as children of the Church. As Saint Paul VI used to say, we are being invaded by the smoke of Satan. The Church, which ought to be a place of light, has become a dwelling place of darkness. It ought to be a secure, peaceful family home, but look: it has become a den of thieves! How can we tolerate the fact that predators have entered among us, into our ranks? Many faithful priests behave every day as attentive shepherds, kindly fathers, and sure guides. But some men of God have become agents of the Evil One.[18]

This "liquid atheism," existing alongside a "radically pagan and worldly way of thinking," in addition to the embrace of a "Neo-Gnostic mythology," in which Bishops also "relativize the Catholic faith," has created a situation in which the "confusion and error" of a "radically secularized culture" has entered, "in a diabolical way," into the Church herself. While the Cardinals quoted above do not name

---

[17] *National Catholic Register*, February 11,2022, "Cardinal Müller: For Faithful Catholics, It's a 'Time of Tribulation and Psychological Terror'"

[18] Robert Cardinal Sarah, *The Day is Now Far Spent* (San Francisco: Ignatius Press, 2019), Intro section, "Alas, Judas Iscariot."

witchcraft directly, all this amounts to at least a subtle collaboration with the occultic mindset which dominates mankind today. An occultic mindset does not have to be one which casts spells or directly fraternizes with demons, but one which sees in this world an end unto itself, the ultimate destination for man, and thus the paradise in which he must enjoy the fruits of his own desires. It is a mindset that does not see God but believes that pleasure is man's end and that man, to go further, is even the *source* of this pleasure. It is a divinization of man without the operation of the supernatural life of grace, one in which man declares himself to be the rule and arbiter of Truth.

The Occultic Infiltration

As man descends further from the Truth, and embraces the ways of the world, the collapse of faith and morals is surely followed by the embrace of occult practices. The rise of the occult today has clearly taken a lot of Christians with it. This is not a unique circumstance in the history of the Church, though it is extremely concerning. Laymen and clergymen alike have felt the allurement of that primordial spirituality of the devil, by which man seeks to ritualize the tendencies of his fallen nature, seeking to control the world around him and make himself the center, the god, of his own universe.

From the research of Sr. Antoinette Marie Pratt, in 1915, in her book, *The Attitude of the Catholic Church Towards Witchcraft and the Allied Practices of Sorcery and Magic,* it is clear that the Church has had to deal with all sorts of issues over the last two thousand years, including witchcraft, superstition, sorcery, enchanters, astrology, amulets, ligatures,[19] nature worship, magicians, divination, Satanic sacrifice, soothsayers, charms, and the conjuring of demons. Of greatest concern is the fact that the Church, in local synods and in Papal interventions, has specifically addressed the situation of clergy involvement in occult practice. Of additional great interest to readers is the fact that the presence of sorcery was often mingled with heretical movements, the latter being something we witness in many areas of the Church today.

---

[19] A spell intended to cause infertility in a married couple.

The historical challenge of the occult is also evident from Sacred Scripture, such as when many who converted in Ephesus confessed their practice of magic and burned a large pile of their occultic books,[20] when St. Paul was harassed by a girl with a spirit of divination,[21] and when the people at Lystra attempted to worship Paul and Barnabas after witnessing the miracles they performed.[22] Purging the occult from the lives of new converts, and keeping it from sneaking back into the lives of Christians, has been one of the principal duties of the Church from the beginning.

As Sr. Antoinette presented, as early as the year 300, Church synods were recorded as having addressed the issue of witchcraft as a practice among Christians.[23] From the fifth century to the end of the 8th century, the Church, in many local synods, condemned a whole host of occultic practices that were creeping into the lives of the faithful. These included the adoration of trees and fields, seeking the help of witches and soothsayers and magicians, wearing amulets, practicing divination, and sacrificing to the devil.[24] The statements of the Council of Toledo in 693 reflect the seriousness of the situation in the eyes of the Church. The Council declared that "bishops and clerics should root out the remnants of paganism, which consisted in making use of charms and exercising magic," further warning that, "if they were not zealous in this work, they were to be deposed and excommunicated for a year."[25]

In 906, Abbot Regino of Prüm wrote a book which reflected the Church's approach to witchcraft at the time. The Abbot was firmly convinced of the ability of witches to destroy crops, summon storms, and cause love and hate among people. He also spoke of the practice of some Christian women who, falling away from the Faith, turned to the worship of Diana, "the goddess of the heathen," as a Queen, or to Herodias. "These women," he wrote, "who have thus fallen away

---

[20] Acts 19:18–19
[21] Acts 16:16
[22] Acts 14:11f
[23] Sr. Antoinette Marie Pratt, A.M., *The Attitude of the Catholic Church Towards Witchcraft and the Allied Practices of Sorcery and Magic* (Washington: National Capital Press, 1915), 33.
[24] Pratt, *The Attitude of the Catholic Church*, 33ff.
[25] Ibid 34

from the faith have not only gone to ruin themselves, but they have dragged many others with them into the destruction of unbelief."[26]

Many Popes also directly addressed the issue of the occult among the members of the Church. Popes Leo IV (849), Stephen V (890), Leo VII (937-9), and Gregory VII (1080), among others, wrote to Bishops of various areas addressing the gravity of the sin of those consulting witches and engaging in sorcery.[27] Further, a number of Popes from the year 1200-1700 "issued decrees treating of the reality of magic and witchcraft."[28] Pope Eugenius IV, for example, in 1434, wrote that there were "many Christians given over to witchcraft, divination, invocation of demons, conjurations, superstitions, use of prohibited arts, by whom simple Christians are perverted."[29]

The presence of occult practice, as could be guessed, did not occur solely among the laity. If the occult is present among the laity, it will likely appear among the clergy as well. This, sadly, has been the case. The synod of Laodicaea in 375, for example, declared excommunicated any priests or cleric "who employed ligatures or amulets and forbade them to be magicians, enchanters or astrologers."[30] Local synods in the fifth to eighth centuries mentioned "perpetual penance for monks" who engaged in occult practice. Further, the punishments listed indicated that some individuals "of high ranks"[31] were practitioners of witchcraft and sorcery, and that some clerics were consulting diviners and witches. The synods also indicated that some priests and clerics were using soothsayers, divination, and ligatures.[32]

In 595, Pope Gregory I wrote to a deacon to warn him about the defilement by witchcraft of his predecessor, and to "take strong measures [himself] against the superstition."[33] The synod of Aachen (789) directly addressed priests and other clerics who were engaging

---

[26] Ibid 39. These references to Diana highlight the historical existence of these two idols, on which modern Wiccans base some of their devotions. Though Wiccans keep the names of these deities, they do not know what practices accompanied the ancient cults.
[27] Ibid 45f
[28] Ibid 86
[29] Ibid 89
[30] Ibid 33
[31] It is unclear if this refers to high ranks in the clergy or in civil society.
[32] Ibid 33f
[33] Ibid 32

in magical practices, forbidding them from doing so, and applying the earlier canons of Laodicaea.[34]

After Pope Benedict XII ordered the Bishop of Paris, in 1336, to correct and punish witches and sorcerers in that area, the Papal Court was convened for the task. From their work, documents have survived which provide an indication of just what sort of people were involved in these practices. Among the others accused of witchcraft were "the rector of a church, a Brother, [and] a cleric."[35] The synod of Regensburg, in 1527, condemned those "clerics who gave themselves to sorcery, magic, and soothsaying."[36]

Of even greater concern is the fact that both heretical practices and abuses of the Sacraments have historically been mingled with occult practices. Sr. Antoinette speculated that the reason witchcraft continued to grow between the 9th and 13th centuries, despite the Church's efforts to stamp it out and purge it from the lives of the faithful, was due to the spread of new heretical practices, which "were mingled with those of sorcery."[37] One example of these being addressed was in the apostolic efforts of Pope Callixtus III, who wrote, in 1457, that he was astonished to hear that some ecclesiastics were teaching falsely about Our Lord and His Holy Mother and were also teaching magical arts to their people.[38]

Further, when Pope John XXII, in 1318, addressed the concerns of witchcraft, which he did on many occasions, he addressed the reality of some Christians making pacts with the devil and of "the abuse by witches of the Sacraments and Sacramentals."[39] He specifically addressed the reality of people abusing the Sacrament of Baptism and the Sacrament of the Eucharist. He also ordered the Bishop of Paris, in 1331, to investigate the accusation that "certain clerics and [layman had] attempted to use witchcraft against the king and his companions.[40] The "abuse of the Sacraments" is mentioned again by Pope Julius II between 1503-1513 regarding those engaged in witchcraft.[41] Thirteenth century synods

---

[34] Ibid 35
[35] Ibid 88
[36] Ibid 98
[37] Ibid 38
[38] Ibid 91
[39] Ibid 87
[40] Ibid 87. This parallels the 17th century *Affair of the Poisons.*
[41] Ibid 95

condemned, among other crimes of witchcraft, "the abuse of the Holy Eucharist or one of the other Sacraments of the Church for some devilish purpose," repeated again in 1321.[42]

As it could be imagined, during these centuries the Church seems to have become overwhelmed by the problems that the occult was presenting. Sr. Antoinette stated that, by the end of the twelfth century, it appeared that the Church, recognizing the reality of witchcraft, "seemed unable to cope with the growing superstition."[43] The Church was not always certain what to make of witchcraft but dealt with it by different means as the evil developed.[44]

Corruption of the Clergy Today

There is evidence that the problems today go much deeper than simply the intellectual and moral compromises previously mentioned and, if we first look carefully at the obvious issues, the depth of corruption is quite clear. Cardinal Sarah, for example, stated in 2019,

> The forgetting of God finds its first and most serious manifestation in the secularized way of life of priests. They are the first to have to carry the Good News. If their personal lives do not reflect this, then practical atheism will spread throughout the Church and society. I believe that we are at a turning point in the history of the Church. Yes, the Church needs a profound and radical reform that must begin with a reform of the way of being and the way of life of priests. The Church is holy in herself. But we prevent this holiness from shining through our sins and worldly concerns.[45]

The "sins" which His Eminence mentioned are today far too often those of homosexuality in the clergy. In addition to Cardinal Muller's statement above, in September 2016, in Pope Benedict's

---

[42] Ibid 96-7
[43] Ibid 50
[44] Ibid 120
[45] *National Catholic Register*, September 23, 2019, "Cardinal Sarah's Cri de Coeur: The Catholic Church Has Lost Its Sense of the Sacred"

book, *Benedict XVI, Final Conversations,* Pope Benedict described the existence of a "gay lobby" which sought power over Vatican decisions. While it is described as comprised of only four or five members, the naming of it *publicly* as a *lobby* would make anyone believe that this *lobby* was just the tip of the iceberg. He also stated that he was able to break up this lobby. However, after his departure, the gay lobby is said to have returned. In June of 2013, Francis also admitted that there was a gay lobby in the Church in remarks he delivered to the Religious Confederation of Latin America and the Caribbean. The existence of this "gay lobby" is evidenced by a host of new stories from the past two decades, still occurring to this day, of wayward priests and Bishops, and of their superiors who have been complicit in their sins or have looked the other way when possessing the power to correct them.

These sins, however, are not just the personal sins of certain clergymen: they represent, and are tied to, a heretical movement and are manifestations of a great many heresies held by some prelates in the modern Church. Given the research of Sr. Antoinette, the ubiquity of the occult and occultic mindsets today, and the many public examples and testimonies of clergy involvement in the occult, we can easily speculate that many more of those modern clergymen engaged in homosexual lifestyles may also be involved in the occult themselves.[46] Likewise, we can speculate about occultic elements among the corrupt clergymen in the time of St. Peter Damian (11th Century). In his famous work, *The Book of Gomorrah,* St. Peter Damian strongly condemned those clergymen who were deeply immersed in homosexual immorality and articulated the many ways in which this sin deforms the soul. We also know that the occult was alive and well in St. Peter Damian's day in Italy.[47]

The effects of sodomy on the individual, in particular on a clergyman, are so much more devastating than many in the hierarchy of the Church seem to accept in our age. This sort of devastation, as Fr. Athanasius explained, can indeed make priests disposed toward occult practices. He said, "Once someone compromises the conscience and habitually lives in sin, the devil's

[46] This reality will be presented further in *Slaying Dragons III.*
[47] *RealPresence.org* presents a Eucharistic miracle which St. Peter Damian witnessed and recorded, involving a Host that was taken from the Church with the intent of being used in sorcery.

suggestions become more constant and acceptable. But consider the interest the devil has in high value targets such as priests.[48] Every mortal sin of a priest is a sacrilege. It makes sense that the Enemy will concentrate on them to bring about *anti-priests, anti-liturgy, anti-Church.* And today we've got a lot of possessed clergy thanks to their sodomitical ways. You'd be surprised." When I further asked if he thought there were occultists in today's hierarchy, he replied, "Absolutely!"

The compromising of the conscience mentioned by the above exorcist is surely accomplished by the enemy through the moral and spiritual effects produced by the sin of sodomy. In *The Book of Gomorrah,* St. Peter Damian presented the evil effects brought about by the presence of this abominable vice within the priesthood in the eleventh century. From these, and in light of the comments by Fr. Athanasius, we can see how this could easily dispose those clergy today to embrace the occult, guilty as they are of the same abominations condemned by St. Peter Damian. St. Peter Damian said that sodomy[49] "evicts the Holy Spirit from the temple of the human heart; it introduces the devil who incites to lust."[50] Further, "It casts into error [and] extinguishes the light of the mind…It defiles everything, stains everything, pollutes everything." The damage done to the priest or Bishop involved in such behavior is immense:

> In fact, after this most poisonous serpent once sinks its fangs into the unhappy soul, (moral) sense is snatched away, memory is borne off, the sharpness of the mind is obscured. It becomes unmindful of God and even forgetful of itself.[51] This plague undermines the foundation of faith, weakens the strength of hope, destroys the bond of charity; it takes away justice, subverts fortitude, banishes temperance, blunts the keenness of prudence.[52]

---

[48] Recall the idiom, *Corruptio optimi pessima* – the corruption of the best is the worst of all.
[49] Specifically homosexual acts, as well as similar sins connected to it, as enumerated by St. Peter Damian.
[50] St. Peter Damian, *Book of Gomorrah*, 63.
[51] Also translated as "Forgets his own identity"
[52] St. Peter Damian, *Book of Gomorrah*, 63–4.

Further, St. Peter Damian added, "This vice casts men from the choir of the ecclesiastical community and compels them to pray with the possessed and with those who work for the devil. It separates the soul from God to join it with devils."[53] With all these negative effects articulated, the mind is quick to respond, "How can a man, given over to this vice, seek to govern the Church as a Bishop or priest, or lead souls to Christ, or protect the Mass, or raise up new holy priests, and avoid leading the people into error?" These men, St. Peter Damian declared, "Try with such desire to ensnare the people of God in the bonds of [their] own ruin,"[54] and lamented, "What fruitfulness can still be found in the flocks when the shepherd is so deeply sunk in the belly of the devil?"[55] Given the rampant acceptance of homosexuality in the clergy today, and the presence of these men even among the Bishops, as it was in St. Peter Damian's day,[56] these criticisms and laments need to be considered as we seek to understand the spiritual fallout which is the result of having these men as the spiritual leaders of the Church today.

As in times past, when the Church has reeled under the weight of sin and corruption, the Holy Spirit provides the grace of encouragement, fortitude, and perseverance. It is by these, and by faith in Christ's promise that He will remain really and mystically present in and with His Holy Church, that we can continue the fight for the preservation of the Faith and the salvation of our souls. In the times when the leaders of the Church are puffed up by pride yet brought down by the idolatry of their sins, we must look not to them but to Christ who operates through them and there behold our peace. Even in persecution, God's will is done. Even in situations so dire that we could never have imagined them to really come about, God's will is done. We, like Christ in His Agony, if we feel abandoned by God, no longer secured by His protection, must nonetheless say, "Not my will but Thine be done,"[57] surrendering, if necessary, all that we have, including our very bodies. Like Our Lord, who, when coming into this world, proclaimed to the Father, "a body hast Thou

---

[53] Ibid 63–4

[54] Ibid 72

[55] Ibid 41

[56] He wrote, "O guilty, carnal men, why do you desire the height of ecclesiastical dignity with so much burning ambition?" p.72

[57] Luke 22:42

prepared for Me,"[58] we must take heed now, with these clear warnings of the signs of the times, and conform ourselves in the same act of trust and surrender as our Master, ready to lay it all down in the pursuit of righteousness.

---

[58] Heb 10:5

Chapter Five

The Situation is Dire

The Church is to be the Teacher of the nations, leading the pagans away from diabolical associations with error and superstition, and pulling souls "into the deep" "living water" that gushes forth in abundance from the Most Sacred Heart of Jesus, "welling up to eternal life."[1] However, the weakness which invades the Church today prevents her from exuding the very wisdom and power with which Our Lord has endowed her. The frustration with the current situation, in which some members of the Church's hierarchy fail to dispense the full treasury of supernatural grace and truth, and in which these clergymen are either scared of the battle or are even fighting on the opposing side, is shared by former occultists, exorcists, and the brave and few priests, Bishops, and Cardinals who have been outspoken against this evil. It is not just a frustration over the failure to maintain the truths that tradition has handed on; it is a frustration over the attitude of permissiveness toward the evil that has invaded the body of the Church; and it is a frustration over the ongoing death of souls, which could easily be prevented if the Bishops, the stewards of the mysteries revealed by Christ, would take their consecration as priests, prophets, and kings seriously, hearing the ancient and enduring call of St. John the Baptist, "Repent, for the kingdom of heaven is at hand,"[2] and responding in deep humility.

As St. Peter Damian said, it is not a sin to expose the grave sins of clergy and monks.[3] For, as he said, if we do not call them out for it, they will die in their sins, as will those who depend on their leadership in order to persevere more easily in faith and good works. Calling wayward clergy to repentance, when done prudently, is not

---

[1] Luke 5:4, John 4:10, and John 4:14
[2] Matt 3:2
[3] St. Peter Damian, *Book of Gomorrah*, 87-90.

an act of pride but of charity, humility, and fortitude. St. John the Baptist did this to the Pharisees and Sadducees who came forward for baptism, announcing, "You brood of vipers! Who warned *you* to flee from the wrath to come? Bear fruit that befits repentance, and do not presume to say to yourselves, 'We have Abraham as our father'."[4] The frustration mentioned above is also the same frustration that Our Lord expressed toward the scribes and Pharisees, and His words are apropos to our current situation, in which too many clergy celebrate what the Church condemns:

> But woe to you, scribes and Pharisees, hypocrites! because you shut the kingdom of heaven against men; for you neither enter yourselves, nor allow those who would enter to go in. Woe to you, scribes and Pharisees, hypocrites! for you traverse sea and land to make a single proselyte, and when he becomes a proselyte, you make him twice as much a child of hell as yourselves.[5]

Holy indignation will rightly stir in the soul that becomes aware of the evils running rampant in the Church today. However, the response which we give should be in proportion to our position within the Church. For the laity, we must sanctify ourselves with a more thorough attentiveness, knowing that, as the Church teaches, Christ has willed to *depend* on us for His continued work of the salvation of souls, and our holiness *matters* to the Mystical Body of Christ.[6] For the faithful clergy, who have been placed in authoritative positions, the challenge is much greater. Entrusted with varying degrees of governance in Christ's Church, much rests on them, and their reward will be great if they lead the charge in the battle for the soul of the Church and the souls in the world whom Christ has entrusted to them. The situation is dire, for the whole world is the parish Church of the Mystical Body of Christ. There is

---

[4] Matt 3:7–8

[5] Matt 23:13,15

[6] Cf *Mystici Corporis Christi*, #44, "Yet this, also, must be held, marvelous though it may seem: Christ has need of His members…the salvation of many depends on the prayers and voluntary penances which the members of the Mystical Body of Jesus Christ offer for this intention."

no soul who has not been given to our collective responsibility, and too many are languishing in evil and ignorance.

A Panoply of Evils

The evils within the Church today are legion. As many Cardinals have implied, a dark shroud seems to blanket the world today, and an evil voice appears to have charmed the minds of men upon whom sacred governance has been placed. This voice has terrified much of the clergy: pushing them away from spiritual warfare; mesmerizing them and enticing them toward embracing what the Church has long deemed to be immoral; brainwashing them and convincing them that the devil does not exist and that all disorders reside, for example, merely within a troubled mind; emasculating them and drawing them into a state of laxity and delicacy, in which they have no courage to stand up and shed their blood in the battle against the spiritual collapse occurring all around them. The result is that many refuse to teach the Faith, others openly oppose it, while others permissively look the other way as the faithful begin to conform themselves not to Christ but to the ways of the world.

Fr. Stephen, speaking about the situation in the Church in the U.S., said that cowardice among the priests and Bishops in the face of the real need for spiritual warfare, deliverance ministry, and exorcism reveals the general lack of a supernatural perspective. Exorcists who work with Bishops and diocesan priests have stated that too many priests are afraid of the devil and refuse to have anything to do with the ministry. As a result, many exorcists have commented that there are not enough of them available to address the needs of people coming with spiritual issues. In many cases, this flows from a heretical denial of the Church's teachings on the devil, which was quite publicly seen in the comments by the current head of the Jesuits, Fr. Sosa, in 2019, in which he denied the existence of the devil as a real angelic person.[7] This comment brought a swift response from the International Association of Exorcists the next

---

[7] "Person" is the theological term used for God as well as for the creatures known as angels (including demons) and men. Angels and men, resembling God, possess an intellect and a will and are destined to live eternally.

day, in which they rejected such a remark and repeated the Church's firm teaching.[8]

The corruption can also be seen in the refusal of Bishops to respond to the presence of morally repugnant behavior and beliefs publicly proclaimed by universities within their jurisdiction, as well as the refusal of the Vatican to take action against Cardinals who promote the same. The former includes situations where Catholic universities have held "Queer Proms," celebrating disorder and the moral collapse of the Faith, which should instead stand strong in places of higher learning bearing the Church's name.[9] The refusal of the Vatican to address wayward Cardinals, to give a very public example, relates to the "wholesale and explicit rejection" of the Church's teaching on sexual ethics by Cardinal Hollerich of Luxembourg and Bishop Bätzing of Germany. Cardinal Pell called them out for this offense on March 15, 2022 and called on Rome to address the matter. Rome, however, did not respond. As a result, similar abominations continue to spread throughout the Church in that area of the world.[10]

The situation becomes one in which false teachings and the failure to teach become the common experience of the faithful throughout the world. Former occultists have often expressed either hurt or anger at the reality of the level of ignorance today regarding fundamental Church teachings, such as those concerning the devil, morality, and the full embrace of the Sacraments. Adelaide said, "Once I realized what I had not been taught, and the richness and depth of the actual Catholic Faith that had been held back from me, I had a very hard time getting that anger under control, and I had a couple of confessors help work me through that. I was [furious]."[11] One of the reasons so many people are drifting off into the occult, she said, is the absence of the power of Christianity in the world. "There's a spiritual vacuum now," she said, "You can thank the Church for that. So, people are seeking other things."[12]

---

[8] *CNA*, August 23, 2019, "Exorcists to Jesuit Head: Satan is Real."

[9] DePaul University on February 24, 2022, St. Louis University on February 25, 2022, and a similar event around that time at Notre Dame.

[10] *LifeSiteNews*, March 16, 2022, "Cdl. Pell: Vatican must 'reprimand' high-ranking clergy for 'explicit rejection' of Church teachings."

[11] The words she used were a bit stronger.

[12] Her words here are an expression of frustration at the many Church leaders who refuse to teach the Faith properly. "Spiritual vacuum" – in the sense that, without the pull which

The Situation is Dire

In my interview with Edith, she volunteered that she felt she had specifically been led astray by the example of Francis, in the way he has taught and spoken about homosexuality. As she drifted into a mind of confusion, without the spiritual support of either of her parents, she embraced a life that was completely defined by same-sex attraction. For her, as she described it, the pontificate of Francis "has spelled a lot of confusion for the gay community, myself included, whenever he was making personal statements on homosexuality that made me feel validated [in that lifestyle]." In a sad but honest statement, she said, "Maybe I'm just bitter I've never really experienced a good Pope."

While it has become objectively much worse today, bad leadership and bad catechesis has been an ongoing thing, having entered the common life of the faithful many decades ago. Adelaide's return to the Church, for example, was through a parish which failed her on many levels. As she said, "I went through my entire RCIA without ever going to Sunday Mass." She rightly assumed, though, that she was being taught everything she needed to know. After her conversion, she would only go to Mass about once every other month. This, and many other issues, would only be resolved when traditional priests entered her life.

Fr. Anselm, when commenting on the impact that the Church lockdowns during Covid had on the faithful's attendance at Mass, placed the blame on Church leadership and on terrible catechesis. He said, "It has really thinned out parishes, and we're not sure if those people are coming back. They were holding on to the Faith because of a presumed obligation to go to Mass every Sunday. This was enough to keep them going, during which time they were, to some extent at least, protected and receiving the Sacraments. When the obligation was done away with, they were cut loose." He continued, "There has been horrible leadership through this. From the Pope all the way down to the priests: horrible leadership." The efforts of many clergy are just to fill the building at any cost, he said. For decades, this approach led to a softening of homilies, a "toned-down" feel-good liturgy, an emphasis on the music and on the people, the reduction of the importance of the priest, the eradication of sin and

the Holy Spirit can have on souls through the Church, fallen men naturally gravitate toward magic and superstition.

69

judgment and Hell, and the effort to be politically and socially relevant in what is truly a Satanic age of the world. He added, "As a result, supernatural faith was stolen from the faithful and, when Covid came, what it really killed was faith."

With his occultic background, one of the things that sets off the alarms for John is the presence of permissiveness, which is clear and visible within the Church's current approach to teaching the Faith in a great many areas of the world. "From heretical priests, Bishops, and Cardinals, espousing and spouting moral and religious relativism, to policies from the Vatican that bless adultery and reception of Holy Communion in mortal sin, to statements from the Vatican and places like Germany that implicitly condone contraception, homosexuality, and transgenderism, we," he said, "are in an age where not only the external disciplines of asceticism[13] have been laid aside, but also the internal spiritual disciplines[14] which supply for the life of grace in the soul."

This sort of permissiveness of evil, by either teaching it, implying it is acceptable, or looking away as it is happening, "smacks of the occult," John warned, adding, "which itself is geared toward the false liberation of the individual, in their own name and unto sin." The permissiveness of the occult, and the indifference and failure to teach and lead and sanctify on the part of churchmen, both lead to the destruction of souls. As John noted, this is all happening in an era where the head of the Church has openly and ceremoniously carried what appeared to be a witch's stang at a Youth Synod,[15] has validated false religions numerous times, has welcomed and defended the Pachamama idol[16] in the Vatican, and has never missed an opportunity to disparage and belittle the Church's Traditional liturgy, even so much as to lead a persecution of the Traditional

---

[13] Fasting, self-denial, abstinence from meat, penance (esp. during Lent), moderation of foods, etc.

[14] Attention to the needs of the soul, including regular Confession, frequent Holy Communion, daily mental prayer, daily Rosary, daily examination of conscience, etc.

[15] At the Youth Synod in the Circus Maximus on August 11, 2018, Francis was handed a *ferula*, the metal staff topped by a Cross and used by Popes, which instead looked very much like a witch's ceremonial staff, known as a *stang*, used in various rituals. Even if it was not a real stang, it was objectively ugly and without any obvious Christian symbolism.

[16] See footnote below for details on Pachamama.

Latin Mass, seeking to abolish it.[17] "It would seem," he added, "that total and complete adherence to the Catholic Faith is missing from the agenda. In its place is confusion and permissiveness. Whatever this ultimately means, the enactment of such an agenda is devastating and disastrous to the state of souls both inside and outside of the Church."

The situation is easily judged to be worse today than in the days of St. Peter Damian, even though it was he who penned the famous *Book of Gomorrah* as a result of the evils he observed. It is worse today since, in his time, while sodomites were rampant in the hierarchy in Italy, there was no "gay lobby" trying to interfere with the operations of the Pope and the Vatican. Further, while even Bishops were involved in moral depravity, there were no Cardinals in his time publicly rebuking other Cardinals for heretical statements on the morality of homosexual acts. Further still, when St. Peter Damian petitioned Pope St. Leo IX, St. Peter Damian was heard and assisted, whereas Cardinal Pell's request for the Vatican to deal with the heretical Cardinal and Bishop, who flagrantly contradicted the Church's teaching on homosexuality, went completely unanswered. In 2015, Cardinal Juan Sandoval Íñiguez offered to write the foreword to a modern translation of *The Book of Gomorrah* by Matthew Hoffman. In that foreword, the Cardinal highlighted the devastation which the embrace of homosexuality is bringing to the Church today, writing, "A thousand years ago sexual vices were being practiced by various sons of the Church that lamentably are present today and have been the occasion of scandal, discredit, and apostasy."

Occultists in the Hierarchy

In the course of interviewing former occultists, I was learning many things about the situation in the world and in the Church which I had never before considered. The thoughts that were stirred by these interviews influenced the course of my research and the questions I was asking, of both former occultists as well as exorcists

---

[17] The latter being a gross absurdity, which Pope Benedict XVI explained in the following words: "In the history of the liturgy there is growth and progress, but no rupture. What earlier generations held as sacred, remains sacred and great for us too, and it cannot be all of a sudden entirely forbidden or even considered harmful." *Summorum Pontificum.*

and experienced parish priests. Andrew, in one of our conversations, made the following bold statement, which initiated one of those thoughts that affected the course of my inquiries:

> With those facts in mind, I have zero doubt there are certainly occultists and subversives in our pews, our seminaries, wearing cassocks, saying Mass, and quite possibly even wearing miters and carrying crosiers. There may be some who believe they are not hostile to God, but I'm sure there are those who are absolutely and deliberately hostile toward God and Holy Mother Church.

In my interviews with exorcists which followed this interview with Andrew, I told them of his comment and asked them what their thoughts were on the matter. Their answers were both disturbing and refreshing to hear. Disturbing because they confirmed Andrew's suspicions. Refreshing because they helped to clarify the evils which the faithful perceive to be blanketing our world and the Church today. At times, the evils we observe are so bad that we want to pretend they do not exist, leading us to experience some sort of Stockholm Syndrome, in which, though we can see that powerful men are working great evils around us, we want to "give them the benefit of the doubt," dismissing the perception of evil as coming merely from "a bad translation" of a speech or residing in a case of "we don't know the full context."

When authoritative clerics, like the Cardinals previously quoted and other experienced clerics like exorcists, who have worked for decades in a direct battle against the devil, all say that a great terror has emerged within the world and the Church, it is comforting to the faithful who have long perceived this to be true yet who are painted as being *backward* for thinking it or pointing it out. When all the other leaders in the Church go around with big smiles on their faces, pretending we are living in an age of great hope and a springtime of grace, and all the while we see the evils which are promulgated by the hierarchy worldwide, and the rise of the occult in our cities and neighborhoods and in the cultural movements of our countries, it can make one feel crazy and confused. However, by looking plainly at the truth of the matter, like a captain studying a battlefield, no matter how evil and dangerous and disturbing the enemy has become, we now *know* that enemy and can take the proper course in fighting against him, come what may.

When I asked Fr. Ambrose whether he thought there might be occultists inside the Church, he said, "Pachamama[18] is evidence of that. Someone in the Church had access to the Pope and set that up. Not some 'Joe Shmoe,' either; someone who worked for the Church." He commented further, placing the situation in the context of all the negative news about certain Vatican officials, living in Rome, where homosexual activity has been documented, and sex and drug-fueled parties have been interrupted in the Vatican apartments[19]: "If they are that deep in grave sin," he said, "it is only one more step to be in the occult, and it would not surprise me in the least!" He further pointed out the fact of the Bishops in Germany who are actively and publicly trying to change the Church's teaching on homosexuality and are embracing that behavior as something good and holy.[20] "How can you be a Bishop and seek to change *that*?" Fr. Ambrose said, adding, "What are you doing in your life that got you to that point?"

I asked Fr. Athanasius if he thought there were occultists within the hierarchy of the Church. He replied, "Absolutely!" Referring to Francis' role in inviting the idolatry of Pachamama in the Vatican, he said, "If he did not welcome them – and he *did* stop talking when he saw the ritual in the Vatican Gardens, and tossed his papers in

---

[18] In October of 2019, a carved image tied to the South American idol associated with "Mother Earth" and known as *Pachamama* was brought to the Vatican by indigenous groups from South America who attended the Amazon Synod in Rome. The statue was worshiped in the Vatican Gardens in the presence of Francis, paraded into St. Peter's on a boat, and given a place of honor in a chapel in a local Church. It drew swift condemnation from numerous Cardinals and Bishops, as well as many exorcists, who warned that this was an act of idolatry which would bring negative spiritual consequences and for which reparation must be done. This will be addressed more thoroughly in *Slaying Dragons III*.

[19] For example, see *CatholicCulture.org*, July 7, 2017, "The truth about the Vatican sex-and-drugs scandal."

[20] Further, the German Bishops were called out by several Cardinals in a November 2022 meeting in Rome and were warned against taking a path into schism. They refused to comply with the call to change their course. Bishop Bätzing, whom Cardinal Pell had called for the Vatican to rebuke, insisted he would personally *continue* to bless same-sex couples. He is the president of the German Bishop's Conference. The Vatican has still not stopped him or the German Bishops. Further, as Fr. Raymond de Souza articulated, this is the latest in a *series* of failures on the part of Francis to enforce obedience to his decrees on these and similar matters. (NCRegister.com, November 22, 2022, "German Bishops Take Perilous Detour from Unity with Rome.")

someone's face – fine, we can accept that story as true. *But* he defended Pachamama and even printed a Vatican coin with Pachamama on it." Even if Francis was taken by surprise initially, Father said, he went along with it the rest of the way.

...It's Not Just About Pachamama

The evil blanketing the Church is not just related to the tragedy of the idol being brought into the heart of the Church, as evil as this event was. A general diabolical oppression appears to be operating over the Church, in particular in the hierarchy. The presence of many and various moral depravities in the hierarchy of the Church, present and public for many decades, as well as rampant heresies embraced throughout Christendom, the fruit of the Modernism warned about by Pope St. Pius X, have all paved the way for a moral descent into idolatry and occultism.[21]

One story illustrates this point. An exorcist traveled to Rome in 2021 and commented to me about how he observed the entire city to be diabolically oppressed. I asked Fr. Athanasius if he also thought that Rome was under a state of diabolical oppression. He replied, "Absolutely," adding, "Of course!" Fr. Athanasius said he had studied with Fr. Amorth in the past and that Fr. Amorth was always talking about occultists in the Vatican, way before the Pachamama idolatry. "And he never stopped talking about it," he said, "That is what got him into so much trouble." Fr. Amorth, in his *Memoirs of an Exorcist*, stated clearly that he knew there were Vatican officials, including priests, Bishops, and Cardinals, who were also members of Satanic sects.[22] Published in the time of Pope Benedict's reign, *Memoirs*

---

[21] In 1972, Pope Paul VI said that something "preternatural" entered the world to disturb and impede the Church (see below). In 2019, a group of exorcists warned that the Pachamama idolatry increased the power of the demonic operating against the Church (see *Slaying Dragons III*).

[22] Many modern examples of priestly occultic corruption give evidence of this reality. Cases include: Spanish Bishop Xavier Novell who, shockingly, was also an exorcist, and abandoned the priesthood to marry a female author of erotic novels with Satanic overtones, and U.S. priest Fr. Travis Clark who was caught in a Satanic ritual on the altar in his parish Church. Many others were accused and found guilty of crimes containing aspects resembling occultic ritual abuse and the desecration of the Sacraments, including Franciscan University priest, (shockingly, also an exorcist) Fr. David Morrier, Fr. Jacob Bertrand, Fr. Jeremy Leatherby, and Fr. Peter Mitchell, among others. The testimony of Rachel Mastrogiacomo has shed light on the occultic elements of the abuse

contains Fr. Amorth's statement that the Pope was aware of all this, saying, "Of course, he was informed. But he does what he can. It's a horrifying thing."[23]

The issue of apostasy, mentioned by numerous Cardinals, was a topic of discussion between Fr. Amorth and St. Padre Pio, when, as Fr. Amorth related, they spoke about the third secret of Fatima and the coming "great apostasy" within the Church. As Fr. Amorth stated, Padre Pio was primarily concerned, above all other things, with this great apostasy and the fact that Satan had been introduced into the "bosom of the Church."[24] Padre Pio was "really tormented" by this great apostasy and told Fr. Amorth that, "within a very short time [Satan] will come to rule a false Church."[25]

Fr. Alphonsus said that the situation with clerical sex abuse, which has been in the news for a few decades, and has clearly been an issue since the 1960s[26], is what caused him to understand the likelihood of occultists in the hierarchy. "The child abuse issues have opened me to this more," Fr. Alphonsus said. "Even in the present day, like the new Cardinal McElroy, a close friend of McCarrick.[27] With the number of things about [McElroy], the media should be all over that, in the negative sense, but instead they praise him. Someone is pulling strings on the human level somewhere. I wouldn't be surprised [if there are occultists in the hierarchy]; it makes perfect sense. Get the wolf in with the sheep and have a field day."

Fr. Alphonsus remarked about how the situation appears to be unstoppable, or that those with authority to stop it refuse to do so, thus echoing the *apostasy* concerns mentioned above. He said, "The man in charge of putting together the Synod is horrible, promoting homosexuality, etc., but he is still in charge![28] Cardinal Marx is

---

which these priests, Bertrand in particular, committed. This will be covered in *Slaying Dragons III.*

[23] *CNA*, March 3, 2010, "Spanish exorcist addresses claims of Satanic influence in Vatican."

[24] *OnePeterFive*, May 23, 2017, "Chief Exorcist Father Amorth: Padre Pio Knew The Third Secret"

[25] Ibid

[26] The time in which homosexual priests and Bishops first began entering the seminaries.

[27] A once-prominent and influential U.S. Cardinal removed from the priesthood in 2019 after countless credible accusations of homosexual abuse against seminarians and others.

[28] The "Synod on Synodality." This man is Card. Hollerich, the very Cardinal whom Cardinal Pell called out for heresy and demanded the Vatican rebuke, to no avail.

horrible but is still the head of Francis' council![29] The head of the German Bishops is the same way – and no correction of any of this! Instead, they are affirmed and picked for Bishops and Cardinals, placed in charge of the liturgy in the Church. We see this massive push against the Traditional Latin Mass and rituals, with even Francis speaking against it. It's crazy!"

The Interference of Grace and the Need for Reparation

The impact of corrupted clergy is greater than people might realize. It is not simply that they fail in their mission or that they cause scandal, both of which are grave sins. Their failure impacts the Church and the faithful on an additional spiritual level. In theology, there is something called the 'principle of redundancy.' "Grace and sin flow downhill," Fr. Athanasius explained. "Grace pours out of the Godhead onto the Church and onto the Vicar of Christ, then down to the Cardinals, Bishops, priests, and laity. But it is not just grace; if there is an interruption of grace or an insertion of grave sin into that chain, that also flows downhill. Thus, we experience the curses and blessings of those above us." One example he gave of this is when Pope Benedict XVI decided to consecrate Vatican City to St. Michael in 2013.[30] "After that," he said, "things started to go faster. Cases delivered more quickly. Then, with Pachamama, we were spinning our wheels in the mud, and things were taking forever. These things don't happen in a vacuum but have an impact on the Mystical Body."

In an interview with Dr. Taylor Marshall, Fr. Chad Ripperger highlighted the fact that exorcisms, as a sacramental, function *ex opere operantis ecclesiae*, which means "from the work of the worker, the Church."[31] He explained, "The state of the Church has a direct impact on how long and how efficacious the prayers [are] that are being said by the priest, who is the public minister of the Church." Theologically, he explained that the prayers offered by the Church Militant which go unanswered retain a spiritual merit, and this merit

---

[29] Cardinal Marx has been called "one of the most influential Catholic leaders in Europe." He is currently a *member* of Francis' "Council of Cardinal Advisers" but he is the *president* of the Vatican's Council for the Economy.

[30] July 5, 2013, with Francis. The blessing of the statue and the consecration of Vatican City were initiated by Pope Benedict and he joined Francis for the actual event.

[31] Or, literally, "from the work of the Church [which is] working."

goes into the spiritual treasury of the Church, from which the Church can pull for various intentions, including exorcisms. However, the amount of merit and prayers offered by the Church Militant today is so little that there is hardly any resource there. The efficacy of the prayers of the Church, he added, becomes reduced when the amount of sanctifying grace flowing into the Church Militant is reduced.[32]

Fr. Ripperger stated that many modern exorcists theorize that the present state of the Church is the reason why exorcisms are taking so much longer. He said it is also due to the evil which characterizes the souls of so many people today. "The Church is much more debilitated and people are just not leading holy lives, that are in the Church (the number is very few)," he said, adding, "As a result, the prayers of the priest are less efficacious."[33] The timing of this weakness in the Church today is dangerous for the growing number of people who are in need of the help of exorcists. Father added that, since exorcists are all having cases come to them that are very difficult to liberate, "that tells you that there's something in the life of the Church that needs rectifying."[34]

Fr. Ambrose said he recently attended a conference for exorcists and noted that everyone was saying the same thing and having the same experience regarding the difficulty with which demons are cast out. "It is getting worse," he said, "and everyone is having difficulty throwing the demons out." From his perspective, while the '40s and '50s saw a general embrace of Christianity throughout the country, the '70s and '80s brought a full reversal of this religious sense. "This has had a big impact on the power of exorcism in these time periods."

"Thank you, Paul VI!" Fr. Athanasius said, jokingly, "who got rid of the minor order of *exorcist*." Those in the minor order of exorcists were the ones who did the pre-baptismal exorcisms in the early Church.[35] With that in mind, he said, "We are in a similar time to the early Church: we are the minority, no longer the mainstream religion. All of these people are coming into the Church with tattoos

---

[32] Dr Taylor Marshall. "Why are Exorcisms Taking Much Longer Today? | Dr Taylor Marshall and Fr Chad Ripperger." *YouTube*, 5 August 2022 youtube.com/watch?v=covnJgIK5Tc

[33] Ibid

[34] Ibid

[35] The traditional Rite of Baptism contains multiple exorcisms of the individual before the Baptism is administered.

and a history [of grave sin] and afflictions, who have dabbled and immersed themselves into the occult."

Fr. Ambrose said that, before Covid hit, it was often the case that one session of the Rite of Exorcism would drive the devil out. "It was not always the case but it was not uncommon," he said. "Now," he added, "It takes two, three, four times, and all the while new cases are piling up." This latter problem Msgr. Rossetti also mentioned, saying, "We just can't deal with all the people coming to us." This he said in late 2021, when Covid's impact was at a high point.[36] In December 2020, Italian exorcist Father François-Marie Dermine echoed these sentiments, noting that more people, as victims of Satanism and Satanic rituals, were coming to see him than in the past. "Unfortunately, I cannot follow all of them," Fr. Dermine said.[37]

A Mortal Wound

The presence of heresy, moral depravity, and occultism in the hierarchy, in addition to a general spiritual laxity and indifference among the faithful, has created a situation which the Church at large, especially in her leadership, has not yet fully perceived. "The Church has to wake up to the situation," Fr. Athanasius said. "It's not 'seventy-two and sunny' like they like to think simply because 'we have Vatican II'." These criticisms by Fr. Athanasius should not be seen as simply the ventings of a frustrated exorcist. Pope Paul VI, who closed Vatican II, suppressed the Traditional Mass, and promulgated the *Novus Ordo Missae*, uttered very similar criticisms in a homily on June 29, 1972. As quoted in the book, *The Barque of Peter*, Paul VI said, "It was thought that, after the Council, sunny days would come for the history of the Church. Nevertheless, what came were days of clouds, of storms, of darkness, of searching, of uncertainty."[38]

---

[36] SlayingDragonsBook.com, October 30, 2021, "Exorcist: "Number of people practicing the occult is astounding" - Exorcists are absolutely overwhelmed." Though, here, he does not directly connect Covid and the occult.

[37] *National Catholic Register*, December 4, 2020, "Longtime Exorcist: Satanism Is Growing in Western Societies"

[38] "The Barque of Peter," by Fr. Leonardo Sapienza, regent of the Pontifical Household, published in 2018.

Further, Paul VI's additional comments in this homily included a very important admission. He began his famous statement, "The smoke of Satan has entered the Church[39] of God" with the words, "We would say that, through some mysterious crack," after which he paused unexpectedly for a moment.[40] "No," he continued, "it's not mysterious."[41] Though he added no further explanation to this change in wording, he stated that the crack that let the devil into the Church is *not mysterious* and, thus, we can conclude, Paul VI regarded the crack to be quite obvious, though he does not identify just what it is. In the same speech, Paul VI later added, "We believe in something that is preternatural that has come into the world precisely to disturb, to suffocate the fruits of the Ecumenical Council, and to impede the Church."[42]

The disturbance that followed the Council was central to the disturbance of the exorcistic work of the Church which also followed the Council.[43] As Fr. Athanasius said, "Thanks to the innovations of Vatican II, we are not equipped. They neutered the Baptismal ritual,[44] giving up the pre-baptismal exorcisms, which is ludicrous! This could not have happened at a worse time. We are the 'odd man out,' the opposite of mainstream, the counterculture; and now we have stripped ourselves of our weapons? It is ludicrous." This deficiency has continued into the current day, he explained, adding a criticism of the new Rite of Exorcism, which was published in 1999. The French theologians who crafted the new Rite of Exorcism, he said, had never seen an exorcism themselves. "It is not ineffective," he said, "but it is not the same and does not have the imperative power of the old Rite." Fr. Amorth had also added that the revision

---

[39] Or "temple" depending on the translation. "Tempio" was the original Italian used.

[40] *VaticanNews.va*, June 2019, "Solennità di Pietro e Paolo nel Magistero dei Papi del passato," second audio clip for "solennità dei santi Pietro e Paolo del 1972." The interruption within his speech is clear in the audio.

[41] Full quote, "We would say that, through some mysterious crack—no, it's not mysterious; through some crack, the smoke of Satan has entered the Church of God."

[42] *Aleteia*, July 6, 2018, "What did Paul VI mean by saying 'the smoke of Satan has entered the Church'?" and a translation of the homily at CatholicStand, January 29, 2013, "Paul VI and the Smoke of Satan."

[43] The ministry of exorcism all but disappeared after Vatican II until, with the help of exorcists like Fr. Amorth, it eventually, decades later, saw a mild resurgence.

[44] The modern Rite of Baptism is very different from the Traditional Rite, lacking the richness of the traditional ritual and the traditional exorcistic focus contained in the prayers of the Rite.

was conducted without the input of a single practicing exorcist. These criticisms are why almost all exorcists prefer to use the Traditional Rite of Exorcism.

Faith in Times of Desolation

There are many verses in Sacred Scripture that bring comfort to those who consistently pursue the holiness called for by Our Lord and, thus, place their confidence in Him and in His Word. It is in these promises of the Holy Spirit that we find our strength and stability in these times when the barque of Peter is rocked by the diabolical storms hovering over the seas of this world. We must not take our eyes off Christ the Lord when the waves and winds begin to beat against the boat, for He is mightier than the seas and the Master over the tempests.[45] Therefore, though the ship may rock, and many aboard, "believing what is false,"[46] may slide off to their destruction, let us "stand fast and hold to the traditions"[47] handed on to us, persevering "to the end"[48] that we may be saved and may say with St. Paul, when the day comes for us:

> I have fought the good fight, I have finished the race, I have kept the faith. Henceforth there is laid up for me the crown of righteousness, which the Lord, the righteous judge, will award to me on that Day, and not only to me but also to all who have loved his appearing.[49]

---

[45] Matt 8:23-27
[46] 2 Thess 2:11
[47] 2 Thess 2:14 DR
[48] Matt 24:13
[49] 2 Tim 4:7-8

Chapter Six

The Occult Among Catholics

The moral and occultic evils that have infiltrated the hierarchy are not limited to Bishops and Cardinals. Naturally, if it is present among them, it is present among priests at local parishes, where all members of the higher orders have their start. Further, if it is present in all levels of the hierarchy, it will inevitably become present in the lives of the common faithful who, without adequate education and direction from the hierarchy, will fall to the errors present in their day. This has been the experience of many former occultists. Camilla, for example, when dealing with several tragedies in her life, sought counsel from a local priest she knew. In his effort to comfort her, he sent her to an ashram, a Hindu house of prayer and communal living, to begin Yoga and meditation. He even gave her books on Eastern meditation and channeling. In that needy state, she latched on to this as a way to find comfort. Eventually, she became an advanced practitioner of Yoga. After hearing about different programs to learn about spiritual healing, she joined one that was engaged in energy work, like Reiki. There, she learned how to "push energy" into other people's bodies to affect them *psychically*, to read auras, to diagnose illnesses psychically, and to talk to spirits. All this began as a result of the occultic counsel of her local parish priest.

Philomena stated that she has observed centering prayer, Yoga, and elements of "earth magic" popping up within local parishes and others throughout the world. One noteworthy incident she mentioned occurred when a church in Germany removed the altar and replaced it with a pile of dirt. On October 3, 2021, in Aschaffenburg, Germany, at the parish church *Maria Geburt*, the pastor coordinated a stunt involving the burial, in the center of what appeared to be the nave[1] of the Church, of a small square table beneath a huge mound of dirt, which they ceremoniously unearthed and then used for Mass. As Philomena said, "This is earth magic 101, but people want to see it as nothing, or just crazy, but not as something of the occult – which it is."

The occultic infiltration of the world, specifically with its "alternative" health techniques, have spilled over into the common life of Catholics. "Catholics have many *new* techniques that are really occultic, that priests, religious, retreat centers, hospitals, universities, and counseling centers have embraced," Camilla said. She added that Catholic health care has also been compromised. "Priests and nuns," she said, "are coming into these places and setting up Yoga, Reiki, 'healing touch,' and touting them as 'healing'." This implicates the hierarchy as well, since the Bishops in these areas both have oversight in these matters and undoubtedly receive complaints about these practices from faithful Catholics, all the while permitting them to continue.

When, in an occultic world, the faithful, especially the lukewarm, do not hear the Truth and are not directed in the right way, many will find the occult alluring. However, they will not simply *replace* the Catholic Faith with this counterfeit; they will mix the occult with the Faith and in their ignorance foresee no problems emerging from this syncretism.[2]

Fr. Dominic has noted that the many common issues which can lead people into the occult are also a concern for those Catholics who are striving to be devout. For them, he said, it is an issue of a lack of knowledge. "In this age of 'do-it-yourself'," he explained, "a lot of people who attend Mass, but know next to nothing about the Faith, will see these occult practices as 'something on the side,' which can coexist with the practice of the Faith." This ignorance blinds people to the dangers of playing with Ouija boards, using crystals, tapping into "energy," and doing tarot card readings, among other things. "They sometimes see this as something distinct from 'selling my soul to the devil'," he said, "but they don't recognize that this is all part of the same nasty stuff."

---

[1] From the Latin "navis," meaning ship, the place where the laity sits for Mass.
[2] The attempted amalgamation of two religions into one, Catholicism and paganism in this case.

Fr. Dominic said that another big concern is that many Catholics are simply unaware that certain activities *are* occult practices and, as a result, are incompatible with the Faith and dangerous. It's not about being paranoid about the devil being everywhere, but if Catholics are aware of what belongs to the occult, he said, "they can spot them when they creep into social interactions and practices." He added, "People in the parish being able to talk about the occult beyond just, 'oh, that's naughty,' is a *must.*"

"A lot of people are not joining the occult willfully but out of ignorance," Fr. Cyprian said. "Still, that causes some knots that are difficult to untie. The objective act," he added, "not the intention, is what demons look for. Such is the case with the Ouija board." Horoscopes, like doing readings for a person, involve getting information directly from demons. "Even if it was not intentional but just for fun with friends," he said, "the door swings open and the demons are ready, with permission." Fr. Ambrose said the impact of the spread of occult symbology and references is also impacting Catholics. He has seen Catholics going into these things, like Yoga, Reiki, psychics, and mediums, and then coming to him saying they did not realize it would affect them in the way it did. Fr. Blaise said that occult interest can begin first with the Ouija board, for example, but then they encounter a friend in school who is involved in Wicca and introduces them to it. They see the structure, the formulas, and think it is simply something neat.

This lack of knowledge is a set-up for disaster for many Catholics. "It's not everyone everywhere," Fr. Dominic said, "but even among striving-to-be-devout Catholics, I've run into people who do tarot readings and such because they don't know there's anything wrong with it." Father explained, "I once blessed an apartment of a lady who was a practicing Christian, very devout, who did tarot readings because she didn't connect the Bible verses against witchcraft and superstition as applying to tarot." Fr. Athanasius agreed and said the occult is widespread and varies by culture and demographics.

Fr. Dominic gave the example of Yoga, a far too common practice among Catholics. Many forms are quite clearly occultic, invoking "namaste," sitting before someone trained in real Hindu yogic practices, taking poses that are named after Hindu demons, and even invoking these demons at the suggestion of Yoga teachers.

Even the "secularized" forms are often gateways into the ones previously mentioned. Camilla said that, after having spent a long time in Yoga and the occult, she eventually left that and returned to the Church. "When I did eventually return to the Church," she said, "I was surprised to walk into Catholic Churches and find so many practicing Catholics going to the same [occult] workshops I was going to." Fr. Ermatinger pointed out that some Yoga disciplines even incorporate Christ, presenting Him as a guru. This has spilled over into Catholic areas as well. "There are even Catholics who portray Jesus as a yogi, and we currently see this in pictures of Jesus in convents, chapels and presbyteries – Jesus presented in yogi postures in meditation."[3]

When Fr. Ambrose has visited parishioners to bless their homes, he said he has occasionally seen pagan altars with strange things like garlic and idols from their home countries. He tells them to get rid of it but a lot of people don't want to. He has seen dream catchers in homes as well. Though he is not sure how those work on the preternatural level, he always destroys them. When he does so, it has brought peace to the home, as his parishioners have informed him.

Clare noted that, despite her father's involvement in the occult, he was also, outwardly at least, a practicing Catholic. He was on the parish council, a Knight of Columbus, and a distributor of Holy Communion. He was a loner in this mixing of Catholicism and the occult and was thankfully not joined by any others from the parish.

The embrace of the occult by Catholics can also be prompted by the culture in general. It was reported to me that Lowe's home improvement store had, in 2022, among its other disturbing occultic Halloween/Samhain decorations during October, a prominent image of the Hamsa symbol, a hand with an eye in the palm, often accompanied by other decorations. It is a superstitious symbol prominent throughout the world, believed to also protect against the "evil eye." The one who reported this to me found out about it because one of his children, who had recently visited the store with a relative, was discovered at home drawing the symbol, at which point this parent intervened and explained it was not a good symbol. The

---

[3] Ermatinger, *Trouble with Magic*, 100. Further, due to the cultural obsessions with Yoga, even Catholic schools that strive to be faithful often face an infiltration of Yoga, through pressure and initiatives pushed by poorly formed teachers and students.

"artwork" was then quietly destroyed. In another report, showing how it is everywhere and tolerated, this same symbol was seen on the back of a kid's sweatshirt during a live-streamed Mass in a Catholic Church.

The youth have an interest in the spiritual world, as many educators have seen, but their great ignorance about how it actually works can lead them to embrace occult errors. Fr. Gregory, reflecting on the interest of students in the topic of angels and demons, said the good thing is that the kids are interested in the topic and can connect with Angels. The bad thing, he said, is that they have a very wrong view of angels which is actually quite pagan. "They think we all become angels," he said. Not only is this an incorrect view of the human and angelic persons, but it also negates the power of sin and grace. When Barbara went through twelve years of Catholic school, she never once thought her New Age beliefs were in conflict with the Faith. "I learned about angels in Catholic school but that was consistent with my view of angels in the *occult*," she said. "I talked to angels, saw them, prayed with them... having no idea they weren't angelic but actually demonic. No one told me not to do those things because we were supposed to talk to our angels, right? There are differences but they were completely lost on me."

Christopher's story provides a prime example of practicing the occult beneath a Christian façade. He said he was once a "Christian occultist" and that he waited for the "providence of God" to give him the right opportunities for casting spells. As preparation for these rituals, he would spend a good amount of time singing and praying to God. At the same time, though, he would also call upon "preternatural guardians" that were related to his spells. His rituals also included a small sacrifice,[4] usually "a belonging of sentimental value," but on the rare occasion it would be some of his own blood. Not only is this a form of superstition, that is, a perversion of right worship, but it is also inherently contradictory: waiting on God's prompting to do something God condemns.

---

[4] Here is another instance of the occult inverting the good. In Christian devotion, we often offer sacrifices to God, but pure and holy sacrifices, such as fasting, charity, renunciation of material possessions, all to help us detach from the world and our selfish interests and cling more to Our Lord.

John said this is not an uncommon occurrence, and that, in various parts of the world, the occult seeks to hide beneath a Catholic façade. This is an historical and present-day reality, sometimes serving as a mask to a full occult religion, or as a parallel religion practiced alongside Catholicism. This includes religions like voodoo (in Haiti and the US), *benedicaria* (Italy), root work (South America), brujeria (Pennsylvania), among others. Fr. Amorth shared his observations of this "mixing of the sacred and the profane" in Italy. He said, "Unfortunately [it] is so present today even in the Christian community – for example, the hanging of a horseshoe around a statue of the Madonna in order to implore good luck – [it] is superstitious. It leads individuals to divination, magic, and witchcraft, with the expectation of gaining supernatural power over their neighbors."[5]

When I asked Helena about the idea of witches visiting Churches in this spirit of syncretism, she said, "I have met those that call themselves 'Christian witches.' They go to Church to worship and overall, their philosophy was more Christian than pagan. Believing in Jesus as the Son of Man and one God. So, they were not polytheistic like pagans. They worked mainly with prayer candles and 'angels,' trying to manifest certain things in their lives – money, family, etc. They had altars at home with Christian symbols. I met both Protestants and Catholics who followed this practice."

A Word about Protestantism

Protestant groups are also not free from the corrosive intrusion of occultic practices which are appearing under the guise of a "method" of prayer or a "technique" for obtaining favors from God. This appears in many forms and some Protestants are likely not even aware of its presence. Gabriel saw New Age mentalities insinuating themselves within the Protestant communities. "Positive thinking," he pointed out, "the idea that, if you want to change your life, just

---

[5] Amorth, *An Exorcist Explains*, 40. Likewise, there is a superstitious practice involving the burial of St. Joseph statues, which even some Catholic bookstores promote, called "St. Joseph kits." Burying blessed items, or placing them in certain areas, for the protection of the home or property, is an acceptable use of a sacramental. When rituals are added that demand odd steps, like burying the statue upside down, facing a certain direction, a certain number of feet from the road, etc., it becomes superstitious.

start thinking positively, is New Age thinking." In this approach, it is believed that "your thoughts can manifest your reality; so, if I just think positively, I can change what is around me."

Helena added that the Protestant "prosperity Gospel," with its "name it and claim it" mentality, is practicing a form of the occult as well. "A reliance on *you* manifesting what *you* want in your life, not a belief in God providing what you need in your life," is an occult concept. Being focused on *affirmations* has many connections with the pagan concept of spells and the ability of our words and wills to create everything in our lives.

"The Charismatic movement in Christianity is the biggest wide-open door to the occult," said Christopher, who had been a "Protestant occultist" for twenty years. *Movements of the Spirit,* Kenneth Copeland,[6] and Word of Faith ministry were three religious organizations he regarded as being problematic. Through these, you are taught to "speak things into existence." This, he said, is an occultic activity. He said it all began with the "power of positive thinking" in the 1970s, where the focus became the power of *believing* what you want to *be* in order to make it *happen.* As he said, "This is what occultists do, speak what they want into existence." Christopher was the first to use the term "Christian occultist" in my interviews. Christian occultists, he explained, merge an apparent Christian belief system with the power to speak things into existence.

He said it all began when he was in his late teens and attended a Protestant charismatic revival during which he witnessed things that he could not explain. Afterward, he began to faithfully attend their Sunday services and began a six-week course on "Christian prophecy." Looking back, he saw that course as a door to the occult. This course promised that he would be able to "learn things about the past and the future with a particular technique by which you open yourself up to the Word of God."[7] It was all placed beneath

---

[6] Beliefs include the blanket statement, "It's God's will for you to be healed, fully and completely. Discover true health today," (KCM.org > Real Help > Healing [video]) and "whatever we set our mind to is what we will receive. If you want God's goodness, healing, peace, joy and healthy relationships, then begin to proclaiming [sic] those things." (KCM.org > Real Help > Spiritual Growth > "How Words Impact Your Life")

[7] The issue here is that the very promise, that "the Word of God" will reveal things to you (secret knowledge of the past and future), is something the Church warns we are not

87

Divine Providence, with an emphasis on statements like "If God wills," "Thy will be done," and "not my will but Yours." Christopher perceived this as a contradiction, which did temporarily block him from going beyond what He thought God would allow. Nevertheless, human nature being what it is, this desire for power and knowledge eventually led him to push the boundaries of what he thought God *was* allowing and into dabbling more directly in the occult.

Helena suggests that many Christians are ensnared by things such as "A Course in Miracles," the Law of Attraction, and the prosperity Gospel. This sort of *easing into the occult* is an essential part of the diabolical ploy. The vast majority of people, Helena said, despite how wicked society is becoming, are not going to jump directly into Satanism, which they will still find unpalatable. However, there are many easy inroads that people, even Christians, are traversing.

---

permitted to know. Thus, this is hijacking a Christian element and merging it with an occultic promise, masking evil with a veil of good.

Chapter Seven

Why People Go Into the Occult

Each age of the world provides souls with temptations customized for the time in which they live. Satan desires to never miss an opportunity to seduce man away from God and into self-worship and, ultimately, toward some form of the occult.[1] His design for our destruction involves a program of perverting and inverting the good things God has made. The world, as God has made it, is good, but our use of the created things He has given us is what turns them into either instruments of virtue and sanctification or idols of abomination and self-destruction. If we, as the Church enjoys doing, consecrate all created things of this world to God and dedicate it to His purpose and glory, in obedience to His laws, there is no sin in using them. Too often, though, our wounded will, seeing the beauty of a created thing, begins to desire it as an end in itself or seeks to use it solely to increase our enjoyment of this earthly life. Both of these examples include the same flaw: God's will has been replaced by our own. When we follow our own wills, they become devils themselves,[2] and make us more like the dark master we choose through sin, which first occurred with the Fall of Adam and Eve.

The whole world is under the power of the evil one, as St. John, the beloved disciple, has said.[3] Thus, in every age, we must be on alert for the presence of evil not just in overt manifestations but also through the corruption of the good. It is through the latter, and not

---

[1] The "occult" really does vary in degrees. Any form of superstition is essentially a participation in the occult. Any form of "magical thinking" is likewise occultic. The danger, it should be remembered, is that when society abandons Christianity and turns toward an open interest in superstition, witchcraft, and magic, those with "merely superstitious" leanings are at risk of giving in to darker curiosities.

[2] St. Alphonsus Liguori. *The True Spouse of Christ*. Ascetical Works, Vol. X, Grimm Ed. (New York: Benziger Brothers,1888), 143-144, "When we do our own will, the enemy ceases to combat us; because then our wills are devils."

[3] 1 John 5:19

through the direct presentation of evil, that the enemy most often seeks to seduce us. He will never walk right up to us and directly ask us to abandon God. He will make false promises, utter lies mixed with truths, and wait for us to desire what is evil, at which point he will gently push us along the path of sin. This is the whole goal: to get us to believe an untruth so that, abandoning the law of God, we will sin. Today, with the occult on the rise as it is, the untruths and the philosophies of Satan are intermixed with a congregating religion of superstition and magic. Many errors of the present day are directly opposed to the teachings of the Church and entice man into varying forms of deviant mindsets and practices.

It has been predominantly through the erroneous philosophies of our decaying culture that man has been led away from the Church and into a self-idolatry in which man is but one step away from open occultic practices. Man's soul will never stop craving spirituality. When this craving is joined with erroneous beliefs about the nature of man and woman, the end for which man is made, the existence of God, the existence of the supernatural and preternatural, and the existence of an objective moral code binding all men throughout time, we have a situation in which our fellow man is in grave spiritual danger.

The paganization of our world is not just a threat to those who have fallen for these Satanic philosophies and actively walk by their supposed wisdom; it is also a threat to the children of the Church, particularly the young ones. Children today are growing up in a toxic environment, one in which these Satanic philosophies have infiltrated almost everything that they encounter. For many, not even their homes are without the stain of superstition and irreligion, even open magic and witchcraft. Thus, it must be understood that even the children of devout families will, at some point, due to the Fall and the decay happening in the world around us, be tempted by the occult. The occult today has achieved, for many, a seductive quality. Only those who have been steeped long in our Holy Faith will be able to sense and reject the superstitious and magical desires which this age has conjured. However, this steeping is difficult to achieve in an age of apostasy, heresy, moral collapse, and the rejection of God. All the more, we must stand fast and be on guard, heeding St. Peter's counsel, "Be sober and watch: because your adversary the devil, as a roaring lion, goeth about seeking whom he may devour."[4] If we do not secure ourselves in God's grace, and make ourselves appear to the enemy as an unconquerable fortress and temple of the Holy Spirit, he will prowl around our souls seeking the most advantageous inroad by which he may work our destruction.

The number and kinds of gateways that are appearing in our world today, through which both young and old are being drawn into the practices and effects of the occult, is astounding. These can include normal teenage angst and rebellion, ignorance of the Faith, feminism, the desire for power and influence, occult dabbling within the family, the unmet need for mysticism, unaddressed wounds, the internet, and encountering the occult in the life of a friend. Fr. Blaise said that the doors that lead to the occult are not all that uncommon and are also those which typically lead to various other spiritual problems. This is a critical point which we must all make note of in an age where an invitation to the occult is being more frequently offered to us. Among the typical things that can be doors to occult interest and diabolical harassment, he mentioned: the feeling of despair, the feeling that things are not going well for a person, the desire to look in a place away from God for a solution, and the search for meaning in the face of a loss of meaning in life.

The Prevailing Culture

The general attitude of a culture, whether good or evil, will be absorbed by the members of that culture, in particular by the youngest. Today, when the culture rejects the reality of sin, feels that individuals may do as they please, and presents the occult and themes of darkness as intriguing, the culture itself becomes an effective gateway to occult curiosity.

When Anna was young, the 1970s American culture in which she was immersed presented Satanic murders, occult-themed shows, and superstitions, all which served as gateways for her occultic interests which, thankfully, only lasted from age nine to thirteen. She said that, in her area, there were several murders related to Satanic rituals or the diabolical, one being connected to a coven which performed Satanic ritual murders. The latter was carried out by a kid

---

[4] 1 Peter 5:8 DR

heavily influenced by certain rock groups and drugs. The other was the "Amityville horror," which occurred not too far away from where she lived. In her area, it was also a common thing to see a Cross and the evil eye horn[5] worn together on the same necklace. People basically dismissed any concern about this symbol, acknowledging the danger while saying, at the same time, that it was "superstitious but harmless."

Anna recalled that there was a big fascination and focus on the occult in TV and movies in the 1970s. *Bewitched*, produced mostly in the 60s but popular in reruns in the 70s, was a popular show about a witch but was regarded as harmless. There was also so-called "G-rated" occult content in lots of movies and other things, even those directed toward children. Lucy's first memory of interest in the occult was also connected to culturally popular entertainment. When she was sixteen, she watched the movie *Buffy the Vampire Slayer*, which sparked an occultic curiosity that lasted for about twenty-one years. What began in Lucy as an interest in stories presented in TV and movies turned into an embrace of a wide spectrum of occult practices.

Bl. Bartolo Longo[6] absorbed both the anti-Catholicism and the spiritualism widespread in the Italian culture at his time, despite having been raised in the Church. He drifted away from the Faith as a result and began searching for meaning elsewhere. The political movements of the day and the spiritualism that was popular began to appeal to him. Surrounded by atheism and doubt, he eventually grew to dismiss the Catholic Faith and completely identify with the anti-Catholicism that was ever-present. He was very drawn to this and, by the time he was in college, he had a firm hatred for monks, priests, the Pope, and the Church herself. At that point, he wanted nothing at all to do with the Church and began a path that would see him eventually consecrated as a Satanic priest.[7]

---

[5] The "evil eye" is a common superstitious belief that someone can issue a curse against another by casting a malicious glance toward them. Various amulets are used to "protect" oneself from this curse, from "eye" symbols to horn-shaped amulets.

[6] A 19th century former Satanist who would become one of the greatest promoters of the Holy Rosary.

[7] Marysdowry. "Bartolo Longo, NEW FULL FILM, biography, power of the Rosary, Mary's Dowry Productions." *YouTube*, 30 May 2018, youtube.com/watch?v=3OQLRndbHIM (see also youtube.com/watch?v=NdR4bn2Bl-E)

Feminism

One of the Satanic philosophies present today is the anti-family, anti-man, anti-woman mindset known as "feminism." It is a self-destructive form of feminine exaltation at the expense of the very nature and purpose of the woman as God created her. It destroys marriages and families and fuels both the abortion and contraception industries as well as the surge in interest in witchcraft today. The influence, attraction, and impact of feminism was a recurring theme in my conversations with former occultists. The emphasis on powerful female figures in Wicca and witchcraft, in popular media and entertainment, and in the culture at large, was a spark that inflamed in many women resentment toward Christianity and a desire for spiritual autonomy.

Adelaide, before she began dabbling in the occult, was filled with a strong spirit of feminism. She hated what she thought was Christianity and was eventually attracted toward a religion with a female-centered deity. Wicca, with its focus on the female and a goddess, satisfied this desire. Her own mother had provided the example of the power of feminism. Adelaide explained, "She went from being a subservient Protestant housewife, back to college, and then her personality flipped one hundred percent. She became a totally different person. It was odd and everyone saw it." After becoming a feminist, her mother eventually divorced her father[8] who, having been brought up as a Catholic, had become an atheist and took no interest in how the children were raised. This set the stage for Adelaide's own strong entry into feminism. As a teenager, Adelaide turned against God, "enraged by Him," as she put it, and pushed against Christianity in particular. "It wasn't much of a leap to go from there to Wicca," she said. She practiced magic and Wicca for over ten years.

Helena was brought up in a Presbyterian home but, after discovering an occult mail-order catalog, she "was immediately

---

[8] Christopher was impacted similarly. His parents, inactive Catholics, were swept up in the sexual revolution and feminism, divorcing when he was very young. This brought an end to all catechesis and paved the way to his interest in the occult.

drawn to it."[9] She began to practice as a solitary witch, quickly became a feminist, and then gravitated toward goddess worship. Like Adelaide's, Helena's father provided a weak spiritual witness. Helena went on to practice as a witch in a Dianic coven for years before returning to being a solitary practitioner. She became disenchanted with this form of Wicca and began studying various occult practices, including hedgewitchery, shamanism, and astral projection, by which she sought to connect with other worlds and spirits. She pursued these occultic paths for twenty-five years before converting to Catholicism.

The spirit of feminism drew Lucy into the occult through an attraction to the strong female figures she saw in movies and TV shows. These appeared in many occult shows, like *Buffy*, *Ghost Whisperer*, and *Charmed*. She was "absolutely fascinated by these," she said, as well as the similar programs *Supernatural* and *Angel*. She loved seeing women battling evil, talking to loved ones who had died, and helping people "move on" to a better world. She thought the attraction to strong female characters may have been tied to her experience of being bullied in primary school. Lucy said she enjoyed having assurances about things in her life and people she could turn to for help, like psychics. The attraction was, essentially, that the occult brought comfort, excitement, strong female role models, and a control over her life, including staying connected with loved ones who had died (such as her father), as well as knowledge about what is beyond the physical world.

Vices Become Demonic

Sin itself is a powerful factor in the emergence of an interest in the occult. Sin begets sin. The more we sin, the more we become sinners, the more we are animated by sinful desires, sinful memories, sinful interests, sinful companions, and a mindset that begins to understand morality in a way opposed to the Truth revealed by God. Further, common sins, such as drugs and impurity, are dangerous not just because they are sinful, but also because of other effects they

---

[9] This was at a time when witchcraft was very much underground; there were no stores or networks to find support, encouragement, or new ideas. Imagine how much more she would have had access to, and how much easier it would have been to fuel this interest, were she a teenager today.

bring. The promotion and popularity of drugs, drunkenness, and impurity make it easier to deceive those who embrace these escapes, as these things all cloud the mind and make it difficult to discern right from wrong, good from evil, and truth from lies. This is one of the many attacks on reason, common both to the experience of those in the occult and to those in the modern secular world, and they are all promoted by the popular entertainment culture that governs the minds of the majority of the population.

"Temptations to sin," Fr. Dominic said, "are the way Satan and the demons attack us most prominently, and these aren't to be taken lightly." Many of the ordinary ways of temptation, "if they get a foothold in serious sins, can be a means of our downfall, even if there aren't the usual Hollywood-predictable occult fireworks shows," he said. He cited pornography and the abuse of drugs as two examples. Pornography witnesses to the power of ordinary temptation to bring us to grave evil. "Pornography," he said, "is demonic in its literal diabolizing[10] of human persons." Those who indulge in pornography, while likely not getting possessed as a result, are, nonetheless, now "open to being compromised by occult influence."

All sins, not just those mentioned above, are dangerous and potential contributors to occult curiosities. Sin in general involves a disordering of the passions and appetites of the body and the control which reason and the human will have over them. In his book, *The Trouble With Magic*, Fr. Ermatinger writes that, when the passions are allowed to dominate, we end up serving them in "a demonic act of false worship...Such a man," he wrote, "has an inward habit of mind and unfettered passion that has claimed the intellect and become an idol in the same way disordered sexuality becomes an idol. The angry person enters false worship in as much as he sacrifices his reason to the blood of passions."[11] St. Alphonsus Liguori presents this same connection between sin and idolatry (obedience to the devil) when recounting the story of Jeroboam:

> When Jeroboam rebelled against the Lord, he endeavored to draw the people with him into idolatry. Hence he placed before them his idols, saying, 'Behold

---

[10] A fancy English word that has to do with perverting, distorting, and abusing the physical human form.

[11] Ermatinger, *The Trouble with Magic*, 73

thy gods, O Israel.'[12] It is thus the devil acts; he represents a certain pleasure to the sinner, and says, 'Make this your god; behold this pleasure; this revenge is your god; adhere to them, and forsake the Lord.' And in consenting to sin, the sinner obeys the devil, and in his heart adores as his god the pleasure which he indulges. 'A vice in the heart is an idol on the altar'.[13]

A devotion to sin leaves the soul with an array of disorders: woundedness, moral weakness, sadness, insatiable cravings for more, cravings for autonomy, and desires for power and control. All these play right into the devil's occultic recruitment and become a gateway for taking up the practice of witchcraft and magic.

Teenage Drama

Normal teenage angst, a sense of rebellion, and even the status of the culture, with everything being confused and "up in the air," even within the Church, has led a lot of youth into the occult, according to Fr. Blaise. "Kids want structure and order and they will seek it even in chaos if that provides it," he said. In his book, Dr. Richard Gallagher agreed about teenage rebellion being an issue. "In my view," he wrote, "these 'neopagan' variants are rarely a rational path nor a simple reversion to cultures that in their day knew no alternatives. Modern regression to such beliefs often seems to arise primarily out of a personal rebellion against monotheistic religions, along with some of their moral codes and demanding creedal systems."[14]

The Beckett's description of their daughter Catherine is a good example of how normal teenage angst can lead to confusion and a dive into the occult. In high school, she was naïve and innocent, often slow to catch on to things but, her parents said, a very sweet girl who was never mean to anyone. Unfortunately, she was also picked on a lot and seen as an outsider. While people did still like

---

[12] I Kings 12:28
[13] St. Alphonsus Liguori, *Preparation for Death*, 157
[14] Gallagher, *Demonic Foes*, 175.

her, she did not fit in with other kids. Toward the end of high school, the teasing became much worse. In spite of everything, she excelled academically and was awarded prestigious scholarships. Nonetheless, within a year of graduating from high school she had plunged herself deep into the occult.

The Monroes believe a spirit of rebellion led to their daughter Ava's exploration of the occult. She is very intelligent which, they believe, led her to think she knew better than everyone else and could figure things out for herself. In late middle school and high school, she met some new friends with new ideas: New Age and "earth love" concepts. She began to experience confusion and question why her religion is right and others are not. She was also insecure about her appearance, not seeing herself as attractive. As a result, she sought to get noticed. This continued after high school when the occult phase began. Now, more mature, she seeks attention on social media using shock value in her attire.

Psychologist Adam Blai, who also works extensively with exorcists, stated in a talk that teenagers are most attracted to witchcraft during the normal phase of individuation. Adolescents feel a lack of control, and this lack makes witchcraft more attractive to them.[15] Philomena explained that this appeal is tied to the promise of obtaining some sort of power, making them feel "different" and "special." Of course, she added, the only thing different is that they have surrounded themselves with demons.

Ignorance of the Faith

The various forms of decline in faith among people is a huge gateway into the occult. Often, this reflects the general abandonment of God by society, the result of which is the lack of religious training in the lives of the youth. In turn, they grow up seeking God but only finding the Ape of God in the counterfeit religion of the occult.

On the question of what sets a person up for a fall into the occult, Fr. Dominic has seen a pattern in the cases he has dealt with, and it all involves a decline in, or absence of, faith. He said, "Almost all the cases I've encountered usually involve a combination of some bad ingredients: (1) poorly catechized Catholics (2) who don't attend

---

[15] *EWTN*, Wicca and Witchcraft, video

Mass regularly or avail themselves of the Sacraments (3) who find themselves dabbling in the occult without necessarily recognizing that that's what they're doing."

Lucy said, "Those who know God's word, know the true teachings of the Church, and focus on the Truth, are at a lot less risk." However, she added, "People who are seeking, and have no idea *what* they are seeking, or those who are purposely seeking to work with Satan," are at a higher risk. "The more lies you are caught up in, the more vulnerable you are to the occult," she said, adding, "I believe kids and youth are very vulnerable as they often don't have a solid foundation of the truth, and are excited by the 'unknown' when it comes to the spiritual."

Anna said that she was seeking mystery and a connection with the spiritual, but she was not raised with a devout practice of the Rosary or other devotions, like Adoration, which were only cursory. This opened her to occultic dabblings, which lasted for many years in middle school. Lucy, likewise, was very drawn to spiritual realities, but not Christianity. "I guess I always knew that there was more to reality than what we could see, and I had a deep interest in seeking out more. Since I'd never really heard much about the spiritual realm, I simply didn't know what to believe."

Gabriel was brought up as a lukewarm and non-practicing Baptist. This left him very curious about the world, including astronomy and the search for aliens. Becoming an agnostic as a teenager, his unmoored curiosity eventually led him to the New Age and deeper. Philomena was left to make the decisions about faith on her own. Her father was in the military and was gone a lot and her mother was a nurse who also worked a lot. This left her, as the oldest, in charge of taking the other children to Mass, but she would often not take them. She said she was raised in the post-Vatican II Church, with a theological emphasis on butterflies and warm fuzzies but a total lack in teaching. It wasn't until her reversion to the Faith in her 30s that she learned not to receive Holy Communion without going to Confession first. Similarly, Edith's father gave no support to her learning the Faith when she was young, even treating it with disdain and mockery. He would not even discuss with her what his religious beliefs were. "Agnostic and anti-Catholic," she said, was a good way to describe him. Her mother told her about the occult instead.

Lucy was brought up as an Anglican by two loving parents, but her mother was a non-practicing Catholic and her father was an Anglican. Her family did not follow a religion or have any strong beliefs. They were good people who sought to help others in the community. She had a few friends who went to Church but she rarely went herself. In high school, she began to dismiss the Church as something not "cool." She heard a few teachings along the way but did not learn much at all about Christianity. As a teenager, she "did as she pleased," including drinking, smoking, drugs, and indifference toward school. She did not regard herself as "bad," taking after her parents and seeking to be helpful, but, in reality, she was becoming a self-absorbed rebellious teenager headed toward the occult.

The absence of understanding regarding how the devil operates is another ignorance that can lead to a dangerous deception in a person's mind. Lucy said that she was not raised as a Christian and, therefore, knew absolutely nothing about spiritual warfare. Andrew, who was raised Protestant, was still not given sufficient understanding about spiritual matters. He said, "As a teenager, I did not have good answers to questions; only pointing to the Bible but *without* sufficient understanding to answer the tough questions." He then added a warning about the need to give youth the answers for which they are looking. He said today's atheists argue about the trustworthiness of Sacred Scripture. They ask, "How can Scripture be reliable and how can you guarantee it has been translated properly?" The answers are available in abundance today, and the youth need to hear these answers. Yes, Sacred Scripture is reliable. Yes, Sacred Tradition is reliable. Yes, Jesus Christ really walked the earth and rose from the dead.

There is a grave danger, Christopher added, of not supplying youth with the answers to their questions. As he said, "If youth don't get a good answer, they are not simply going to stop thinking about it – they are going to look elsewhere. You can't just say, 'It's in the Bible,' when you and they *both* cannot actually find it there!" Sending a youth to the Bible to find the answer to all his questions is not the way to handle these dilemmas. Sacred Scripture, Sacred Tradition, verified history, logic, reasoning, and discussion, are all necessary to answer these important questions. This is why all Christians, the young and the old, need to constantly study the Faith and obtain a deeper understanding of the many intricacies in the Truth Christ has brought to us. This deeper knowledge will not only serve to keep us as fruitful branches in communion with Christ the True Vine, but it also makes us always "prepared to make a defense to any one who calls you to account for the hope that is in you."[16]

Many former occultists are convinced that people go into the occult looking not only for the Truth which has been withheld from them but also to satisfy the need for mysticism in their spirituality. Concerning the desire for mystical experiences, Andrew said, "I would say the vast majority of those you see practicing some sort of occultism or paganism are certainly seeking a 'divine' or 'mystical' experience." People are seeking this through the occult because, Adelaide said, even more than offering power and fame, "The occult offers to satisfy the hunger for mystical union." People in our post-Christian era, deprived of the riches of the graces of Christ, are going to seek to satisfy that hunger with *something*: addiction to drugs, loose living, or a foreign religion. "We can't just be *human*," Adelaide said, "There is always something [greater] above you. It's always going to be there. If it's not God, it's going to be something else, and there are only two camps to choose from."

A major reason for Helena's interest in the occult was the lack of mysticism in her Protestant upbringing. "It seemed very beige, very shallow," she said. "I found much of the occult to be far more interesting. It was transcendent, something beyond the ordinary. I felt a connection to everything in a way that I had never felt before." When she was young, Christianity never appealed to her. "It always rubbed me the wrong way," she said. "I loved nature and being outdoors. It was one of the few places where I felt the presence of the Divine." Since most forms of witchcraft have a strong connection to nature, it appealed to her specifically for this reason.

Introduced to the Occult

With all these spiritual deficiencies in place, it often only takes someone to introduce the individual to the occult in order to hook them with this "new and exciting" spiritual world. The introduction to the occult is often done by the presentation of the "soft" side of the

---

[16] 1 Peter 3:15

occult. This can include a focus on "angels"[17] or "self-help"-style "New Age" philosophies which are both very disarming. Further, with no intellectual structure in place to discern the good from the bad, nor a belief in the existence of "good and evil" at all, the person is highly likely, today, to take the bait.

After Adelaide got married, the mother-in-law that came with her marriage was, in fact, a witch who had been practicing the "craft" since she was a teenager. Adelaide was still a bit afraid of witchcraft so her mother-in-law, and a witch friend of hers, gave Adelaide a book on "Angel Magic," designed to introduce her to the craft with the help of "angels." To someone like her who knew nothing about Christianity, this appeared innocuous. She later understood this to be a clever technique to get around her initial fears. However, this occultic use of "angels" became Adelaide's entry point into witchcraft. From there, "I had a knack for it," she said, "and I loved the way it made me feel." As a result, she easily went deeper into the practice, pulling from the Greek and Celtic pantheons as a Wiccan. She was a solitary practitioner and not a member of a coven, though she would get together on occasion with her mother-in-law and her friend. She realized she was quite good at magic and was soon writing her own spells and incantations.

In a similar way to Adelaide, Andrew, having already embraced a soft interest in magic, was introduced to Wicca by the mother of a girl he was dating. He began to practice that for a while and then moved on to study influential occultists like Madame Blavatsky, Eliphas Levi, and the notorious and highly influential Aleister Crowley. Crowley became his primary fixation. By early college, he had fully embraced this form of the occult, living by the so-called "Law of Thelema," and identified as a Thelemite[18] until he converted to Catholicism. It was over a four-year period that he progressed

---

[17] This points to a modern tendency to regard everything spiritual as good, without distinction or discernment. It also highlights a point of concern: the occult often incorporates "angels" into prayers and rituals, which is a means of deception to uneducated Christians. These "angels" are not the Christian spirits who are given by God to assist our salvation. They are demons and this is clear when looking at the fruits produced when a person incorporates them into his life. Many Christians stray into practices tied to these occult "angels." This includes the practice of giving names to guardian angels, forbidden by the Church but a common occultic practice.

[18] One who embraces the occultic religion of Aleister Crowley in which, as one element, the personal will is the principal power by which one lives.

from an active curiosity, study, and exploratory practice to a serious dedication to the occult as a Thelemite.

Catherine Beckett's embrace of the occult began when, after taking a break from college as a result of suffering a breakdown, she was introduced to "mindfulness"[19] by coworkers at a new job she started. During that time, her parents observed that she was still praying the Rosary with the family, going to Mass, and even going to Adoration on her own. When they later realized she was also into some form of Wicca or witchcraft, they noticed that, while she was still going to Mass on Sundays, she would now hold her head down the entire time, refusing to look up. She would still receive Holy Communion, despite being well-formed on *not* receiving in a state of sin, and, as the parents noted carefully, would always consume the Host. Even when her work schedule prevented her from going to Mass with the family, she would still go on her own.[20]

Having a moment of *introduction* to the occult is something that even "high profile" occultists have in their background. Zeena LaVey, the daughter of Anton LaVey, the founder of the Church of Satan,[21] said that, in her youth, her natural inclination to magic was influenced by the self-identified witches and warlocks who joined the Church of Satan in its early days (1970s). The Church of Satan itself was not truly spiritual, instead focusing on Satan as a "metaphor" or "archetype," but these additional influences pushed her into the practice of real magic.[22] Similarly, the modern-day Satanist, David Sinclair Smith, of the Church of Satan, said, in a 2021 interview with Ciaran Lyons that he was given a copy of the Satanic Bible by a friend in 1992. "It resonated with David as soon as he read it," Ciaran said, as the narrator. Now, as Ciaran worded it, "he's an expert in the church and its practices, which include spells, magic, and rituals."[23]

---

[19] A Buddhist technique of Eastern meditation in which the practitioner seeks to observe his thoughts and feelings in order to control them and attain peace.
[20] Catherine is still in the occult. This sort of back-and-forth with Catholic devotions has been very confusing for the family.
[21] Important to note, though not a Christian, Zeena has renounced all forms of Satanism as well as her last name. She now goes by the last name "Schreck," from her former husband.
[22] *Vice.com*, September 25, 2012, "Beelzebub's Daughter."
[23] 7NEWS Spotlight. "'SATANISTS NEXT DOOR' | Our cameras capture a secret ritual as a 'curse' is cast | 7NEWS Documentary." *YouTube*, 27 February 2021. youtube.com/watch?v=Wqa5F6vWWXM

Zeena's former husband, Nikolas Schreck,[24] also a prominent and public Satanist at one point, shared a fascinating anecdote on the power of horror movies to stir an interest in the occult when he was young. This presentation of the devil in film, combined with curiosity and an ignorance of the True Faith, had the power to send a young man off the deep end and into decades of deep occult practice. Discussing the impact of horror movies on him in his youth, he said, "Growing up in the '60s, occultism was everywhere and I was drawn to it immediately." He had a regular babysitter who was a self-identified witch, before it was something common to encounter. They shared an enjoyment of horror movies and would stay up late watching them. One movie was the 1931 Bela Lugosi *Dracula*,[25] during which the babysitter harped on the line in the film, which Dracula spoke to another character, *All these things will I give you, if you will obey me.* "The babysitter treated watching these horror films as if we were at a university seminar on occultism. It's like 'These are the things you need to know in life.' For some reason," Schreck said, "that statement, *All these things I will give you,* as a little kid, that appealed to me. The other religions weren't giving you anything."

He then began to study the Bible to learn more about who the devil is, this being who will *give you everything if you serve him.* "This is how upside down and 'bizzaro world' my perspective on the world was," he explained. All this happened at a time when 19th century occult books and magical books ("grimoires") were being published and his parents were encouraging him to explore occultic practices. His parents, on a trip to Haiti, even took him to participate in a voodoo ceremony. "So," he said, "I grew up not even thinking the devil was evil, or that there was anything wrong with it. I lived in, like, an alternate universe."[26]

---

[24] He, like Zeena, has also strongly renounced all forms of Satanism. While not a Christian, his eventual condemnation of Satanism, which he embraced for close to twenty years, is important for people to hear. It will be addressed in *Slaying Dragons III.*

[25] The book *Dracula,* by Bram Stoker, has a lot of fascinating Catholic themes in it and is recommended for Catholics to read. That being said, movie presentations can stir the imagination differently than books, and a curious soul, seeking occult enticements, can still latch on to something unintended by the author, such as Schreck's attachment to Dracula's evil.

[26] YouTube, The Nikolas Schreck Channel, "Nikolas Schreck Interviewed by Legs McNeil THE DARK SIDE OF THE SIXTIES PT 2 HOLLYWOOD SATANISTS," April 17, 2022

Built on Sand

Our society has forfeited the offer of building itself on the solid rock of the good, the true, and the beautiful.[27] In settling for, and even willingly electing, to build itself on the counterfeit, pursuing not the glorification of God and the fulfillment of the human person in the Truths revealed by God, it has built itself up into a mighty city of man built upon sand. What we are seeing today could be described as a testing, permitted by God, where the devil has come against us as he once did against the Apostles on the Sea of Galilee.[28] When Our Lord slept peacefully, the storm came upon them and the Apostles fell into fear. Stirring Our Lord by their petitions, He arose and "rebuked the winds and the sea," imparting a sudden and complete calm. Our society, having "built [our] house upon the sand,"[29] is now suffering the onslaught of the devil's presence. As in the parable, when the "rain fell, and the flood came, and the winds blew and beat against that house,"[30] our nation, even our world, which has rejected Christ as King, does not have Him with us to stir by our petitions, for we have refused to cry out to Him, having turned our backs by our infidelity. Therefore, we see the fall of the culture and the entrapment of too many citizens in the lures of the enemy. Without an effort to reorder our world and place ourselves, individually and collectively, under the reign of Christ the King, we will continue to watch as our friends, families, neighbors, and fellow citizens are seduced from sin unto sin.

---

[27] Matt 7:24-25
[28] Luke 8:22-25. Exorcists see in this scenario an exorcism of a tempest stirred up by demonic agency.
[29] Matt 7:26
[30] Matt. 7:25

Chapter Eight

The Occult Plays on Our Wounds

The power of sin, articulated so well in Sacred Scripture, is on full display today in our very broken world, and in particular within the scourge of the occult, which calls out to wounded souls and feeds on their brokenness. We are all, therefore, in the sights of the diabolical, which seeks to draw every one of us away from God and the right worship which will fulfill our souls. It is not simply through the sins which we commit ourselves, which do in fact create an emptiness and a wound, that the diabolical will seek to ensnare us. It is also from the effects of this fallen world, the discord within mankind, the separation we feel between ourselves and God, between ourselves and others, between ourselves and the created world, and the internal discord which burdens us on a daily basis.

Even though a Christian may be risen from the death of sin through Baptism, he remains a wounded soul, carrying the burden of concupiscence until the moment he departs from this earthly life. Through these wounds, we tend to hide our true selves from God, from others, and even from our own personal reflections. We need to be re-oriented toward God, to be taught how to love Him, to be taught that He loves us, and to be taught how to be virtuous and how to live by virtue in order to peacefully navigate this valley of tears. When we do re-orient ourselves toward God, we will see that everything we endure in this life, including the wounds from our sins and our sufferings in this fallen world, can be redeemed, joined to the sufferings of Christ on the Cross, and can propel us, through His healing love, further forward on the path of sanctification.

The Christian is led through this valley of tears by the hands of a Holy Mother, which is the Church and Bride of Jesus Christ. It is only with this companion that the soul can avoid the pitfalls of temptation and diabolical deceptions and grow into the image of Christ, breaking free of the hold of concupiscence, and re-establishing the unity he needs with God, man, creation, and himself. It is only through this total healing, brought about by sanctifying grace, that a man can resist the pull of our fallen nature, whose vices are celebrated by the world and the devil. But "men loved darkness rather than the light," and, due to the power of sin, we resist the call of the Light of Christ.

St. John, the beloved disciple, spoke of the power of sin to draw men into the realm of darkness, in which, wounded, they hide so as not to be seen by the light.

> Men loved darkness rather than light, because their deeds were evil. For every one who does evil hates the light, and does not come to the light, lest his deeds should be exposed.[1]

The discord described above, and the wounds which it and personal sins bring, cause us to turn away from God, in ways small and great. When a man lives apart from God, he lives with a blinded conscience, attachments to evil, festering vices, and a confused mind. Further, when he remains in a spiritual situation where grave sin has been permitted to reside in his soul, which is the case for too many people today, he lives, as the Church says, in "a state of sin." This is the name for the "darkness" in which men who love evil hide. This state of sin is a perpetuated spiritual dilemma which can give rise to a whole host of new evils and new attachments to sin. Even those who seek to love God, as a result of the wounds they carry from enduring the discord in this world, often turn to sin and vices in order to escape the pain they endure.

All these sins and experiences of the brokenness of the world can cause or feed a disorder within our souls. This disorder becomes a wound which then inclines us to turn away from God to avoid His presence, as Adam and Eve did in the Garden after the Fall.[2] Shame, lack of trust in God, lack of faith in God, self-obsession, and a preference for created things over God, all overpower our will and prevent us from repenting of our sins. When the wounds flow from sins committed against us, they can harm our trust in God, our trust

---

[1] John 3:19–20
[2] Gen 3:8–10

in others, and our belief that there is any good in this world or in the next. All these wounds dispose us toward a consideration of the offerings of the devil, both in ordinary temptation as well as that of the occult.

Wounds flowing from personal sins can be likened to a residue of evil in the soul. On this point, St. Louis de Montfort said, "The actual sins we have committed, whether mortal or venial, even though forgiven, have intensified our base desires, our weakness, our inconstancy and our evil tendencies, and have left a sediment of evil in our soul."[3] Wounds that flow from the brokenness of the world can function in a similar way, when their presence in the soul taints our belief in the goodness of God. Exorcists state that these weaknesses and wounds become the focal points of the devil's temptations[4] and the targets of the demons.[5] Fr. Maximilian said the diabolical plays on our weaknesses and is able to leverage those against us one hundred times better than anyone else. This should greatly alarm us today. "There is a lot going on that is creating a general weakness that the whole culture is experiencing," he said. This includes the lack of understanding regarding religious authority, lack of education on foundational truths, and a tendency toward sloth and entertainment.

As I discussed in *Slaying Dragons*, demons are dedicated to ensuring that we are affected by wounds. One of their tactics is to seek to orchestrate external events in a person's life in order to bring harm upon that person, either internal or external, creating a wound through which the demons can then get a better hold on the person and more easily manipulate them through temptation. Trauma, whether occurring in the natural course of life or instigated by diabolical agency, can have spiritually dangerous effects. Exorcist Fr. Carlos Martins said that trauma "can lead to losing faith in the goodness of God and the world He created." Trauma, he said, can "leave a wound and that wound can shake us in the goodness of reality." He added that a spirit of fear can latch on to a person as a result.[6]

---

[3] St. Louis de Montfort, *True Devotion to the Blessed Virgin Mary.* (New York: Montfort Publications, 1996), 79.

[4] Fr. Amorth, in *Slaying Dragons*, 116.

[5] Fr. Ripperger, in *Slaying Dragons*, 14.

[6] Fr. Martins, in *Slaying Dragons*, 111.

Andrew, from his experiences in the occult, observed that people who live outside of the Church, or live in a state of sin, or are too curious, or who lack proper spiritual guidance, are all in a state of vulnerability to the temptation toward the occult as a result of the spiritual weaknesses that these will likely bring about in the soul. The world is in such a state that even a member of the faithful, if they go astray from the Faith, could wind their way into the occult. Lucy observed that people are drawn into the occult, or disposed favorably and receptively toward it, through fear, anxiety, needing to know the future, loss, rejection, doubt, and the promise of something greater/better than what the person has at the moment. These are not always conscious choices and, thus, something to which Christians also need to be attentive. Satan, she said, "Taps into areas that people don't fully understand or even realize about themselves, their weaknesses, their desires, their past, etc."

"It's like the island of misfit toys"

In my conversation with John, he made a remark which I have shared with people in various situations and which has rung true for all of them. The occult, he said, "Is like the island of misfit toys." This image comes from the 1964 *Rudolph the Red-Nosed Reindeer* stop-motion animation film, in which there is an island where all the broken or improperly assembled toys go to live. John's point is that everyone in the occult, likewise, is wounded, broken, or feels rejected in some way, and they are all gathered on the one "island" of the occult. Converts from the occult are not the only ones who make this observation. In an October 31, 2020, article by the *Guardian*, titled "My Life as a Teenage Witch," the author stated, "The pagans I met in real life didn't look like people who had harnessed the unseen currents of the universe...I began to wonder whether people drawn to mystical realms really were charmed souls, or *misfits who had struggled to find a place for themselves* anywhere else."[7]

When I mentioned the reference to the occult as the "Island of Misfit Toys," Adelaide reacted strongly. She said, "Absolutely. Absolutely, I've got to agree with that. That's actually a really good

---

[7] *The Guardian*, October 31, 2020, "I Became Convinced I was Channeling Powers: My Life as a Teenage Witch." *Emphasis* mine.

way to put that." In light of this and given the statistics on depression and anxiety in the culture, it makes the occult seem much more formidable of an enemy, since there are so many who are positioned to feel the occult has something beneficial to offer.

"The One Thing We All Have in Common"

Therese said that nearly everyone in occult groups has serious wounds, whether from rape, abuse, childhood trauma, depression, or bipolar, among others. Helena agreed and noted that abuse, family disharmony, same-sex attraction, drugs, low self-esteem, and loneliness are doors by which the devil lures people into the occult. Therese said that, when she left the occult and became Catholic, it was "like breaking up with a violent ex-boyfriend that no one believed existed. It is hard to get help when people don't think he's there."

Riaan Swiegelaar, a recent convert from Satanism, said, "I got involved with Satanism because at the time it resonated with me, being very broken and sad without realizing it. I think the reason why a lot of people resonate with Satanism is they come from a very broken place. I have met thousands of Satanists over the last three years and I'm not saying their intentions are bad, but they are extremely broken and extremely hurt ... that's the one thing we all have in common." "In my own experience," Andrew said, "[occultists] tend to be very much traumatized and damaged individuals." Helena agreed, noting, "There were a lot of troubled people involved with the occult. A lot of mental issues that I would say came about because of demons.[8] Then they thought the occult could help them with these issues, so they just went around and around as a result." "It is very clear to me," Christopher said, "that there are some very deep spiritual and emotional wounds that undergird the Satanic movement, and the occult movement as a whole." Unlike people who seek to heal those wounds, he said many occultists use these wounds to fortify their wills and often let the

---

[8] While natural causes for mental illnesses should be assumed, demons are capable of creating mental disturbances that imitate true psychological problems. From Helena's experience with people in the occult, she saw enough to be convinced that many of these psychological issues, at least among those in the occult, were actually caused by the diabolical.

pain drive them mad in the process. "At no point," he added, "is there a willingness to suffer out of love for what God has done for them."

The people Fr. Dominic saw who were involved in Satanic and pagan rituals "were desperate individuals with lots of depression, abuse, and/or drug use who were seeking to bend things to their wills – that is, there was more heart-felt dedication in their giving themselves over to the occult." This eager desire to use the occult to find a solution will only more deeply entrench the individual in its servitude. Philomena said that the initial responsiveness of the demons, granting so many desires of the occultist, eventually stops. This leaves a new void, in the absence of this reciprocity from the "spirits," on top of the original void or wound which the person brought with them. As a result, people indulge themselves in various ways to fill this new void, including alcohol, drugs, and impurity. "You think you have all this [power in the occult]," she explained, "but you don't, so [once you realize it] you add vice and sin on top of it, and they compound each other. When the occult starts to fail, the resulting desperation starts to grab on to other vices...and it gets heavy." Everyone Philomena knew who was in the occult had struggled with attachments to alcohol or drugs or impurity.

Msgr. Rossetti, a very busy exorcist in Washington, D.C., stated that many of the people who come to him with demonic afflictions have experienced some sort of trauma in their youth. They retain a hatred and desire for vengeance and are, essentially, "poisoned" by a lack of forgiveness toward certain people. To truly experience healing and liberation, an expression of forgiveness toward these people is necessary.[9] A false religion that offers you the ability to tap into secret powers ready to do your bidding, and to which are attached no governing morals, can be very appealing to a person who carries around an unaddressed hatred.

Many occultists developed a hatred for God as a result of misfortunes in their lives and were driven into the occult because of that anger. Others were angry at their misfortunes and sought the power to change the circumstances themselves. Once they settled into the occult, the anger often became inflamed and uncontrollable. One piece of evidence of the presence of this anger in the occult pertains to the writings within Satanism. Riaan Swiegelaar said that

---

[9] Rossetti, *Diary*, 117.

these writings, such as those which state the philosophy and purpose of Satanism, are written from a place of anger. As someone who was himself sad and broken, he said that is why the philosophy initially resonated with him.[10]

It seems, as Swiegelaar further described, that a *lot* of Satanists end up in that dark realm partly as a result of not knowing how to deal with the hurt and pain they have accumulated in their lives, and not knowing how to properly turn to God for significant healing and peace. He said, of the times when he was helping to lead the South African Satanic Church, "[There were] thousands and thousands of applications to the Satanic Church that I've seen," adding that the *majority* of the applications say, as the reason for seeking out Satanism, "I've been hurt by Christians," or "I hate God" because, as he himself can relate, "that has been their experience – that's how people get lost."[11] Therese also noticed that there were an awful lot of wounded Christians[12] in the occultic groups she frequented.

The Gate is Wide

The number of sins and wounds and misfortunes that can be taken advantage of by the world, the devil, and our fallen nature is sadly quite large and varied. Fatherless homes, abuse, injury, experiences of death, rejection, isolation, and anger are just a few of the many that are brought forward by former occultists as reasons why they were vulnerable to the temptations of the occult. These causes do not automatically produce an interest in the occult. With the help of God, we can overcome every obstacle. However, that is part of the point. When we reject God and live *without* Him, the obstacles in life can easily trip us into falls for which there is no power, either within our souls by grace, or from above by His extraordinary intervention, by which we can rise again.

The world today, greatly destabilized as it is, has added a dangerous new ingredient to the general spiritual battle which all men face, making it much easier to fail and much harder to succeed: isolation. This isolation has been growing in recent decades as

---

[10] Riaan Swiegelaar video #1, Facebook, July 4th, 2022.
[11] Riaan Swiegelaar video #1
[12] She specified "mostly Protestant."

families are increasing broken apart, grave sins skyrocket,[13] pornography becomes ubiquitous, and the internet in general lures people into a dark light of solitude. This situation mushroomed into an unimaginable danger during the reign of Covid. One exorcist, Fr. Ambrose, observing the nightmarish situation, said, "I could not dream up a scenario that would be this damaging."

This isolation, according to Msgr. Rossetti, is a tactic of the devil. He observed that the possessed, and other afflicted souls, will experience a feeling of isolation, as if they were cut off from everyone and their situation unintelligible to others. Thus a key means of hastening their liberation was to incorporate them into a community of worship and of nurturing relationships. "Living a life of isolation," he stated, "feeds the demons."[14]

"Demons seek to isolate people more and more in order to destroy them," Fr. Dominic said. As a result, the people who are particularly targeted by the demonic are often those who are already somewhat isolated. This also includes those who are "not integrated well in the life of the Catholic parish," he said, adding, "Such as people who have stopped practicing, people who have just moved to a new city, etc." This can easily lead the person to an experience of sadness and depression, another tactic of the enemy. St. Francis de Sales described the misery of the demons as "sadness and melancholy" and that Satan uses sadness and depression to lead good men to give up the pursuit of doing good. He said, "The Evil One delights in sadness and melancholy, because they are his own characteristics. He will be in sadness and sorrow through all Eternity, and he would fain have all others the same."[15]

Isolation can be experienced in a variety of ways. Riaan Swiegelaar, in his public testimony, appeared to place some of the blame for his atheism and Satanism on people of faith rejecting him as unworthy of religion because of his homosexuality.[16] Isolation can

---

[13] Think about abortion, which creates a grave sin and a grave wound in the soul of a woman who is then taught by the culture that there is no shame but actually more power and personal autonomy as a result of this "choice." All the while, unable to express her pain and anguish, she becomes internally isolated. Likewise, all mortal sins sting the conscience and, unresolved, place a burden on the person's soul which, without the grace of Christ, will never be removed.

[14] Rossetti, *Diary*, 93.

[15] St. Frances de Sales, *Devout Life*, 192.

[16] Riaan Swiegelaar video #1

also include the absence of a father, such as in the situation of Margaret, whose husband abandoned her when her three kids were very young. Margaret said that, as a single mom, "I raised them as well as I could." She relied on the help of a lot of people so she could protect and homeschool the children while working to provide for them as well. Despite the effort, their isolation from the positive and protective influence of a father allowed the culture to find far too many significant inroads into her children's minds, such as through abuse, fraternal discord, bullying, drugs, addiction, and a soft embrace of the occult.

In one account of isolation from a father, impurity and same-sex attraction emerged in a boy as a result of the complete absence of the father from the boy's life. The boy, as he later admitted to his mother, was desperate for his father, but the father refused to be around him and the family. As a result, the boy became very wayward, falling into dangerous homosexual activities. Once the mother became aware, nearly ten years later, the boy was able to explain to her that he felt his disordered attractions were from the lack of satisfaction of the emotional need for a male in his life. He then sought, even as a youth, through many and reckless homosexual encounters, the filling of that void in the only way he could find it, which was disordered, dangerous, and damaging. As exorcist Fr. Gary Thomas said, demons are always looking for people with broken relationships or no relationships.[17] At these moments, the devil appears with a counterfeit good, wrapped up to look like the perfect and very enticing solution. Satan says to us, "Here, kid, I'll help," and extends this enticement, which only brings new pain and sadness, such as became the case in the boy mentioned above, whose life later crashed into all forms of sin, including witchcraft.

Suffering from abuse, such as occurred in the families mentioned above, is another source of isolation as well as for the emergence of occult interests and diabolical harassment. The one who suffers abuse is not guilty of any sin, but the wound is very powerful and healing must be quickly sought in order to allow God to bring about the healing that is needed. However, a lot of people who suffer from abuse feel unsafe, ashamed, or scared, and do not quickly seek help as

---

[17] Fr. Gary Thomas, from *Slaying Dragons*, 14.

a result. Abuse is a common factor for people in the occult as well as for people afflicted by diabolical harassment. For example, exorcist Fr. Gary Thomas said that *eighty percent* of people who come to see him are victims of abuse.[18] They do not all need an exorcism but they all present serious wounds and need help in some way, either spiritually or psychologically.

Abuse was the final spark which initiated Catherine's descent into the occult. When she went away to college, her parents stopped hearing from her. The parents decided to give her space and freedom and not bother her. She had met a good group of Catholics at this college, including many traditional Catholics. It was after she met a guy through her job that communications ceased completely. When she came home for one of the breaks, they noticed she had lost a significant amount of weight. Despite that red flag, she told her parents that everything was fine, which was one of the many lies she would tell them during this period of her life. The parents eventually received a phone call from a school representative explaining that Catherine had suffered a breakdown while on campus, was not going to class anymore, and would not seek help. Catherine eventually opened up and admitted that she had been sexually assaulted while at college. This abuse immediately preceded the downward spiral into the occult the parents would soon witness. This same report of abuse in college was given by the Monroes, which also accompanied their daughter's embrace of the occult. Likewise, John, who later spent several decades in the occult, said that he was exposed to pornography at a very young age and was abused before he graduated from high school.

Among the Youth

The youth always struggle to "fit in" and figure out "who they are." A true and vibrant faith in Christ is the only way by which a young person will find this answer. These struggles are particularly difficult today, in a society hyper-reliant on the internet and living in the aftermath of the Covid era. Isolation, for the youth, is also an instigator of grave problems. Further, an openness to the occult is more likely when a person is in his youth, and the world and the

---

[18] Fraune, *Slaying Dragons,* 111.

devil are actively targeting them at this age. The results, as experience demonstrates and studies verify, is that the youth today are plagued by wounds.

A Pew Research study in 2019 found that seven out of ten youth, from what is called Generation Z, said that anxiety and depression are significant issues among their peers.[19] According to the American Psychological Association, also in 2019, they are also more stressed than adults by various issues in the news and are more likely to report that their mental health is poor and that they have received help from a mental health professional.[20] The Guardian UK reported in 2016 that the youth are pessimistic about the future, extremely anxious, distrustful of the government and businesses, think "the system is rigged," but, as a positive, they are not as selfish as one would expect.[21]

The Institute for Family Studies (IFS) added to this list by stating that this group is also suffering from an "epidemic of loneliness, social isolation, and disconnection." Part of this is due to the fact that they are more likely than previous generations to be raised in a single parent home. A lot of the blame is also placed on social media, or on the reign of Covid, or on both of them together.[22] According to the IFS, the social media app called TikTok in particular poses a unique threat to children but is definitely not the only threatening social media platform. TikTok has a uniquely powerful algorithm which has led many people to express the same reaction: "TikTok can read my mind."[23]

Further, as IFS stated, the way TikTok operates can drive girls into eating disorders by convincing them that physical perfection is just a few steps away. It also drives girls to post sexually inappropriate videos in order to increase their popularity on the site. The director for a program addressing eating disorders found that sixty percent of the girls treated in the program had posted sexually inappropriate videos. Some parents take the approach of trusting their kids instead of heavily monitoring their internet usage. The author of the IFS article stated that he has seen many teens who

---

[19] February 20, 2019
[20] January 2019, Vol 50, No. 1
[21] March 12, 2016, as summarized by Inc.com, by Jessica Stillman
[22] IFStudies.org, April 6, 2022, "Growing up Lonely: Generation Z"
[23] IFStudies.org, March 29, 2022, "Is TikTok Dangerous for Teens"

simply have two accounts, one clean and the other one not so much. Despite this, proper and advanced internet monitoring systems have proven to be effective, and the benefits are worth it, the author noted.[24] It is important to note that all this is happening in what is now the *#1 most visited website on the internet*, and all this is creating very wounded young people.

A startling example of the power of social media to wound the youth is in a new and increasing phenomenon of TikTok-induced tic behaviors in teenage girls, which are "severe, frequent, and disabling." Oxford Academic and *Brain*, a neuroscience medical journal, said this is appearing in many countries, and described this appearance not as Tourette's but as "the 'modern' form of the well-known motor variant of mass sociogenic illness." They added that it can be seen "as the 21st century expression of a culture-bound stress reaction of our post-modern society emphasizing the uniqueness of individuals and valuing their alleged exceptionality, thus promoting attention-seeking behaviours and aggravating the permanent identity crisis of modern man." Boiling that down, it is not Tourette's or mass hysteria but a "mass social-media induced illness."[25]

The American Psychiatric Association said researchers "looked at data from eight Tourette syndrome clinics in five countries." The number of referrals for this behavior, before the pandemic, "accounted for about 1% to 5% of cases, but now account for 20% to 35% in these clinics." The author said that the "functional disability" brought about by this disorder is "extreme." The uncontrollable motions "included large-amplitude arm movements, hitting and punching self or family members, and blurting out obscenities or bizarre words or phrases." The rise in cases coincided with the increased popularity of videos featuring people with tic-like behavior, leading to a situation known as echo-phenomena, where a person picks up the behavior of another person. This usually occurs through in-person contact; its occurrence through social media is new. Doctors noticed that contributing factors, such as isolation, stress from the pandemic, and loss of routine, made the brains of those

---

[24] IFStudies.org, March 29, 2022, "Is TikTok Dangerous for Teens"
[25] Academic.oup.com *Brain*, Volume 145, Issue 2, February 2022, pp. 476–480, "Stop that! It's not Tourette's but a new type of mass sociogenic illness."

afflicted highly suggestible. This is also occurring alongside a "surprising" rise in the number of young people engaging in self-harm and experiencing suicidal thoughts.[26]

Death

Unsurprisingly, alongside the experience of intense disruptions to life, and of sadness, anxiety, and depression, *death* is also a factor that makes souls vulnerable to the offers of the occult. The experience of death was an important element of trauma that helped push a lot of people into the occult. Bl. Bartolo Longo, who became a Satanic priest before his extraordinary conversion, experienced the death of his mother at the age of ten. This is said to have had a strong and negative impact on him. By college, he had become completely disillusioned by Christianity and was filled with hatred for all things related to the Church.[27] When she was still just a teenager, Lucy's father suddenly passed away from a heart attack, at a point in time where things were otherwise very happy for her. "From that moment, I decided that there was no God, and if there was, I didn't like Him. What God would take a dad away from his daughter, especially on such an important day?" This death fueled existing occult interests, especially in mediums and the ability to contact the dead. Her prior reliance on psychics became even stronger after her father died. Believing that she could connect with him after death was a great comfort and increased her positive view of psychics. She already had a slight attraction to psychics, but not in the serious way that would emerge as a result of his death.

Ava experienced three deaths of very close, often young, friends and family, in the same year that she was early in her occult dabblings. Shortly after high school, a good friend of Ava died in a drug-related incident. Ava was deeply affected by everything and, as the parents said, "She could barely keep it together." When Ava was visiting with the mother of a close family friend who had suddenly passed away, she began to use her occult ability to try to explain what the deceased was going through prior to the sudden death. "She was almost trying to channel her," Ava's mother said, "and

---

26 The American Psychiatric Association, "Outbreaks of Sudden Tics Among Teen Girls", June 14, 2022.
27 Mary's Dowry, Bl. Bartolo Longo documentary, YouTube

fascinatingly trying to explain to the mother what led to the girl's death. She was trying to get into [the deceased girl's] head and it was almost like she could understand the girl's mental state prior to her death. It was very scary to watch." Ava, it turned out, was actually quite accurate in what she was saying, based on some journals the deceased's mother found later on.

After dealing with the traumatic death of her child, Betty Brennan, an eventual convert from Satanism, held on to a strong anger toward God. Soon after this anger surfaced, she became acquainted with several Satanists through her work in an orchestra. One of them befriended her and became a consoling acquaintance who helped her process her wounds and pains (though it truly amounted to what she called "negative inner healing"). She happened to later encounter him in the context of a Satanic ritual, to which she had been invited. From that point forward, she became deeply involved in the Satanic group, participating, she said, in everything shy of human sacrifice.[28]

Redemption

One of the things that the rise of the occult, and its appeal to the many who are wounded, reveals to the Church today is that the healing power of Christ is not reaching the number of souls who need it. As the following story reveals, wounds of all sorts, even together within one man, are not beyond the power of God to reach, redeem, heal, and transform by His grace. What must happen, though, is that wounded souls come within the reach of Christ and His Holy Church. It is only through Him, and the instrument of salvation which He willed to use, that mankind can be redeemed. Let us pray constantly for those souls who need Christ but who are not currently in communion with Him. Let us pray that He will "send laborers into His harvest" for we see clearly that "the harvest is plentiful, but the laborers are few."[29]

---

[28] Saint Joseph Studios. "'Former Satanist Becomes Catholic,' Betty Brennan." *YouTube*, 10 April 2013. youtube.com/watch?v=-hudedR2iPM

[29] Matt. 9:37-38

A Story: Death Leads to Resurrection

Death does not always bring the destabilization of the soul such that it propels the person away from God and makes them vulnerable to the occult. Often, God uses the experience of death to purify a person's soul and prepare them for a conversion which He could not bring about in the absence of such an experience.

The following is the story of Vincent, a typical American *nominal* Catholic boy, whose deficient spiritual life left him unprepared to handle a sudden and traumatic encounter with death. By God's grace, however, clearly perceived to be operating in his life, Vincent was able to emerge from this taste of despair as a new man, risen to a new and abundant life through Christ.

A Wounded and Idolatrous Soul

Vincent was a wounded man who had turned away from God in a variety of ways. His family life was one of the many avenues through which significant wounds had been created in his soul. A final wound, the divorce of his parents, occurred just before this pivotal encounter with death occurred. Even prior to the divorce, Vincent did not value his family nor seek to nurture any family relationships.

Unbeknownst to Vincent, God was already at work in his life, preparing a powerful conversion that would set him onto the path toward the priesthood. Football was the idol that God first tore down, and this began a few months before the death he witnessed. Vincent suffered an injury that ruined his hopes of playing football in college. It was because of this injury that he happened to be in the exact spot to encounter this woman on the day of her death.

Encountering Death

"It was a wake-up call to come back."[30]

Vincent was on his way to physical therapy for his leg injury when he noticed a car coming down a road that typically had no traffic. That made him curious. Eventually this car, after turning onto his road, was in front of him at a stop sign. He noticed that the car was stopped for a really long time, which made him even more curious about the person driving. Then, he saw the car go into park, the door open, and a lady look out. She looked out, then back, holding the door open. Then, she fell to the ground. His first thought was that it was not something too serious. He is a trained first responder, and he got out and moved the lady parallel to the car. He used her phone to call 911. He checked her pulse, which was weak, and then her eyes. She was awake and aware but did not speak. Eventually, she stopped breathing, so he began CPR. After checking the pulse again, he found nothing. At that point, the emergency personnel arrived and took over. They pronounced her dead at the scene.

The Impact

The impact of witnessing this woman die in his arms was "earth-shattering," Vincent said. He began to see the world in a very bleak way. He became very sad, and angry. "Why her?" he wondered, focusing especially on the fact that she was only in her thirties. Selfishly, he was also sad and angry because he saw it as an inconvenience to him, which was forcing his own life to change.

He became transfixed by death. Death is going to happen, there is no getting around it, and there is no hope within it, he thought at the time. He got to the point of absolute despair. He was obsessively depressed about death. He held this struggle with the meaning of all things privately. His mind was haunted by the question, "Why is the world this way? Why do we die?" At this point he was completely

---

[30] Lucy also described her mental breakdown and time in a mental facility as a supernatural event God used to save her.

away from the Sacraments and had pushed away a priest who had been reaching out to him.

As a Catholic high school student, he said he received support from adults in ways he did not expect, which helped him know he was cared about. The priest also reached out to him numerous times, but given his indifference toward God, Vincent always refused to talk. His friends were also supportive and his friend group slowly began to change, revealing the quality of the people, and the life, to which he had been devoted prior to the encounter. He also began to change, flipping from being a rambunctious and talkative kid to a very quiet individual. "You're different now," everyone told him. "Yes," he thought, "I am different. Everything has changed."

Exposing the Wounds

In order to avoid a complete spiral into self-destruction, he needed to be broken down by an act of grace. He admitted that he was already very broken on a spiritual, moral, and human level. "God used the dust to build up the pot," he told me. The death he encountered and the subsequent despair crushed his reliance upon these false gods, bad friends, and vain pursuits. At the same time, they revealed to him the many wounds which drove his selfish and sinful behavior. Christ and the friendship of the priests who would soon enter his life would help to highlight and begin to heal the fatherly wound that he knew also resided in his soul.

Steadied against Despair by the Faith

When I asked him what anchored him so he did not "go off the rails" after witnessing this lady's death, he credited the Catholic environment of the school. "Being around the sacred," he said, "despite being in sin – you are still receiving the promptings. Even if you are not making use of it, you still could not get away from it."

In the days and weeks following the death, he was primed for total despair. "I remember being so lost. I could have gone off the deep end easily," he said, "My moral life went down before it went up. It was already bad and then it just got worse." That, of course, was his spiritual state for the month between the death and a pivotal Confession.

Drawn to the Church ... and Confession

In the lead up to deciding to go to Confession, he could feel the emptiness, the hollowness of his life. "I had a greater awareness that my life was built on sand," he said, "and I knew, after I saw that woman die, that my life would be meaningless if I did not change." The biggest thing at this moment was the meaninglessness of his life and his conviction of the truth that there had to be something that would truly grant meaning to his life. The Catholic environment helped him feel a pull toward the Church, causing him to consider Catholicism as a viable way of living.

Fear Before Confession

He eventually decided that he did indeed need to go to Confession. This would be his first Confession in seven years. He told me that he was shaking in the line going in to Confession, but completely calm and at peace once he went in. "I was mostly afraid of the penance," he said, "which was only one *Our Father.*" He also had doubts about the "supposed mercy" of God, he said. However, his doubts would be substantially resolved. Going to Confession was, as he described it, a watershed moment in which a deluge of grace entered his soul. People speak of a weight being lifted through Confession and this is absolutely what he experienced.

The Power of Confession

Primed, as it seemed, by his encounter with death and the despair of a soul without grace, God found his soul open and receptive, and was able to enter triumphantly and lavish him with His mercy and grace. "I saw the omnipotence of God," he told me, "and it crushed me to receive that mercy. I don't deserve all this. It was more of the surrendering – I am so weak, but 'Here it is.' From that moment, the gates were opened, and He swooped in with His power, bringing me out of the dirt and into a divine life."

Confessing his sins brought him to tears and the priest could easily see the contrition. "When I was in the confessional, I could not imagine a life without God, but my life up until then was completely without Him," he told me. "If I had not had that experience, I think my conversion would have been much different from what it was. I needed that, though, that grace. I was so weak; I needed something to propel me."

He described the Confession as thorough and that the priest asked a lot of clarifying questions. Once the priest began talking, after he had confessed his sins, he said, "I could feel the reordering of my soul. I had released all the idols and said, 'Nope. No more. Not doing this anymore.' I had to break the idols in that Confession. That was my moment of destroying the golden calf."

Let God Rescue You – Or Something Else Will Try

"It very much felt like I was rescued," he said, "Without it, something else was going to come in and address that wound. Without that, I would not be where I am today." Seeing this as an issue that effects everyone, he said, "You have to go through these things. We have to confront the wounds. Some are so deep that you can't see them until you are broken down – I was a leaning tower – it wasn't going to work. I was the definition of an indifferent soul."

~~~

Seeking Healing

When people incur a wound in their soul, it is necessary for this wound to be addressed and properly healed. Exorcists emphasize the importance of this in order for the person to be able to grow spiritually and to be more protected from diabolical temptations. When these wounds are not addressed, the soul can become vulnerable to negative thoughts and emotions,[31] and the occult can become a more appealing option for healing. Unfortunately, the pursuit of healing is often a moment the Enemy takes advantage of to trap souls in yet one more of his deceptions. Also unfortunately, it is a common occurrence that those who have wounds, even some Catholics, will seek help from spiritual powers outside of the Church. Exorcists note and report this concerning trend in the modern world.

---

[31] Fr. Grob, in *Slaying Dragons*, 111.

Fr. Anselm said, "People fall into the occult because they want a quick answer and a fast solution to their situation, but they have no idea what they are doing. It is only later on that they realize that the 'fix' was only an *apparent* fix, and a temporary one at that, because the problem was never healed. Only the *appearance* of healing was given and the success brought by dabbling with evil did not last."

As a kid, Gabriel experienced some unexceptional trauma which brought some emotional baggage with it. This was the first avenue by which he was led into the New Age. He sought a way to heal himself and not feel so bad on a day-to-day basis. With that as the starting point, he said, "Then they start teaching you about all the chakras in the body which control different things like emotions, healing trauma, healing your heart." Camilla's descent into the occult followed a similar path. She said, "The reason why I went into the New Age is that I was seeking a lot of healing." This all began with a well-intentioned pursuit of healing with the Charismatic renewal at her parish. In that Catholic environment, and through the Charismatic services, she experienced a deep healing. This prompted her to start exploring spiritual healing, but not just for herself but in order to become a *spiritual healer* for others. This then took her outside of Christianity completely and into the occultic energy healing practice called Reiki.

Our Lord Pursues Us

Some people are tempted to feel that, invisible as God is, He has no cares for us: He is distant, absent, and quiet. But this is not so. Our Lord is not deaf to our petitions nor ignorant of the struggles which characterize our life in this passing world. By His Incarnation, He demonstrated that He truly possesses a knowledge of our plight, not just from His omnipotence but also from His participation in our existence as a true Man Himself. Among the many titles given to Him, "Man of Sorrows" is one which our lost world needs to contemplate. The prophet Isaiah gives Him this title, saying, "He was despised and rejected by men; a man of sorrows, and acquainted with grief; and as one from whom men hide their faces He was despised, and we esteemed Him not."[32] Further, Isaiah said, "Surely

---

[32] Isaiah 53:3

He hath borne our infirmities and carried our sorrows: and we have thought Him as it were a leper, and as one struck by God and afflicted."[33]

All those who feel themselves to be despised by others, to be rejected, to be without a friend or companion, or to be alone, must know that the Lord God Almighty was like them when He walked this earth. Now, risen in glory, Our Lord looks kindly upon those who suffer, seeking to accompany them as they carry their crosses, lightening their burden and being their Companion on the way. He can take these wounds, these burdens, and the sufferings that they bring and, binding them to His Cross, grant them an eternal and salvific power. It is then that the endurance of the darkness of this world will not be one that will defeat us but one which will unite us more fully to "Jesus, the author and finisher of faith, who having joy set before Him, endured the cross, despising the shame, and now sitteth on the right hand of the throne of God."[34]

---

[33] Isaiah 53:4 DR
[34] Hebrews 12:2 DR

Chapter Nine

The Occult Plunges the Person into Darkness

Our Lord's desires for us are so intensely wonderful that the whole world would be converted if they were to understand them. Far surpassing the promises of any other religion on the planet, and far more glorious and inspiring, the promises made by Jesus Christ to those who love Him and keep His commandments are truly a source of ecstasy to His friends.[1] If only all mankind could have these explained to them, and have the message proven to them to be trustworthy by the accompanying miracles which have been collected throughout the life of the Church, they would surely be convinced and converted.[2] This, as a *hope*, must be the hope of all who love Our Lord: that all mankind would receive the reward promised to those who love Him.

Of the many glories promised to His disciples is a rich and diverse kingdom in which we will be placed, each justly rewarded for the deeds which we did in imitation of Our Lord and Redeemer. In this kingdom, we will be made to be like unto God Himself,[3] transformed from glory to glory,[4] raised to new and immortal life, fit to behold the Face of the Creator of the Mysteries of the world, and endowed with supernatural dignity through our participation in His own divine nature.[5] All the good that we have done as His disciples

---

[1] I Cor 2:9 DR, "That eye hath not seen, nor ear heard, neither hath it entered into the heart of man, what things God hath prepared for them that love him…"

[2] I Cor 2:10 DR, "…But to us God hath revealed them, by this Spirit. For the Spirit searcheth all things, yea, the deep things of God."

[3] I John 3:2 DR, "Dearly beloved, we are now the sons of God; and it hath not yet appeared what we shall be. We know, that, when He shall appear, we shall be like to Him: because we shall see Him as He is." Cf. also 2 Peter 1:4.

[4] 2 Cor 3:18, "And we all, with unveiled face, beholding the glory of the Lord, are being changed into his likeness from one degree of glory to another; for this comes from the Lord who is the Spirit." "glory to glory" in the DR translation.

[5] 2 Peter 1:3-4, "His divine power has granted to us all things that pertain to life and godliness, through the knowledge of him who called us to his own glory and excellence,

will receive the corresponding reward that He promised. There, in eternal joy, we will live as His own children, transfigured by His gift of sanctifying grace.

Satan was promised these very things by God when he was first created, but the full experience of them was withheld until his own will chose them freely. Receiving his great dignity at his creation, and the invitation to loving humility before His Creator, Satan, from the very first moment of his existence, noting his own glory and beauty, refused to agree to the situation. Desiring to be like unto God but through his own nature alone, not as a gift of grace, Satan refused to be obedient to the plan of Divine Providence. Turning away from the offer of fellowship with God, Satan was cast down to the earth to await his consignment in the eternal punishments of Hell. In the interim, he has become an invisible tagalong to all men who walk this earth, and he, filled with rage and malice, has concocted a plan in order to prevent us from receiving what God deeply desires to impart.

Satan's Funnel Model

One of Satan's desires is to bring about, in our souls and in our destinies, the exact opposite of what God desires for us. Instead of allowing us to be taken up into the high places of Paradise and transfigured in divine glory, Satan wants to tear us down, and tear us down again, debasing us into animalistic behavior and making us a mirror of his own diabolical malice. To do this, he uses the same thing that trapped him into his own Fall from grace: pride and a desire to achieve a self-imaged godhood[6] on his own terms.

In my interview with Gabriel, who had started with what he thought to be "safe" New Age beliefs, only later to realize that he had begun to embrace the same sorts of practices as those of witches and Satanists, I began to use the image of a "funnel" to describe the

---

by which he has granted to us his precious and very great promises, that through these you may escape from the corruption that is in the world because of passion, and become partakers of the divine nature."

[6] Man is called by Christ into divine union and offered the gift of sanctifying grace by which man *participates* in the divine nature, becoming *like* God while remaining a creature. Contrarily, Satan and the occult seek *godhood* and to become G/gods, seeking this by their own power and means.

diabolical technique I perceived to be at work. As in the same model often used in business and marketing, Satan uses what is called the *soft occult*[7] as a bait and a *funnel* and a lure to drag those who are initially merely curious deeper into his grip. This "mere curiosity" is already a problem, for it is itself the pursuit of divine glory and power and knowledge apart from God. Dabbling in "hidden" techniques and "religions" in order to conjure up a power that supposedly lies dormant within man, or within the elements of nature, is a Satanic enterprise in itself, but it is presented so subtly that, like Eve, people often don't recognize it for what it really is.

The outer ring of this *funnel*, as I discerned in my conversation with Gabriel, could be said to be the New Age, or even "positive thinking,"[8] the occult fixtures that amount to a free, no-ritual, no-demon (it is said) sort of dabbling. At this level, the practitioner typically denies he is doing anything nefarious, and would never identify himself as an occultist. Despite that appearance, the New-Ager has taken the first step in responding to Satan's marketing strategy. At this point, Satan "has his number" and is beginning to build a file on him, so to speak. This "free" occultism offers just enough of a taste of hidden powers to open the practitioner's curiosity to take the next step and find something just a *bit* more powerful, but, of course, still "safe" and "without demons." Here, the stage is set for the slow decline of the practitioner into a more dedicated and darker ritual.

Here it would be helpful to think of what is called the "trumpet pitcher plant." It is a carnivorous plant, shaped like a vertical tube, with a greased and hairy inner lining and an enticing scent that lures insects to it. In one variety of the plant, the entrance to the tube exudes copious amounts of nectar, drawing the insect to set foot on the upward-facing rim of the plant. Here, the insect quickly loses its grip due to waxy deposits, sending it plummeting down into the tube, the lining of which has tiny downward facing hairs that prevent the insect from turning back and escaping. As the insect, exhausted, inevitably descends further, it meets its destruction in the digestive enzymes at the base of the plant, at which point the tiny

---

[7] An expression sometimes used to denote the entry-level or superficial occult practices, like a casual use of Ouija board or tarot cards or astrology, or other half-hearted embraces of what in reality are occultic practices.

[8] A New Age technique similar to *manifesting*.

downward facing hairs are so thick that escape is impossible. I know of no better natural image of the dangers of the occult than this. Likewise, in the occult as a whole, the vast and diverse "New Age" is like the outer ring of the funnel, or the enticing scent of the pitcher plant: it is free, out there everywhere,[9] and is perfect bait to lure the practitioner deeper into the craft. As the practitioner descends further, he finds the occult to be addictive and alluring and, as his descent escalates, he soon finds himself entering into a dark spiritual world which was never his original intent.

Those who enter the occult, like those who enter deep into sin, step into a realm of darkness. Some do so thinking that, by simply dipping their toes into these black waters, they can merely glimpse this mysterious reality from a distance, enjoying just a bit of the thrill of the dark side. What they don't know is that the black waters are but the edges of a tarry sea which will not clean off without a supernatural solution, and whose tide is aggressive and unstable, risking becoming overwhelmed unexpectedly. This plunge into darkness brings about many negative effects, such as the disordering of the intellect, opposition to truth, a disordering of beliefs and morals, and a generally self-destructive path that eventually tears the person's life apart.

The Eclipse of the Truth

A hallmark of Satan's activity is the inversion of the truth, the twisting of reality, the tainting of the good with evil, the reversing of the moral order, and the mockery of the sacred. These are lamented by former occultists who have seen and experienced the consistency of this diabolical tactic. The principal thing that the occult robs, Andrew said, is the truth. It robs the truth on all levels: supernatural, natural, personal, and historical. It is a parade of lies, a piper of deception, after which souls, dressed in the garb of deceit, are running toward damnation. In the occult, he added, "You have to have a misconception about human history, metaphysics, and cosmology, among other things. Further, if, as the occult makes you

---

[9] Not just through its infiltration into the culture but also because it can be practiced anywhere, even in the privacy and solitude of a person's home, making it, as modern witches like to point out, accessible to everyone.

130

think, you can bend reality to your will, do things and change things through rituals – why is your life not the perfect dream?!"

Man seeks greatness, beauty, truth, honor, recognition, and security, Christopher said, but the truth of these has been obscured by the Fall and the work of demons. They have been inverted from what God intended them to be and are now all self-serving. They end in our destruction instead of our glorification. The fingerprint of demonic activity, John added, is in the inversion of the good, such as when love becomes obsession, anger becomes wrath, admiration becomes envy. On the issue of anger, obsession, envy, and other *wounds* such as these, witches are trained by their "craft" to take their wounds and make them their occultic *strengths*, the thing that animates their intention.[10] Further, hatred is one such wound, as Fr. Ermatinger pointed out, that witches use to seek to *increase* the efficacy and gravity of harm that their spells can bring.[11]

Satan wants us to do the opposite of what Christ wants, John pointed out. Satan wants to invert the path that God has established for us, to take us down to a lower form of being, to a materialistic, vegetative existence. As a result, we lose the supernatural vision that God has inclined us toward by our nature and has supplied by His grace. Satan inverts this supernatural vision and tries to make us see the supernatural *seat* as residing within ourselves, to see things only as our senses perceive them, and to feel things only as our human emotions would feel them. In the occult, he said, you are a powder keg of emotions.

A Mockery of the Sacraments and Doctrines

Occultic rites are, themselves, an example of this diabolical inversion of the good. John said, "In the Mass, there is silence. The Saints find God in the silence, but the devil is always talking." Occultic rites, which John himself created when he was in the occult, are often psychologically manipulative and provide the opposite of what is anticipated.[12] "Looking back," he said, "everything looks like

---

[10] The will of the witch in each specific ritual or spell.

[11] Ermatinger, *The Trouble with Magic*, 61.

[12] "The great patristic tradition teaches us that the mysteries of Christ all involve silence. Only in silence can the word of God find a home in us, as it did in Mary, woman of the Word and, inseparably, woman of silence. This principle – that without silence one does

a perversion of the Sacraments." This is not the perspective only of former occultists. Exorcist Msgr. Rossetti commented that the popular cultural observance of Halloween has become an inversion of the Church's feast of All Saints, a "demonic distortion."[13]

Andrew agreed that occultic rites are inversions of the Sacraments. He said, as an example, that the kinds of incense he used in his rituals were frankincense and myrrh, a mockery of the gifts of the Magi. He also used chant, which was in Latin, Hebrew, and Greek, the same sacred languages on the placard nailed to Our Lord's Cross.[14] He also pointed out that Aleister Crowley, whose occultic religion is referred to as "Thelema," stole the word "thelema," meaning "will," from the Agony in the Garden, where Our Lord used it in the context of the acceptance of the Father's will that He be handed over and crucified.[15]

In addition to the Sacraments, the occult inverts the teachings revealed to the world by Christ. Lucy, speaking about the occult and New Age in general, noted lots of clear signs of the diabolical inversion of these truths: "my body, my choice" of abortion vs "this is My Body, given up for you" of the Holy Eucharist; souls stuck in an "in-between" world vs Purgatory; burning sage in a house to cleanse it vs having a priest bless it with holy water; witches and spells vs priests and prayers; and fairies vs angels. Many inversions, such as fairies for angels, make the true reality (angels) then look just as silly and easily dismissible as the counterfeit (fairies), further eroding truth in the mind of someone who might become open to it. She added, "Satan knows what is important to us as God's people and knows what the important things are in the Catholic Church, so he has a contradictory, yet corresponding, teaching for it."

---

not hear, does not listen, does not receive a word – applies especially to personal prayer as well as to our liturgies: to facilitate authentic listening, they must also be rich in moments of silence and of non-verbal reception." Pope Benedict, General Audience, March 7, 2012.

[13] Rossetti, *Diary*, 249. Further, this is why we need to consider assigning a new name to the cultural, and depraved, celebrations that occur during the sacred days around All Saints.

[14] Luke 23:38 DR

[15] Matt 26:42

The Eclipse of the Intellect

As occultists continue with their spiritual endeavors, many eventually become presented with the gravity of the situation and the fact that they have entered into a relationship with a "malevolent spirit," that is, a demon. This usually comes about when the demons begin to remove their masks but the person has already invested so much in the relationship that they do not want to end it, despite now knowing this reality. Persisting in evil at this point, knowing it is wrong, can bring an added level of damage, what Fr. Ermatinger called a fragmentation of the intellect and the will. This can only do harm to a man's psychology and his future ability to assess reality properly.[16] Though the natural law present in the conscience eventually convicts occultists of the evil of their actions, those occultists who are, or who become, aware of the danger and evil of their practice, and yet continue, are the most negatively impacted in this way.

Christopher, explaining how the occult damages your reason, said "Often occultists believe contradictory things but call them *paradoxical.*" As an example, when he was a "Christian occultist," he held to two mottos which guided his occultic commitments: 1) "I will serve God by taking my life and destiny *into my own hands,*" and 2) "I will do Your Will, even if it means *becoming the devil himself.*" In the first, he claimed to serve God, which implied a surrender of his own will and an acceptance of God's will but did so by "taking my life into my own hands," which implied serving himself alone. In the second, he claimed to do God's will even if it meant "becoming the devil himself," which means he is setting himself completely *against* God's will. The absurdity of believing there to be any truth in these beliefs should be plain to see, yet it was not apparent to Christopher until he got out of the occult.

Andrew said that the principal form of diabolical attack he experienced in the occult was the clouding of his intellect. He experienced a profound darkening of his mind which, as he said, "made it difficult to discern truth from lies." He added, "This was the chief abuse I experienced." During the time he was in the occult, he

---

[16] Ermatinger, *The Trouble with Magic*, V.

endured a lot of dark emotions and thoughts, which he thinks highly likely originated from the demons with whom he interacted.[17]

The eclipse of the intellect can also appear in an experience of mental chaos. While Lucy was in the occult, she said that her mind was regularly filled with many different thoughts at the same time. "I thought it was normal," she said. "I used to have a lot of thoughts in my mind; sometimes five at once, maybe even more." Once she converted and found healing, the thoughts began to subside. The change from chaos to clarity was so drastic, she explained, that she was quite surprised by the difference. "I was used to having so many conflicting thoughts, that when I started to get less of them, it was like something was wrong," she recounted.[18]

Destructive Beliefs

As the occult begins to form the mind, the connection of the mind with the Truth, the natural law, and the dictates of the conscience begins to erode. In the absence of these inhibitions to sin and error, the occultist starts to enshrine falsehood and celebrate iniquity. John, who was once a psychotherapist, noted that, in his practice, he originally addressed homosexuality as a personality disorder related to trauma, but the deeper he went into the occult, the more he flipped to viewing it through the lens of "love is love" and homosexuality is just fine. John then began to advocate for his patients to *embrace* the way they felt, believing that there was no moral absolute, or natural law, that governed or guided sexuality.

The "Law of Thelema," which Andrew followed, as laid out by Aleister Crowley, states, "Do what thou wilt shall be the whole of the Law. Love is the Law, Love under Will." As a result of seeking to embody this philosophy and mindset, a key virtue became very difficult for Andrew to fulfill. He said, "This has made *humility* very difficult at times, and it has made surrendering myself to Divine Providence particularly difficult, especially in light of the crisis in the Church." The reason for this is that, by following the Law of

---

[17] Similar to Helena, who also observed that certain mental issues, among people in the occult, were caused by demons.

[18] Psychological issues like these could have natural or diabolical causes. Therefore, it is important to be put in communication with a Catholic psychologist to help properly diagnose the issue. Many do telemedicine today.

Thelema, the individual self is "deified" and the practitioner comes to see reliance on oneself, and living out one's *True Will*, as the highest virtue. This is quite Satanic or, better, Luciferian[19]: it directs the practitioner to imitate the self-idolatry and self-exaltation of the devil himself, by which Satan rebelled against God and turned in on himself, declaring that his high angelic glory proceeded from his own nature and perfection, instead of from God as his Creator. Andrew added, "As an occultist, I believed I was immortal and would survive death, not knowing how. So, if I am *not* small (i.e., I am powerful), how could I *be* small (i.e., humble, a simple piece of this puzzle)?"

The occult, as Fr. Verlinde experienced in his time dedicated to Eastern meditation,[20] offered him the supposed "truth" that "there is no love." He explained how disturbing this was for him to accept. The goal of Eastern meditation, he explained, was to annihilate all activity in the subject, which is himself.[21] First, during these meditations, he had to stop moving, which he accomplished through adopting the *lotus position*. Then, he had to calm his breathing, to the point that it was veiled and indetectable, which he did through breathing techniques called *pranayamas*. Then, he had to control his thoughts, to the point where there were none, which he did through a trance state, achieved with the use of repeated phrases used for meditation called *mantras*. Visual concentration techniques were also employed until, eventually, his *self* seemed to disappear from his awareness. At that point, there was supposed to be no more suffering, since there was no more *self*. This is where he became very disturbed.

In the process of doing this meditation, he had to give up all verbs, even "to love," since there is no more *self*, which is the subject who loves. If he could no longer suffer, he could also no longer love. This disturbed him a lot. As Christians know, *love* is central to God's revelation, to humanity's fulfillment, and to God's relationship with

---

[19] "Lucifer" means "light-bearer"; "Satan" means "accuser."

[20] Fr. Joseph-Marie Velinde spent years studying and exploring Hindu and Buddhist religious traditions in India, including serving as the secretary of Maharishi Mahesh Yogi, the Yogi of the Beatles. He eventually encountered Christ and renounced his Eastern practices, slowly making his way into the Catholic Church and on to the priesthood.

[21] One could also say that the goal of Eastern meditation is confusing. The goal is what is called "self-extinction," which is principally an annihilation of all forms of desire.

man. Without the ability to love, there is no real ability to live, and the destruction from the occult will be swifter if that philosophy is embraced. Gabriel was also disturbed by the philosophies of the occult, and reflected on one particularly destructive New Age belief, *reincarnation*, highlighting its ability to disorder a person's desires. "You think you are doing a good thing [by believing this to be true]," he said, "but the impact of accepting reincarnation means this life doesn't matter: you can do whatever and hope for a better life next time."

The Eclipse of Morality

The disorder which flows from the eclipse of the intellect manifests quickly in a disordering of personal morals. The occult is truly a religion of subjectivism and subjective morality. No practitioner of the occult follows a creed which absolutely restricts his behavior under a specific moral code. The closest thing is the *Wiccan Rede*[22] and the *Rule of Three*[23] in Wicca, which are only pieces of loose guidance and not binding authoritative moral statements. Thus, occultists are free to reject all morality, which most end up doing.

In the 1989 interview of Zeena and Nikolas Schreck,[24] we see one stark example of this in their discussion about Adolf Hitler. When Bob Larson asked them about Hitler, and the murder-driven reality that Hitler lived within, Schreck labeled Hitler as "a masterful black magician." When asked if Hitler's reality and beliefs were evil, Schreck stated, "I am telling you that I don't believe in good and evil, and nor can anyone decide what is good and evil. It's all based on historical and cultural values. In my point of view, Christianity is 'evil' because it is negative." Larson pushed again, saying, "You won't call Hitler evil?" "I'm not going to bow down to your level of good

---

[22] The supposed governing code of conduct for Wiccans, a poem which has the essential line, "An harm ye none, do what ye will." It was invented in the 1960s and is very similar to the principles of Aleister Crowley's Thelema.

[23] The supposed rule which states that what you do through spells and "workings" will return to you three times as powerful. It is supposed to encourage a Wiccan to avoid doing evil spells or curses.

[24] This was when Zeena was still associated with and representing the Church of Satan.

and evil. That's so primitive," Schreck responded, adding, "No act of any human being or animal can be judged good or evil."[25]

Former Yogi, Alex Frank said that Yoga is also an example of this collapse of morals. In Yoga, there are very few ethical constraints. For example, the manipulation of energy through Yogic practice is often, for example, used by men to manipulate women and stir attraction. *Siddhis* are a further example of this. These are occult powers that practitioners of Yoga gain from their practice. These are obtained by individuals who might start on the traditional Yoga path, with its strict moral restraints, but who, after attaining these occult powers, throw out those restraints, inclining them to use these powers for evil ends. This can be glimpsed in the modern *left-hand* Yoga, where it is common to hear someone say, "I satiate [indulge] all my lustful desires so they don't inhibit my consciousness." Yoga also flouts boundaries. One example he gave is the immodesty of Yoga classes, in which men and women contort themselves in awkward poses, in tight clothing, in the same room. This is occurring in the context of a philosophy which instructs them to "be open to everything," without discernment, and, believing themselves to be gods,[26] to see the oneness they have with everyone, with few moral constraints. As Alex added, "There may be moral constraints even in the *left-hand* version, but they are much more pragmatic with them. The moral constraints are usually temporary and can be discarded once they inhibit the practitioner's growth in power. They may impose them [simply] to avoid bad press."

Alex's old Yoga teacher told him, "A lot of people who follow this path become a sort of *dark sorcerer*." Through the intensely introspective work of Yogic meditation, the individual discovers a lot of dark sinful desires inside himself. Christianity seeks to temper these and guide these disordered passions through moral truths and moral constraints. Yogis do not have these moral constraints. As a result, they will collapse *into* these dark desires. When they combine this with the belief that they are gods, they will become this *dark sorcerer* to which his old Yoga teacher referred. The story of Matsyendra, the founder of Hatha Yoga, is a good example of this. Matsyendra, and his disciple Gorakshanath, using their Yogic

---

[25] Larson video #1

[26] As clearly seen in the tradition of bowing to each other and saying *namaste*, which means "The god in me bows to the god in you."

powers, became involved in an infamous scene of debauchery and immorality with the queen of Kadalidesa and the king's large harem.[27]

It is not just Satanism and Yoga, but the occult in general, which has a corrosive effect on morals. Ava's efforts to get noticed, in the context of drifting from the Church and entering the New Age, "led her away from the good morals of our religion," her parents explained. "She was trying to find happiness in other avenues, dabbling in some drugs, not heavily but likely spiked with things." She also began to embrace the New Age sexuality, stating, "I love people, I love souls." She wanted to identify as bisexual and pansexual mainly because it was trendy and she simply did not want what was traditional. A bisexual interest was not consistent with her previously healthy orientation, so it made no sense to the parents. "She is convinced by the culture that this means it is her identity," they added. "But it's *you do you,*' with shock value as well."[28]

Fr. Cyprian told the story of one lady with whom he worked whose embrace of the soft occult eventually destroyed her sense of self-identity and sexual morals. She had started messing around with tarot cards after she lost her job. She asked someone to show her how to do it and she was, then, not only *told* how to do so but *trained.* In the process of that training, she was attached to certain spirits in order for her to acquire occult knowledge of other people's lives. It was not merely "reading cards," Father pointed out. "The demon places the knowledge of the other person into the mind of the card reader which allows the reader to predict things to come in the future, with exactitude and often with great accuracy."

As soon as the woman in Fr. Cyprian's example started doing this, she suddenly had sexuality and "gender fluid" issues, he said. Prior to that, she had had healthy relationships with her family and at school. "Sexuality is the most intimate thing," he said. "When we are not guarded, we will be attacked there." She eventually gave up the cards and returned to Mass, abstaining from Holy Communion at first. Once she went back to Confession as well, it was like a fog was

---

[27] This is recorded in many different books on the history of Hatha Yoga, such as James Mallinson, *The Khecarividya of Adinatha: A Critical Edition and Annotated Translation of an Early Text of Hathayoga.* Routledge (2008).

[28] "You do you" is a modern expression meaning "do what you want, what you alone decide is best."

lifted. She then became disgusted when hanging out with her old friends in the LGBT community and she no longer saw why she had found them to be such a welcoming group in the first place.

Sexuality, John observed, is a powerful example of diabolical inversion in the culture. Sexuality is the "thing that connects us, body, soul, and mind, to another person; that creates life, like a divine spark," as John put it. The sexual revolution in the '60s was a conditioning for the full perversion and diabolical degradation we are witnessing in our occultic age today, he added. This doorway of evil was fully open and dumping perversion across the earth. Members of the Church, as we sadly know, were not immune to the poison that was released. "The diabolic wants to degrade everything," he added, "make it dirty, debased; to do this to everything God made, giving God the finger, so to speak. They take delight in debasing all the good things that God has given us."

The Eclipse of Love

Satan, through the guise and mystique and mask of the spiritualities of the occult, offers a person everything he wants. Though, when it happens, it may at first appear positive, he then quickly leads the person down into darkness, turning around at that point to destroy him with shame and self-defeat, and often real violence.

In our discussion of what love *really* is, Margaret posed the question, "If you love someone, wouldn't you give everything for that person?", referring to Our Lord and how much He does to reach us. I remarked, "Yes, thus, the Eucharist. He became man, died for us, ascended into Heaven, with our nature, *and* stayed here with us until the end in the Eucharist, *and* made an abundance of things on this earth holy, even water.[29] No other God would do this." Satan, she countered, seeks to do for his followers the exact opposite. As their "companion," instead of doing anything *for* them, he takes everything *from* them. He makes them "pretty" to show *his* love, but in doing so, he adorns them with tattoos of grotesque images, piercings all through their bodies, strange nails, eating disorders,

---

[29] Through the blessings of the Church and the use of water in Baptism. One significance of Our Lord's own Baptism in the Jordan River is that He left the "cloak of His divinity" in the waters that we may take it up, by participation, through Baptism.

oddly colored hair, ripped up clothing, and the like – making the person the opposite of how they were born and how God desires them to be adorned. Margaret's own son, she said, hates himself so much that he cannot stand seeing himself without clothes on, and he blames everyone in the family for how much he suffers. He is currently covered with tattoos, even on his face, many of which are Satanic in their look.

"With very rare exceptions, occultists decay in appearance quite rapidly," Christopher admitted. "The darker the arts, often the faster they decay." Occasionally, drug use contributes to this but, as he said, "almost always with the Western occult, there's a 'detectable off-ness'." Those in Voodoo, Macumba, and Satanic practitioners "dress to intimidate and are rarely...beautiful." He added, "Within the occult, I'd say that's how the Devil marks his own."

The devil also seeks to steal joy from those who enter the occult. Catherine, for example, claimed she wasn't doing anything bad as a witch but her life was filled with negativity, her parents stated. As her mother said, she had no peace or joy and was often argumentative. She used to be happy all the time, one of the happiest people around, but now she was a miserable person. While living at home for the time, her parents watched her life crumble. She slept all the time, was vaping and drinking a lot, would leave the house and not come home, was dressing in a very strange manner, and had become angry and bitter. Later on, when she would return home to visit, her head would be half-shaved but she would hide it in a beanie.

Even in the founding of the Church of Satan, we see the presence of this eclipse of love. According to Zeena Schreck, the daughter of Anton LaVey, the founder of the Church of Satan, "They had other people caring for me [as a child] since they [her father and his mistress] were too wrapped up in their own problems and fought constantly. This mentality – along with our dysfunctional relationships and my father's violence, fear, and paranoia – were the forces behind his teachings."[30] Helena observed that the effects of the occult include "damaged family relations, anger and distrust toward anyone outside of your circle, and a despair that can cause you to

---

[30] *Vice.com*, September 25, 2012, "Beelzebub's Daughter."

believe nothing."[31] When the occult began to take over Ava's life, her parents noted that indicators of depression, reckless behavior almost leading to death, and suicidal talk began to appear in her life.

The movement toward despair and total self-destruction is what exorcists see to be the motivation behind diabolical attacks, reflecting the personal state of mind of the demons themselves. Msgr. Rossetti observed, "[Satan] is in a rage and believes he has been victimized by God. He is narcissistic, arrogant, and violent. He is emotionally isolated and has no connection with other beings. He seeks revenge." He added that the demons, when assaulting the minds of the possessed, impose their own disordered minds upon the individual, making them suffer in the same way they themselves suffer. He said, "A common message that the possessed hear in their brains is a prompting to do violence to others and to kill themselves."[32] Though most occultists do not become possessed, they associate themselves with these same demons, thus exposing their souls to a similar evil influence.

The Eclipse of Self

Those who enter the occult begin to lose a connection with who they really are. They lose their joy, break off connections with others, engage a fantasy as reality, and become oblivious to the fact that their lives are falling apart through fear, depression, anger, addiction, anxiety, and selfishness.

When I asked Lucy about the kinds of damage people suffer in the occult, the list she wanted to give was endless! "Where to start?!?" is how the conversation began. Lucy observed that fascination with and involvement in the occult leads to damage to our relationship and connection with God, failing at relationships or watching them break down, selfishness, an increased need for power and knowledge, a decline in mental health, the hardening of the heart towards others, and damage to one's soul on many levels.

To put it in a more complete list, Lucy's thoughts included: the occult attacks the mind and soul, which gives rise to mental health issues; causes feelings of doubt, fear, dread, anxiety, depression,

---

[31] There are several recurring themes among occultists: despair, frustration with losing the power, and difficulty surrendering.

[32] Rossetti, *Diary*, 138.

anger, frustration; perpetuates the need for control; enslaves the person to all the different elements of the New Age and the occult; turns the person against holy things, i.e. people, teachings, language etc.; can instill a lack of care for others; can cause selfishness and a vicious sense of 'me'; sows confusion in many areas; ruins relationships; instills a sense of need to solve your own problems using occult idols such as crystals, incense, magic, spells, etc. "So much damage!" Lucy said, adding, "The worst, I guess, is essentially ensuring that people lose their mind and their soul."

People who get immersed in the occult can suffer from the loss of their family, their job, and even their sanity, according to Fr. Blaise. It brings chaos into their life and a sense that nothing is going right for them and everything is falling apart. When this attitude persists, it can cause them to continuously go back to the occult to find a sense of security, desiring this more than before and ending up progressing into deeper occultic associations, including making pacts of some sort. The occult is a downward spiral marked by a series of deep wounds, each of which propels the individual further along this damnable course.

As is evident in the cases of former occultists, the retaliation[33] they experience is typically proportionate to what they have invested in the occult. This investment is not simply an issue of time, but primarily an issue of the will and their personal intentions when dealing with the occult. Fr. Dominic described it in a similar manner. He said, "Those who experienced the 'lighter' side of the occult had confusion, anxiety, and fear. If it progressed beyond this, they found their relationships affected: deep confusion, bouts of anger, fights out of nowhere, etc. If it progressed further, isolation and deep depression set in, as well as alcohol and/or drug abuse, and beyond that, in the dark cases, complete confusion, deep depression, and suicidal ideations."

After Lucy's initial conversion in a mental health facility, but before her liberation from diabolical possession and her entry into the Church, she was released and returned home. However, externally, she said the damage from her extensive engagement with the occult was visible and led her family to think she was lost for

---

[33] Retaliation from demons as the individual seeks to quit his occult affiliations and activities.

good. Internally, she was in a fog of confusion, unable to separate reality from fantasy, experiencing disturbing visions, hearing voices and, at times, unable to control her actions.

Bl. Bartolo Longo, in his days as an occultist, bore witness to these things as well. After his consecration as a Satanic priest, and with a specific demon now living in his life with his consent, everything began to fall apart. The documentary stated,

> From that moment on, a great feeling of dread, sadness, and exhaustion took hold of Bartolo and he felt the continuous presence of a being with whom he now spoke. Bartolo asked this angel of darkness for guidance in everything he did and began to exist in a world of nightmares and visions. He started to feel insane, especially as his angel gave him contradictory answers to those that his friends received from their spirits.[34]

Though the diabolical will respond to the requests of witches, Adelaide said the demons also blind them to the impact of their dabbling. "The thing about witches," she said, "is, even when you are good at it and your work produces results, your life is just burning down around you, and no witch I have ever known has put the two together. Health problems, money problems, relationship problems, *to the extreme*, but, to the witch, there is never a correlation. It's just, 'Oh, this happened, so I've got to do a spell about that,' or 'I need to do a ritual about that and that caused this…so, oh, I gotta do a ritual about that'." In the occult, the witch is helplessly blind. "It's hindsight," Adelaide said, "It's after getting out; you turn around and you're like, 'Oh, my, it was *killing* me and it was destroying everybody I love'."

A May 2021 article by the *National Catholic Register* described the observations of Matthew Arnold, a former member of an occultist group who received messages from a medium. As the article stated,

---

[34] Mary's Dowry, Bl. Bartolo Longo documentary, YouTube

While they were not told to harm anyone or do anything clearly evil, the end result was that Matthew and the others became obsessed with their supernatural experiences. They neglected their personal duties and withdrew from those who were not part of their small group. Karen's[35] marriage, for example, fell apart and she eventually lost her sanity. Another group member's business went under. "What was really bizarre is that they couldn't see that their lives were falling apart," recalled Matthew.[36]

"Dabbling in the occult is like playing with a loaded gun," Andrew stated, adding, "Someone is going to get hurt." The most dramatic moment of retaliation that he endured was the destruction of his home as he and his wife were in the process of abandoning the occult and seeking to join the Church. He saw this as not just diabolical retaliation but as "God burning away my false gods." Andrew warned that the diabolical will also attack other people in your life while you are dabbling in the occult. "Demons are not nice," he added bluntly. "Anyone not in a state of grace who is living in that home, can be driven crazy, even to the point of suicide. This stuff," he added, "not only impacts the practitioner but also anyone they come into contact with.[37] If you take your occult practice seriously, you know it is dangerous." He added that he himself was fully aware of this danger. He also brought up the fact that one of Aleister Crowley's students went insane as a result of not being careful with the occult, which resulted in his death.

When John was an occultist, he said he never looked in the mirror and saw himself as the *bad guy*, even though he had begun advocating for disordered lifestyles as a psychotherapist, was manipulating people within occultic rituals, and was fraternizing with demons on a regular basis. Satan is a master of deception. Now,

---

[35] A member of this group, who would go into trances and communicate messages.

[36] *National Catholic Register*, "Magician Turned Catholic Recalls Bizarre New Age Experiences," May 8, 2021

[37] While diabolical harassment and possession are not *contagious*, when a person is demonically afflicted, they carry demons around with them until they are freed. These demons can harass others in that person's life if those people are not spiritually protected.

John looks in the mirror and sees how much he has to atone for. "That is what is ruling [the culture] right now," he said, "and it is Satanic."

That None Shall Perish

The dire situation of those who go into the occult should stir the hearts of all Christians. Like Our Lord, our hearts should be moved to pity, especially when we behold those who are like sheep without a shepherd. As the Gospel of Matthew describes Our Lord, "[He] went about all the cities and villages, teaching in their synagogues and preaching the gospel of the kingdom, and healing every disease and every infirmity. When He saw the crowds, He had compassion for them, because they were *harassed and helpless*, like *sheep without a shepherd*."[38]

"Harassed and helpless" is an adequate description of those trapped in the occult. For them, His sheep as well, He also has compassion. They, like the Apostles aboard the boat on the Sea of Galilee, are swamped by waves of evil. If they would, like the Apostles, but cry out, "Save, Lord; we are perishing," Our Lord would gladly "rebuke the winds and the sea" and bring "a great calm" into their lives.[39] St. Peter himself adds to this reality, stating, "The Lord is...not wishing that any should perish, but that all should reach repentance."[40] St. Peter, as one of those Apostles saved by Christ from the storm, knows even better the power of Christ to save, and Our Lord's desire that none who call upon Him should perish, for he himself was saved a second time from a storm on the Sea of Galilee. After Our Lord had commanded him to walk toward Him on the water of the sea, Peter then became afraid, noting the power of the wind, and began to sink. Crying out, "Lord, save me," Jesus "immediately reached out His hand and caught him."[41]

Many testimonies of former occultists have indicated that Our Lord is ready to reach occultists where they are, in the darkness of the errors and sins of the occult, and save them. Our Lord is also, they testify, inclined to use rather miraculous means to rescue them.

---

[38] Matt 9:35–36, *emphases* mine.
[39] Matt 8:25–26
[40] 2 Peter 3:9
[41] Matt 14:30–31

No matter how deep into the occult they have plunged themselves, it is still possible for Our Lord to save them. This, though, will indeed require repentance, a desire to reform one's life, and a true calling out to Christ, as St. Peter did, saying, "Lord, save me!"

Chapter Ten

The Allure of Occult Power

Sacred Scripture mentions the devil's power and authority to act on the earth and to build up his kingdom on many occasions. The devil's temptation to Our Lord...

> To you I will give all this authority [of the kingdoms of the world] and their glory; for it has been delivered to me, and I give it to whom I will. If you, then, will worship me, it shall all be yours.[1]

...is not offered to Him alone. It is offered to all mankind. Those who take the devil up on this offer end up within the occult, as practitioners of diabolical arts, or as members of "the wicked," fulfilling Psalm 73,[2] which speaks of the prosperity of the wicked. St. Augustine, commenting on the fact that "Asaph" is mentioned as the author of this Psalm, stated that "Asaph" is to be understood as the Synagogue, "they that worshipped God after a godly sort, but yet for the sake of earthly things, for the sake of these present things."[3] Thus, the Synagogue observed the prosperity of the wicked who, not following God and His laws, had no pains, were healthy and fit, avoiding troubles and afflictions, "always at ease," and "increas[ing] in riches," all the while wearing "pride [as] their necklace" with "violence cover[ing] them like a garment."[4] Further, these wicked "scoff and speak with malice," "setting their mouths against the heavens."

It is in this structure of what might be called "diabolical providence," in mockery of Divine Providence, that the occult

---

[1] Luke 4:6–7
[2] RSVCE, or Psalm 72 in the Douay Rheims translation.
[3] *NewAdvent.org* > Exposition on the Psalms (St. Augustine), Psalm 73
[4] Psalm 73:4–9

operates. The occult combines man's fallen desire for an earthly paradise with man's natural desire to worship a higher being. In joining himself to occult practices, a man truly does experience this "diabolical providence" in some sense. This must not be overlooked, for the devil really does *share*[5] his power with those who will do his bidding. The end result is, of course, self-destruction, but the taste of Satanic glory in this life is, for the many who imbibe it, too intoxicating to ever let go of.

Exorcist Fr. Ambrose said occultists are attracted to this power. "The devil is quick to respond so he can ensnare them," he added, "whereas our use of sacramentals does not deliver us immediately from [the sufferings of this life]." The Cross is essential to our happiness but the general society hates suffering, seeking pleasure at all costs and avoiding suffering at all costs. The occult is quicker and more visible; it has a quicker payoff, he said, adding, "Whereas we have faith and trust and wait for God and His timing." The occult and the devil's offerings, in this sense, is clearly a mockery and a counterfeit of the Truth. St. Thomas Aquinas, referring to St. Ambrose, highlighted that the basis for all temptations was contained in the three temptations presented to Our Lord in the wilderness. He said, "For the causes of temptations are the causes of desires – namely, 'the lust of the flesh, hope of glory, eagerness for power'."[6] All these, it is obvious today, are what the occult offers and what those who chase after it desire: pleasure, glory, and power.

Andrew's description of his slow descent into the occult is helpful to hear at this point. He first went into what he called a "soft atheism": he was processing so much doubt that he just could not be religious, so he fell into a mindset similar to agnosticism.[7] He added, "Atheism did not satisfy my underlying curiosity." For example, he still believed in ghosts but thought that there was perhaps a rational explanation for the phenomenon. "There is a spiritual mystery to

---

[5] "Share" in this sense is, in the end, only an illusion. All magical *powers* a human appears to possess or wield are simply the actions of the *demons* with the goal of seducing the occultist into thinking he has control over them, all the while leading the occultist into grave sin and damnation, which is the ultimate reason for permitting the occultist to "taste" this power in the first place.

[6] ST III, Q. 41, A. 1, ad. 4

[7] The belief that there is no truth that man can clearly know.

human existence that atheism cannot satisfy," he said, adding, "Stating that the universe is a 'happy accident' is *not* satisfying!'"

As he looked for ways to satisfy his curiosities about the mysteries of life, he eventually reached occultic conclusions. "My basic conclusion," he said, "was that consciousness made up reality – a dream within a dream. I make up my own reality. However, there are countless things that are independent of my own personal consciousness and awareness. Since I did not believe in God, I was looking to satiate that curiosity and I became *my own god*, determining my own destiny and how things work." He said that this brought him a "feeling of empowerment, so lacking today." He added, "People feel vulnerable and small, just an evolutionary accident, a random existence in an evolutionary chaos. This makes people feel small and meaningless." Feeling small can be a good and a bad thing, he added. Feeling "small" can be a form of humility, where you come to know who you really are, your limitations, and how much you need God to give you strength and guidance. This only occurs in a Christian context. In the spiritual void of the post-Christian nihilism which dominates today, feeling "small" can be joined with a feeling of being oppressed and neglected, being overlooked and dismissed, which can brew feelings of retaliation and self-assertion, provoking the individual to demand to be regarded *not* as small and, perhaps, going so far as to be regarded as a threat instead.

Power

With the *offer* of power comes the strong desire on the part of the occultist to actually *attain* that power; this is a key draw of the occult. The occult promises power over yourself, power over your future, power over your needs, and power over others. Adam Blai said that the experience a person may have of being hurt or neglected, feeling that world has hurt them, can draw them to the occult, with its claim to give power to the powerless.[8] For people who are wounded and carrying all sorts of moral and spiritual baggage, these offers of power are more than enticing: they are addictive as well, often maddeningly so.

---

[8] Blai video

Fr. Alphonsus, who worked as a chaplain at a high school for many years, observed a growing trend of attraction to the occult for this reason, especially among girls but also among boys. This attraction originated from one thing in particular: a desire, in the face of a feeling of insecurity and weakness, to possess the same powers that witches are claimed to possess. Likely, this feeling of insecurity comes from a weak or nonexistent faith in Christ as well as the brokenness flowing from a life of sin, so common in our secular world. Together, particularly in spiritually curious youth, this is a dangerous setup. He said, "Among teenage girls there is a strong pull towards occult practices because a lot of the movies and TV shows they're watching show witches. And what do they have? They have power. They make you strong." This attraction toward the occult then plays on their wounds. "So many teenage girls are insecure and feel weak," he continued, "so they are very attracted to something that seemingly gives them power and protection and influence over others. So, they end up going after it."

In an article in the Washington Post, in 2021, the opinion was presented that magic enables young people to gain control of their lives in a world filled with unrest and uncertainty. It said, "For young people, the boom in witchcraft allows you to change your circumstance, versus that feeling of being helpless. [*sic*] Where you're relying on some outside source. Look at the political unrest, prices rising, Covid – magic helps you get through it. It gives you a sense of stability, to ground yourself, and to take control of your situation."[9] Allure.com had a similar article, in which "astrologer" Aliza Kelly stated, "But now, folks are more interested in the mystical realm than ever, and it's become clear to me why – astrology provides comfort in a world that's chaotic, and right now, it's a comfort that's sorely needed." She added, "Whether you're exploring astrology or recharging healing crystals, magick[10] provides a steady anchor during difficult times."[11]

Helena experienced this pull of the appealing power of the occult. "Being able to control your own destiny," she said, was

---

[9] *Washington Post*, Oct. 28, 2021, "From spellcasting to podcasting: Inside the life of a teenage witch"

[10] Occultists will often spell magic with a 'k' in order to distinguish occult magic from stage magic.

[11] *Allure.com*, Dec. 26, 2018, "Astrology Offered Comfort in a Chaotic World."

something that she latched on to. "Childhood was a bit chaotic, and I did have a lot of anger. I wanted to change circumstances, be in control and witchcraft was a way to do that," she said, adding, "I was a bit, ahem, rebellious." She added that a main interest in the spellwork was "the thought that you could take power and guide your life rather than just being passive. This was a main interest." Anna, who practiced the occult as a youth, said that she was picked on and regarded as a nerd, so she was seeking power from witchcraft as a result, and wanted to feel special. At one point, a friend of hers dressed the two of them up like witches. Anna described this girl as a "spoiled rich girl who was trying to get attention" through the occult.

John said that the goals of the two paths of the occult, the right-hand and the left-hand, are different. Witches, on the right-hand path, he said, are trying to get back personal empowerment for things they lost or are self-conscious about. They may be burdened by a dislike of their physique, or are wounded by a relationship, or feel alone. Magicians, on the left-hand path, which tend to be men, want enlightenment. The difference can be seen in the story of Adam and Eve. "Eve," he explained, "said, in response to the serpent's offer, 'Hey, this is good to eat,' and Adam said, 'Cool, I want to know stuff'." John was seeking hidden power, the preternatural power that Adam and Eve had, not just power in this world but occult powers also.

The lure of occultic power, in a way similar to Eve, has the power to infect the practices of Christians as well. Christopher admitted that he likely had a very different experience in the occult than the other occultists he knew because he was, at the same time, a Christian. He was firm in his Christian beliefs but admitted that his trust in God's Providence was presumptive, as if God would simply do whatever he asked. He said, "I told myself that I started studying the occult to understand the ways of the Enemy. The truth was that I wanted the power to make my own destiny." The reader might recall the story of Saruman, a celestial figure like Gandalf in the epic story, *Lord of the Rings*. Saruman was assigned to study the ways of Sauron, a figure of Satan in the story. As a result of studying

Sauron's ways too deeply, and with a hidden pride, Saruman himself was lured beneath Sauron's power and became corrupted.[12]

The Power of the Occult Backfires

Often, when the occultist interacts with these secret rituals and practices, demons will respond and grant the power they are looking for, but the results of this dabbling are often very unpredictable. Fr. Alphonsus told the story of three high-schoolers, two of whom were practicing Catholics, who fell into the occult "in a big way." It all started with a game they played in the woods, popular with young adults, where they would dress up like witches and wizards and do these imaginary games. At one point, they all thought, "Well, why can't we *really* have these powers?" So, they started their own occultic group. A girl, the one with the most dominating personality, became the occult leader and the two Catholics abandoned the Faith completely. "The last time I saw her," Fr. Alphonsus said, "she looked like something out of a horror movie. Ya know, dark eye shadow; just looked very scary, but also very sad, very very sad."[13]

In another situation, two girls sought out Fr. Alphonsus' help when they were diabolically attacked after playing with a Ouija board. Fr. Alphonsus mentioned how, as in the above example, it doesn't always end with an attack. "If the devil hadn't seemingly overplayed his hand there," he explained, "in other words, making it a negative experience, it might have led the girls on to worse things. Other times, what kids will do is find, 'Oh, now I can read hearts!'[14] But they can't! It's the demons whispering what they themselves know about people. Then they'll think, 'Ooh, I have this power,' and that's very attractive, particularly to teenage girls, but also increasingly to boys."

---

[12] This highlights the importance of prudence when researching matters of the occult. There is a secret appeal to superstition and magic within the fallen human nature of which we must all be aware. Even when researching the topic for the education of others, one must be careful to do so prayerfully, avoiding following one's disordered curiosities along the way.

[13] This exemplifies the reason why even simple occultic curiosities can be dangerous: they appeal to our fallen nature which, at present, is surrounded by a culture that is actively promoting the occult as an alternative and exciting religion.

[14] A supposed spiritual gift by which you can perceive the secret thoughts and feelings of another.

Pure Power

An article from Allure.com, writing about the occult under the theme of self-empowerment, said, "If you feel an urge to exert your will and get what you want, you qualify [to be a witch]. A witch is simply someone who is aware of their power and puts that power into action. If that's you, then congratulations, you're witch-material."[15] The occult, as another Allure.com article explained, offers the person a power that becomes his own. It said,

> One of the best parts of esoteric practices is that they offer a language of self-empowerment. Astrologer Analisa Six, explains, 'Occultism allows for freedom... it only makes sense that young people searching for a spiritual anchor outside of tradition would gravitate towards it.' Potter [a tarot card reader] agrees and tells *Allure* that esoteric practices offer power that doesn't require you to ask for permission.[16]

This power is very addictive. Exorcists often encounter individuals who, though they want help to be freed from the diabolical effects of dabbling, do not want to give up the power that comes with it. Msgr. Rossetti told the story of a man in his thirties who had been practicing witchcraft for seven years. He came to Monsignor because he feared he was becoming possessed. The man clung tightly to the power that witchcraft had granted him and, though he attended a few sessions with Monsignor, he did not want to give up his witchcraft and eventually stopped returning.[17] Dr. Gallagher, in his work with those afflicted with diabolical harassments, helped a woman who viewed herself as a Satanic priestess in her cult. In the course of their conversations, she told him, "Do you think we become Satanists because we're stupid? It's

---

[15] *Allure.com*, December 17, 2021, "We Asked Real Modern Witches to Debunk Magick's Biggest Misconceptions"
[16] *Allure.com*, December 26, 2018, "In 2018, Astrology Offered Comfort in a Chaotic World."
[17] Rossetti, *Diary*, 133.

because we get a *lot* in return. We worship Satan because he looks after us and grants us big favors."[18]

Damien, the Satanist that Elizabeth became involved with, eventually admitted to her that he knew he was possessed and had no problem with it. He said it gave him powers, including speaking foreign languages, allowing him to see vices in other people, and being able to tell whether people were lying to him. He was drunk on the power but the rest of his life was out of control. For example, he was such a pathological liar that she could not believe a single word he would say. After she got away from him and later spoke to him on the phone on one occasion, she told him she thought he was possessed. He said, "I know, and I like it that way."

Fr. Alphonsus was once helping a young woman, from the "big-time" business world, who was dealing with psychics and was clearly under their control. He recalled his meeting with her, stating, "I said to her, 'You are under demonic influence – there's demonic stuff here – and you need to let me pray prayers,' and she wouldn't let me, because she knew that all the stuff she had been given, the gifts and everything, it would all stop." Similarly, as Christopher made an observation about the number of Satanists he knew who were in the military, he reflected, "Particularly when you have to go to war, you want all the power that you can get, it's that simple."

Another exorcist told a story about a young boy who was in a juvenile detention center after assaulting a police officer. Father went to visit him to discuss his situation and offer his help. In the course of the conversation, the boy admitted that, when he was younger, Satan had appeared to him as a father figure, and had offered him powers to assist him. The boy told the exorcist that he could never let go of all the power Satan had given him, and he refused to let Father help.

Striking Fear

Fr. Louis, who had spent time as a priest in Africa, said, "Some use [the occult] in Africa to make people afraid. No one doubts the existence of the devil there. People go into this out of fear and fright

---

[18] Gallagher, *Demonic Foes*, 52. Nevertheless, this woman still sought out Dr. Gallagher and the exorcists because she was suffering so much from Satan's attacks and abuses.

– but if you are of the light, you are not driven by fear." Former occultist, Rigo Cambray, admitted, "When I was in [the occult], I felt like I was someone else. People were afraid of me, and that felt good."[19] Elizabeth quickly learned that Damien was driven by many evil motivations. He was seeking revenge, had an extreme sense of entitlement to a degree that everyone owed him something, and was angry and vindictive toward the whole world, God in particular. He wanted to hurt people in order to get revenge on God.

Philomena said that her first husband, the Satanist, was seeking power and wanted everyone to fear him, to be "devastatingly afraid of him." Like other occultists, he had a daytime and nighttime persona. For the most part, people did not see the "nighttime persona" that desired to instill fear, though people did catch glimpses of who he really was, then only thinking he was weird. He sought true power, power in this world. He already thought that he was his own god and was very adamant that he wanted people to turn and run from him out of fear.

Narcissism

All forms of the occult, Satanism in particular, create a disordered mindset in the occultist based on their desire to possess and to wield this power on their own terms. This condemnation of Satanism as narcissistic is something that Satanists themselves agree to be true. The daughter of Anton LaVey, the founder of the Church of Satan, is one such person. As part of the fascinating story of her renunciation of Satanism, about which more people need to know, Zeena, now formerly LaVey, stated on her website, "LaVeyan Satanist behavior in practice is best understood as Dark Triad personality disorder with cosplay and ritual fetishes."[20] This personality disorder is described as a combination of three negative personality traits – narcissism, Machiavellianism, and psychopathy – each labeled as *dark* because each is considered to contain malevolent qualities.

Zeena is not the only one who has described Satanists in this way. "Satanists are quite possibly the most insufferable occultists I

[19] Rigo testimony
[20] Zeenaschreck.com/general-info.html

have ever encountered," Christopher remarked. He said that, from his experience, they are arrogant and manipulative and despise the truth. He saw in them an attitude of vehement opposition toward God and of resentment toward the Church and the God who guides her. They desire to have the freedom to decide what is good and would love not so much to "reign in Hell" but to storm Heaven and replace God.

The narcissism of Satanists very much resembles the personality of Satan and all demons. Msgr. Rossetti explained this, describing how, in one session, the demon kept correcting Monsignor's pronunciation of the demon's name, even while the demon was screaming from the exorcism and about to be cast out. Father said, "This was narcissism beyond belief! Demons are complete narcissists, and Satan is the biggest narcissist of them all. In Hell, no one thinks of another's good. It is pure self-focus."[21] He added, "Because of the demons' wickedness, narcissism, and consuming hatred, authority is exercised in Hell in the most brutal of fashions. It is self-serving, harsh, and sadistic."[22]

A Satanic mindset is indeed self-serving and sadistic, as we see in Nikolas Schreck's 1989 presentation of the philosophies of Satanism.[23] In his interview with Bob Larson, Schreck responded to Larson's mention of the effect that the philosophies of Satanism might have on the masses of the general population, saying, "The masses? We have no regard for the masses. Satanism is a religion for the elite. A religion for leaders. A religion for competent people." He added, "Back to Social Darwinism again: in the animal kingdom, you preserve what is strong." Taking care of the homeless, he and Zeena both said, produces more homeless and extends the problem. Among the animals, they don't do that. Zeena said, "How does the animal kingdom survive? There is no such thing as homeless." Nikolas added, "In the animal kingdom, you preserve what is strong, you give more food to the stronger animal; you don't feed the weaker ones. There is no welfare in the animal world."[24] Nikolas, when clarifying that acts of charity and altruism are not part of his spiritual path, stated, "My spiritual path, which is the way of the

---

[21] Rossetti, *Diary*, 216.
[22] Ibid 44.
[23] Since that time, Schreck has also renounced all forms of Satanism.
[24] Larson video #1

Prince of Darkness, is my primary concern, [and] is the development and empowerment of myself, not of others."[25]

Worship of the Intellect

Many "baby occultists" are initially led onto the occult path by a spirit of intellectual pride. Helena saw this herself and said that those who "have large egos, want to control everything around them, and aren't that interested in strong social connections," are vulnerable to going down the path of the occult. Margaret, who had been brought up in a solid and holy Catholic family, which provided a good human and spiritual foundation, was the only child to show a rebellious spirit, which led her to dabble in New Age ideas. She said she eventually thought her devout Catholic parents "did not know the whole truth." She was then determined to find it herself. At another point, Margaret fell into a very bad relationship because she was drawn to the man's intelligence. "I was attracted to smart people," she said, "and intelligent humor, but if it is not grounded in God, you might as well throw the key away and head downstairs, because that is where you're going."

Throughout my research, it became apparent that the worship of the intellect is quite Satanic. Not only did Satan do this, preferring his own mind and truths to the reality that God had created, but modern Satanists, such as the Temple of Set, are also quite adoring of the intellect. The Temple of Set is very much an elitist group for "very intelligent people" which restricts who can enter based on that criterion. As Nikolas Schreck stated in 1997, "There are extremely accomplished and powerful people in the Temple of Set, because the Temple of Set is based on intellectual knowledge."[26] With these considerations, it could be concluded that the final fruit of rationalism, with its renunciation of faith and its hyper-focus on the intellect, is the "religion" of Satanism.

Many atheists, too, as we often see when they seek to debate Christians, are dedicated to pure intelligence, without faith and humility, and, like the previous examples, can be quite conceited about their personal possession of this quality. On a related note, in

[25] Larson video #2
[26] Larson video #2

Catholic seminary formation it is mentioned to the young men to be careful that they ensure they are worshiping the Person of God and not simply their own intellectual knowledge *about* God. Often, in the intellectual journey, given our fallen state, even devout young men will turn in upon themselves and hide within a pursuit of intellectual knowledge rather than within the Sacred Heart of Our Lord. The ideal for Catholics is to join excellence in faith with excellence in reason and intelligence. All men can attain to the heights of faith and grace, but natural intellectual powers are neither as universally accessible as the latter two nor are they necessary for salvation. While many Saints have had some of the finest intellects in the history of mankind, others have been notably simple, St. Bernadette as one example among many. Regardless, the joy and glory that they all attained was through faith in Christ and the reception of His grace.

Superior to Others

Arrogance is not exclusive to the extreme occultism of Satanism. Witches, Wiccans, and New-Agers all confessed to having been animated by this vice. This superiority can manifest in feelings of hatred, rage, desire to control others, and a desire to have no need for others. When Gabriel was in the New Age, he felt like he was easily triggered and angry with everyone. In conversations, he would often snap back with a dismissive "I'm right, you're wrong; you don't know what you're talking about." He felt like the anger was feeding off something. A spirit of hatred was certainly present in Andrew's life when he was in the occult, though it disguised itself as a sense of superiority over the "uninitiated." "I saw myself as better, and more powerful, than them," he said. "I was closer to my 'divine nature'[27] and could bend my reality, as well as powerful entities, to my will."

This superiority appeared in many of the stories of the former occultists interviewed. Alex Frank, for example, said the meditations of Yoga train the individual to attain what they regard as a "superior consciousness." This superiority allows them to manipulate and

---

[27] A counterfeit to the "share in the divine nature" (2 Peter 1:4) that Our Lord offers through grace. Here, Andrew believed that he possessed a divine nature on his own.

control others through an occultic "energy" and their own will.[28] Though Margaret's exploration of the occult began with dabbling in crystals, "I wanted to live on a higher plane than everyone else," she said, adding, "I was looking for truth." Camilla said, "I thought I was a Catholic but a *larger* Catholic – I understood the deeper mysteries more than most people." Timothy, as a pagan, attended some Christian fellowship events in college, though he said he was not there to learn from them, believing at that point that he had more spiritual wisdom than they had.

Interestingly, the Church acknowledges that Baptism results in the exaltation of the human nature of the one who receives it. Whereas the occultic belief that personal greatness is self-acquired and leads to superiority over others, the Christian is reminded that this exaltation is a gift, freely given by Our Lord, which requires work on the part of the Christian. Further, their failure to mold their lives to correspond to this grace will result in the loss of this exaltation. As *Lumen Gentium*, of the Second Vatican Council, states, "All the Church's children should remember that their exalted status is to be attributed not to their own merits but to the special grace of Christ. If they fail moreover to respond to that grace in thought, word and deed, not only shall they not be saved but they will be the more severely judged."[29]

Becoming a God

For many occultists, the desire for power culminates in the belief that this power is something that actually resides within themselves. As a result, they seek to tap into this limitless energy and power, believing that they themselves are actually divine. This concept appears in more occultic practices than people realize.

Allure.com's article on astrology had a very revealing comment on this issue. It said, "Find something that speaks to your soul and practice the art of manifestation. Within each person is their own cosmology – an individual universe that has the ability to expand exponentially. Don't be afraid of your power, cosmic warrior. You

---

[28] Certain forms of Satanism seek this power as well, as will be discussed in *Slaying Dragons III*.
[29] Lumen Gentium, 14.

are magick."[30] This is a very loaded quotation. It is saying that, within the soul of the witch is their own universe of truth, which is unlimited, powerful, and magical. It is difficult to come up with a better way than that to say "You are God" without just saying it.

According to Alex Frank, the main goal of the common forms of Yoga is to recognize the practitioner's supposedly true identity as god. Yoga teaches that when a person identifies with his "partial ego," it is this that is the cause of all suffering, whereas "enlightenment" only comes from the realization of their "infinite" and "divine" identity. Through Yoga, an individual's pursuit of power and enlightenment is a statement that they believe they are god and is an effort to feed this supposed divine nature. This is a reflection of the meaning of the word *Hatha*, meaning *power*, which is the style of Yoga that predominates today. Turned in on themselves, and identifying themselves as the central focus, and essentially as the authority, they view themselves *as god*. Further, through the practice of Yoga, they seek to grow into an even more powerful god.

In 1997, Zeena and Nikolas Schreck gave a second interview with Bob Larson. At the time of that interview, they had left the Church of Satan and embraced the Temple of Set, rejecting the psychological Satanism of the Church of Satan and embracing "the real thing" as followers of the "real" entity named Set. Calling themselves black magicians, they explained very clearly that they believed they are gods. In doing so, they even brought Our Lord into the discussion, blasphemously using Him as an example of a *black magician*. Given the powers and abilities which Jesus demonstrated, Schreck stated that Jesus resembled a black magician, explaining, "He himself was a cosmic rebel like Lucifer. He declared himself a God, and the point of black magic, left-hand path Satanism is to make oneself a God."[31]

Schreck then said that Set, who lived, so they claimed, thousands of years before Christ, is like Jesus as a *black magician*. "Set was the first to create himself and thus set the model for all black magicians to come; this example, through willpower, of creating yourself and making yourself into a god. This creation of self, ex-nihilo," he

---

[30] *Allure.com*, December 26, 2018, "In 2018, Astrology Offered Comfort in a Chaotic World."

[31] This belief about Christ as a *black magician* is a great example of Satanism's inversion of the Truth, aping of God, self-exaltation into the place of God, and the belittling of God in the process.

explained, "is the magical process." Schreck added, "We believe that we have created ourselves and that we are developing our knowledge of that godhood further," which they do as members of the Temple of Set. He added, "If you're saying, 'Are we denying that God, Jehovah, gave us life?' Yes, we are." When Larson asked who Zeena believed is the one who gave her life, she said she believed that she had the special will to draw her mother and father together in order to create herself, "therefore, making me a purely magical child."

Schreck stated further, "The value of what we are doing is to transform ourselves into the masters of our own destiny and self-deify ourselves, actually become a god. That is what we believe is the value of black magic and of our religion." They said they are striving to create their own destiny, their own existence after bodily death, in order to continue their power in the world.

This belief persists to the present day. In 2021, a fresh statement on the matter was given by a current leader in the Church of Satan. In a Rolling Stones article, magister of the Church of Satan, David Harris, said, "Basically, we worship ourselves. We refer to ourselves as *I-theists*. We see ourselves as our own god."[32]

Though Wicca and witchcraft are often portrayed as summoning the powers of nature, spirits, or deities, thus placing themselves beneath some sort of higher being or power, within Wicca and witchcraft is the same Satanic belief, ultimately, that they are gods. To illustrate this reality, consider the following example. A witchcraft and Wicca website discussed the fact that atheists can also be Wiccans. It stated, "Wiccans hold reverence for Nature and accept the existence of a Goddess and/or God," but it then added that atheists can also practice "spirituality without religion." The goal here, it stated, is to "connect with your *inner world* and *awaken the powers* that live within you. You don't need to seek out any Higher Beings because you can always find your Witchcraft inwards through deep meditation." Directly mirroring Satanism, which also rejects any dependence on a Higher Being, Wicca clearly sees that the *power* they pull from for their magic resides within themselves, thus making themselves into gods.

---

[32] *Rolling Stone.* March 26, 2021, "We Asked Satanists What They Think of the New Lil Nas X Video"

In the Light of Truth

Though the desire to attain to such earthly power can be alluring, particularly when life is burdensome and appears to be filled with suffering, Psalm 73 adds further clarification on the truth of the matter. Wearied with seeking to understand the dilemma of the prosperity of the wicked, Asaph was illuminated by entering "into the sanctuary of God." There he perceived the true end of the wicked. For, while they currently enjoy freedom from the burdens of life, they reside "in slippery places," soon to "fall to ruin," and to be "swept away utterly by terror," for "those who are far from [the Lord] shall perish." Asaph sees that he was "stupid and ignorant" when he was bitter about his own lot, for, speaking to the Lord, he said, "I am continually with Thee; Thou dost hold my right hand. Thou dost guide me with Thy counsel, and afterward Thou wilt receive me to glory. Whom have I in heaven but Thee? And there is nothing upon earth that I desire besides Thee. My flesh and my heart may fail, but God is the strength of my heart and my portion for ever."[33]

---

[33] Psalm 73:13-27

Chapter Eleven

The Occult is Dangerous and Destructive

The soul of man was made by God for union with Him and eternal life. Man, fallen and wounded by sin, can easily stray from the path that Our Lord laid out before him to accomplish this end. Deviating from the dictates of the natural law, his conscience, and the divine laws revealed through Christ's Holy Church, man instead embarks upon a path which cuts through the dark valley of sin, under the shadow of death, in which only falsehoods and lies echo against the hills.[1] Here, man enters into a state of oppression as life's mysterious end tempts him to despair. Only in Christ is the answer given to the meaning of life and, in particular, to the enduring question of where we go after death. When this question goes unanswered, it hovers over all men like a thick shroud, obscuring the light of reason and faith, and making them blindly grasp in the darkness for the answer to this riddle.

The men who wander from Christ, or who remain separated from Him, and who grab hold of the occult, in its soft or deep varieties, are grasping what has presented itself to them in the darkness[2] as the answer to all their problems. Along that path, men are promised to find peace, power, fulfillment, and answers, but *not* from God. What they are not aware of is that, by doing so, they have laid hold of the rattle of the ancient serpent, who lurks in that darkness with a shimmering offer and with the appearance of truth, disguised as he often is as an angel of light.[3] The devil, further blinding the intellect and seducing the will by his offer to give them "all the kingdoms of the world and the glory of them,"[4] beckons men

---

[1] 1 John 1:6. This refers to all mankind who wanders in sin, not just the issue of dabbling in the occult.
[2] Eph 5:8
[3] 2 Cor 11:14
[4] Matt 4:8

deep into superstition and magical thinking. It is here that men become compromised, sensing their slithering master and the danger of this endeavor, nonetheless persisting along the way. What they eventually find, inevitably, is the serpent himself, coiled before them, glaring and ready to strike with his fangs.

This is the reality of the occult. The dangers which it presents to the soul are the same dangers which came to Adam and Eve when the serpent promised them divinity if they took from the Tree which God had forbidden them to eat. By heeding the voice from below, they shunned the Light from above, and fell into the darkness of Satan's own rebellion and separation from God. Only misery, illness, discord, vice, death, and eternal perdition came to them as a result. The shocking reality of this danger within the occult is that most occultists *understand* there is a danger and yet persist in the practice, despite the presence of many indicators of evil emerging in their lives.

The truth that there is an evil presence within all occultic practices makes itself known, sooner or later, to every practitioner. Whether or not this is alarming to the individual will depend on many things, including the manner of the diabolical manifestations and the degree of the alignment of the person's will with that of the evil of the practices and beliefs. Occultists typically become alarmed by the diabolical presence within their practice only after initially thinking that what they were engaged in was completely safe and innocent. "Most are just curious," Fr. Sebastian said, "but once the reality sets in, it puts a stop to [their occult practice] before they get too involved." From my interviews and research, while the dark reality can pretty effectively scare away the curious, it often only slows them down a bit, or gives them pause, but it takes many moments of realizing the dangers before these individuals actually make the decision to turn around and exit the occult.

The ultimate danger of the occult, as exorcists warn, is that it is a prime way for a person to become possessed, or to suffer from a variety of diabolical afflictions and risk eternal damnation. Adam Blai noted, "A lot of our cases are witches or Satanists. The consent needed to get possessed is at the level of black magic."[5] Fr. Fortea added to this, stating, "Even if those who practice magic – witches,

---

[5] Blai video

sorcerers, seers, etc. – deny it (or are even unaware of it), the devil is behind all their works. And the very magic they practice in the end opens them up to demonic influence and even possession."[6] Magic is so bad because it is a violation of the First Commandment.[7] The individual, Blai explained, is saying, "I don't trust You. You're taking too long. I want what I want *now* on my terms. I'm gonna turn to this other spirit to get it."[8] Breaking the First Commandment leads the person into mortal sin and turning to the spirit then initiates a relationship with a demon. The first destroys the life of grace and removes God's protection, while the second directly associates the person with an aggressive and malevolent entity who now has an open door into the person's life. While Blai singles out *black magic*[9] above, all forms of occult dabbling are grave and place a person into mortal sin and a state of spiritual vulnerability.

While the occult is an evil and effective tool of entering into a relationship with a demon, all the rituals and philosophies and spells involved are arbitrary concoctions encouraged by demons or crafted under their influence. The rituals have no power in themselves other than to destroy one's relationship with God. Adam Blai said that, at the start of an exorcism, the demons will often say to Blai's exorcism team, "Do you believe this one fell for it too? I can't believe this _____[10]!" Blai added, "They mock them and think it's just really pathetic that they fell for the black magic lie. Demons mock and denigrate people who think black magic controls them; they think this is hilarious – that people think that they can draw a circle on the floor and wiggle their fingers and say some mumbo jumbo and that the demon suddenly is going to obey them as a powerful witch or magician. They think that is hilarious. They don't *serve* people; they only pretend to [serve them] in the beginning to draw the person in deeper until they are in so deep they cannot get out on their own." Andrew is a case in point: the demons actually did refer to him with exalted honorific titles and pretended to obey and even fear him.

---

[6] Fr. Jose Antonio Fortea. *Interview with an Exorcist* (West Chester: Ascension Press, 2006), 114

[7] "I am the Lord thy God; thou shalt not have strange gods before Me." (Exod 20:2-3; Deut 5: 6-7).

[8] Blai video.

[9] "Black" magic here refers to spells and rituals where the person knowingly interacts with a demon.

[10] Blai said the demons use derogatory language to refer to the possessed witch.

The Occult is Dangerous

Fred Wolff's story, in which he ventured from Wicca into a shared curiosity about summoning a demon, is a good example of the danger that occultic interests can ultimately bring. While not every occultist has such a strong encounter with a demon, some do. One day, Fred's original mentor in Wicca invited Fred to join him for a new ritual that he had just learned, which involved summoning a demon. "Rich told me that as long as we were in the circle[11] inscribed on the ground, we were safe," Fred recalled. As the ritual progressed, various demonic manifestations occurred in the room, taking hideous forms, clearly intent on scaring them. At one point, it appeared they were being shown a glimpse of Hell. "The smell was atrocious," he said, "Rotten eggs, sulfur; I can't begin to describe it." When the specific demon which Rich had summoned finally emerged, it said to them, "Do you really think that circle could stop me?" Then, according to Fred, his friend "was picked up off the ground and slammed into a wall fifteen feet away." Fred bolted, locked himself in a nearby bathroom, and waited. When he emerged later, Rich was "foaming at the mouth and babbling incoherently." When the police arrived, they determined that Fred was not guilty of causing any harm that resulted in Rich's condition. Rich, however, "had apparently lost his mind," and spent the next twenty years in a psychiatric hospital, at the end of which he sadly committed suicide.[12]

The ability of demons to toss people in extraordinary ways has been witnessed by exorcists in many cases of possession. In these cases, it is the demon acting within the body of the possessed by which they observe such strength. However, this can happen by the external action of the demon as well, as was presented above. The angelic nature has the power to move matter in a variety of ways. In *Slaying Dragons*,[13] the story was presented of exorcist Fr. Truqui, who worked with a possessed man who first realized he was possessed when he fell into a trance and then suddenly grabbed his friend who was next to him and threw him in a way completely

---

[11] A protection circle; a very common practice among all occultists.
[12] Chnetwork.org/story/freed-from-the-occult. *Coming Home Network*, Fred Wolff, July 18, 2016, "Freed from the Occult."
[13] Fraune, *Slaying Dragons*, 80.

impossible for a normal person to do. Fr. Amorth's mentor, Fr. Candido Amantini witnessed a case that resembled the Gerasene demoniac from the Gospel of Mark, in which a possessed girl was able to break leather straps and pull strong ropes so fiercely that the iron rods on the bed were broken. Exorcists occasionally witness levitation during an exorcism, which is a clear sign of the demon's ability to effortlessly lift a human body off the ground.[14]

The Occult Harms the Occultist

The gravest danger of the occult is the harm it brings upon the occultists themselves. This includes those who engage in both the *soft* and the *dark* occult. All forms are tied into the same *funnel* strategy of the devil and are, as a result, risking the same danger and harm. This harm can range from the superficial and annoying to the dangerous and terrifying. The former can disrupt a person's life and drive them into bad decisions; the latter can lead to the complete destruction of the individual, from which they may never recover.

Lucy's story is one of the latter. After years, perhaps decades, of admiration and appreciation for psychics, Lucy eventually decided to become one herself. This was one of the occultic decisions that immediately preceded the mental collapse that would send her to a mental health facility. "One of the things I did, not long before I was admitted to the mental health facility, was attend a 'course' to become psychic," she explained. "It's where you empty your mind[15] to give access to the 'source.' I do believe that was a catalyst for the possession."[16] The possession either accompanied her "mental collapse" or was the actual cause of the observable signs that mirrored the psychosis with which she was diagnosed.

---

[14] Here, it is obviously the work of the demon who is possessing the person's body. Levitation can also occur by the work of holy angels. This is the case in famous stories of the great Saints, like St. Joseph of Cupertino.

[15] *Emptying the mind* is also one of the occultic dangers of the general practice of Yoga. Further, this emptying is not what Christians do in prayer: the Christian *calms* his mind so he can then fill it with sacred thoughts, doctrines, and images.

[16] As in many occult practices, ranging from tarot card readings, to psychics, to Reiki, to Palo and Santeria and Voodoo, the practitioner opens himself to a "source," a spirit who will communicate knowledge and/or powers to the person. This spirit is a demon, for the souls of the dead are not capable of doing this and angels are not permitted to.

The mental collapse came about because, as she herself said, "Then one day, it all went too far." Her deep dive into unreality in the New Age led to a true break with reality. She had come to a point where she was reading for hours and hours about ungodly topics and filling her mind with unholy thoughts. "I was fascinated with aliens and fairies and believed that both were in our home," she said. "I was also doing meditation a lot, trying to connect to 'sources', learning how to read tarot cards and more. I filled so much of my mind with so many lies, let Satan into so many areas of my life, that he ended up taking over."

She was then, at the age of thirty-six, committed to a mental health facility following the mental breakdown. As it turned out, though, her "mental disorder" appeared actually to be diabolical possession. She was hearing voices, was confused, could read people's thoughts, had horrible thoughts in her mind, and was paranoid. In the facility, she said she was so drugged up that she could barely carry on a conversation or respond to her own name. The facility gave her no way out of taking the medication, but it only made things worse.[17] She described the situation in this way: "I could no longer function. I had gone from a busy mom of four, a business owner, a loving wife and community volunteer, to someone who could not put a sentence together. It was the most horrifying and hellish time of my life. I truly was in the pits of hell. Satan had me, and he wasn't letting go. I felt empty, like I had no soul. My heart was empty, but my head was full of Satan."[18]

Yoga, whose spiritual dangers have already been touched upon, has additional harmful elements of which readers should be aware. A specific form of Yoga, called *kundalini* Yoga, is a deceptive form of Yoga that has bewitched many, even Christians, into embracing its practice. The concept, details, and purpose, however, should frighten any observant and thoughtful person. The end goal of Kundalini Yoga is stated, by exorcists and by those who observe it, to resemble possession. Anyone can look into this on the internet and find alarming details everywhere. Websites which promote Yoga, Hindu

---

[17] This was a rather unfortunate experience. Not all mental health facilities are like this. It should be noted that mental health in an individual is regarded by exorcists as highly important and helps them rule out natural causes at play.

[18] As sad as the story of her collapse is, the story of her conversion is correspondingly beautiful.

meditation, and specifically kundalini, speak of it as a primal energy, a "serpent" coiled at the spine, released by the meditation, which can then positively impact a person's life if the person approaches this *energy* properly. However, if done improperly or without the proper motives, it can cause all sorts of harm. The numerous negative effects of Kundalini Yoga include searing sensations, intense spasms, vibrating, jerking, uncontrollable emotions, visions, headaches, heart problems, screaming, laughing, and symptoms resembling a psychotic breakdown. Some of these symptoms are only experienced short-term while others remain long-term and are destructive to a person's life.[19]

Several of these negative effects of releasing the "serpent energy" of Kundalini resemble what exorcists report as symptoms of possession. As Fr. Amorth stated, the possessed are subject to interior assaults of the devil, including trembling legs, headaches, and other pains and illnesses. In the more serious cases, the person is unable to have a stable life as a result. Each case is different; some are able to pray and go to Mass, while others are not.[20] Dr. Gallagher stated, "The experience of many exorcists is that possessed individuals may indeed shake or exhibit tremors."[21] He also added that, in his work with the Satanic princess, Julia, she "complained about experiencing a burning sensation from her own diabolical tormentors." She described it as a kind of spiritual fire. "But it does hurt," she added, "*like Hell*, I was going to say!" Julia is not the only one who has told Dr. Gallagher about experiencing a burning sensation from demons.[22]

The Occult Impacts Others

Occult dabbling can also have an impact on those within the person's life. The Becketts told me that, even before they knew their daughter Catherine was into the occult, they picked up on a spirit of

---

[19] An internet search for "Kundalini ruined my life" brings results that repeat a theme: this "awakening" is actually a psychotic episode that is *supposed* to destroy your understanding of reality, in keeping with the Hindu pursuit of "no-self" and "self-extinction" and "the world is illusory." This dangerous and rude awakening is the fulfillment of humanity, according to this false religion.

[20] Fraune, *Slaying Dragons*, 44.

[21] Gallagher, *Demonic Foes*, 124

[22] Gallagher, *Demonic Foes*, 67

oppression in the home. There was a lot of unrest, anxiety, everyone was at each other's throats and rude, short with each other, curt. There was a lack of love in the home. They admitted they are not a perfect family but they do eat dinner together every day and the kids support each other all the time. Before this evil arrived, love was there but alongside normal family squabbling. The mother remembered noting at that time that the kids were struggling with their normal support of each other. It was a very rough time, but it was only after the daughter left the house, and they started blessing the home, that they realized how bad it had gotten.

Ava's family was likewise impacted by her occult dabblings. On one occasion, Ava did a "reading" in a room in the family's house. The family home, being very devoutly Catholic, had already been blessed and exorcised several times. The night after this reading, the younger brother woke up seeing a black cat on the other side of his room, staring at him. He stared back at it to see if it was the family cat but realized it was not. He turned on the light and it vanished. When Ava found out, it really affected her, the parents explained, since she loves her brothers a lot, and this one in particular. She was disturbed by the idea that her activity might be bringing bad things into the house. She most likely did not understand this could be diabolical but possibly simply "negative," given her New Age inclinations, the parents said.[23] This last detail is very common and highlights a dangerous ignorance which blinds many occultists to the dangers that are present.[24]

It's not only children's occultic dabblings that impact the family. In Clare's situation, it was her father's occult interests that brought spiritual problems into the home. Growing up around her father's explicit occult practices, she, alone among her four siblings, began to experience regular diabolical manifestations and harassments, lasting for decades. It eventually also appeared in the life of her children and, once her husband Lawrence finally began to take the spiritual lead in

---

[23] Those in the *soft occult* often do not regard spirits as "evil" but as "negative" and disregard the distinction, in all areas, of "good and evil."

[24] *Slaying Dragons III* will contain the story of a popular online witch discussing the presence of "difficult" spirits in her home, which have the tell-tale signs of being demons. Similarly, *Teen Vogue*, in September 2022, had an article on "signs that your house may be haunted" which does not distinguish between "good and evil" and actually coaches the reader to think that tell-tale signs of a demonic presence are actually those of a ghost, further coaching them that there is a low likelihood of it being an "evil ghost."

the family, it appeared in his life as well. Specifically, the diabolical attacks[25] began to impact Lawrence when Clare's brother, who is married to a Wiccan, visited and began to attack Lawrence for his Catholic faith. "The attack was very diabolical," she said, "[My brother's] face changed from normal to filled with hate, accusing Lawrence of 'abusing' the children by raising them according to the traditional teachings of the Church." This was during a vacation that included the entire extended family. On that trip, Clare's brother had also been trying to corrupt her teenage boys, trying to get them to watch impure movies and encouraging them to look at the indecently dressed women on the beach. Clare said that the attack was so bad that Lawrence had to kick her brother and her brother's wife out of their house, something he would have never otherwise done. Clare speculated that this beginning to the manifestations was either the result of a curse from her father, a curse from the Wiccan wife,[26] or some other "spiritual junk" left behind by her brother after the visit.

Occultists Know the Occult is Dangerous

What those curious about the occult might not encounter on the surface level, they quickly find out about when, with interest already piqued, they look deeper to see how this "New Age" or "witch" or "occult" thing is supposed to be done. Only when they meet with the counsel they find in books and online, do they hear that there are actually *dangers* in this new and mysterious spirituality they have embraced. However, at this point, they are hooked and want to keep going, regardless of the "red flags" that have now emerged about this new practice. Once they are in, they will join the other occultists who, despite encountering these dangers and their risks, find themselves addicted to the experiences.

---

[25] The diabolical attacks began with his own experience of seeing the same *shadow people* that Clare had seen since her childhood. She described it, saying, "He woke me up one night and said, 'Do you *see* that?' I certainly saw it. A shadow person is pacing around our bed while a dark cloud ebbs and flows in the corner of our room, and two orbs of light seem to be attacking it." I have learned through my research that "shadow people" and such apparitions of "orbs of light" are more common than I was aware of, reported by exorcists and former occultists alike. There always seems to be a connection to the occult when these manifestations are present.

[26] As former Wiccans testify, though Wiccans profess to "do no harm," many still venture into issuing curses.

Angela Ucci, in her interview with Michael Knowles, perhaps best addressed the issue of the presence of dangers within the occult. She said,

> It's interesting how, even in the realm of New-Ageism, you understand that there's negative energy and negative and demonic influence. Like, why is it that – every time we did Reiki, every time we did a moon circle, every time I practiced with my crystals or my tarot, every time I did Yoga – why is it you always have to *pray for protection?* Why is it you always have to call in an *angel team?* Why is it you always have to set up *pillars of light* around the room? Why do you have to prepare yourself for the *worst* with all these practices?[27]

Witches, surprisingly to those who have not done the research, will readily admit that there are risks involved in this practice. One witchcraft website said that they protect themselves by "directing our energy and creating an energetic shield that will safeguard us from different types of evils." They also create "protection circles" before invoking "spirits or external forces." They say it is important to protect yourself when casting spells because various things, like psychic attacks and "disruptive energies" are a risk. I have heard from former occultists that they, while members of these occultic groups, endured these same psychic attacks. John described this scenario and also mentioned that it was common for infighting within these occultic groups to include accusations that one person "psychically" attacked someone else or attacked them through astral projection.

When I asked Helena about her experience with the goddesses of Wicca, and about a comment she had made concerning the

---

[27] Michael Knowles, "Former Astrologist Explains Danger of New Age Practices, Angela Ucci." *YouTube,* 21 October 2022. These "protective" actions on the part of occultists should be seen in contrast to how exorcists protect themselves before going into an exorcism, which is through prayer and the reception of the Sacraments, because the exorcists are very much aware of the dangers involved. Further, this activity of the occultists should stand in contrast to Christian prayer which, even more than *not needing* any protection beforehand, is itself a *source* of protection.

dangers of these practices, she explained the situation very candidly. There are a lot of different flavors of paganism, she told me, and a lot of different tenets, so to speak, within witchcraft as well. "As someone who followed the Celtic goddess Morrigan, speaking from my direct experience," she added, "yes, the goddess can absolutely be dangerous. She was a goddess of war, battle, death – we considered her to be frightening in many aspects and she demanded respect. That being said, we didn't cast a circle to keep her out. We *wanted* her to be there and have our power combine with hers. She is asked to come. Our circle was protection against having any unwanted entities come into the ritual."

One example of the danger within witchcraft is in the risks involved in making "moon water"[28] on Halloween/Samhain when there is also a full moon at the time, as happened in 2020. A certain online witchcraft forum contained a warning from an experienced witch that, since the upcoming full moon at the time was a blue moon, falling on Halloween night, it posed some dangers to those trying to make "moon water" that night. *Moon water* is made by witches by leaving a jar of water out under the moon at different phases. This supposedly makes the water sacred in a specific way, which varies based on the phase of the moon at the time. *Ghost water*, which is regarded by witches as effective for hexing,[29] is usually made by leaving a jar of water out in a cemetery. The warning was issued because, apparently, since, as witches believe, the veil is so thin between the visible and invisible world at Halloween/Samhain, the practitioner might end up making "ghost water" instead of "moon water." The danger is that the energy from ghost water has the potential to go badly if mishandled, so she urged caution. Since ghosts, she claimed, are attracted to reflective surfaces, you might mistakenly attract them to your jar of water. She also reminded the reader that "not all ghosts are friendly," so this situation might pose a hazard.[30]

---

[28] Moon water is a witchcraft practice that claims that water left out during different phases of the moon absorbs the moon's power for different intentions. It is then used in various rituals.

[29] Another term used for "cursing."

[30] Of course, the Church rejects this portrayal of ghosts. Ghosts are souls from Purgatory and are not interested in their reflection. Any invisible entity acting in this manner is a demon, albeit one pretending to be a "friendly ghost," which is a common ploy they incorporate in their deception.

In the *goetia*, the ancient occultic texts containing the names of demons and how and when to invoke them, Christopher mentioned that the texts themselves "are explicitly warning that if you do these things and you are not prepared, you will get possessed." This reality frightened him enough that he created lines that he never crossed, and he never ventured beyond a certain point, though he continued with his other occult practices. Even though he did not know whether he believed in those things or not, he did not want to take that risk.

Gabriel shared an interesting observation about an experience he had after visiting a psychic. He said that, when he went to see the psychic, he picked up on a very "weird vibe" from the psychic and everyone who worked there. When he finished speaking to the psychic, he saw the man who was the "boss" over the whole business. Gabriel noted that the man's eyes had a really strange look to them. "It was almost like there was no soul there," he said, "like you are looking into nothing, just a vessel, like he was not a real person." It reminded him of a YouTuber that he followed a lot in the New Age who had similar eyes and a similar look. "It is odd," he remarked, "how the masters have a soul-less look to them, almost an enticing look."[31] Signs of diabolical influence in the "masters" of occultists is something that Camilla also noted. While attending a weekend New Age workshop, Camilla observed that one of the instructors, who was channeling a spirit, began to go in and out of that new personality, "as if she were crazy," she stated. At that point, Camilla admitted, "The veil was lifted. It was not beautiful, incense, angels, etc. – it was terrifying."

Satanists, like other occultists, will also admit that their practices involve a real danger. Even before their more recent condemnations of Satanism,[32] Zeena and Nikolas Schreck, back in 1997, were already aware of the dangers of black magic, as they explained to Bob Larson in their interview. In the discussion of their worship of the entity known as "Set"[33] and their practice of black

---

[31] Exorcists report that possessed people, when the demon is manifesting, often have a unique look to their eyes, in which it appears that the demon is looking back at the exorcist through the person's eyes. *Slaying Dragons*, p 69–70.

[32] Perhaps as early as 2012, or earlier. This will be presented in *Slaying Dragons III*.

[33] A supposed ancient Egyptian god, image for Satan, and viewed as "another name for Satan" by some.

magic, Zeena and Nikolas both spoke plainly of the dangers of doing black magic. While not admitting to belief in demons *per se*, they did admit to "forces" that will "come back to them in a very negative way." In their description of the danger, they were quite clear and plain in their tone. Zeena said, "Based on our particular religious belief system,[34] [black magic] is not at all evil to us. I wouldn't recommend it. I have to say, here and now, to work with these forces is a very precarious thing that I would not recommend." Schreck chimed in, explaining, "We don't proselytize; we are not trying to convert others. Black magic is probably the most dangerous undertaking a human being could work with." Larson, picking up on the obvious unexpected admission of the pair, said, "You're telling me black magic is *dangerous?*" Schreck emphasized the affirmative, "Extremely dangerous." Zeena spoke further, explaining, "Not only is it extremely dangerous, and not only would we say obviously the people here tonight wouldn't tamper with it ... I would even go so far to say people who just dabble in it or experiment with it, without fully understanding what they're getting into, are really doing themselves in. It will come back to them in a very negative way."[35] Larson responded, "Are you saying there are demons that could get them?" "I don't believe in evil entities," Zeena said, "I believe that through one's own abuse, use and abuse, of such forces, that is what will do them in."[36]

Story – The Danger of "Metaphorical" Satanism

The following story is from a 2021 interview with David Sinclair Smith, a current and prominent member of the Church of Satan, conducted by Ciaran Lyons.[37] Ciaran went to an awkward and dangerous depth with this Satanist, and there he confronted what the "dark energy" of "atheistic" Satanism really produces.

In discussing the issue of the meaning of Satanic rituals, David's seriousness and animation in giving his answer is very telling. He is obviously not one who thinks this is all for show. Ciaran, the

---

[34] They did not believe in the concepts of "good" and "evil."
[35] This warning is similar to the warning given to the practice of Kundalini Yoga.
[36] Larson video #2
[37] 7NEWS Spotlight, Interview by Ciaran Lyons, "Satanists Next Door," *YouTube*, 27 February 2021.

interviewer and narrator, stated, "A lot of this is performance but David believes these rituals can have real world consequences." David described the presence of a reality conjured by the rituals, saying, "You can feel it in the air, you can feel the buzz." David explained that numerous rituals he has performed have brought about their intended real-world results. He mentioned specifically "anger and destruction rituals."

As he explained, David did a curse against a neighbor who would play music very loudly, during the week, at night. About a month later, the two individuals in that house hanged themselves. "So that stopped that music," David coldly stated. Ciaran, puzzled, asked, "Do you feel guilty?" "No," David again stated plainly, adding, "Why would I cast a spell if I didn't want an outcome?" The Satanist explained his reasoning further. "I didn't go up and kill that neighbor myself, so there's no repercussions of the law coming to me and arresting me. Most people go, 'Oh, that's interesting, that's just a coincidence.' It's like, 'yeah, cool, it's a coincidence,' I don't care. The outcome, I got. So, in my view, I got a cathartic release. I got my anger out. When they played their music, I was like, 'Uh, whatever,' but eventually the music stopped."

After David finished that last statement, "eventually, the music stopped," the interviewer, Ciaran, was aghast, staring bug-eyed at the Satanist, who was quite pleased that, it seemed, his Satanic ritual led to someone's death. The hiddenness of diabolical agency becomes crystal clear in accounts like this. Ciaran's final thoughts are important to hear. He said, "Satanism surprised me. I went in thinking it was all about worshiping the devil, but it's not. Satanists don't believe in the devil, God, heaven, hell, anything. Satanists like David believe you are in control of your own universe, which is great, but I still can't get my mind around the fact that David thinks one of his curses may have ended someone's life, and he seems fine with that. There's definitely a lesson in living for now and putting yourself first, but at what cost?"

Delighting in the Danger

When many witches and other occultists perceive the danger of their craft, they often experience a sense of delight as well. "Real power can bring real change in my life," they might be thinking.

They are often blinded as a result of the many wounds which have driven them in the direction of the occult, and they either do not see, or do not want to see, how dangerous it is.[38] One witch said, "When a money spell led to me finding £10 in the street, I became convinced I was channeling powers – dangerous ones – beyond my comprehension. I was delighted."[39]

In 1997, Zeena and Nikolas Schreck believed the "powers of darkness" they were working with were their "friends and peers." Eventually, they came to realize this was not the case, and that Satan is a very dangerous force with which to work or to be associated, and with which they no longer desired to be connected. Exorcists are very clear on this reality about the motives of demons. "Demons are not your friends," Msgr. Rossetti said. "They even hate each other. They are vicious sadists and enjoy making people suffer."[40]

Dr. Richard Gallagher, who has worked with exorcists for decades on cases of diabolical harassment, in telling the story of the Satanic "princess," said that she, while addicted to the power granted through the devil, knew Satan was dangerous. As he wrote in his book, when the two of them were discussing her work with the exorcists, she said, "But Father Jacques keeps telling me I have to turn to them [Jesus], whatever that means, and renounce Satan. Renounce Satan! Are you kidding me? How can I do that? Who knows what will happen to me? This isn't someone you want against you. Trust me, I know. He's punished me plenty already."[41] In the end, hooked on the power of the occult, she stopped returning to meet with Dr. Gallagher and the exorcist, and was never freed from the cult or liberated from the possession.

I asked John if he ever had a dread of the diabolical when he was deep into the occultic practices that specifically summoned demons. He stated that he rarely had a dread of the demons he worked with, which he blamed on a poorly formed conscience. He also explained that occult practice included a process of desensitization such that, by the time you should be feeling dread, you are not. It created a bit

---

[38] CCC 1791. Repeated sin can lead to the blinding of the person's conscience, leading them to willingly commit more and perhaps greater evils in the future, for which the person *will be* morally responsible.

[39] *The Guardian*, October 31, 2020, "I Became Convinced I was Channelling Powers: My Life as a Teenage Witch."

[40] Rossetti, *Diary*, 173.

[41] Gallagher, *Demonic Foes*, 67

of a split personality: you are not afraid of the thing even though you know you should be. John pointed out that, like angels, an unveiled encounter with demons would terrify us. Sacred Scripture depicts numerous encounters with even good angels in which the person who beholds them is struck with fear, though not terror, while encounters with a demon bring both. As a result, he said demons will put on "masks," disguising themselves as benevolent spirits in order to communicate with us in a manner that does not scare us away.

Therese shared a similar view of demons. She added that she would have terrifying experiences when it was not expected, so she would talk herself through it, convincing herself that there was really no need to be afraid if she simply understood better what was happening. She spent a lot of energy trying to make things make sense even though there was a division in her mind and she knew it really *didn't* make sense. Evil things would happen to her especially at night (which is very common with the diabolical and not to be confused with normal nightmares), but she would not connect it to what she was doing as an occultist during the day.

The invocation of spirits and demons, as one would expect, and as depicted in Fred Wolff's story above, can still appear in more frightening ways than expected, even if the occultist has grown numb to the danger. Therese once participated in a ritual in which she summoned a demon to come into her house. When the entity manifested, the whole house creaked and groaned as if some great weight had come to rest upon it. It was clear to her, and to the others in the house, that the demon had clearly responded to the summoning, and that they had made a big mistake. This summoning marked a turning point in their spiritual journey, which, by God's grace, would soon lead them out of the occult.

Blessed Bartolo Longo, and the story of his consecration as a Satanic priest, provides another example of how occultists see the danger and yet, knowing this, persist in the practice. The documentary described it in the following way:

> At his Satanic ordination, he fell into a trance and communicated with numerous spirits. At the moment of his Satanic consecration, there was an enormous bolt of thunder, blasphemous disembodied shrieks filled the air, lightning flashed, and the building shook,

terrifying Bartolo. Later on, Bartolo would describe how, in the rites of his blasphemous ordination, he promised his soul to a spirit guide, a demon which shook the walls and manifested itself with blasphemous shrieks.[42]

It should be noted that these sorts of encounters, terrifying with inexplicable preternatural manifestations, are not uncommon in the occult. In the stories of Therese summoning a demon into her home, and of Bl. Bartolo Longo summoning a demon as his spirit guide, the diabolical presence appeared in strikingly similar and horrifying ways. The point here is clear: occultists are all in over their heads and many stay in the occult until an extraordinary grace from God is offered and accepted. To the occultists, the diabolical is both extremely enticing and also cripplingly terrifying: a religious slavery with no match in the visible world.

What occultists need to hear is that the One True God, the Most Blessed Trinity, is not like any other "god" they have experienced. As He made clear in the test of Abraham, He does not desire the vicious sacrifices of the pagan religions. As He makes evident in the Sacraments, He wants to gently bring us into communion with Him through the comforting means of the various elements of the earth. He makes us His children through the pouring of water and the sacred words of His Holy Name. He feeds us His supernatural life through the appearance of the common food of bread and wine which He, by a gentle but almighty power, has transubstantiated into His very Body and Blood. He speaks to us of love and obedience to laws which protect us from, rather than expose us to, harm and evil. He promises to transfigure us into His own image if we become His friends in love and obedience. He promises that the way of being His disciple is not burdensome, saying, "My yoke is easy and My burden light." He, who is "meek and humble of heart," proved His love by both dying for us and breaking us free from the bonds of death in His glorious Resurrection. There is no other God like this, and those who embrace Him fully, as the great Saints have done throughout history, have left a stunning testimony

---

[42] Mary's Dowry, Bl. Bartolo Longo documentary, YouTube

of the truth of Christ's promises. This is what occultists need to know, and what former occultists have already encountered.

Chapter Twelve

The Occult vs. The Church

A big concern of people who are both familiar and unfamiliar with the occult is whether the occult is motivated by a specific agenda to attack or destroy the Church. Prior to doing this research, I could only speculate, and that speculation leaned in the affirmative. Why would groups who, knowingly or unknowingly, summon and fraternize with demons, cast spells, celebrate immorality, seek power and control over the world and over others, and celebrate the image of Satan as the eternal rebel, not also, at the same time, possess a secret or public hatred for the Catholic Church? The work of exorcists, which I sought to collect in *Slaying Dragons*, makes it clear that the demons know the truth: the Catholic Church possesses the supernatural power, communicated through her Sacraments and sacramentals, to impart the sanctifying Truth about God, and to undermine and totally decimate the Kingdom of Satan. With these things in mind, one would think that, within the occult, there would indeed be a hatred for the True Faith. Anyone thinking this would be correct.

Since the occult is clearly a diabolical fabrication and spiritual counterfeit used to pull souls away from God and into perdition, any hatred for the Church would first begin within the demons themselves, the ones who "pull the strings" within the occult. The Church is fully aware of this hatred on the part of the demons and has no fear about it. Our Lord made a decisive promise to the Church in the person of St. Peter when He said, "Thou art Peter; and upon this rock I will build My Church, and the gates of Hell shall not prevail against it."[1] A successor of St. Peter, Pope Leo XIII, explained this further when condemning the occultic Freemasonic organization in his encyclical *Humanum Genus*. "The race of man," he

---

[1] Matt 16:18 DR

explained, after the Fall, split into "two diverse and opposite parts," one being "the kingdom of God on earth, namely, the true Church of Jesus Christ," the other being "the kingdom of Satan, in whose possession and control are all whosoever follow the fatal example of their leader and of our first parents, those who refuse to obey the divine and eternal law, and who have many aims of their own in contempt of God, and many aims also against God."[2]

The occultic Freemasons, the primary motivator for Pope Leo XIII's explanation of the "two kingdoms," is also a "behind-the-scenes" source of inspiration for many forms of the occult, ranging completely across both the *soft* and the *dark* occult. In 1884, when this encyclical came out, Leo XIII observed that "partisans of evil" were combining together, "led on or assisted" by the Freemasons. These groups were "no longer making any secret of their purposes" and were "boldly rising up against God Himself, ... planning the destruction of holy Church publicly and openly." Their purpose was of "utterly despoiling the nations of Christendom, if it were possible, of the blessings obtained for us through Jesus Christ our Saviour."[3] Looking back, from our day to his, we can see the wars and uprisings, the rationalism and destruction of faith, the restrictions on the Church and the cowardice of some of her own shepherds, and the weakness and compromise on her ability to communicate the True Faith in the face of an apparently unstoppable secularization of the world. All this may rightly be attributed to both the activity of groups like the Freemasons, effectively secularizing the nations,[4] and the growing weakness of the Church as she imprudently sought to build bridges and establish dialogue with a world that was no longer interested in her message.[5] As a result, the occult and the secular world feel empowered both to ignore the Church's teachings and to actively work to undermine her presence and influence in the world.

---

[2] Leo XIII, *Humanum Genus* 1.

[3] Leo XIII, *Humanum Genus* 2.

[4] As seen in the details of the warnings and criticisms of the sect by various Popes.

[5] As seen in the warnings of Pope Paul VI about the "smoke of Satan" that entered the Church after the Second Vatican Council. This smoke was rising within the world itself when Pope John XXIII said he wanted to "open the windows of the Church" to interact better with the world.

Occultists are Within Society

Exorcists, experienced pastors, former occultists, and active Satanists all state that Satanists, as one branch of the occult, are in every level of society. Their ultimate agenda, and the means of carrying it out, are not publicly stated but we can easily discern its nature and its purpose, and can often easily discern its presence and activity, in the same way that the Popes have been able to do with Freemasonry. Freemasonry itself, like the occult in our age, is also widely present within the culture, on a level that easily surpasses that of occultists.[6]

Betty Brennan, a convert from Satanism, has given numerous testimonies about what she learned in her time with this religion. Referring to people in the "upper echelons" of Satanism, she said, "In the fourth, fifth, and sixth levels," this included doctors, lawyers, physicians, and psychologists. These are the ones calling the shots and pushing a higher agenda, but, she said, people in the world are distracted by the lower level Satanists who are hooked on drugs.[7] Satanist David Sinclair Smith, in his interview with Ciaran, claimed there are people in all fields of business, including politicians, who are Satanists, many of whom he has seen at Church of Satan gatherings.[8] According to Geraldo Rivera's documentary, Anton LaVey, the founder of the Church of Satan, and Michael Aquino, the founder of the Temple of Set, have both said the same thing.[9] Fr. Louis has also pointed out that, in his home country in Africa, in order for people to excel in business and politics, it is often demanded that the person engage in occultic rituals.

John gave his explanation of the structure and diabolical nature of occultism as it is organized in the world, especially the explicitly darker forms like Satanism. Satan, he said, works through human channels, placing himself at the top. It is like an organization with a hierarchy, where a man progresses to higher authority and privilege through various means. The higher he rises, the more he becomes aware of, the more benefits he accrues, and the more danger he is in. It is very much like the known structure of Freemasonry, with the

---

[6] According to msana.com, there are roughly one million Freemasons in the USA.
[7] Betty Brennan testimony
[8] Ciaran YouTube docuseries
[9] Geraldo documentary

degrees by which a man, through various oaths and curses, rises to higher awareness of the secrets of the craft, binding himself to greater retribution for defection, and acquiring the benefits of the power of the organization.

Most people do not make it to the higher levels of the occult, John added, and most people would not want to if they understood what it meant. At the top is Satan himself, in the middle is the pleasure and power that the true devotee is seeking, and at the bottom are the "useful idiots," similar to those Betty Brennan mentioned above. As a man works his way up the occult ladder, he becomes possessed by the Satanic entity that has chosen him.[10] John shared an enlightening anecdote about his personal experience climbing the occult ladder. In one occult system, when he was being trained to be a leader, John was taught to do the *opposite* of whatever anyone asked of him when they came to him for a spell or a ritual. If they asked for a ritual for health, he was taught to impart an illness instead, for example. He refused to comply with this and was, instead, cursed by his trainer and spiritually attacked by another magician, who broke up his marriage, caused health problems for him, and attacked him in his sleep.[11] "To climb the ladder in the occult is an idiotic decision," he said.

Not All Occultists Have the Same Goals

A key distinction needs to be made since the occult is such a wide and varying conglomerate of spiritualities. Despite the over-arching anti-Catholic goals of the occult, most low-level *soft* occultists are not particularly concerned about the Church one way or the other. These include the common New-Ager, Yoga practitioner, astrology-seeker, and relatively new Wiccan. When you analyze the perspectives of experienced witches, it gets much more complicated. Many witches, like the soft occultists, are completely uninterested in the Church. However, some witches do have a strong aversion, even a hatred, toward Christianity. Similarly, there is more

---

[10] This stage is not one which the common occultist reaches. This is usually achieved in darker rituals of more explicitly demonic forms of the occult.

[11] An example of the "astral attacks" that occultists are on guard against. This, of course, is done through the agency of the diabolical.

likely either a mockery or a hatred of the Church present in the philosophies and rituals of black magic and Satanism.

Christopher explained what he saw, stating, "Most occultists are unaware of a specific antipathy to the Catholic Faith. It's dangerous[12] to associate the *many* occult groups and practitioners with the specifically Satanic occultists." Among the many occultists he knew who rejected Christianity, they did not specifically reject the Faith itself but the poor example given by Christians who were behaving, as he put it, more like Luciferians.

Witches, for example, vary greatly in their thoughts and interests related to the Church: some witches, filled with an aversion to Christianity, will not go near a Church; others simply have no regard for Christianity at all; others never give it a thought; while others will attack the Church but only indirectly. Helena said that Dianic Wiccans would target pro-life groups, but not for the reason a Catholic would expect. "From what we did," she said, "it wasn't just this idea of targeting pro-life groups, and it wasn't usually against the women who participated in such groups. Our focus was on the *patriarchy* in general. Cursing them, driving our energy and various entities to make them fail: bring about a matriarchy and everything will fall into place."

Andrew, as a Thelemite,[13] said that when he was in the occult, his greatest hatred was reserved for Christianity, a manifestation of his hatred for "conventional religions" and his having been brought up in the West. Further, he was still filled with resentment for his Protestant upbringing, which increased that hatred. Thus, for him, the occult that he practiced did not *explicitly* stir a hatred for the Church, though the devil will seek to fuel a hatred for the Church whenever, and by whatever means, he can, the occult being a prime place and opportunity for doing so.

The Mission of The Occult

The goal of the occult, as Andrew described it, is essentially to dissolve Christendom completely and recreate the world in its own image. In the world today, everyone can see the proposed "New

---

[12] In the sense that it will lead to unnecessary judgments upon low level occultists, who have no agenda against the Church.

[13] A follower of the occultism of Aleister Crowley.

World Order" and the "Great Reset" on the lips of basically all global elites and leaders. The "New World Order" is part of the continued effort to dissolve the Church, eradicate Christianity, "reset" societies across the globe, and impose a new moral system on the world that is built upon man and not upon God, Andrew observed. The "Old World Order" would thus be Christendom and the Church, the Reign of Christ in both the spiritual and the temporal spheres. The modern strength of the occult, he said, we must understand to be *not* a random appearance at a time when there is a clear global shift toward what may be the final inauguration of the sought-after "New World Order," but rather as part of this very effort.

These strong views of Andrew's should not be dismissed as the "confused ramblings" of someone who was once wrapped up in the occult. Whether he realized it or not, Andrew's views are congruent with Pope Leo XIII's views, who spoke similarly in 1884. He said,

> Now, the masonic sect produces fruits that are pernicious and of the bitterest savour. For…that which is their ultimate purpose forces itself into view – namely, the utter overthrow of that whole religious and political *order* of the world which the Christian teaching has produced, and the substitution of a new state of things in accordance with their ideas, of which the foundations and laws shall be drawn from mere naturalism.[14]

This condemnation of Freemasonry must raise an additional red flag against the modern occult movements, whose founders were all influenced, in some way, by this secret society bent on destroying the Church.[15] In light of the concerns about both the rise of the occult

---

[14] Pope Leo XIII, *Humanum Genus*, 10. *Emphasis* mine. "Naturalism" refers to a belief that rejects the supernatural destiny of man, seeing nature to be all that is needed, where nature is without defect and all natural instincts are legitimate to follow.

[15] Significant leaders in the modern occult movements were members of Freemasonry or indirectly associated and influenced by it, such as "irregular Freemason" Aleister Crowley (modified Ordo Templi Orientis and founded Thelema), Freemason Gerald Gardner (founded Wicca and influenced witchcraft), Helena Blavatsky and Freemason Henry Steel Olcott (founded Theosophy, influenced by Spiritualism, which influenced the New Age movement), and Freemasons Woodman, Westcott, and Mathers (founders of the Golden

and the rise of the New World Order, I once asked an exorcist if the religion of the Antichrist could possibly be witchcraft, Satanism, and the occult, and, during that reign of evil, might we see pentagrams and other occultic symbols all over society. He replied, "Absolutely."

Larger occultic groups, Andrew observed (from his perspective as a former practitioner of Thelema), gave the clear impression, from their practices and rituals, that they held a strong hatred of God and sought to mock the Catholic Church. Here, he referred to the Ecclesia Gnostica Catholica, the "ecclesiastical arm" of the Ordo Templis Orientis (OTO), the international fraternal society dedicated to Crowley's "Law of Thelema." He also expressed a certainty that there are explicitly malicious occultists in the world that "seek nothing more than chaos, destruction, death, and damnation for others." Here, he referred to those who actually worship the devil, which would include many forms of Satanism, and, he said, likely include even the so-called "atheistic" Satanists, when the facts are analyzed.

Philomena described the occult as the counter-revolution against the Church, the latter being God's revolution against sin and death. The occult is undoing everything that is a fruit of the Incarnation.[16] "Once you bring together all the information, the light bulb goes off and it all makes perfect sense," she said. "Remember the testimony from Bella Dodd, for example.[17] Those infiltrators went into parishes and now we have the mess we have."

One American exorcist said that exorcists are currently concerned about the confrontational and "in your face" attitude that a lot of occultists, including Satanists and witches, have adopted in recent years. This shows that they are not hiding anymore, they feel equal and empowered to be in the culture, and they are comfortable insulting the Church in public. It appears that they have crossed a

---

Dawn, which influenced Wicca and Thelema). Anton LaVey states (in *The Satanic Rituals*) that every occult group has Masonic origins and that he pulled some of his rituals (for *The Satanic Bible*) from the texts used by the Golden Dawn.

[16] Again, this is the precise aim of Freemasonry.

[17] Bella Dodd was a Communist who converted to Catholicism through Ven. Fulton Sheen. She testified to Congress about the plan of Communists to infiltrate different facets of the country. She also told various people that Communists placed their members into seminaries and claimed that some of these Communists had risen to the ranks of Bishop and Cardinal. This was stated in the 1950s and 1960s. Though there is some uncertainty about her statements, the bad fruit we see among the Catholic hierarchy today would easily support their accuracy.

line very recently and have taken the level of their confrontation up several notches. All this, as the exorcist said, "means something." Italian exorcist Father François-Marie Dermine, who has worked as an exorcist for close to thirty years, said there is a growth of "real Satanic groups," which used to be merely the exception, and that this indicates that "Satanism has come out in the open." He added, "We must be very careful about it."[18]

John observed that most of the occult activity is directly against Catholicism, not Protestantism. From the mockery of the Church's rites and liturgies, to the undermining of the Church's morals, to the inversion of all the good that the Church brings to cultures and societies, the occult's *modus operandi* is to eradicate the Catholic Church. A good historical example of this Satanic hatred for the Catholic Church specifically is in the life and times of Blessed Bartolo Longo in the 1860s. After his consecration as a Satanic priest, he began offering Satanic worship and preaching against the Catholic Church. He would publicly ridicule Catholicism, priests, and everyone who was connected with the Catholic Faith. The whole thing eventually took a great toll on him physically and psychologically. Another interesting point to his story is that, similar to today, the Catholic Church was battling, in the time of Bl. Bartolo Longo, an increased interest in Spiritism and the occult. The occultic practices of people at that time, also similar to today, were coupled with an attitude of hostility against the Pope and the Church.[19]

A further historical example, which gives significant evidence of the occultic and anti-Catholic aims of Freemasonry, comes from St. Maximilian Kolbe. He reported that he witnessed, in 1917, the Freemasons parading through the streets of Rome, even in front of St. Peter's Basilica, declaring, "Satan must reign in the Vatican. The Pope will be his slave." In addition to this, St. Maximilian Kolbe said

---

[18] *National Catholic Register*, December 4, 2020, "Longtime Exorcist: Satanism is Growing in Western Societies." The statements in this paragraph mirror the concerns of Pope Leo XIII quoted earlier, in which he sounded the alarm about the "bold" opposition of the Freemasons in which they "publicly and openly" worked to destroy the Church. Further, while modern Freemasonry has sought to put on a friendlier face, hiding behind a philanthropic façade, the occult appears to have taken over the role of leading the direct confrontation against the Church.

[19] This was also during the time when Freemasonry was open and hostile to the Church, receiving condemnations from Pope Bl. Pius IX.

that Freemasonry openly professed, "We will conquer the Catholic Church not by argumentation, but rather with moral corruption."[20] The moral corruption, which is intrinsic to the occult, and which is rampant in the world and in the Church today, is a clear indicator of the success of this effort.

The Occult Mocks Catholic Rituals

Andrew said that, while the occult draws people in through the claim of revealing what is hidden and introducing them to secret truth and power, Christianity is the true religion of mystery. The Sacraments themselves communicate this, called *mysterion* in Greek, drawing us in to the sacred mystery of God Himself. In the words of Institution during the Mass, the expression *mysterium fidei,* the "mystery of faith," is inserted, referring to the True Presence of Christ in the Eucharist. In one of the most popular and powerful Catholic devotions, the Holy Rosary, the Church refers to the events in the life of Jesus and Mary as "mysteries." These *mysteries,* thanks to the Incarnation of Jesus Christ, are not secret but public. In this public revelation of the mysteries of God, it must be understood that no aspect of the power of those mysteries is lost. They are now made manifest for the whole world to embrace. The occult, as an inversion of the Truth, actually proclaims that the mysteries, the supposed truths about life, are *hidden* and only accessible through dark and esoteric rites which also necessitate certain perversions of Truth and goodness and the human person.

Andrew said, "I think, in terms of the occultist and the magician in particular, the demons are making a mockery not only of the good things God has promised us through His Church but also of the priesthood." He was referring to the fact that the famous occultist, Eliphas Levi, was actually in seminary to become a priest before leaving to pursue occult studies. He highlighted an important example, stating, "Levi wrote in one of his works that to be a magician is to be in direct competition with the Catholic priesthood." This mockery of the priesthood extends to a mockery of the sacramental practices of the Church as well. Lucy, now that she is

---

[20] Br. Francis Mary Kalvelage FI, *Kolbe: Saint of the Immaculata.* (Ignatius Press, 2014), 31-32

Catholic, and still uses incense in her home devotions,[21] "for prayers, not spells!", sees the devil's mockery of the True Faith quite clearly. She said, "The direct twisting of what the Church does, in what Satan does, is very telling."

From her time in a Satanic group, Betty Brennan said she realized that Satanists truly knew the value of the Church's Sacraments. "Every Satanic ritual, in the higher echelons," she said, "is a take-off of the sacramental rites that are used in the Roman Catholic Church. And that is a powerful testimony, because they know, and they understand, and they're terrified of, the power within the sacramental Church."[22] Andrew gave some examples of this from his own experience with Thelema. The rituals he practiced used Greek, Latin, and Hebrew, as well as incense. In the language of this occult group, the word "Thelema," meaning *will*, was stolen from Our Lord's usage of the term in the Garden of Gethsemane.[23] Further, the Thelema principle, "Love is the law, love under will," uses the Greek word *agape*. This, as he said, is "another bastardization of the Faith," because, he added, "'Love,' in this sense, is but a slave to the individual 'Will,' and therefore serves the individual and is *not* self-sacrificial, as it is in the Christian sense." The twisting of these concepts, he said, can be confusing and deceiving to poorly catechized Catholics who wander into the occult, see the language, and notice that it sounds very familiar.

Andrew also noticed that the occult inverts the image of Our Lady. For him, it began with his exposure to Wicca. In Wicca, practitioners venerate a horned god and a goddess, and deities from various pantheons, including many other goddesses. A constant element in Wicca is something called the divine feminine. In this, they worship the sexual and fertile nature of woman, the fact of her carrying a child in the womb and giving birth. He saw this as an obvious parallel to Our Lady. Some Wiccans, he added, see Our Lady as an icon of the divine feminine, almost a Gnostic interpretation, while other occultists revile her with horrendous insults.

There is also a parallel to Our Lady in Thelema which is a serious perversion. Thelema employs the image of "the whore of

---

[21] "Three Kings," from a Church supplier, she added.
[22] Brennan testimony
[23] Matt 26:42

Babylon," again stolen from Sacred Scripture.[24] This feminine image is perverse and liberated, "very coarse, straightforward, and brash – an inversion," he noted. "This is what demons really like to do: take the holy and flip them in a mockery of God and the Church. Rather than a straight-up attack on Our Lady," he added, "they take the image, give it another name, flip it upside down, and use that to mock her – that is how they acclimate you toward an aversion to Our Lady – you have this perverted and distorted image of her place in reality." "Demons," he added, "rather than attacking Our Lady directly, distort her ever so slightly. They are slightly poisoning the water, the teaching, and the image."

The inversion of Catholic devotions also includes that of the desire to have a patron Saint interceding for you and watching over you. Philomena said that when you are practicing Thelema or earth magic, you think it is your *personal spirit* guiding you (like a patron Saint) but it is not. Andrew, in his practice of Thelema, sought to enter into conversation with his HGA, or "Holy Guardian Angel," a very specific diabolical mockery of the guardian angel Our Lord gives to each of us.[25] The spirit guide or HGA, Philomena said, is structured in a similar way in earth magic and any kind of paganism, in imitation of the Catholic concept of a patron Saint, but clearly different in the way things play out. "There were weird things happening in the house that were clearly demonic," she said. "When you connect with a spirit guide, a dangerous thing occurs, especially when they give you a name and claim to be your own personal 'spirit guide'."

Fr. Anselm warned that, in light of this mockery of the Catholic Church's rituals and devotions, it *must not be thought that we must abandon such rituals* in favor of the bland, or non-existent, rituals of the majority of Protestantism and of many modern expressions of Catholicism, as if this blandness or absence is now justified in light of the fact that the occult also enjoys the use of rituals. The truth is that the occult makes a mockery of the Church as Satan makes a mockery of God, seeking to make himself *as* God, and have us serve him *instead* of God. Satan perverts and inverts all that is good; he creates counterfeits in order to deceive. Satan proposes alternative

---

[24] Rev Ch. 17
[25] Matt 18:10

"goods" that appear to be or to resemble the real thing, but which contain a bitter poison. In seeing what Satan hates, we can learn more clearly what we must love.

Occultists Attack Churches

From the testimonies of former Satanists and witches, supported by the experiences of exorcists, we have learned the shocking truth that, yes, many occultists seek to infiltrate, disrupt, and desecrate Churches. My specific questions along these lines, to former occultists and exorcists, about the reality of occultists seeking to steal consecrated Hosts from Churches, opened up the conversation to all sorts of other things that occultists seek to do against the Catholic Church.

The theft of consecrated Hosts is indeed a reality though not a thing in which all occultists engage.[26] Philomena clarified, saying, "Yes, people really do sneak into Masses to steal Hosts. It is the greatest prize, so to speak, for groups like Thelema, Satanic groups, and other forms of black magic." Fr. Stephen told me the story of an incident at his parish where a man once walked off with the Blessed Sacrament. The priest blamed it in part on strange local practices that were in place during the Covid era, where priests allowed people to take the Eucharist back to their pews and consume the Host on their own. There was a concern that the man was doing the same thing at other parishes and had some connections to the occult, though his connection to the occult remained speculation. The man also exhibited violent tendencies and there was also the thought that he was primarily motivated by a mental illness rather than malice. Despite this lack of clarity regarding his motives, the local police, when speaking "off the record" to individuals at the parish, shared that they had been coming across occult and black magic groups in that area, and had been finding the remnants of the presence of these groups and their rituals in places such as cemeteries. The police also said that they had been assisting other Churches who had also had encounters with occultists trying to steal the Blessed Sacrament,

---

[26] For more information on the history of the occult seeking to steal and desecrate consecrated Hosts, look into the "Eucharistic Miracles of the World" on the website TheRealPresence.org and read through the accounts, many of which contain such stories.

unrelated to Fr. Stephen's case. Over the last ten years, the police said there had been more than just this one individual, though they did not elaborate further.

It is claimed by some that Satanists can tell the difference between a consecrated and an unconsecrated Host, while others, like Fr. Andrew Trapp, have wondered whether this is really true. Fr. Trapp, spending a brief time in France many years ago, and leading a prayer group there, met a man named Nicolas who eventually told the group that he had been a Satanist in his past. Fr. Trapp, having never met someone like Nicolas, began to ask him several "burning questions." One question was whether, as a Satanist, he could determine whether a Host was consecrated or not. Nicolas stated that, yes, he was able to know if a Host was consecrated. Fr. Trapp recalled, "I asked him in amazement, 'But how were you able to know?!?' He looked at me and the words he spoke are forever burned in my memory: 'Because of the hate,' he said. 'Because of the burning hate I would feel toward that host, apart from all the others'."[27]

Not every occultist is interested in stealing the Blessed Sacrament from Churches. Adelaide said that, as a witch, she was clueless about the Blessed Sacrament, thinking it was just a symbol. Helena said, "Myself, I didn't go into Church at all. The thought would make me feel sick." She was involved in Dianic Wicca, traditional witchcraft, and was also a hedgewitch. A hedgewitch is a solitary witch, very involved in herbs and healing; a "kitchen witch," the old healer in a village. It is hedgewitches who are more likely to say they could be a "Christian witch." Dianic Wiccans, she said, "wouldn't be anywhere near a Church." Those in traditional witchcraft would be very few in number in a Church, she speculated, while you may have ten or so hedgewitches in a Church. However, she added, "I do know people that did both. There were those that went in for the specific reason of working magic – usually we were against the patriarchy as we saw it. We wanted to bring about a matriarchy and going into a Church, working your energy, was a way to do this." Within Dianic Wicca, she added, some Catholic groups would be targeted. These primarily included pro-life work. Outside of Dianic Wicca, and among other people she knew, there

---

[27] Fr. Andrew Trapp, SaintFactory.com, April 24, 2004, "Satanism and the Eucharist"

were witches who would attack Christian organizations more frequently and more broadly than just regarding pro-life activity.

Though it is apparent that many Satanists target the Blessed Sacrament for desecration, even if they claim to be merely "metaphorical" Satanists, others appear to not be focused on it at all. Elizabeth said that, when she was living with the Satanist Damien, she was able to get him to go to Mass with her on two occasions. From these experiences came some interesting observations. On one occasion, they went to the modern Mass. He was able to remain in the Church all the way until the Consecration of the Precious Blood before he couldn't tolerate it any further and had to leave. She also took him to a Traditional Mass, which was a much different experience for him. He was not able to endure the *Asperges* at the beginning and had to come in after that had finished.[28] The blessing of the incense at the Offertory was the final intolerable moment, which she thinks is due to the invocation of St. Michael which that blessing entails. After this, he left, much earlier than at the modern Mass. On neither occasion did he express an interest in trying to acquire a consecrated Host.

Fr. Ermatinger pointed out that occultists do not limit themselves to the Blessed Sacrament when they desire to desecrate something. "Satanists," he wrote, "will often sacrilegiously use holy water stolen from churches in the carrying out of these types of rituals."[29] In a post on January 15, 2022, Msgr. Rossetti told a story of this very thing. A deacon once came upon a witch inside his Church (who later admitted to worshipping Satan as well) who was trying to gain access to the Blessed Sacrament but had settled for stealing holy water instead. The deacon was also a police officer and was able to convince the woman to leave immediately. When the deacon told his pastor about the incident, the pastor told him that a priest-friend of his had a parish secretary who was a Satanist. The Satanist had taken the job specifically in order to try to gain access to the Blessed Sacrament.[30]

Occultists have also been known to defile sacramentals. The Becketts told me that, among the many witchcraft items they found

---

[28] The rite, at the start of Mass, involving the sprinkling of the sanctuary and people with holy water.

[29] Ermatinger, *The Trouble with Magic*, 124.

[30] Msgr. Rossetti blog, January 15, 2022, Exorcist Diary #173

in their daughter's room, they also found a jar containing a St. Benedict medal in some sort of liquid or sludge. This idea fits with the surprising admission of a Satanist who was once handed a St. Michael medal. As reported by *Tradition, Family, and Property* (TFP)[31] Student Action, in a video on February 20, 2022, one of the members of the TFP, in conversation with a Satanist attending the *SatanCon* convention in Scottsdale, Arizona, handed him a blessed medal. As soon as he handed it to the Satanist, the latter changed the topic and said, almost spontaneously, "I'll probably defile this thing, though." When asked why, he said, "I was raised Catholic, and I am anti-Catholic with a vengeance."[32]

Fr. Maximilian reported two incidents where he learned that occultists defile sacramentals. He said there was once a woman who had been in prison and teamed up with a witch she met there. They began going to RCIA meetings together in the prison. The reason for attending these meetings, she later admitted, was to acquire blessed medals, which they then used in their rituals. Many years later, she showed up at a parish seeking to get married and to go through the RCIA process legitimately. In speaking with the priest, and admitting to this background, they realized she had a lot of diabolical issues still pursuing her from her time as a witch. In another situation, a man came to see Fr. Maximilian stating that he was possessed. The man told Fr. Maximilian that he wanted a specific number of blessed medals. He was very specific, and insistent, about the number of medals and this made Father even more suspicious than he already was at first speaking with the man. Father then refused to give him the medals and, shortly afterward, began to experience a very clear diabolical oppression, which lasted for several days. At times, it would begin to make him very irritable and agitated and he would have to run to the Chapel and pray in order to feel better. He prayed the Rosary and the Divine Mercy Chaplet over and over. He wasn't able to even talk about it with priest-friends due to the strange feeling it gave him.

Msgr. Rossetti told a disturbing story which exemplified one of the dangers of the occult and showed the extent to which God allows

---

[31] Founded in 1971, TFP "is an organization of lay Catholic Americans concerned about the moral crisis shaking the remnants of Christian civilization." (TFP.org)
[32] TFP Student Action. "Satanic Temple Event Hits Big Wall of Prayer." *YouTube*, 20 February 2022, youtube.com/watch?v=9R1vg5y4HDg

demons to act. An exorcist, who is also the pastor of a parish, annually sets out relics of the Saints for the faithful to venerate in early November. This year they were stolen by what appeared to be an occultist of some sort. As the security cameras captured, a woman in a dark coat, sitting near the relics, began to approach them. At that moment, all the security cameras went out – but for only five minutes. The film showed that, when the cameras came back on, the relics *inside* the reliquaries, but not the reliquaries themselves, had been stolen. The conclusion was that this was a theft of something sacred, not a robbery, and the malfunction of the cameras, occurring for just that key moment, pointed to the startling cooperation of the diabolical.[33]

Riaan Swiegelaar, a recent convert from Satanism, said, in a Facebook video on August 26th, 2022, that theistic Satanists "enrolled themselves in the devil's army, like Christian spiritual warriors, but as spiritual warriors for Satan." These Satanists, he explained, actively try to infiltrate Christian churches,[34] targeting the biggest ones first, which are easier to sneak into. They would disrupt the services and create chaos, but not in an obvious way. These Satanists practice chaos magic, he added. He said these big Protestant communities don't understand what is happening, adding that one "mega-Church" pastor dismissed the concerns about Satanism in the area, saying that the "New Age Jesus"[35] is the real problem. As Swiegelaar said, "No, no way, wake up!" Protestant communities like this one are specifically targeted because, he said, the Satanists know that the Protestant group is all about prosperity, and that the leaders are not filled with the Holy Spirit but are all about money. It is easy for them to infiltrate these groups and operate there. Another thing he said people are blind to is the fact that most Satanists look like normal people. Very few of them wear all black or are covered with tattoos and piercings. As a result, someone in one of these "mega-Churches" might be sitting right next to a Satanist and have no idea.

---

[33] Msgr. Rossetti blog, November 19, 2022, Exorcist Diary #216

[34] He appears to be speaking about large Protestant communities, not Catholic Churches.

[35] The false presentations of the Person of Our Lord by both heretical Christian movements and the occult itself. The latter takes Our Lord and makes a mockery of Him, presenting Him in a variety of ways that resemble Hindu religious concepts, for example.

This concept of disrupting Churches is a reality to which many others can also attest. Betty Brennan told the story of how she sought to disrupt a Church when she was a Satanist. By an arrangement of Divine Providence, she said she found herself taking a friend, Pat, to a healing Mass at a Catholic Church. At these Masses, Brennan would go inside and attempt to spiritually disrupt the Mass with certain Satanic rituals.[36] The lights in the Church would go out when this would happen, but, she added, the priest just continued with candles. Other things would occur as well but it did not stop the Masses. Pat told her once, "I go here all the time and nothing happens; but only when you're here…and you act very strange. You look terrified, sweating, and then take off."[37]

Fr. Alphonsus told me that exorcists and priests in deliverance ministry have noticed what he called "minions" hanging around Churches and seeking to cause spiritual disturbances. Father had one who would park his car in the parking lot and just sit there. After the minion left, Father would pray over that parking spot and, on the following day, the car would always be parked somewhere else.[38] Father said he knows of another pastor who had the same thing happen at his parish. Another exorcist, whom Fr. Alphonsus knows, has had a lot of experience with occultists coming into the Church and onto the parish campus, some with the ability, similar to Betty Brennan, to turn out all the lights in the parking lot.

These attacks on Churches are not random or simply out of spite toward the Faith, though the latter is definitely a motivator. An American exorcist said that the common way for a new witch to be initiated into a coven, or to make a pact with a spirit, is to desecrate a Catholic Church or commit a sacrilege on some level. He mentioned that this can include destroying a Church Missal used for Mass, defiling a Confessional in some way, or breaking into the Tabernacle. Often, the witch will document the incidents with pictures to prove that they actually had the resolve to carry out the desecration. John told me that there were sacrifices that he was required to offer as part of a ritual, which then had to be dropped off somewhere on a Church's property as the required final element of the ritual. Fr.

---

[36] She called these "endowments."

[37] Brennan testimony

[38] Eventually, one evening, he approached the car and the man gave some excuse for sitting there, drove off, and never returned.

Blaise confirmed this, stating that he had seen those ritual offerings on his own parish grounds on a few occasions, often with a red string on it, or containing parts of an animal. He knew of other priests who had found them as well, sometimes literally on their doorsteps, which would then be accompanied by some form of extraordinary diabolical activity at the parish.[39]

The Battle

"Christians are born for combat," proclaimed Pope Leo XIII, the same Pope who vehemently condemned the occultic Freemasonic organization and, by extension, all occultic groups whose aims are the same. In his 1890 encyclical, *Sapientiae Christianae*, the Holy Father called on all Christians to be bold and courageous against the enemy, lest that wild fire of error spread, destroying the intellectual habitations of man, preventing him from attaining to grace and truth and, wayward, causing him to depart from the path of salvation. The words surrounding the above quoted sentence are powerful and, issued by the Vicar of Christ, impressively encouraging:

> As St. Thomas maintains: 'Each one is under obligation to show forth his faith, either to instruct and encourage others of the faithful, or to repel the attacks of unbelievers.'[40] To recoil before an enemy, or to keep silence when from all sides such clamors are raised against truth, is the part of a man either devoid of character or who entertains doubt as to the truth of what he professes to believe. In both cases such mode of behaving is base and is insulting to God, and both are incompatible with the salvation of mankind. This kind of conduct is profitable only to the enemies of the faith, for nothing emboldens the wicked so greatly as the lack of courage on the part of the good.

---

[39] In one case, it was a diabolical infestation in the rectory, where the electrical and plumbing systems began to mysteriously malfunction until it was resolved by an exorcist.

[40] ST, IIa–IIae, qu. iii, art. 2, ad 2m.

Moreover, want of vigor on the part of Christians is so much the more blameworthy, as not seldom little would be needed on their part to bring to naught false charges and refute erroneous opinions, and by always exerting themselves more strenuously they might reckon upon being successful. After all, no one can be prevented from putting forth that strength of soul which is the characteristic of true Christians, and very frequently by such display of courage our enemies lose heart and their designs are thwarted.

Christians are, moreover, born for combat, whereof the greater the vehemence, the more assured, God aiding, the triumph: 'Have confidence; I have overcome the world.'[41] Nor is there any ground for alleging that Jesus Christ, the Guardian and Champion of the Church, needs not in any manner the help of men. Power certainly is not wanting to Him, but in His loving kindness He would assign to us a share in obtaining and applying the fruits of salvation procured through His grace.[42]

The attacks against the Church, appearing on many different fronts, including those internal to her earthly existence, must stir those who love Our Lord to greater knowledge of Him, greater love of Him, and greater dedication to His glory and the salvation of souls. Our Lord said, "With God, all things are possible."[43] St. Paul, the one who followed Him well, from his own experience confirmed, "I can do all things in Him who strengthens me."[44]

---

[41] John 16:33
[42] Pope Leo XIII, *Sapientiae Christianae*, 14.
[43] Matt 19:26
[44] Phil 4:13

Chapter Thirteen

The Occult is Full of Lies and Manipulation

Our Lord teaches us that the devil is "a liar and the father of lies." When the devil speaks, he does so "according to his nature" as a liar. The devil does not simply *tell* lies, he has become, by his corrupted nature, a *being* of lies. Just as God is Truth and, when He speaks, He speaks what is true, likewise the devil has become deception and, when he speaks, he utters only what is false. "There is no truth in him," Our Lord states. In the case of those who become bewitched by the forked tongue of Satan, such as the Jews who argued with Our Lord in the Gospel of John, they "cannot bear to hear [Christ's] word," since the will of such individuals is to "do [their] father's desires," "[their] father the devil." As a result, since they have been trained by the devil's voice, and have grown to hate the Truth and recoil from it, their corruption is so deep that Christ says against them, "*Because* I tell the truth, you do not believe Me."[1] This dangerous spiritual situation, in which the individual has developed an *aversion* to the Truth, explained to us in Our Lord's warning to the Jews, applies to all men who refuse to hear Him when He speaks.

We also see, from Sacred Scripture and from observations of the occult as it is, that Satan is also the author and master of the occult. Therefore, the occult is saturated with his lies, half-truths, deceptions, poisonous gifts, and false friendships, together creating a fantasy world in which the occultist begins to dwell. Within the occult, the first ploy of the demons is to convince the occultist to believe in an unreality: that magic is natural and uses a real (and safe) power, that occultists can control demons, that morality is dependent on the practitioner, that demons and "spirits" and "goddesses" are here to help us, and that we have the power in

---

[1] John 8:39–47

ourselves (and with their help, of course) to discover the truth and become gods. Once the occultist accepts this structure of reality, he is easily manipulated because the demons possess much greater intellects, an ability to influence us and the world around us, and a crafty and malicious will unimaginable to us bodily creatures.

The occult should be regarded as a real and complicated danger. Dabbling in it can be explained through a variety of metaphors which highlight the naïveté of playing or associating with elements evidently dangerous. The occult is also very subtle in the beginning. The devil wants to establish a presence in the person's life first by enticing them through certain "innocent" behaviors. He then latches on in a secret place in the soul, often completely hidden from the person. From there, the demon will pull and tug at the person's mind and heart, and the more open and responsive the person is, the more this particular temptation will be successful. The demons are dedicated to getting results, and they will patiently chip away at a person's resolve and conscience.

Fr. Cyprian said it is common for a person to have a diabolical influence in his life as the result of simply a casual encounter with the occult. "They may not even be aware of the influence but it is there because they have not fully repented of the occult involvement," he said. The influence could appear as an oppression or a bad relationship with a relative that spans a long time. Fr. Ambrose added that approaching the occult with ignorance and naïveté is like approaching a lion in a cage and sticking your hand in to pet it. "Ignorance," he said, "does not keep the devil, the lion, from biting off your hand!" The people that Fr. Dominic assisted who had been using Ouija boards or doing tarot card readings, "were dabbling or seeking entertainment out of boredom or a much-less-severely-felt need and found themselves dealing with things beyond what they'd bargained for."

Bait and Switch

As with Eve, the first step for the demons is to convince the person that the occult is safe and will bring them happiness and fulfillment. Some occultists begin with the impression that they can use the occult for good, to help others; others simply want the power to control their lives and obtain happiness by their own means.

"There is power in the occult," they think, "which does not have to pass through an institution or higher authority." They feel like they can tap into what amounts to limitless power and potential and, for the majority, as with every man's thought should he win the lottery, he will use this power only for good. This does not apply to all occultists, as some do have malicious intentions, but many are at least partially blinded by the thought that they might be altruistic in their practice.

When Lucy began her occultic practices, she had a desire to know the future, control things, help others, and have knowledge of the supernatural. The allure of being a psychic presented a perfect inversion of all these desires, which the devil indeed manipulated as he led her into the occult. Her goal then became to open a business helping herself, loved ones, and other people by being able to tell them what the future would bring for them. She said she was never afraid of what she was doing because she was convinced that what she was doing was not wrong. When Helena began her occult practices, and attempted her first spell, she said, "I was overcome with a deep feeling of oppression and that what I was doing was wrong." Despite that, she continued. She dismissed that fear as simply her "programming." "After all," she added, "Christianity was pervasive in society and I just thought I was letting it color my thoughts."

Regarding the appearance of goodness in the occult, Lucy said, "While some individual practices might not seem evil, they are simply part of a much bigger plan to destroy, wreak havoc and essentially lead a soul to hell. So yes, it is evil." The occult, as is clear from these and other examples, only leads to misery. It promises to be exciting, empowering, and thrilling, but, as Philomena said, "There is nothing good about being in the occult – I mean absolutely, 100%, unequivocally – nothing good!" Despite what occultists think they are getting, "What they really find is an empty void." For Philomena, this manifested itself by bringing "abuse of all kinds in the house," in addition to stranger things. She added, "There were things happening in the house that were weird and clearly demonic."

For Andrew, the absence of joy or true pleasure in what he was doing was not apparent until he left the occult. Looking back, he can see this clearly. He added, "The enjoyment of my occultic practice was solely the illusion and the thrill of basically having what I considered to be manifest *proof* that the supernatural and preternatural do exist." However, simply knowing that these demons were real did not steer him toward happiness and fulfillment or joy but plunged his life into lies and darkness and diabolical oppression.

The Pseudo-Miracles of the Demons

In the occult, the "dark powers," goddesses, energy of the Universe, spirits, demons, or whatever the occultist might call them, promise to impart gifts and powers and often do. One danger of the occult is that the demons do give occultists some of what they ask. However, these are not miraculous abilities of "the gods" but abilities natural to the demons. As Msgr. Rossetti pointed out, "What seems miraculous to us when demons are acting is really just natural for them."[2] Thus, people need the wisdom and teachings of the Church so they will know how to discern the pseudo-miracles paraded before them meant to deceive them in their naïveté.

This apparent miraculous power of the demons was described by Fr. Ermatinger in the story of a man who, venting to another man at a bar about his employment woes, was taken by the stranger back to his house in order to "help" him. There, the new acquaintance opened a Satanic altar, performed some rituals, and then promised the man that he would receive money and a job offer in the next few weeks. These two things then happened exactly as the Satanist described. The man then went and asked a priest if he should keep the money (a legitimate refund check which came in the mail) and the job (which he had earlier applied for) or if they were gifts from Satan which he should reject. The priest counseled the man that, while demons often *predict* the future and promise good things to come, as if they themselves are the source of this thing, what the demon is actually doing is simply telling the person what the demon knows is already happening elsewhere in the world and which will soon impact the individual. The knowledge which the demons possess, about our world and all that is happening in it, is vaster and more

---

[2] Rossetti, *Diary,* 85.

comprehensive than we could imagine, and they know exactly how to use it to deceive.[3]

Situations like these can be analyzed rationally which will allow the truth of the matter to become clear. From Andrew's experience, curses and spells do not reside in the realm of objective reality. There is no way to verify that they operate as a cause which produces an effect. He said, "There is no way of telling if it works because bad things happen to people all the time; there is no way to connect it back to the issuing of the curse, no way to ascertain that there was a connection."[4] The impact of believing there is a connection takes one into the realm of fantasy. "It causes you to lie to yourself," he said, "and believe things that don't make sense and don't hold up to scrutiny."

Despite the fact that the deception can be unmasked, demons will still respond when people cast spells, summon them, or make pacts with them or "spirits" in order to become wealthy and powerful. Exorcists frequently observe this to be the case. Fr. Louis said, "People will make pacts with the devil and wealth will come quickly." This has lured many people deeper into the occult. Often, the demons will use this ability to attempt to persuade a person to stay in the occult, at the moment they might be considering leaving, which would have removed the person from the demon's reach.

Demons can also conjure up these gifts without even being invoked, in an attempt to orchestrate external events and steer someone away from a holy path. Fr. Alphonsus was working with a man who his deliverance team had concluded was possessed. The man was living in another state where there was no exorcist, so the man decided to move to Fr. Alphonsus' area to get the help he needed. Father and others helped him find a place to live and work for that time. Father warned the man that the devil would likely do certain things to try to stop him from getting to the exorcism, and he was one hundred percent correct. As soon as the man quit his job, determined to move and look for work near Fr. Alphonsus, all the "dream companies" and "dream jobs" the man had always wanted began to contact him. They were calling and begging his parents to get his number to call and offer him these dream jobs, which were

---

[3] Ermatinger, *The Trouble with Magic*, 26.

[4] This is a good example of a former occultist sharing the perspective that curses are not real.

nowhere near Fr. Alphonsus. Seeing this as exactly what he had cautioned the man about, Father warned him, "This is demonic. They would never give you the time of day beforehand and now they are begging?"

Deceived

Lucy said she did not realize that she was making the decision to delve into occultic practices when she first started dabbling. At the time, she did not see that what she was doing was that unusual. Gabriel said the descent into the occult can begin with very subtle things like *manifesting change* in your life, *positive thinking* to cause the change you desire, astrology, and Ouija boards. All these things are looked at as fun games, but, he stressed, "they are really doorways to the demonic and the New Age." He added, "They won't tell you it's a religion but these things are practiced by Wiccans, witches, and Satanists, and it could lead you down that path." The occult, as Andrew said, is objectively evil, but many who are involved in it don't really know what they are doing. "Many participants," he said, "believe they are merely exploring the mysteries of reality and navigating hidden secrets of human nature. As we know, intention does not always equal effect." Catherine's mother said, "The threat of the occult is beyond real; the slightest little New Age thing is a wormhole. It will suck you in." "People don't start right away with saying, 'Let's summon demons!'" John explained, adding, "Demons play the long game. Time is different for them, and they work on us over the decades."

Gabriel highlighted that astrology, often regarded as a more innocent occultic practice, and widespread in the general population, is truly a gateway to greater and more evil occult practices. He said, "if someone wants more than that, they can get more, and that's what takes you deeper into the rabbit hole." Astrology, as he has seen and experienced, can be an easy gateway into darker spiritual realities. "It's very subtle things, you don't see it," he added. "When they say *the devil is in the details*, the devil is in the details." As he emphasized, it is a subtle trap that lures people in and they go deep into it before they realize it is problematic. He said, "Subtle things that you don't think are demonic, you don't think are bad. You see it as a fun hobby but you start craving more of it and you want more answers."

Gabriel's own attachment to astrology led to him giving himself over to the powers that resided within it, allowing these forces not only to tell him his mission in life but to give him his very identity. As with other aspects of the New Age, having all this information about the influence of the heavens on your personality made him feel really special. Not only did it make him feel special but, as he said, "It defines you much more specifically. It looks like it explains so much, but not really!" Buying into all this gives the New Age the power and permission to tell you who and what you are, replacing the role of God the Creator to do so, and providing a lie in place of the truth.

As a result, people in the occult become gullible because they eventually accept the idea that they themselves are special, in some mystical and unclear way, and that they are the authority and can determine what is good and what is evil, what is safe for them and what is dangerous. This gullibility becomes extremely dangerous since the entities the occultists are working with are demons who will take advantage of every possible weakness they detect. Former Yogi Alex Frank raised the issue of how practitioners of Yoga also think they have the ability to properly discern what is good and what is bad in their spiritual practice. Even Christians, he pointed out, have difficulty discerning these spirits, and are warned by St. Paul and St. John about it:

> Do not quench the Spirit, do not despise prophesying, but test everything; hold fast what is good, abstain from every form of evil.[5]

> Beloved, do not believe every spirit, but test the spirits to see whether they are of God; for many false prophets have gone out into the world. By this you know the Spirit of God: every spirit which confesses that Jesus Christ has come in the flesh is of God, and every spirit which does not confess Jesus is not of God.[6]

---

[5] I Thess 5:19-22
[6] 1 John 4:1-3

Discernment of spirits follows principles that must be taught and learned and which require humility to understand and consistently obey. Yoga, ignoring the need for these principles, which only Christianity can teach, trains the individual to see himself as the authority, leading him to discern the good from the bad by disordered standards, and placing him in a situation of spiritual recklessness and subsequent danger. In discussing the dangers of Yoga, Alex Frank shared an insight that applies to all forms of the occult. The purpose of Yoga and mindfulness, he explained, is to enter into a more profound relationship with ourselves. This is done through "enhancing your consciousness" and gaining self-awareness, which is done through a deep entering into oneself. However, it is difficult to wade through the troubled waters of our fallen human souls without the help of God. Yoga provides no guides except, potentially, a guru or a Hindu spirit or yourself, none of which are truly safe to follow. Without Christ to guide us, the One who made us and who knows us, we are lost in a stormy sea and will only find darkness there. At that point, we won't know what to do to resolve these issues and we will be tempted, and *taught*, by Yoga and any branch of the occult, to use this darkness to help accomplish the personal goals we have for ourselves.

When Gabriel was faced with the reality that the New Age was not actually helping him, the gullibility which Alex Frank warned about drove him to look deeper within the New Age movement for a compelling answer. He was then counseled about "light paths" and told to seek out those who are "higher in consciousness" and who, as a result, possess "spiritual powers." These are the psychics and mediums and people of that sort. His addiction to the New Age, and his desperation to be able to find what he was looking for through these practices, eventually led him to visit a psychic. He had hit a low point regarding a situation in his life and did not know what else to do. He went to speak to her to see if he was on the right path in his life, doing so because he felt enticed by the offers and had become willing to do anything to feel better.

In his description of the encounter, his desperation and gullibility are palpable. The psychic was reading tarot cards and spraying incense as she sought to read his situation. "I can see you are very hurt in your heart," she told him, as she drew something, an image of a heart, on a piece of paper. Vulnerable as he was, he was

The Occult is Full of Lies and Manipulation

elated by the image she was drawing. "Oh yes," he said to her, "that's my heart there!" Calling upon the beliefs he had acquired in his New Age formation, he asked her if she could talk to his spirit guides to see if his life would improve. She told him she was able to see them in the room there with them and that they are laughing at him because he is so worried about the wrong things. Instead, she told him, he needs to focus on his "mission" and on "being loving," classic New Age philosophies that simply sent Gabriel further into his confusion.

Demons Play Along

Those who spent time in the occult and have, by the grace of God, been able to escape it, have provided many anecdotes about their interactions with the diabolical and how demons will play along with the *big game* of the occult that they have invented. When witches, magicians, and Satanists cast spells and seek to acquire higher and higher magical abilities and ranks, demons will assume their part in the game. They will pretend to be able to be manipulated, pretend to fear the witch or magician, obey commands, and give every impression that what the occultist believes is true. For example, Adam Blai, who has worked with exorcists for over a decade, discussed the fact that Wicca is a big made-up system in which people think that, if they follow these strange rituals, they can acquire whatever they want. He said, "The demons couldn't care less about that, but, if you're breaking the First Commandment, they'll step in and play the role. 'Sure, I'll be your guardian angel,' 'Sure, I'll be your grandmother,' 'Sure, I'll be the Horned god of the green forest or whatever you want to call me'."[7]

Andrew, whose occult practice involved directly summoning demons, experienced this sort of treatment himself. He said, "Obviously, I thought I was in control and [the demons] would often act angry, as if I was holding them against their will. I believed I was, and that I could punish them and force them to do my bidding." The diabolical ploy of being weak and submissive was quite elaborate at times he said, adding, "Sometimes, the demons would put on a show of 'respect' and refer to me with titles, such as 'Magus'

---

[7] Blai video

209

or 'Master of the Temple'." The show of respect or weakness before the occultists was obviously insincere. As Andrew said, "This was obviously a mere display to play on my pride, and to convince me I had such power over them and other people. It was nothing more than one big act of deceit in an attempt to keep me performing these rituals and magickal practices, with the hopes I would die in my sin and be condemned to Hell forever."

"Here's the thing about demons," Adelaide commented. "Whether you want to call them demons, or you want to call them Celtic gods, or whatever you want to call them, here's the thing about them: they hate you, more than anything else – *they. hate. you.* And while they will give you success and do your bidding to keep you where you are and make you go further down the rabbit hole, they will torture you every chance they get. Their goal is not just to drag you to Hell, but to make sure you drag as many people with you as possible. That's the only goal – and your misery is icing on the cake." Mirroring what Blai said above, Philomena added, "Demons think you are stupid – that you are the dumbest life form on the planet, because they know the Truth." She continued, "Will they answer some things for you, nonetheless? Yes: love, money, etc., they will toss out the line but will jerk it back, then toss it out again."

Not What They Wanted

Fr. Ermatinger wrote that fallen man's ability to properly discern what is good and what is evil, what is of God and what is of Satan, is severely hampered as a result of the Fall of Adam and Eve. "Adam and Eve," he wrote, "had wanted to determine *for themselves* what was good and evil, and they got their wish. They could no longer easily, or without error, determine what was of God, what was sustained by Him, or what actions or things resulted in Him being the end." This includes not only a proper understanding of cause and effect, and of the nature and purpose of all created things, but also the awareness that man himself is capable, through the nature of the human soul, to possess God Himself within them by the gift of grace.[8] As a result of this confusion, fallen man can easily become deceived, abandon the hope brought by Christ, and sink

---

[8] Ermatinger, *The Trouble with Magic*, 63. *Emphasis* mine.

again into the depths of superstition and the occult, believing and chasing after lies and falsehoods.

As with Adam and Eve, so with the rest of mankind: when a man engages the diabolical through the occult, he will usually not get exactly what he wanted; but, even if he does, it will not be exactly what he expected. The tactic of the diabolical in the occult is to come close and then back off, dangling the enticing bait before the occultist but demanding a sinful servitude in order to get to the sought-after gifts. As angelic beings, the diabolical can produce powerful enticements which can enchant the occultist, causing them to be irresistibly fixated on continuing to engage the demons, no matter what comes as a result.

This powerful enticement can be glimpsed in the experience of Ciaran Lyons, who interviewed the Satanist David Sinclair Smith. Ciaran naively agreed to perform a ritual himself, under the guidance of Smith. In the ritual, Ciaran pointed a sword toward an image of Baphomet,[9] and "projected his desires" in that direction, with the hope of "manifesting" them into reality.[10] At the end of the ritual, when the Satanist asked Ciaran, "How'd you feel?" Ciaran, speaking at a noticeably accelerated pace, said, "Oh, just such a big adrenaline rush like, you know, I was, I was in the moment, you know. You just sort of forget about everything else and like the blood's flowing and, yeah, it's powerful, like, you know, there's nothing else around and you're just so focused on what's going on. It feels powerful, like *you feel like you're part of something and something is happening even though you're not seeing anything around you.*"[11]

Occultic rituals are often addictive simply because they give the *appearance* that there is a power at work through the ritual. Like Ciaran, who was given a strong *sense* that "something was happening," Andrew said, "Often, it is just close enough to keep you looking for more." Andrew told me the story of a ritual that gave him a similar and equally addictive feeling, which involved his desire to win the lottery. To do so, as an occultist, he decided to perform an astrological ritual, involving certain planets that are supposedly connected to wealth and fortune. He carefully followed a specific

---

[9] The demon which modern Satanists have gravitated toward and which appears in numerous images and statues in their practice.

[10] Take note of the general occultic wording which this Satanic ritual includes.

[11] Ciaran YouTube docuseries. *Emphasis* mine.

rubric, trying to "manifest" the numbers needed to win the Powerball. When he went to buy the ticket, he let the machine pick the numbers, thinking some spirit would pick the right numbers for him. When the numbers came back, and the winning numbers were announced, he was off by just one number on each of the five numbers on the ticket. He was very close to winning fifty thousand dollars. It was so close that the ritual and the effect seemed very compelling to him. So, even though the ritual failed to produce the desired result, in its deceptive nature it did produce an effect: as he said, "It does not even need to succeed, but just come close, in order to be satisfying to an occultist."

Philomena commented on this manipulative response given by demons in answer to the spells and rituals of occultists. She said, "Sometimes the spells you are doing won't work. If you get to a point where you say, 'ugh, this is stupid, it doesn't work,' *that* is when you start noticing that it is actually starting to work. Then you say, 'Oh, maybe I tapped into something, I figured it out,' 'success finally!', but it is all a trick to keep people in it." Further, she added, "When it works, it is just a manipulation that makes you think you can do all this stuff, 'this is cool,' and you stay in and try to gain more knowledge and more power and you go to a new level. You ride the wave of success until it cuts off and then you look for things that are more dangerous to keep it going."

Gabriel said he went into the New Age because he wanted to learn how to be healed and happy and more loving toward others but ended up chasing this goal through ritual after ritual. To obtain what he sought, he was being told, "you need to get your chakras healed." This, the online New Age world told him, would not happen overnight, but would take years. "Then," he explained, "they said that crystals will help more, or you can talk to mediums about whatever is causing you pain or burdens. If you have trauma, well, that could be from a past life because reincarnation is a thing." He added that, in this phase of his exploration, these things began to seemingly answer his questions and help him make sense of things, though, in the long run, it brought nothing helpful.

Bl. Bartolo Longo, after his initial experience with mediums, was drawn deeper into the occult by a desire to have clearer answers to his questions. Through the medium he consulted, the demons presented themselves to Bartolo as spirits, ghosts, guides, deceased people, and angels of light, and answered all the questions he asked. However, the answers that were given were often contradictory, which left Bartolo confused. Delving deeper into the occult, and desiring to receive the communications himself, he decided to join a Satanic cult. In that cult, he dedicated himself to the study of esoteric teaching, intense fasting,[12] and preparation for consecration as a Satanic priest. It was in that role that he hoped to obtain the answers and power he had desired, answers which, still, would never come.[13]

In addition to leaving occultists without the answers they sought, the diabolical will also manifest in unexpected and dangerous ways. At Samhain, the pagan holiday which occurs at Halloween, and which is the biggest Wiccan "holy day" and one with lots of occult activity, Helena encountered what was certainly "something evil" as they went about the prescribed rituals on the day when, they believe, "the veil between the corporal world and the spiritual world are at their thinnest." In preparation for that day, she and the other witches would cover all the mirrors in their houses because they believed that the spirits could enter our realm that way. "Although connecting with them was something you did," she explained, "even witches wanted to do it on their own terms; not be surprised by unexpected guests." These spirits indeed came around for them on Samhain but, as she described, "It was a very dark feeling and despite what we did, you felt a presence and I could sense that they were not all 'family,' that it was something evil; not just Aunt Sue coming around."[14]

When Therese summoned a specific demon to enter her home as part of a ritual, the effect of doing so was anything but comforting. When she did the ritual, the demon made it clear that he had arrived. "A behemoth settled on the house, a heavy presence," she said. "The house groaned; there was no mistaking it." It was not a good thing. After it occurred, things would happen around the house that would agitate Therese and everyone else, and wear them down, like the appearance of vermin, cockroaches, pests, and anything unclean.

---

[12] Fasting is a universal spiritual practice. Thus, false religions and the occult also embrace fasting in order to enhance the soul's receptivity to whatever spiritual world with which they are engaged.

[13] Mary's Dowry, Bl. Bartolo Longo documentary, YouTube.

[14] This parallels the story of the witch Lola and her unwanted ghost guests, and the naïve idea that witches can create "rules" that bind the spirits to obey them. This will be presented in *Slaying Dragons III*.

These manifestations very much resemble classic signs of a diabolical infestation of a home.

When demons do respond to spells and rituals, the answer comes in a way that the occultist never desired, often bringing with it a great deal of damage. "You learn to be concise with your intent," Christopher said, "because you often get exactly what you request, which can derail your whole life." Adelaide's experience was very similar. She said, "[The demons] also give you what you want but in a twisted way. I did a spell on my husband before he was my husband. I thought I was a genius; I worded it perfectly. So, I did the spell and bound him to me. But then, we could not stay away from each other and we made each other miserable. Eventually, he was stalking me. So, it worked, and it was a nightmare."

"The demonic will bait you. You get attention," Philomena said, "Then they back off. Then to get their attention again you have to go deeper." She was looking for peace within herself but did not realize she was being so influenced by what her first husband, a Satanist, was doing. She looked for peace and kept going deeper and deeper to find it. There was an oppressive sense the whole time and her search in the occult brought no peace but she kept going, looking for it, following the diabolical bait. She went from centering prayer and New Age stuff to earth magic, grounding,[15] and on to a pantheon full of death and power and war, among other things. "It is a progression," she added.

There was one time when Philomena was offered a very high-paying job working at a casino without even going to look for it. She saw it clearly as a demonic gift flowing from her occult practice. Despite these "gifts" which the demons arranged in her life, there were countless negatives. She was depressed a lot, had things happening in her life that didn't make sense, and negative influences in her thoughts. She was plagued by feelings of despair, which hit her through thoughts like, "you're not worth it," "your husband hates you," with the final temptation, "maybe do a spell about it." As Philomena said, when you are in the occult, you don't pay attention to these things. All the while, as the last temptation mentioned above reveals, "you are being coached by the demons to go further into the

---

[15] Where a witch will "discharge" excess energy that they collected for use in a spell, which may now be causing a feeling of agitation.

occult, to get you to the point of despair – there's no turning back from that."[16]

Lucy decided to become a psychic at what would turn out to be the end of her occult practice, and just before her physical and spiritual collapse and subsequent conversion. She said, "I expected to achieve a sense of lightness, some sort of positive changes in my life, as I would be able to tell the future and help others with theirs. I expected a lifetime of great things. I got much more than I expected." That "much more" was diabolical possession and confinement to a mental health facility.

Andrew's motives were not to help others, just himself, but with a similar illusion of making himself a better person. The rituals Andrew engaged in were done in an attempt, usually, "to gain some further knowledge of my *True Will,* and to attain knowledge and conversation with my HGA [Holy Guardian Angel]." This HGA, of course, is *not* his real guardian angel but a spirit guide of a sort and, thus, something diabolical which pretended to be benign. Though he sought "knowledge" and "conversation with his HGA," he never achieved it, though he met people online who claimed to have done so. However, he was able to make contact with "various entities, usually demons," as he put it, especially through automatic writing and talking boards.[17] Even before he became a Thelemite, he said he used talking boards "to try to barter with the demons for power and secret knowledge. I'm not particularly convinced it ever had any effect other than clouding my intellect and playing into my pride. I expected to learn the secrets of human nature," Andrew admitted, "to explore the dark, unknown recesses of my mind and soul. In a word, I was looking for total clarity. Instead," he added, "what I found was chaos and confusion, debauchery and debasement."

This bait and switch tactic of the demons occurs in all aspects of the occult. Msgr. Rossetti told the story of a woman, a practitioner of Reiki, who tried to contact her deceased father through automatic writing.[18] For a long time, she was receiving long and loving

---

[16] While God is always ready to receive us when we repent and turn to Him, despair, by definition, is our refusal to turn to Him. As a result, when we despair, we push God away and block His ability to help us. God will not help us against our wishes.

[17] Another way to refer to Ouija boards.

[18] An occultic practice where the individual opens themselves to a spirit and allows their (typically non-dominant) hand to move on its own, at the spirit's prompting, communicating various sorts of messages.

messages from what she thought was her deceased father. Then the messages became "ugly and threatening," revealing to her that the entity with which she was communicating was not her father but a demon, leaving her terrified. After renouncing necromancy[19] and confessing her sins, the demon departed.[20]

Lucy experienced this same underlying reality in the New Age. She said the devil begins with offering a sense of liberation, knowledge, understanding, and solutions to your problems, such as the Reiki practitioner thought she was attaining through the automatic writing. Then, Lucy said, it flips to an oppression and a burdensomeness that is enslaving. It will fluctuate just enough to keep you seeking further. The demons will torment the mind and the soul, she said, sowing doubt, confusion, anger, and resentment. The more you use the occultic practices, the more you feel you need them.

In the end, the addiction to the occult will only bring misery, as the life of one of the greatest modern pioneers of occultism reveals. Andrew was a devotee of Aleister Crowley as a part of his practice of Thelema and he discussed how Crowley's life ended, in light of the supposed powers of the occult which he had mastered. Andrew, remarking how Crowley, who was super rich and, as a result, was able to dedicate himself to his magical system full-time with no obstacles standing in his way, posed the question, "Wouldn't having a lot of money make it possible to achieve this spiritual end?" Aleister Crowley, who was very smart, a polylinguist, and very rich, and who travelled everywhere, focused solely on achieving his occultic spiritual goal, nonetheless died in poverty from drug addiction. "If I am a *god*, why can't I make lots of money? A prophet of a new religion," Andrew said, "ushering a new Aeon of humanity, would not go from millionaire to poverty to death as a drug addict." John agreed with this, pointing to the truth of the matter as seen in the case of the famed Blues guitarist, Robert Johnson, who supposedly made a pact with the devil in order to acquire fame. John said there are always strings attached to a deal with the devil: Robert Johnson died young. The devil will give the thing which you requested but will bind you to all sorts of things that you did not sign on for.

---

[19] Summoning and communicating with the dead.
[20] Rossetti, *Diary*, 39.

Sliding Deeper

One of the dangers of being in the occult is that, like the insect inside a pitcher plant, anyone within the occult is slowly sliding deeper into it, whether they realize it or not. Occultists often realize they have gone to a deeper level of occult practice only after they have arrived there. The lure of the occult, with Satan as an "angel of light," like the enticing aroma of the pitcher plant, is blinding and powerful. Speaking about witchcraft, Helena said that, though Satan is not considered to be a part of that religion, "I think that Satan and demons do their best to make sure that you have success with your spells. You have success, you feel powerful, you go into it all even deeper."

Gabriel said he intended to stay away from "the occult" when he was in the New Age because he truly believed in the evil power of darkness and the devil. Nevertheless, the New Age was itself a vehicle for him into the occult, something he neither realized or admitted until much, much later. "I am doing all this stuff but 'I will never touch a Ouija board'," he said, describing the stopping point he had established for himself.[21] "I did have a line, and I was not going to cross that line, but I probably did without knowing it, because I did try to contact spirits 'from the other side,' which is the exact same thing as a Ouija board!"

The deeper Gabriel went, the more "adventurous" he was becoming. Eventually, he was trying to get his soul to leave his body so he could travel around the universe. He even sought to meet his spirit guides and encounter his past lives and deceased family members. When he was having trouble with these things, and with channeling and meditation, he said, "They get you to go deeper by telling you your *spirit energy* is low." As a result, in order to have these special experiences, he was advised to do more meditation and more practices. Through this, he could make his soul leave his body and attain to all these "secrets." John's experience in magic was similar. In the early stages, John explained, it is often said that the magician is just working with angels, and this appears in early stages

---

[21] Another example of the arbitrary self-magisterium. In the occult, the individual makes himself an authority, but it should be obvious how ridiculous it is to do that.

of interest in Wicca as well.[22] After expertise is acquired in that work, the magician is then taught how to work with demons. "The insatiable desire for more leads a person to consent and keep moving where more power is promised," he added.

Enticed to Perform Still Greater Evils

The addiction to the power and promises of the occult leads many to consent to still greater evils than they had already committed and than they had ever thought they would do on this "spiritual path." Many commented that, around the time they decided they needed to stop the occult practices, they looked around them and could not believe who and what they had become.

Fr. Blaise said that people will open themselves up through these occult practices, but when they willingly do so, their defenses are gone. The initiatory levels always seem benign or even good. Take the Freemasons for example, known to present themselves as do-gooders in society. As they move up the ranks and progress into the higher degrees, they take oaths and invite curses upon themselves for violating those oaths. It is the same in Wicca: they can never get enough and always want more. It is just like drug addiction: start with something lighter and safe but, once that high is not sufficient, they begin to try the harder stuff to get a better high. Pornography is also like that: the more time a person spends, the deeper they go into stranger and weirder things to get the next level thrill.

As was previously mentioned, Wiccans will start with prohibitions, such as regarding curses, but many eventually compromise and do things that they once regarded as evil. With no true moral authority or conscience established to guide the practitioner in making decisions, there is absolutely nothing within that religion to stop them from progressing in evil. "Wicca," Therese said, "is the soft sell. It presents itself like, 'We won't harm anyone – the Law of Three says, 'if you do anything bad, it will come back to you three times,' so we don't do that!'" Wicca boasts of being part of the *right-hand path*, the path of light. It focuses on worshipping "the

---

[22] Remember Adelaide's story, in which she was introduced to witchcraft first through the "innocent" Angel Magic.

Lord and the Lady," with the Lady having a greater preference. Therese, who was in Wicca for several years, and was also a practicing witch (in addition to darker things) for over twenty years, added, "Eventually, you will move up the ranks [in Wicca] and find out that you actually *do* do black magic and curses. We just don't tell the youngin's. Oh, and 'we only do it for good,' like when all those witches across the country cursed Trump." Wicca, she said, "is a bunch of nonsense" and has no true history, no tracing back to the Celtic religions of long ago, but the Wiccans believe it anyway.

One danger of Wicca, Therese said, is that, after spending time in it, practitioners will begin to realize that there must be more to it, there must be witchcraft without the naïve Wicca movement. This draws people beyond the pseudo-religion of Wicca into the practice of magic, while still working with spirits and doing spells. The morality within witchcraft is then found to be much greyer, and the witch is not as upset if they do something bad because the magic itself is said to be morally grey and without any moral governance. Besides, as she pointed out, the witch is likely using it to try to help a friend or help themselves which, they will argue, "can't be a bad thing."

As this justification of the person's actions kicks in, she added, they start to go down the left-hand path looking for more, and real, spiritual power. This leads them to cross over from Wicca to witchcraft and then ceremonial magic. "If you stick with Wicca long enough, you will flip from the right-hand path to the left," she added. In the mind of the Wiccan, the left-hand path was forbidden…at first. This will take them into the Luciferian cults with warlocks and brujas.[23] Brujeria stores, she said, are becoming more common in cities across the country, and are just like the kitschy witchcraft stores popping up everywhere. So, if a person were to visit a brujeria, he would be in the presence of one of these brujas.

In the Christian spiritual life, Philomena pointed out, in order to go deeper and grow in holiness, you have to dedicate yourself more and more to doing *good* and *holy* things, like increased prayer, fasting, and almsgiving. However, in the occult, to go deeper and tap into more "power," you have to increase the kind and number of *evil*

---

[23] A witch or witch doctor associated with Latin American occultism like Voodoo and Macumba.

things you are willing to engage in. John agreed and said that, as you progress further, the evil of it all becomes quite obvious; the mask comes off and the diabolical reveals itself. To advance to a new level in magic and attain to a higher level of power, you are required to perform ceremonies that are more and more perverted, blasphemous, and disgusting. By doing these, you acquire the personal assistance of a demon who leads you deeper into the practice. By this point, you have already compromised so much on morals, have gone against your conscience and better judgment so frequently, and have seen the diabolical power at work so often, that it is quite difficult to "hit the brakes" and turn back, or even stop going deeper. At this stage, as John said, "You start to change: the bad becomes the good and the good becomes the bad. You are eventually doing the very things that, five or ten years ago, you would have never done."

As he descended further into darker rituals, John eventually confronted this reality when he hit the point of using human bones and sacrificing animals in order to obtain further progress and stronger pacts with the diabolical. "It was that bad," he said. Other rituals involved being "crowned" with a demon and cutting his skin with occult symbols, combined with dirt and fire pressed into the wounds. "What started with Eastern meditation [as a youth] became, decades later, drinking rum with poison and herbs, staring in an altered state into a pot of dead things, talking to demons, in an old shed, surrounded by roaches and ants." While the evil can then become more obvious, the "waking up" is a heroic feat for which many cannot muster the strength.

Point of No Return

"Then, you realize you are so far gone and there is zero turning back."
-Adelaide

Adelaide mentioned that there is a "point of no return" that occultists can reach. This does not mean that God will not forgive them and welcome them back, but that the demons eventually successfully instill despair in the soul. At that point, by consenting to the idea that you are trapped where you are, there is no option within the occultist's mind, no thought that it is a choice, of turning back to God. Fr. Louis affirmed that it is only when the danger becomes oppressive that individuals will seek help. He said, "People come to you for help when it has reached that radical stage."

Dr. Gallagher said, "Strange paranormal experiences, associated with the variety of spiritual or esoteric traditions, are unusual but hardly as rare as most people today believe. People who venture into the occult too often get trapped in a world beyond their imagining."[24] One aspect of this "world" is the fact that demons are very possessive. Exorcists note this reality all the time in their work. Fr. Ripperger said that Our Lord will, in His Providence, permit demons to possess people and that demons, being impulsive, simply cannot resist seizing the opportunity. The furthering of the Kingdom of Satan, by associating as many men with it as possible, is a key part of their objective. Fr. Fortea added that demons, enslaved as they are to the evil which they freely chose in the beginning, are often quick to attack, seeking the immediate gratification from the harm they can inflict.[25] Another reality that exorcists speak about quite clearly is that demons will viciously defend their claim over the possessed person, who, through whatever sin, had been delivered to them. "He's *mine*!" they will state, angrily, when the exorcist attempts to cast the demon out, arguing that they now have rights over the person. Regarding one case of possession, Dr. Gallagher said that, during the exorcism, "[The demon] protested that no one had a right to liberate this woman because she had freely promised herself to Satan, a typical sentiment of evil spirits."[26]

In explaining this, Adelaide likened the soul to a window. Covered in sin, the soul, like a window, is dirty, and no light can get through it. To clean that window would then, as a result of the layers and layers of old and hardened dirt, take a tremendous amount of time and effort. Likewise, the liberation of the soul from the occult, as a result of the number of sins accumulated therein, would take so much time and effort, while actively in the midst of diabolical attacks to stop you, that despair would set in and the person would simply quit trying to leave. As she said, "It hits you like that, so you quit trying to leave and you stay in it, and keep going with it." In Fr. Dominic's work, he encountered a few people who were so deep into the occult that they could not get out. He said, "There were two

---

[24] Gallagher, *Demonic Foes*, 162
[25] Fraune, *Slaying Dragons*, 6-7.
[26] Gallaher, *Demonic Foes*, 63

cases in which someone *deeply* embroiled in the occult reached out in desperation, but they had gone so deep that it seemed their will and hope had been severely compromised. Despite all my attempts to tell them this was the right path, these people dropped off my radar and I don't know what happened to them."[27]

"One important thing," Fr. Louis said, *"Don't go into the occult.* It is difficult to get out; it gets wrapped up with your psychology." One man he knew, who was striving to become a better person, was also hanging out with some friends who were into weird occultic things, like trying to strangle people in the night with some sort of power. These practices eventually became a part of him but he wanted to get out. Father decided he needed to send the man to counseling due to the psychological impact these practices had had on the man. When a person strays into the occult, Fr. Sebastian explained, God is working to free him, such as through the activity of his guardian angel, who is working to get a foothold in his life in order to bring him back. At a certain point, Father said, "[The guardian angel] has been ignored for so long that it is nearly impossible for the angel to do so." The demon will also be working on the person's mind, trying to close off any openings to the angel, getting him to think that any spiritual considerations are silly, and inclining him to mock them instead.

The Retaliation Begins

The deeper the occultist goes, following the lead of the spirits he is fraternizing with, the more apparent the evil of the situation becomes. "The demon always wants more," Fr. Sebastian said, "and keeps demanding more and more. He also threatens to take away what was first given." Eventually, the person will reach a point where they don't want to go any further and seek to get out of the pact. That is where the retaliatory behavior begins.

Msgr. Rossetti said, "In lower levels of demonic possession or oppression, demons are typically hooded and their faces are not seen. If the person enters more deeply into a relationship with the demons,

---

[27] Sadly, this is all too common. Julia, the Satanic princess in Dr. Gallagher's book, disappeared. Therese, John, and others expressed the sentiment that they almost did not escape, and most occultists they know have not been able to.

and thus more inured to evil, the horrible visage of demons becomes increasingly revealed."[28] This more personal experience of the demon is never enjoyable. He added, "When demons manifest, the afflicted person typically feels some of what demons feel and often experiences their dark world. Thus, they experience aspects of being in hell."[29] This experience ends up becoming the "lot" of the person, from which they feel they can never escape. Fr. Ermatinger described this attitude in the presence of one woman, stating, "She came to expect the nightly attacks, convincing herself the problem is contained – or at least bearable."[30] However, when the occultist begins to resist this awful situation, the attacks from the demons only get worse.

Edith described how her immersion in the New Age slowly led her into darker practices, which took her into a situation where she began to experience diabolical attacks. The intrusion of New Age beliefs into her mind led her to eventually think of herself in a God-like manner. In her early twenties, she said, after all the New Age things became boring, she decided to take it further. Dealing also with same-sex attraction for many years, she was tempted toward the mutilation surgeries of the transgender ideology and briefly embraced magic in order to manipulate and seduce the women to whom she was attracted. She began to desire to be more "God-like" and also to become a "shape-shifter." Going further, Edith made a pact with the devil in order to perpetuate her desire for fame and access to women. Eventually, she saw the emptiness of it, gave up the pursuit, and dropped the transgender mutilation considerations. From the moment she made the pact, though, she was flooded with "unreal" demonic dreams and night terrors. The very night of the pact, she said, "I felt a lingering presence in the air and in the corner of my room." She also felt like someone was always watching her at night.

Therese described, from her own experiences, the way in which demons will attack women. She said that women are more likely than men to believe in spirits because they are more relational. Those

---

[28] Rossetti, *Diary*, 203. As described in *Slaying Dragons*, demons can take certain visible forms in their extraordinary activity. These are *apparitions* and not incarnate forms that last beyond the vision which the afflicted person experiences.

[29] Msgr. Rossetti, blog, February 2022

[30] Ermatinger, *The Trouble with Magic*, ix.

spirits are like the abusive boyfriend: attentive, they hang on to every word you say, stroke your ego, give you what you want. However, the moment you try to leave them, things get really ugly really fast. For example, when she began to think about converting, the spirits said "it's just a phase" until it was obvious that she was converting. Then, she said, "It was wild what was happening. There were death threats, where the spirits were saying, 'come back or we will kill you or [your boyfriend] or your loved ones'."

It is no surprise that the resistance on the part of the occultist, who begins to seek to move away from these dabblings, pacts, relationships, and the routine of rituals, all which amount to mortal sins, would stir a great anger on the part of the demons. The ultimate goal of the occult is to ensure the damnation of the person. Demons gloat over our misery in this life and ever moreso in the next. From what exorcists have learned, demons obtain more glory in Hell each time they are successful in deceiving man. When this plan begins to fail, and the time invested appears to have been wasted, the demons who once showered gifts upon the person will waste no time taking those away, as well as destroying everything else they can get their hands on in that person's life.

Chapter Fourteen

Why Occultists Leave the Occult

The initiation of the journey *out* of the occult has many causes and is taken along many paths. From the stories I have heard, the desire for Truth and for fulfillment according to the human nature that God has given us eventually wins out, casting aside the promise of fulfillment according to the lies of the devil and the world. The experiences of occultists testify to the presence of the conscience within man. Deep in their souls, beneath the attachment to power and pleasure in the occult, is a true desire to find and embrace the Truth. However, the occult is an entangling web which does not let go of its prey easily.

The importance of making a clear and solid decision to depart from the occult can be seen in two perspectives that were shared with me. Fr. Dominic, to whom many people have come asking for help escaping the occult, said the people who came to him were reaching out in desperation. "They were wanting healing at whatever cost," he said. This points to the need for healing and to truly be *saved* from the dangers of the occult. Another perspective is that of Christopher, who had many friends and acquaintances who were in the occult. He highlighted the reality of the need to make a *break* from the occult. Everyone Christopher knows who has left the occult is not, at this point, practicing any religion at all. "The occult," he said, "is most alluring to those trying to come of age, trying to establish power and where you sit in the world. After age forty or fifty, they don't really cast spells anymore (unless you make money off it), but only do it in severe need." For the majority of these people, the interest in the occult just fades away and they tend to forget about it." Then he made an important point. "Unfortunately," he continued, "this reality leaves them still very much morally and spiritually attached to the occult, and the slow fade out of it prevents them from seeking a conversion to the Truth."[1]

Disillusioned by the Occult

Many of those I interviewed approached a point where their occultic practices began to objectively fail to fulfill their spiritual desires. This appeared in both subtle and dramatic ways, depending on the person and the type of occultic practice they had embraced.

Yoga

Alex Frank said that the lack of moral structures, and the dangers of what Yoga was actually seeking, caused him to become disillusioned by the practice. He agreed that the modern parts of Yoga parallel the occult and said that the desire to manipulate the *energy* within you eventually takes the practitioner to dark areas. Yoga trains the individual to fully enter these dark desires, transmute them,[2] and gain more power from them. However, people get fully possessed by them instead, as is seen in the story of the founder of Hatha Yoga, Matsyendra, who now has a pose in his honor in Yoga.[3] Alex saw these dark aspects of his own soul and realized he wanted, and needed, real structures to keep him from following them. These, he realized, are the ethics that are missing from modern Yoga. At that point, he started to turn away from energy manipulation and made his journey toward the Church, in which he found the structures he desired.

The Pagan Community

Timothy hit a point where the pagan community, and the beliefs that he had formed for himself from within that system, were no longer fulfilling. He realized they were all lacking something and that, even in his role as a father, which he cherished so much, he felt

---

[1] This is true from the perspective of exorcists as well, who say that these occult attachments, even from minor dabbling, need to be repented of and healed in order to free the person from any diabolical influences that came with it.

[2] Harness their energy and redirect it for another purpose.

[3] See Chapter Nine for a brief mention of the story that made him infamous.

like he did not know what he was doing. This introspection eventually left him feeling really depressed. The depression was so intense that it became difficult for his wife to be around him and for him to even get up in the morning. He felt lost and close to despair; it was the most severely depressed he had ever felt, bordering on suicidal. Despite how close he came to giving in to the despair, he knew there must be an answer to his dilemma. He looked at the Twelve Steps program again since he had once found elements of truth there. He discussed everything with his wife, principles about truth and morality and all the craziness of the world.

At that point, they had been attending a Unitarian Universalist community but were not very fond of it. Some friends had invited them there and, though they stayed a few years and it had a lot of spiritual elements that the pagan groups lacked, there were some serious morality issues within their beliefs. There was also a pervasive relativism, especially regarding its comments on Christianity. They focused on being kind and loving, which appealed to him, but the sexual morality which the community taught became intolerable, especially as they learned of the teachings that were being given in the youth group meetings which his daughter was attending. In that regard, it was obviously no better than the pagan communities they had been in.

Soon, his wife was getting more and more opposed to attending the Universalist community on Sundays as they had been doing. Further, she was feeling drawn toward the Catholic Faith, so they started looking at Churches in their area. After attending a Palm Sunday Mass, they went over to the Universalist community as usual. His wife was folding palm fronds in the hall there and a lady asked her what she was doing. After hearing "What's Palm Sunday?" in the course of the conversation, his wife knew they no longer had any reason to stay with the Universalists. Interestingly, at that moment his wife began to have very intense anxiety and felt that bad things would happen if they remained at that place.[4] They left that day desiring to never set foot there again. He agreed to the search for a new spiritual home, but did not feel the same urgency that his wife had. He knew that the spiritual component was missing but was

---

[4] This could be seen as an indicator of the activity of her guardian angel, who had been able to work with her more easily now that she had opened herself up to the graces flowing through the Church.

indifferent to joining the Church. He had an openness to the Church's social teachings already, so conversion was not out of the question, though it was not yet a necessary thing in his mind. This, of course, would turn out to be the beginning of their journey to the Catholic Church.

Foundation of Sand

For Helena, the occult did bring a sense of peace and joy, which seemed authentic at the time. Her dissatisfaction with it began from an intellectual perspective. "I felt so much of what I practiced was based off shaky research: people trying to rewrite history to fit a particular narrative," she said. "It was all made up and ultimately false. I began to feel that I was standing on a foundation of sand and I wanted rock." Helena referenced St. Paul, who stated, "Be not conformed to this world; but be reformed in the newness of your mind, that you may prove what is the good, and the acceptable, and the perfect will of God."[5] The renewal of the mind through the pursuit of Truth opens up the soul to the unlimited power of God to transform it. When she started doing the intellectual work necessary to arrive at the Truth, she not only realized the occult was an invention of man and a lie, but that the Church was the answer from God and the Truth. "That was one of the main reasons," she added, "that I started entertaining the idea of Christianity. When I did that, I knew it would have to be Catholicism. It was rooted in deep history, understanding, and was solid. I also began to understand that there *is* an objective truth, that some things do not change, and that there is a danger in people twisting certain things around to make them 'their truth'."

Seeking a Better Environment

As part of her break with the occult, Philomena decided to move to a new state, where she would be around family who were Catholic; yet, without that shared religion, she felt left out. It was at this time that she met her new husband, a proud Protestant who was adamant that the Christian faith was the foundation of their marriage. She did

---

[5] Rom 12:2 DR

not oppose that but, since she was so ignorant of the Faith, they began attending a non-denominational community ("a Baptist group with a coffee shop"). After their first child was born, getting her newborn baptized was important to her, so she became more open to Christianity, but with a very weak understanding of how things work.

The pastor was very knowledgeable, and being a Protestant for that time ended up making her a better Catholic in the end. The reason is that, while she was there, listening to that pastor, she fell in love with Sacred Scripture. As a result, things began to click in her mind regarding the connection between Catholic practices and the Bible. It was at this point that she started praying, or, as she described it, "Started praying for the first time – without any deities – just God." Aside from God's intervention, she said that, had it not been for the positive influences in her life, like her husband and their newborn son, she may have never left the occult. "It was hard," she admitted, and said she "needed a full and clean break or it never would have happened."

Child-like Faith

The first crack in Helena's dedication to the occult appeared following the birth of her daughter, after having spent twenty years in the occult. "I had every intention of raising her as a witch and did so according to her age," she said. "Honestly," she added, "I think that part of my thoughts in the beginning about raising her pagan had a lot to do with pushing against society. I was still very left-leaning and was not at a point to start accepting any Church teachings." Eventually, Helena said she slowly began to feel a dread that she was on the wrong path and would end up in Hell. "Even worse," she added, "that I would damn my child."[6] With all this in her mind, when her daughter was still very young, she realized it would be good to give her some more socialization. After looking around, they found a Presbyterian preschool which her husband thought would be good.[7] When she went to see the school, she said,

---

[6] Having been raised in the Presbyterian community, she was exposed to the teachings of eternity, Heaven and Hell, and the possibility of eternal damnation.

[7] Her husband was a non-practicing Catholic and apparently indifferent to her occult practices.

"I had a literal, visceral reaction; my skin crawled at the Bible verses on the walls." Despite its connection to her childhood religion, and this immediate reaction, the people were so genuinely good and loving that she felt comfortable allowing her daughter to attend. Due to the goodness of the teachers and the great atmosphere, "My heart began to soften in regard to Christianity, whereas before I was a very outspoken critic of it."

At one point in her daughter's schooling, they discussed Baptism. Eventually, her daughter asked her about it, since she was the only child in the school who had not been baptized. The daughter then said she wanted also to be baptized. "Again," Helena said, "at first, I wasn't ready for that but after a while, thought, 'okay, maybe we can do this. It doesn't mean anything and the grandparents would all be happy'." From this point, she began to do a lot of research on Christianity and realized that Baptism in the Catholic Church was the only baptism that made sense. As her story reveals, this was the first step in her own eventual conversion.

As for Helena, so for Adelaide: her son's resistance to her practice of Wicca convinced her that she needed to give it up. When her son was turning thirteen, she was preparing a ritual to induct him into Wicca. Before that could occur, she said, "He looked me right in the eyes and said, 'no'." It was out of character for him to be so blunt, she said, adding, "At that moment, I was suddenly able to see it for what it was, and I stopped practicing, but I didn't know what to do next." Unable to make a clean break and enter the Church more promptly, Adelaide's occult attachments would linger as she slowly made her way into the Church.

Aided by the Algorithm

Since so much criticism is rightly given to the internet as a tool for evil, it was quite fascinating to hear numerous accounts of the "algorithm" actually aiding occultists in their journey toward salvation. The online world is a prime culprit for luring people into the occult and immersing them in a virtual occultic world and virtual occultic community that never sleeps. This proves to be one of the real dangers of the online world. However, many former occultists have mentioned the internet as a key vehicle in presenting the Truth to them, which eventually awakened their souls and got them out of the occult. For Andrew, an online debate between a Mormon, a Norse pagan, and a Catholic eventually led him into Catholic forums and down the path to his intellectual conversion and renunciation of the occult. As Philomena dove into more research about the Church, her Kindle app began suggesting more books on the subject, which led her steadily into a deeper study of the Truth. For Gabriel, the YouTube algorithm helped him by suggesting more and more videos on the topic of leaving the New Age.

For Gabriel, the internet was truly a weapon of evil in the beginning. The majority, if not all, of his formation in the New Age was occurring through the internet and online videos. Eventually, he stumbled upon a video of Ed and Lorraine Warren speaking about their experiences in deliverance ministry with the Catholic Church. In the video, Lorraine spoke about her lack of fear of evil which sprang from her Catholic faith, and that she had always been a strong Catholic. As he listened to her speak, her Catholic faith really stood out to him. "If you believe the darkness exists," he said, "the light must also exist." That night, after watching that video, he prayed for God to lead him in the right direction. The next day, the YouTube system began to recommend videos to him that were a bit different from the New Age videos he had been focused on for the last three years or more. The first one that he noticed on that day was called, "From New Age to Jesus Christ." It was a personal testimony, just shy of one hour long, about a man who almost got possessed from his time in the New Age. A lot of what the man was saying was very similar to his own experiences. Subsequently, the system began to recommend more and more videos. After watching three more videos similar to the first, Gabriel sat back and said a prayer of conversion to Christ. As he told me, "Someone in a video said, 'Guys! You have to get out! You have to give yourselves to Jesus!'"

Occultists are Looking for the Truth

Many people in the occult are simply seeking genuine answers to the meaning of their lives, lost as they are in this rotten generation of lies and scandal and bad examples. As Andrew said, "Looking back, that is what my soul and mind were deeply yearning for all that time. All it took was exposure to the Truth, and it eventually led me here." As Andrew wandered through the occult, and fraternized with demons, he was not seeking to be a malicious person and to do harm. He had succumbed to the trap and the temptations surrounding the vice of pride, and thought the truth lay inside of himself, instead of in God. This, however, was a wrong turn in the pursuit of the right thing. He said, "The fact that my former religion was centered around what I thought was the pursuit of *truth* was precisely the thing that ended in my conversion!"

Andrew said that one of the problems today is that, in schools, an idolatry of the human mind, and a "scientistic" mindset, has replaced Christianity as the "guiding light" in the search for the answers to life's biggest questions. This idolatrous replacement claims to provide the truth but gives no answers to the fundamental questions. Even more so, "It leaves more questions than answers," he added. "It does not satisfy the human mind." As a result, modern education does not even seek to provide the answers to the questions of man's existence. In the end, this void of wisdom and Truth naturally causes people to go and look elsewhere for answers. Andrew was led to the occult as a result of searching for this answer. "Youth," he said, "will seek constantly for the Truth. Our post-Christian society no longer offers an answer, but the occult is bubbling up and claiming that it offers answers."

Margaret is another individual who stated she was looking for the Truth when dabbling in the occult. The expression of that search was tainted by the occultic desire for power and superiority. "I wanted to live on a higher plane than everyone else," she said, but then also added clearly, "I was looking for truth." The pairing of *truth* with *superiority* was due to believing the occultic lie that the Truth is relatively inaccessible and can only be found through obscure, secret, hidden, esoteric rites, often only by those with higher intellects.

Bl. Bartolo Longo's venture into occultism was done for the same purpose: the pursuit of truth. However, the anti-Catholicism and hatred that came with it eventually left him in a state of depression. As he continued this search, and to counter the interior darkness that was coming with it, he took the advice of a friend and began attending séances and consulting mediums. Despite his hatred for the Church, he still had a thirst for the supernatural, but this was being turned to the dark religion of the occult. He began to experience clear encounters with the "spiritual world," and thought that he would surely find, among these occultic practices, the truth that he had been pursuing, but he did not.

"Life is a mysterious and confusing thing," Andrew said. The search to understand what it means to be a human person, and to understand the purpose for our existence, "is a driving factor for the search for the occult. People in the occult want discipline and regiment," he said, "but they won't necessarily admit it; but that is what they want. They want the sacramentals, but they seek them in the occult altar and trinkets. Those are just a forgery of the Catholic sacramental system." Gabriel's conclusion was that if there is someone who will preach the Truth of Christ in the hearing of occultists, they will come into the Light of faith.[8] As a child, Gabriel was interested in astronomy, which was an aspect of his search for the Truth. Now that he has entered the Church, he sees clearly that "people who do that eventually find Christ. We are trying to figure out this whole world, why are we here, how do I get out of a depressive state, like life is not going in the right direction," he said.

Encountering the Truth

"People can't make a choice [of the truth] if they don't know what [the truth] looks like," Riaan Swiegelaar said, "So, for me, when I saw [the truth] and I knew this is my choice – I didn't know that choice was an option before because I never experienced it. I always tried to reason it out and I did not believe that [the] unconditional love of Christ and grace is a choice – I never knew there was an option for me, so when I saw, it I chose it."[9]

In college, Timothy had joined the Twelve Steps program just as a precaution given his exposure to drugs. The program essentially became his religion for a while. The "Higher Power" element was confusing for him but he latched on to the other elements like the daily routines and the meditations. There were genuinely good people there who helped him stay on track, finishing college well as a result. The various cultural phenomena and insanities in recent years led Timothy to a place where he knew he needed to look for the

---

[8] Rom 10:14–15
[9] Swiegelaar video

truth. The Twelve Steps program began to appear lacking and, with various career shifts, he began to question who he was personally and spiritually. An awareness that something was missing emerged and became very strong. Even in his role as a father, which was of great importance to him, he began to realize that he did not know what he was doing.

Timothy said that, while he remained in the pagan community, he was never closed off to any belief. He often said prayers to God asking Him to reveal Himself and was open to believing in God, whatever the truth might be. When he found the Truth in the Catholic Church, the teachings on concupiscence, the Fall, and the Redemption provided a lot of clarity on his own wayward youth and the weaknesses he saw, and detested, in himself. He longed to find real spiritual strength. It wasn't just this issue though: the Blessed Trinity, the Incarnation, the intimacy of Christian prayer all made a lot of sense and were very exciting to learn about. As RCIA progressed, his decision to enter the Church was a no-brainer.

As I noted earlier in this chapter, Andrew's search for Truth began to accelerate when he was observing the online religious debate between a Mormon, Norse pagan, and a Catholic. He said he was likely drawn to this debate by the inclusion of the Norse pagan. The Catholic pulled from St. Thomas' "Five Ways"[10] and, essentially, introduced this concept to him for the very first time. The Catholic was intelligent and articulate and clearly and convincingly presented his view. When the debate came to a close, the Catholic asked him, through the chat room, if he would like to join another forum and look around there. This other group was a debate forum for Catholics and Protestants. He stayed in that forum for months, listening attentively to their debates. As he did so, he also got connected to multiple traditional catechetical websites, where he read profusely and became increasingly convinced of the Catholic position.[11]

---

[10] His famous five "proofs" for the existence of God.
[11] Fisheaters.com and NewAdvent.com "Catholic Encyclopedia"

The Truth Will Set You Free

Thanks be to God, when a person truly sets their mind and will on the Truth, provided they are within the avenues of grace flowing from Christ's Church, they can be set free. Truth and freedom are joined together in Christ our Redeemer, who said, "You will know the Truth and the Truth will make you free." Further, He gave this teaching in the context of slavery to sin, the very plight of those trapped in the occult. "Everyone who commits sin," Our Lord said, "is a slave to sin." Slaves do not abide in His Father's house forever, He added. If a man perseveres in sin in this life, he will eventually lose his soul and the chance for salvation. However, if a man turns to Christ, the Son of God, he will become a son of God himself. Then, what applies to Christ will apply to the man: "The son continues [in the Father's house] forever. So if the Son makes you free, you will be free indeed."[12]

---

[12] John 8:31–38

Chapter Fifteen

Leaving the Occult is a Real Battle

A critical element of education on the occult is the fact that no one enters it without implicitly signing on with an organization run by the diabolical. When a man steps into the occult, he is pushing open the door to the kingdom of Satan and walking right in. The door swings open easily and the initial environment is quite relaxing and enticing. Typically, the hostile agents are waiting behind another wall, giving the man a chance to get comfortable. When the man begins to come to his senses and realize he is in an evil place, he will slowly begin to understand the extent of the danger in which he has placed himself: demons run the occult, they want him to stay, they are incomparably smarter and stronger than he is, and the door by which he entered only opens from the outside.[1] Thus, someone must *enter* through that door, looking for him, in order for him to obtain his release; the man's will alone is insufficient.

Thankfully, this is essentially the same image that Our Lord used to describe His destruction of the Kingdom of Satan. "By the Spirit of God," Our Lord said, "I cast out demons." Therefore, He added, "the kingdom of God has come upon you." With this coming, and with the establishment of His Holy Church, against which the "gates of hell" will not prevail, Christ came not just to oppose but "to destroy the works of the devil,"[2] and to break into the Kingdom of Satan, "binding [Satan] the strong man...and plunder[ing] his goods."[3] Thus, Our Lord is the One who breaks against that occultic door of the Kingdom of Satan in which many souls are imprisoned

---

[1] Demons, as fallen angels, retain the angelic nature and the powers proper to it. They lack the power of grace which the angels possess, making the demons weaker than the angels. However, the angelic nature of the demons brings intellectual powers much greater than those of men as well as the preternatural ability to influence created elements in the world.

[2] 1 John 3:8

[3] Matt 12:28-30

and, with power, robs Satan of all the captives whom he has trapped in his snares. Any man, then, who has entered the occultic realm of the kingdom of Satan, can be liberated by Christ who perpetually bombards that accursed kingdom with the redeeming power of His Most Precious Blood. That being said, getting out will be a memorable battle, one which will provide a particularly focused story of redemption.

The Attacks by Demons

When leaving the occult, occultists can suffer from a variety of diabolical attacks that resemble all forms of extraordinary diabolical influence: infestation, vexation, obsession, oppression, and even possession. This is due to the gravity of the situation, which the image above highlights. Associating oneself with occultic powers places oneself outside of the protection of God and inside a relationship with the hosts of Hell. To get free from that involves the endurance of a wrestling with evil. Our Lord showed us that any successful wrestling with evil, whether it is with the world, the flesh, or the devil, will involve some degree of suffering. The very means by which our liberation from sin and death was accomplished was through the suffering and death of the Son of God on the Cross. When we bind ourselves to Him, we become part of His Mystical Body and our share in these same sufferings becomes salvific. We all must endure certain sufferings in this world, in the degree that divine justice requires, if we wish to save our souls.

The diabolical retaliation experienced by those seeking to leave the occult is proportionate to the amount of evil they committed and the depth of their involvement in the occult. It also varies based on the intensity and power of the specific extraordinary graces freely given by Our Lord in the process of bringing about their conversion. Some former occultists experience truly miraculous conversions and suffer very little afterward. Others slowly or steadily leave the occult, and the demons pursue them for years, if not decades. It is also interesting to note that, in my conversations with former occultists in the process of writing this book, many of them have stated, within communications via text or email, that they were currently enduring particular diabolical attacks at the moment and could use the support of my prayers.

Fr. Amorth addressed the issue of the difficulty of breaking free from occultic affiliations which comes about because of the nature of these actions. When speaking primarily about Satanists, he said, "All these cases concern a true and proper selling of the soul to the devil, who maintains his tragic promises, but without ever giving any happiness but only innumerable sufferings. In a word, being consecrated to the devil guarantees a life of pure hell on earth and an eternal hell in the afterlife. In my experience, these persons do not ever receive peace, and they leave behind them a trail of sorrow, solitude, and death."[4] Here, *consecration to the devil* is referencing a literal consecration or pact with Satan, though an underlying principle would apply to *all* occultists, even those who do not believe the devil exists.

Fr. Amorth added to this warning, connecting it to the danger of the occult in general. He said, "I wish to conclude with an important observation. It is not necessary to become a Satanist in order to serve the devil and become one of his followers. There are many, alas, who do not officially consecrate themselves to Satan but choose to follow his basic principles, and as a result they place their souls at great risk."[5] Speaking about Satanists specifically, he added, "For this reason it is necessary to think of the consequences of such a choice, which is often irreversible or at least very difficult to reverse."[6]

From my research I have learned that occultists will suffer to the degree that they got involved in the occult, with Satanism bringing the most suffering and a most difficult liberation, though all forms of the occult share in those problems to some extent. Msgr. Rossetti also observed this reality, stating, "It is unrealistic to think that someone who has practiced witchcraft, divination, or other occult practices over several years would be liberated quickly. They have immersed themselves in evil for many years. It is reasonable to expect the cure to take some years as well."[7] Fr. Blaise agreed, adding, "It makes sense that the diabolical retaliation, when seeking to leave the occult, would be proportionate to the depth of involvement in the occult. Nonetheless, it all falls under the

---

[4] Amorth, *An Exorcist Explains*, 32. It seems that these individuals never abandon Satanism.
[5] Ibid 34
[6] Ibid 33
[7] Rossetti, *Diary*, 140

permissive will of God and should be embraced as a penance in reparation for the sins committed."

In light of the above warnings, it should be understood that dedication to, or "working with," any sort of "spirit" or "deity" implicitly involves some level of consecration, pact, or relationship with that entity. These arrangements with spirits, as exorcists state, are also made more powerful and more binding if they are "enhanced," so to speak, by the inclusion of money, blood, sex, or a signed pact as part of the ritual.[8] These are not uncommon in modern occultic movements, thus the danger is higher than many realize. Further, while the diabolical retaliation which a Satanist may experience should be more intense than, for example, a New-Ager, it has proven to be the case that the latter can still suffer acute, though short-lived, retaliation as well.

Retaliation can also come to those who, simply in passing in their youth, dabbled in the occult merely in the form of playing around with a Ouija board once or twice. Dr. Gallagher told the story a woman who came to him experiencing signs of a diabolical infestation in her house. She thought it was due to a conversion she had recently experienced in which, after neglecting her faith for many years, she had started going to daily Mass. However, that was only part of it. Dr. Gallagher stated, "Almost in passing, she mentioned how as a teenager, she had fooled around with her friends with a Ouija board and tarot cards."[9] This, however, is sufficient to bring diabolical problems and is something that the priest will need to know about in order to help the person break any possible connections.

The dangerous affiliation with Satan can also occur when a person has been in a relationship with someone in the occult. Elizabeth, who was in a relationship with an abusive Satanist for almost a year, said that, after she left him, she was plagued by suicidal ideation and began taking lots of medication as a result. Despite the medicine, the thoughts would not stop. After reaching out to an exorcist, she was advised to use the binding prayer against the demon of suicidal thoughts and drink some holy water over the

---

[8] These additional steps include sins of a certain gravity, damaging the soul in a particular way, as well as a turning of the will toward the demon, which deepens the bond the occultist establishes with it.

[9] Gallagher, *Demonic Foes*, 184

course of three days. After significant improvement, she continued with the binding prayer and, after two weeks, the suicidal thoughts vanished.[10] Msgr. Rossetti commented on similar situations, where a person's spiritual problems were tied to immoral relations with a witch. This immoral behavior caused the person he saw to be "deeply bonded with evil." Further, he said, "This evil is hard to root out…the final liberation will likely be a long fight."[11]

While most occultists do not become possessed (though many suffer from some form of extraordinary diabolical influence as listed above), the specific experiences of those leaving the occult resembles what the possessed also experience. The possessed may endure scratches and bruises from the demons, which appear inexplicably and suddenly, as well as nighttime attacks and home infestations. Fr. Blaise added that many people who are under the influence of demons, especially from possession, suffer from sexual assaults by invisible entities during the night. In his book, *Rescued from Satan,* Italian exorcist Friar Benigno Palilla presented the stories of individuals he had helped liberate, many of whom endured such attacks. Another form of attack, falling under the category of *vexation,* is the experience of being choked, which is not an uncommon experience in a diabolical attack. When discussing why demons choke people, Msgr. Rossetti compared this behavior to how animals kill their prey. Since demons are not allowed to kill people, they try to at least choke them, but are only permitted to do so in limited circumstances.[12]

Demons are also permitted to attack homes and appliances and other possessions. Msgr. Rossetti told the story of a priest who was assisting his work and was having problems with the plumbing in the rectory. The toilets would not flush and the pipes were clogging. Plumbers looked at it and said there was nothing wrong with anything. Monsignor advised the priest to use holy water on it and everything started working immediately.[13] This resembles, in great detail, a similar diabolical attack reported by Adelaide,[14] as well as an

---

[10] She was also regularly visiting a medical provider or counselor, which is important in situations like this.

[11] Msgr. Rossetti, St. Michael Center blog, May 2, 2021, Exorcist Diary #136

[12] Rossetti, *Diary,* 23

[13] Ibid 33.

[14] See below

encounter with a "demon of destruction," which Fr. Ripperger spoke about, in which the plumbing in the rectory and the hard drive of the pastor's computer were destroyed during an exorcism.[15]

Diabolical Response to Leaving the Occult

If the demon sees that the person is inclined to leave the occult, or God has begun to open doors for him to see the light of Truth, the demon will go into a full attack. These attacks can vary quite a bit in the beginning, but all turn violent and dangerous eventually. "The devil," as Fr. Louis said, "knows when you are trying to leave and he gets into you more." The demon does not want to lose the territory he has gained and, if he becomes aware of this spiritual shift, the person will begin to suffer from a lot of diabolical attacks. When the person persists in trying to leave, the retaliation begins, taking on such forms as nightmares, depression, and suicidal thoughts. The demon will use anything to try to bully them to stay in the relationship.

Demons also adopt the tactic of reminding the occultist of what he stands to lose if he leaves. "When they try to get out," Fr. Sebastian added, "the demon does not want to scare them away. There is a pact and a promise that was made, and the demon makes good on it." Here, Father referred to the "gift" the demon gave to the occultist in the beginning, to bait the person into the pact. At this point, as they seek to leave the occult, "that one [core] promise is threatened to be taken away, especially if it was something big in their lives." An American exorcist said that the demon will also take the approach of trying to trick the possessed into pitying the demon and wanting it to stay. This is all part of the abuse relationship. The demon threatens the person that they will be all alone after liberation: the priest will be gone, the demon will be gone, and they will have no one. He said this happens a lot.

When Christopher got into the occult, he knew that diabolical attacks were possible, and expected them, so when they appeared he was not surprised. As he grew closer to converting, he realized that he had been burdened by diabolical obsession for most of his life. "I'd be willing to bet," he added, "that most of the occultists I knew were

---

[15] Fraune, *Slaying Dragons*, 83.

subject to [experiences of diabolical obsession]." He said his life was near constant despair as far back as he could remember. He felt nagged toward despair regularly by a thought in his mind that kept pointing it out to him.

When Philomena told her husband that she needed to become Catholic, a spirit of division emerged in their marriage that they both recognized as demonic. As she spent more time going to Mass, before returning to the Sacraments, though she was feeling better about everything, things were getting worse at the same time. She started to get really sick and could not figure out what was wrong. Then, she was diagnosed with a chronic disease, seemingly "out of nowhere." In addition, little things were occurring, "not the *extreme* parlor tricks of the Enemy," she said, but things like car accidents, illness, anger, attacks on the home and an internal struggle in the family. The more dedicated she became to returning to the Church, the more she realized she had to accept the attacks that were coming.

Sometimes the attacks by the demons can *prompt* the desire to depart the occult. One night, the entity that Rigo had been speaking to, that he thought actually cared for him, came inside him and told him to commit suicide. He woke up holding a knife to his chest. The tip of the knife was in his skin but something was blocking it from going all the way in. He became fearful and said that that was the turning point, the moment in which he decided to leave the occult.[16] Fr. Blaise commented on this tactic of the diabolical, stating, "The devil will often overplay his hand and the individual will see he is in trouble, but, unfortunately, not always. When they do notice the devil's presence in this way, they become open to getting help and the Church can assist them. They often reach this point only after they have begun to see the toll the occult has taken on them."

---

[16] *CBNNews.com*, July 6, 2022, "A Warlock Got Him Hooked on the Occult – Then He Was Hounded by Demons Until the Power of Jesus Set Him Free."

Stories – Diabolic Retaliation when Converting

Adelaide

"The conversion to Catholicism made all the crazy start," Adelaide stated. After her soft conversion to the Faith,[17] the diabolical retaliation became intense. Her family moved shortly after this and the new house became a classic example of a home infestation. After the move, "All hell broke loose," she said. "There were whispers and footsteps in the hallway, the shower turned itself on and off, a phantom cat appeared, one of the kids woke up with bloody claw marks down his back, and another kid suffered a superficial cut straight down the middle of his eye, from top to bottom, while walking down the hall."

Considering the incidents to be caused by the presence of a demon attached to the house itself, they moved to a new home, where things were initially quiet. Then, a few odd things occurred, followed by the appearance of a very large black widow on the stairs. While these spiders are not uncommon in her area, there were a few things that raised a red flag for her. "It was big," she explained, "it was in plain sight, and it gave me a warning feeling." Further, the next day, copperheads appeared on their third-floor balcony, which meant the snakes would have had to climb up three stories to get there, all the while not being seen by any of the neighbors. "We were surrounded by poison, literally," she said, "and I knew, beyond a shadow of a doubt, that it was an attack."

Still unaware of the cause of these manifestations, they decided to move again, thinking they would be safe this time. Things got quiet and they thought it was over. When the manifestations begin at this third location, she finally realized that the house was not the cause – *she* was. Doors were unlocking and opening on their own. Random things went missing. One evening, they came home and found the eyes of the stove[18] turned on. When one of the kids was home in the shower, he heard what sounded like a gunshot. It was actually the moment that every cabinet in the kitchen suddenly flung

---

[17] She entered through a modern Church which did not teach her properly, bringing her into the Faith with a very weak understanding of the obligations and the knowledge necessary to receive the fullness of grace Our Lord wanted to give her.

[18] A common name for the stove top burners, often resembling the shape of a human eye.

244

open. An entity was breathing on the neck of one of the children at one point and calling out to them in her voice when she wasn't home. Leaving a recorder running while they were away, they picked up the sound of laughter and other voices. Before this period of retaliation concluded, she was lying awake in bed and had "a terrible, terrifying vision," she said, adding, "The thing pinned me down and took my breath. Just as I thought I was going to pass out it let go of me and I vaulted over the bed like a rubber band that had been shot." Adelaide said that, after this attack, she began to suffer from new and ongoing problems with asthma.

Andrew

The diabolical retaliations that Andrew endured were quite extensive. Before his Baptism, and that of his wife and daughter, as his interest in converting to Christianity emerged and began to grow, the diabolical retaliations came in swiftly, he said. His wife had also been in the occult and, within a week of attending their first Mass, they joined RCIA. A few days after the first class they attended, their house burned down, taking all the lingering occult paraphernalia with it. No one was harmed; his wife and daughter escaped as soon as the smoke reached them inside the house, but the fire was already widespread at that point. "The only things that survived were my wife's and my first rosaries. All my ritual tools, tarot cards, etc., were totally destroyed by fire, water, and smoke. I never saw any of those tools again."

People might argue that it was a coincidence, but that is not how it looked or felt for him. He explained, "That really was the big event that proved to me 1) that we had to continue moving forward with RCIA and enter the Church, and 2) that what we had been participating in for most of our young adulthood was not only false, but dangerous and even evil." The evil of his involvement in the occult would continue to play out in various forms of retaliation until his whole family was baptized. This evil, as he reflected on it, emerging just after starting RCIA, caused him to be rather fearful of what he had gotten into. Thankfully, there were a few priests in his area who worked in deliverance ministry. He was able to get in touch with a good priest who led him, and his wife, through deliverance prayers.

Andrew has also concluded that, before his and his wife's entrance into the Church, the devil tried to disrupt their home through influencing their daughter on a few occasions. As catechumens, before being baptized, he and his wife began their first family rosary with their little girl. As soon as they began, he said, "Our daughter became completely distraught and was screaming wildly at the top of her lungs and flashing the lights in the bedroom off and on over and over again. We couldn't get her to calm down so we just kept praying and she eventually was back to her totally normal self." The incident, he said, "Freaked me out."

They experienced a similar incident at the actual Baptism, which was done in the Traditional Rite. First, his father-in-law began to experience a sudden migraine, forcing him to leave the Church during the initial prayers. Then, his mother-in-law received what turned out to be false alarm notifications from their home security system. Finally, the daughter was again acting in a highly unusual manner, running around the Church, yelling, and talking back, despite the fact that she had been coming to Mass for months and had never had an issue. At the moment of the girl's Baptism, she had to be held by three people to keep her still enough yet was completely calm afterward. Further, at their private Confirmations, just minutes before they were Confirmed, they received word that a close friend was being rushed to the hospital, only to be told later that she was completely fine. Isolated, these could be dismissed as mere coincidences; collectively, this is clearly, especially to him, something else entirely. It is reasonable to conclude that his many sins, and those of his wife, especially while unbaptized, had brought in certain demons, who manifested in these ways when they knew their hold on the family was being broken through their entrance into the Church.

Gabriel

After making the spiritual shift away from the occult and toward Our Lord, Gabriel began to clean things up in his life, such as the way he spoke to people, the language he used, and bad habits. One of the things he had to purge from himself was a lingering attachment to pornography. Among the physical items he removed from his life were impure posters on his walls. When he started doing that, he noticed a resistance, and then he began to have nightmares. He began to be awakened at 3am or 5am every morning, with terrible dreams, often of a sexual nature, "like something was trying to pull me back into what I was doing before." He added, "And that was really upsetting me, because that starts to make you think, and this is what the devil wants you to think, 'God has abandoned me;' 'What happened? I thought I'm good now;' 'He's left me, He doesn't really love me'."

After this, he started looking into whether anyone else had ever experienced what he was going through. "Sure enough," he told me, "people had been through that same thing, people who were in the occult, or who were in these spiritual practices, or people who actually literally worshipped Satan. They were having similar experiences of being pulled back in. I noticed it was the night that I had pulled down my posters, that's when the dreams began. Maybe I made something angry," he said. "When I was quitting the New Age, I did not feel like anything was pulling me back in. It was like, 'Okay, you can quit the New Age, but you're still not saved.' But once I started praying to Jesus, they started to get mad."

In addition to the nightmares, he experienced a disturbing sleep paralysis on multiple occasions, like an energy in the room that would start creeping up on him: he could feel it coming, like it was seemingly feeding on his fear. He would be suddenly paralyzed, like he could not breathe, like something was choking him. He felt like something was on him; there was pressure on his chest or back or something clawing up his spine. After it happened several times, he realized it must be demonic. "The demons don't mess with you while you are still in the occult," he said. "Satan already knows you are going to Hell, but when you turn to Jesus, he seeks to drag you back into what you were doing before."

Helena

The first big moment of doubt or spiritual difficulties did not occur until Helena's first Confession. "It was what cast doubt in my mind, although I could not pinpoint a reason," she said. She mentioned how she heard so many people talking about the joy and lightness they felt after Confession, "while I," she added, "ended up in utter misery." For two weeks afterward, she could hardly sleep and her mind raced about what she had done and if it was right.

Compare Vincent's story[19] of the breakthrough which Confession was for him, aiding his pursuit of meaning in life and peace. It is important to note, though, that he had never dabbled in the occult. It seems that, while Confession remained effective and powerful for Helena, she had also provoked a demon by this sacramental action, which then retaliated against her. Reflecting on her case, it is important to understand that, from the experience of exorcists, different demons react differently to different Sacraments and sacramentals. Some demons, for example, can tolerate the reception of Holy Communion by the possessed person, while others will be tortured by the presence of Our Lord in the person's body through that Sacrament; some demons can tolerate the person going to Confession, while others will experience a crippling of their power over the person as a result.

Christopher

When Christopher decided to leave the occult behind completely, he "declared war" against it. Regarding the occult, he said, at that point, "I have had enough of your influence in my life and now I am going out of my way to break it." That night, he began a serious spiritual warfare practice, which included the *Auxilium Christianorum* prayers. The next morning, as he was heading out of the house toward his car, he witnessed what he was certain was a diabolical attack against him. A six-foot long stick suddenly crashed through his back window, going straight in before stopping at the head rest of the driver seat. As he said, "If I had been in the seat, it would have impaled me." He caught the whole event on video through a home security system and, looking quickly between the frames on the video, he could see the stick suddenly appear. The natural causes are easily dismissed: there were no other people at his house, the wind only pushed against the house from the opposite direction as that from which the stick came, the back window was made of a special tempered glass, the stick would have naturally slid

---

[19] From Chapter Eight. Vincent is the young man who was changed by witnessing a young woman's death.

over the car after first making contact with the window due to the window's curved shape, and the stick turned out to be rotten, shattering into pieces when he removed it from the car and tossed it into the yard.

Pondering the event, and the situation in general, Christopher reflected on the fact that he had just recently begun studying the Faith, having stepped away from the occult after many years. He had also just made the decision, that prior night, to push away the entire evil affiliation. It was then, only nine hours later, that the stick inexplicably burst through his car window.

Diabolical Attacks After Leaving

Once the person has left the occult and entered the Church, diabolical attacks can take on numerous forms. They may appear in the form of nighttime attacks, mysterious scratches and bruises; demons may also stalk the person, manifesting as shadowy figures; they can strike the person with mysterious illnesses or drive them into depression; they can wage various attacks on the home, such as knocking over items, breaking plumbing and fixtures in the home, and disrupting technology used for communication.[20]

The former occultists I spoke to shared their experiences at this point in their conversion. Years into the real spiritual warfare, a priest came to bless Adelaide's house.[21] The demonic theatrics picked up as he arrived. She said, "As he was pulling up in the driveway, an unused toilet suddenly overflowed, and a clock flew off the wall and smashed into the wall on the other side." Christopher experienced diabolical apparitions, diabolical obsession, inexplicable issues with his finances and car and relationships, as well as bouts of anger that nearly landed him in jail. The biggest form of retaliation Andrew experienced came in the form of strong temptations, in particular the temptation to pride. This, as he mentioned, has been a big struggle for him, devoted as he was to the prideful exaltation of his own will as a Thelemite for many years.

---

[20] Some exorcists and priests assisting afflicted people report unusual interruptions in cell phone communications with the afflicted.

[21] They were now attending a traditional parish and had met priests trained and knowledgeable in both the Church's traditions and spiritual warfare.

After leaving the occult and as she was on the verge of entering the Church, Philomena suffered from ailments that made no sense but that eventually led to a diagnosis of a chronic illness. She also suffered from particularly acute disturbances at night, where she would wake up and see things or suffer from terrifying dreams from which she awoke disturbed. They were such that she said she was afraid to close her eyes because she feared something was right there with her. Many relationships suddenly fell apart after being infected with anger. In addition, before her Satanist first husband died, but after they separated, he would contact her and say things that made her fear for her safety. At the time, it did not make sense, but now, she can see it clearly as a diabolical attack.

Dr. Gallagher said that, in analyzing an individual named Steve who had ventured into the occult, he concluded that there were no signs of psychiatric problems. "The context for his strange condition was clearly defined by a phase of serious occult involvement…all the criteria for a genuine diabolic attack were occurring." Though Steve had left the occult, "he continued to experience visions of spirits and other paranormal images," including dark shadowy figures. As in other cases Dr. Gallagher observed, the spirits turned hostile and violent and often struck Steve on the head.[22]

One tactic of the diabolical at this stage in the former occultist's life is to call in the debt that the occultist owes the demons as a result of entering into a pact or other agreement and accepting gifts and favors from them. This is aimed at convincing the person that they cannot turn to God anymore because they belong to Satan. Msgr. Rossetti told the story of a man who had once asked Satan to grant success in his business endeavors and who had later repented and returned to the Church. He came to Father because the devil was now attacking him at night and speaking into his mind, saying, "You belong to me."[23] Bl. Bartolo Longo, after living a real life of faith and devotion for a number of years, was hit one day with very strong doubts, which left him close to despair and suicide. He had begun to reflect on his consecration to Satan and feared that he was now eternally bound to the devil and unable to be saved.[24]

---

[22] Gallagher, *Demonic Foes*, 162.

[23] Rossetti, *Diary*, 135.

[24] At the point of considering suicide, he remembered one of the promises of the Blessed Virgin Mary to those who propagate her Rosary, that those who do so will be aided by

Some of the kinds of retaliation that Philomena experienced included mental obstructions and extreme depression to the point of despair, and in a way that was uncharacteristic of what was normal for her. She typically did not struggle with depressive tendencies at all, so this stood out as very unusual. She was also plagued by such abhorrent thoughts that she wondered if she needed therapy. Philomena said, "The whole game of the occult is despair." The mechanism and the intention of the diabolical, she said, "is to lure you in with power and power and power, and the moment you want to get out, they attack." She suffered from despair as well, but not the "point of no return" kind. She was very aware that she had to suffer in order to get out, and she was willing to do so. Edith, for the six months that followed her return to the practice of the Faith, specifically the Traditional Latin Mass, would wake up at least once a month with strange bruises on her arm in the shape of handprints or fingerprints holding onto her and digging into her arms. In addition, infrequently and sporadically, she also had moments where she felt strangely suicidal and hopeless.

John pointed out that those who leave the occult, who were deep into it, also fear retaliation from the occult groups themselves, who fear that the secrets of their groups might be exposed. These retaliations would be in a similar manner to diabolical retaliations, appearing as "magical attacks" or "astral attacks." While some pacts made within the occult compel the practitioner to speak publicly about the occult, in order to win favors from the demons, other pacts bind you to silence and secrecy. In dealing with a pact with a demon, Therese said she was commanded to tell at least ten people all about the demon that she was invoking. However, in another group she joined, she was bound not to talk about the magic they practiced or anything else they were doing. Now, however, she feels it is important to bring all this into the light, though prudently.

Fr. Amorth said, "I know persons who have left [Satanism], but only after an enormous struggle, and often while being threatened by the followers."[25] Looking at the current situation of the rise of occult practice and the subsequent flood of people fleeing the occult

---

her to obtain their salvation. He then vowed to spread her Rosary for the rest of his life and, now filled with a great peace, realized that he had also finally discovered his vocation. (Bartolo Longo documentary)

[25] Amorth, *An Exorcist Explains*, 33.

and seeking the Church's help, John said he believes there will be retaliation against the "first wave" of people who seek to leave the occult. "These [occultic] groups," he said, "consider themselves families, but like mafia families, and there are vows taken of silence and secrecy, especially in the *goetic* groups."[26]

Ongoing Retaliation

An occultist's conversion process adds to the demon's suffering because, despite all the demon's efforts, the person rejects them. This resembles what happens in an exorcism. The demon, who is losing his grip and rights over the person, is suffering and lashing out at the same time. Having left the occult after such a deep involvement with the demons, Therese said her redemption is a thorn in the demon's side. "It is painful to them to see me out of the occult," she added. "God uses that to highlight their fallen situation: there is no redemption for them and that is painful to them." This suffering on the part of the demon, as former occultists experience, causes the demons to lash out against them even more. Regarding the issue of ongoing retaliation, Lucy said, "The Sacraments of the Catholic Church, Jesus, Our Lady and the Saints, are instrumental in saving people; and no doubt, as long as I stand for the truth, Satan will retaliate. But that's OK; fighting Satan is the least I can do, when our good Lord has saved my mind, my life and my soul."

Adelaide was told by one priest that the target on her back is likely to never go away. She explained, "He said I was never going back to life the way it was," she added, "and that I now have to practice a militant Catholicism; 'it is the only protection you have,' he said." He also told her that she needs to focus on making reparation for her sins, and that the issue of justice is very important in deliverance ministry. Once in a while, Adelaide added, "Things happen that let me know that the target on my back will always be there." Items will fly off the wall or a shelf, once barely missing her head; her room was once suddenly filled with the smell of smoke with no source; unused toilets inexplicably overflow; electronic communications are frequently compromised, and messages and calls

---

[26] The groups that explicitly invoke and employ the help of demons.

do not go through; but thankfully, she and her family no longer experience any physical attacks.

Reflecting on her ongoing retaliation, Adelaide referenced the famous story of St. Paul's lament over a persistent suffering he was enduring:

> And to keep me from being too elated by the abundance of revelations, a thorn was given me in the flesh, a messenger of Satan, to harass me, to keep me from being too elated. Three times I besought the Lord about this, that it should leave me; but He said to me, 'My grace is sufficient for you, for My power is made perfect in weakness'.[27]

Adelaide said, "God allows a little activity to remind me of what I was into. St. Paul never got rid of that demon either. No one is ever off the devil's radar – that's normal temptation; but after getting into the occult, it does not go back to normal."[28] Occasionally, she said she would have a "pity party" about the whole ordeal. "I want it to go back to normal," she said. "Sometimes I think, 'Perhaps, if I am good enough, practicing my faith enough, atone enough, I will have a normal life.' But that is not how that's gonna go down." Philomena compared the occult to a time-share presentation. People go to these things, get all excited and sign up, only to then realize it was a bad deal and you want to get out. As difficult as that process can be, once you do get out, they still have all your information and don't really let you go. "It is the same thing here," she said, "They will continuously show up, they have your number!" Andrew also felt that these attacks would never stop so long as he was alive. He said, "The demons aren't exactly happy that my wife and I are no longer living that lifestyle. We were deep in their clutches and they must have thought our damnation was absolutely inevitable. They never stop attacking."

John said he has been under constant affliction since he became Catholic. "Once you convert, the façade is over and demons do not let go of you," he said. "They threaten that they are going to try to kill

---

[27] II Cor 12:7-9

[28] Though this was Adelaide's real experience, some priests believe this resistance on the part of a demon is rare and that, once established in Christ, the person is freed from evil.

you or everything else around you in order to bring you to a point of despair. They will seek to counter every good thing in your life with something bad for that same purpose." Despite this malicious response from the demons, he can see that God is still in control of all of it. All of it is within God's permissive will. John understands that his actions have consequences. Being in the occult is like being in the mob, he said. "When you get out, you either die or go into witness protection." He believes that he will never be free from the retaliation as a result of his deep involvement with the occult. He would like to get some more advice from a priest, but there are no good resources in his area.[29]

When Therese expressed to a priest her own concern about ongoing retaliations, he unfortunately dismissed her. He told her that, since she had converted and was now in a life of grace, "everything was fine" and there was no atonement nor penance for her to worry about. Therese humbly admitted that the punishment inflicted by Our Lord allowing this diabolical retaliation is medicinal not only for her but for other souls as well. As she remarked, "Had all of it disappeared, the constant affliction and oppression, and everything gone back to normal, would I be doing this interview, or any others?" Likely not, she added, and, as a result, there would be no warning offered to others because, as that priest implied, her experiences and sins in the occult would not have really mattered.[30]

Thankfully, from my research, there have been a few people who have not experienced much in the way of ongoing retaliation. Their stories are still being written, however, and it has yet to be seen whether the demons will seek to re-enter their lives or bring their attacks through some new open door. Since leaving the occult, there have only been two occasions where Helena experienced some form of retaliation. In these, she awoke at night with, "The overpowering feeling of an evil presence in my room, an actual physical entity standing at the foot of my bed. It was horrifying. I didn't look but instead just prayed the Hail Mary and Our Father, over and over and

---

[29] NB: You can summon demons all over the world, but there aren't priests all over the world, nor many knowledgeable enough to undo it.

[30] To understand better how some former occultists are attacked by demons perpetually, consider that the great Saints have also been tormented by demons most of their lives. Both came onto the devil's "radar" but for two different reasons. As a result, neither will be delivered from this harassment very easily.

over again until I felt that it was gone." Other than this, she stated that she had not experienced any sort of extraordinary diabolical retaliation after leaving the occult.[31] Gabriel, when I followed up with him after his entrance into the Church, said he felt that he had been completely freed from all his occult entanglements as a result of the graces he has received from Our Lord and Our Lady. He is now free of the recurrent despair that plagued him for many decades and he sees no signs of ongoing diabolical retaliation.

The Power of Grace

Those who venture into the occult, and seek to get out, exemplify the true dangers of all forms of sin. Sin is an association with Satan, the first rebel against the Lord. Sin is also, for Christians, a regression back to the lineage of Adam, in which man is a prisoner of the kingdom of Satan. All forms of sin pose threats against our earthly and eternal peace and happiness. Sin, also, is no small matter: to destroy its power, Our Lord deemed it necessary to endure the ignominious death on the Cross, Himself suffering as a sacrifice to obtain the forgiveness of all the sins which mankind would commit. Sin, therefore, not only harms the individual but it necessitates a solution which can only be found in God Himself. If man stays alienated from God, there is no way out of the downward spiral into which sin, the occult in particular, drags him. However, though "the sting of death is sin,"[32] those who welcome Christ as their Savior will eventually, by experiencing the power of His liberation, cry out with St. Paul and say, "Thanks be to God, who gives us the victory through Our Lord Jesus Christ."[33]

---

[31] It is important to clarify that, while the retaliation is not as strong for Helena as it is with others, it is still there in the strong temptations she experiences.

[32] I Cor 15:56

[33] I Cor 15:56-57

Chapter Sixteen

By the Power of God

Sacred Scripture is filled with images and stories and doctrines which highlight Our Lord's power to act in our lives and save us from the evils that surround us in this fallen world. One story in particular is that of Peter being saved from drowning beneath the waves of the stormy sea of Galilee. Graced with the unique power to imitate Christ by walking on top of the sea itself, St. Peter became distracted by the wind and the waves and turned his eyes, and his heart, away from Our Lord. At that moment, he lost his connection with the One who upheld him and he began to sink beneath the waves. With faith still in his heart, he cried out, "Lord, save me." St. Matthew lays out an important doctrine when he writes his next words: "Jesus immediately reached out his hand and caught him."[1] When we turn to Our Lord, He desires to save us without delay, particularly if our repentance and prayer is sincere and our situation involves a need to move from a state of sin into a state of grace.

In the lives of those trapped in the occult, Our Lord is ready to act. In many cases, He indeed *does* act in extraordinary ways. In these modern-day stories, Our Lord reveals the truth of the words of the Holy Spirit given in St. Paul's letter to the Colossians. Through His victory on the Cross, Christ "despoil[ed] the principalities and powers,[2] he hath exposed them confidently in open shew, triumphing over them in Himself."[3] This triumph manifests often in great display, cutting the occultists free from Satan's iron grip, and launching them into the ocean of Christ's healing mercy. However, just as it is required from all His disciples, even more so is repentance, humility, and a desire to cooperate with His grace required of former occultists.

---

[1] Matt 14:28-33
[2] Two of the higher ranks of fallen angels, just above angels (lowest) and Archangels.
[3] Col 2:15 DR, containing "shew," which is an older style of writing "show."

To leave the occult, Fr. Blaise said, occultists need to be willing to renounce it and turn away from it. The prayers which the Church can utilize at this point are sacramentals, which rely on the power of God and require the person to be open to God's action and willing to cooperate with it. As St. Augustine said, God created us without us: but he did not will to save us without us."[4] Fr. Louis observed that it is difficult for many people in this situation to do the work that is necessary. "Getting out of the occult and diabolical influence is a process, not a one-day thing," he said, adding, "People need to cooperate, but most don't want to cooperate." One approach he commonly takes is to have an individual see him every day for a novena. However, most don't return after one or two days.

The need for repentance, cooperation with God's activity, and a full surrender and trust in Our Lord, are things that all Christians must incorporate into their spiritual lives. This includes exorcists as well, who experience, firsthand, the need for these forms of humility. Fr. Alphonsus, for example, shared an anecdote from his time in formation for the priesthood which highlighted the effort of Satan to undermine this trust and the need for this full surrender to Him. In seminary, during a time when his spiritual life was growing, he began to see strange shadowy figures. The shadowy figures, appearing everywhere, were intimidating, making him think he was going crazy and afraid he might get kicked out of the seminary. He discussed with his spiritual director what they might be and he concluded they were either products of his imagination, souls from Purgatory, or perhaps demons. Soon, he began to see the negative effects of these manifestations, which were slowing him down spiritually and pulling him back from the path of spiritual growth. In reference to the fact that these disturbances caused him to reduce his prayer life, he said, "I noticed as I withdrew spiritually from giving myself [to God] as fully, they stopped appearing." As a result, especially as he looked back at the experience, he determined that this was the goal of the demons in appearing as they did.

All his experiences as a seminarian and as an exorcist, while uncomfortable or frightening in the moment, taught him to love and trust in the Lord, in His goodness and power and strength, more

---

[4] CCC 1847

than he ever could have otherwise.[5] "I was put into places where no one could help me, not even another exorcist," he said. "I was the one there with a possessed person," referring to a time when a possessed person was manifesting in a rage and he was alone. He explained that his trust in the goodness and the power of God unlocked the wonders of God's love and His fidelity to His promises.

The Power of Christ in Action

Those who seek to leave the occult, repentant and humbled and with a determination to do so, are often aided by Our Lord with very special graces. To leave such an extraordinarily dark world, it makes sense that an extraordinarily bright Light is required. Part of the reason for this extraordinary grace is that the demons are still maintaining a hold on the individual occultist. As all exorcists state, demons are very legalistic: they will hold the occultist to all the demands and punishments from their time wandering in the dark world. Thus, it is often only by an extraordinary action of God that the occultist can be set free. Thankfully, Our Lord is so good that He freely and often acts in this way.

Fr. Stephen told me the story of the unexpected arrival at his parish, and the subsequent remarkable conversion, of two occultists. Due to the situation in that diocese, the priests had no recourse to an exorcist, since their Bishop refused to appoint one. Fr. Stephen feared that one of the cases would move very slowly as a result. An exorcist he consulted had cautioned them that the Satanism element in one of the cases could bring lingering influences as the person was trying to leave it, which would make the whole process more complicated. There were a lot of things loosely connected which created violent attitudes in the person. Father said he was prepared for a years-long process as a result, and that it would be a long-drawn-out conversion. "At each step," he said, "something intervened that allowed [the Satanist] to just shed this stuff. It was very childlike. To be honest with you," he told me, "I still have not figured out how Jesus broke them out of this, but He did, very, very powerfully. I really don't understand how Jesus led them to us; but

---

[5] As in Vincent's story, only through the extraordinary grace he received could he have grown spiritually as he did.

then we had the role of leading them closer to the Gospel, and they have responded in all humility. It is incredibly humbling for us.[6] It's incredible what Jesus does."[7]

Jesus Inspires Hope

One Sunday, Rigo joined his mother, who had been praying for him and hoping for him to be liberated, and went to her Church with her. Though, he said, the deliverance he would eventually go through took a long time, he was quickly given a deep peace that Sunday as he listened to his mother and the congregation worshipping God. One of the big aids to his liberation was that Our Lord convinced him both of His own reality and existence and that Rigo was a child of God.[8] Anna had a similar experience of Christ's encouragement after being Confirmed, which led to her occult activity coming to an end. She believes that the grace of Confirmation gave her a spiritual instinct to leave the occult behind her. She did a strict fast during the Lent before her Confirmation, the latter being very important to her and something about which she was very excited.

When Betty Brennan was leaving Satanism, she stated it was not an easy deliverance, but Our Lord took over. "I just had to make one slight movement toward Him," she said, "and He came surging in." The deliverance prayers brought greater and greater freedom, and more Truth. She realized she was not actually angry at Our Lord but needed healing for the hurts and wounds she was carrying. She needed the strength to make better choices and the wisdom to understand life the way it really is. God provided all these things, she added. While she did have a good Catholic upbringing, she felt like she drifted away because there was no Christian in her life whom she could really love, which would have forced her to open up.[9]

---

[6] He and his pastor have both been coming to this new awareness together.

[7] This simplicity is also apparent in Lucy's story, in her reaction to God's grace while in the mental health facility.

[8] *CBNNews.com*, July 6, 2022, "A Warlock Got Him Hooked on the Occult – Then He Was Hounded by Demons Until the Power of Jesus Set Him Free."

[9] Brennan testimony (St. Joseph Studios, YouTube). See Riaan's story below, which is very similar.

Jesus Destroys Occult Power

Alex Frank told me the remarkable story, recounted in the book, *From Tibet to Mt Athos to Elder Paisios*, about the power of Christ working through a monk, destroying the occult abilities of a man, and converting him to Christianity in the process. It concerned a three-year-old boy who was kidnapped by a relative and taken to Tibet, where he was brought up in the occultic ranks of Tibetan Buddhism. The boy thrived and became excellent in the practice. Eventually, when older, the boy, possessing strong occultic powers, went to Mt. Athos where an Orthodox monk named Elder Paisios lived. As Alex recounted, Elder Paisios witnessed the boy's occult powers, including the ability to walk through walls. In response, Elder Paisios said "I can make you *not* do those things." The boy responded, taunting him, "Can *Christ* make you do these things?" "No," Elder Paisios said, repeating, "but I can make you *not* do these things." At that point, Elder Paisios was permitted to put a wooden cross over the boy's neck and the boy immediately lost all his occult powers and abilities. Apparently, the boy also had a personal demon and, after he started praying with Elder Paisios, and staying at the monastery, the demons would beat him up to prevent him from progressing spiritually with the monks. In the end, the boy stayed and became a monk himself.

In a different manner, Christ destroyed the occult power that latched on to a girl who was lured toward fame in Hollywood and who sacrificed her soul to get it. Kyle Clement[10] and a team of exorcists worked with a girl who chased an acting job in Hollywood, eventually compromised all her morals to get the job, ending up in the middle of a Satanic ritual during the party the crew put together to celebrate. When the girl finally realized just how deep into evil she had entered, she quickly left the party. Suicidal ideation emerged at that point, she said, which was overwhelming until she got to the border with Arizona. Here, the thoughts lifted a bit. Arriving in Kansas, she returned to her home parish and entered the Church. At this point, she was possessed but was resisting the possession. There just so happened to be, by Divine Providence, a traditional priest there, visiting the town to see his dying mother, who was also the

---

[10] Works with Fr. Ripperger at *Liber Christo*.

assistant to a well-known exorcist. The priest heard her Confession and, in the process, due to her contrition, she was liberated from the possession. An exorcist later did three solemn Rites of Exorcism just to be sure the demon had departed.[11]

Jesus Acts Quickly and Decisively

As a result of watching a video about Ed and Lorraine Warren, Gabriel began feeling an attraction toward the Catholic Faith. He said he then "opened up just a little and asked God to lead him in the right direction." The next day, everything began to fall into place. He decided it was time to leave the occult and run to Christ, and he offered a prayer of trust and surrender to Our Lord. When he did so, "the whole house," he said, "felt clean or clear. I don't know how to describe it." He added, "Before, there was something, or an energy, or a vibe, in the house, something on me. When I was alone in the house, the dark corners seemed like something was there, watching me, but I did not realize it until I said those words, and then later that night, it felt like my whole house was empty."[12] "All the New Age stuff," he said, "was taking forever; I was making no progress. Jesus, however, did it *just like that*! There was an immediate impact. I felt complete, content, safe, and now had a hunger for Scripture and knowledge. I wanted to know, 'Who is this Jesus guy?!'" He said he knew only the main stories at that point but was then ready and eager to dive in.

Story – An Unbelievable Transformation

After hearing her story, I asked Lucy if she thought her conversion and healing from the occult was due to an extraordinary grace. Compared to the stories of others, it seemed to me that her healing was much quicker and more complete. She said, "Sometimes,

---

[11] Jesus 911. "06 May 2020 The Most Evil Woman in the World." *YouTube*, 7 May 2020, youtube.com/watch?v=krLGDzFdbR4

[12] His experience is similar to that of Andrew after he went through deliverance prayers with a priest. Both cases resemble the impact of minor exorcisms on situations of home infestation. In *Slaying Dragons*, (p21): "Adam Blai says that, when the entity present is a demon, the minor exorcism prayers of the priest will have the effect of lifting an 'evil pressure' from the dwelling and imparting a 'noticeable lightness and clarity in the air'."

when I think how much I have changed, and how much God has done for me, it is nearly unfathomable. It's like something out of a book, or a movie – that someone can change so much, can have such a different way of looking at life, that so much peace can be found, that God truly saves someone's soul and delivers them into peace. But He did. He does. I have no doubt he will continue to."

Lucy said she did not realize how bad it had gotten until she was in the ambulance and being taken to a mental health facility. While there, a true search for God began, in which He found her and saved her in an extraordinary way. "That's when I realized that something supernatural had happened," she said, "and that me being in the facility was more than because I was overworked, and had too many late nights, which is what the official reasons were for my breakdown." One day while she was in the mental health ward, she experienced a mysterious, if not mystical, attraction toward God, which assured her that, if she could simply get to Him, she would be saved. Slowly, she realized that she did not need to try to get to *Him* because God could come to *her* on His own in the facility. As she was reflecting on this, she saw the sun through the window and began imagining that God's power was in the sun. Captivated by the idea, she entered into a sudden and powerful supernatural moment, where her soul was completely filled with what she described as a "heaven-sent energy." She described the experience in the following words:

I then had a realization that God could reach me inside the building. He could save me. It didn't matter where I was, He could save me. Then I looked up at the sun, which was so bright and beautiful. I thought at that moment that the power of God was in the sun. The sun went behind a cloud, and I asked for it to come back out. It did so immediately. The sun shone strongly and, suddenly, I felt a huge internal explosion within my chest, which radiated throughout my body. It was like a 'boom' that was completely soul-filling. It radiated warmth, it was powerful, it was energizing, and somehow, I just knew it was divine, heaven-sent. The words that I spoke out loud were, 'I have the power.' I didn't know exactly what that meant, at first. I just knew that something phenomenal had happened.

I realized later that it was the Holy Spirit: 'You will receive power, when the Holy Spirit comes upon you' (Acts 1:8). In that moment, I heard words in my heart: 'Convert to the Catholic Faith and you and your family will be saved.' I couldn't explain how I could hear words that were impressed on my heart; I had never experienced anything like it. But I knew that I needed to convert to Catholicism.[13]

The change in her personality was a sign that the mystical experience was truly an extraordinary grace from God. She was moved into a state of enduring peace and joy. With this, though, she knew that a spiritual battle was now raging within her. She was then prompted to leave the occult as a result of her breakdown and God's divine intervention, in which He promised that He would save her if she converted to the Catholic Faith. "In saying that, it also led to a miracle, a chance at a new life, grace like I never knew existed, love deeper than I'd ever experienced, a family raised in the Catholic Faith and a connection with God, Mary, the Saints and the Angels, and a wonderful range of new friends. My life is so much better than I ever expected."[14]

Christ Intervenes Within the Occult

Shockingly, to those who have never heard of it, but also unsurprisingly to those who know the extent of His desire to save us, Our Lord has, on many occasions, entered into the lives of occultists, while they were still practitioners, and converted them on the spot. Some of these accounts are quite remarkable.

Father Joseph-Marie Velinde, a convert from a life dedicated to Yoga and the New Age, shared the story of his initial conversion to

---

[13] This should be seen as a slow awakening which was not clear at the beginning. We do not believe that God's power resides in the sun in some supernatural way. Lucy *felt* these things, such as feeling power within herself, as the true reality slowly became clear to her. As she said, "I didn't know exactly what that meant, at first."

[14] An interesting detail to recall is that Lucy was brought up as an Anglican by nominal Christian parents. Spiritual seeds were likely planted in her soul because her children were enrolled in a Catholic school, with which she was very impressed.

Christ, a return to the faith of his childhood, and what would be the first step in a long journey into the Church. He said,

> One day, a doctor of natural medicine came to visit the Guru,[15] because we were suffering physically from the very intense exercises that we were practicing over there. The naturopath was a Christian and, as I was the personal secretary, although that's not what they called me, he had to pass by me to meet the Guru. He asked me, 'Were you a Christian? Are you baptized?' and I said, 'Of course.' He continued, 'So you *were* a Christian. Who is Jesus for you *now*?' And here, I experienced something that's not easy to express…but I sensed the presence of Jesus, very intensely, and He was asking me, 'My child, how long am I going to have to wait for you?' I understood that I was loved unconditionally, that I was not being judged in the slightest, that He was very close, there was only compassion and mercy. And suddenly, my God!, I was standing upright with incredible strength and, standing, I understood, 'You know what you need to do now?' Yes, I knew that I could not stay with the Guru after such an experience.[16]

After this, Velinde left and returned home, but his journey was not complete. It was many more years, after a long time wandering in pseudo-Christian occultic practices, before he would arrive at the steps of the Church and enter.

Fr. Velinde's story is very similar to the following, presented here at greater length. This next story, which occurred in May 2022, is still very much a "work in progress" and will hopefully, God willing, follow a path similar to that taken by Fr. Velinde, who, after his initial conversion, still had a long way to go. Nonetheless, we can see the evidential power of Christ acting directly to convert a practicing Satanist.

---

[15] Maharishi Mahesh Yogi, the yogi of the Beatles.
[16] CheminNeuf NetforGod. "A Guru or Jesus Father Joseph-Marie Verlinde." *YouTube*, 20 June 2017, youtube.com/watch?v=kHoKWxp8Imo

Riaan Swiegelaar[17], a recently converted Satanist, said he is convinced, now, that God is reaching out to try to save everyone. "God is everywhere," he said, "He is omnipresent. That means, at every Satanic ritual, at every interaction with another human being, everywhere – God can reveal Himself to anybody, at anytime, anywhere." When God appears, Swiegelaar said, it is the opportunity to receive His grace. "We constantly get opportunities for that," he said, "and this was my opportunity and I took it. I made the choice – I choose Light – I am living for light, and it is because of that grace that I can do that."

The story about this "choice" is quite remarkable. Earlier this year, he left the South African Satanic Church, which he had co-founded, and began his journey toward Christianity. Listening to his story, it is evident that his conversion is not complete, as he still hangs on to certain language that is not Christian. We must not pass judgment on his mind and mission at the moment, though, as it is all still fresh for him and he has not articulated all his new beliefs. However, his initial conversion is indeed fascinating and has merit on its own. In his conversion testimony video,[18] with great emotion, he said, "I've never known unconditional love in my whole life, and up to today, there's only four Christians in my whole life that have shown me what unconditional love is. I want to thank those four people. Words cannot express what you have done for me," he said. This unconditional love, as with Fr. Velinde, is at the heart of his conversion, and reached its peak in his interaction with a lady named Amy.

The story began when he did a radio interview about the South African Satanic Church (SASC), with which he had worked for four

---

[17] An important note on Swiegelaar, when looking into his testimony further, is that, at the time of his interviews, within a few months of his conversion, he still held to many rather strange and New-Agey doctrines. This demonstrates the damage which Satanism brought to his intellect. Hopefully, in time, as with Fr. Velinde, he will come to reject those and completely convert to Christianity. Nonetheless, his testimony is worth hearing, because Our Lord can do these things.

[18] Posted on his Facebook page and referenced in many news articles. Possibly due to an overwhelming response on his social media sites, this and other subsequent videos were taken down, but after this research was conducted on them. One interview remains posted online, which can be found at the YouTube channel Wide Awake Podcast, July 10, 2022, "Founder of Satanic Church in South Africa Gives His Life to Jesus" as well as the channel Bachan Tv, July 9, 2022, "Satanist Co-Founder Meets Jesus in Supernatural Encounter"

or five years and was helping to take public. Amy was a lady at the radio studio that he had only been able to correspond with via email ahead of the interview at the station. After the interview, she came over to him to say, "It's nice to meet you in person," and gave him a hug. When telling this story, he is constantly interrupted by tears, because he is telling this a month or so after it occurred, on the other side of what was a powerful moment of conversion. Riaan stated, again with great emotion, "This lady came to me – in the interview I said, 'I don't believe in Jesus and I don't believe Jesus Christ exists,' because I didn't. And she came to me, after the interview, after I said that, and she hugged me, and she held me in a way that I've never been loved. That's all she did, didn't say anything, just that 'it's nice to meet you in person'." A week later, he noticed on her WhatsApp profile that she was a Christian. "I couldn't believe it, because I've never had a Christian do that. I've never had a good experience…a Christian showing that much love and acceptance unconditionally ... *after* I said the things I said, she did that. And it stayed with me. I said, 'OK, cool, she's a Christian, whatever'."

Shortly after this interview and encounter, he decided to do a ritual to figure out what the next step would be for him and for the SASC, "How do I get more," he said, "more power, more influence." When he began the ritual, "I opened myself up [to converse with a group of demons] and…Jesus…appeared…and I was extremely cocky, and I said, 'Whatever, if you are Jesus, you need to prove it." He then added, in a separate interview, that he began to feel scared at that moment, as he began to consider that this may actually be Jesus standing before him. He said, "I began to feel scared because, if this is Jesus, I'm in trouble. So, I said to Him, 'I'm scared'."

At that moment, Riaan said, "And He flooded me with love, with so much love, with the most beautiful love and energy…and I recognized it immediately…because that woman at the radio station showed it to me. That's how I recognized the love of Christ. Because four people, four Christians, showed it – not the others. So, I recognized it." He added that Amy loved him at a time when he was a "monster and an ugly person," and when he did not respect Christians like her. Amy did not understand and said it was just such a simple thing she did, showing him love. He said, "To show someone love is everything – it's not just a simple thing. It's everything. You've shown me the love of Christ. I've seen it in you."

Protected by Formation and Mysterious Moments

Echoing Riaan's experience, John stated that God is with us even when we go into the darkest mess, but we have to be willing to see that He is there. As an example, something would occasionally happen to John which would block him from going further into the occult, such as at one point when, during a ritual, he was about to be "crowned" and receive a demon into him. Further, as a result of his upbringing learning Buddhist meditation practices, he felt he had a keen mental focus and awareness and a great enough intellectual power to resist similar diabolical approaches. He credited God and his guardian angel with this power to resist the demons. He also said he has noted, throughout his life, several occasions when he was prevented from joining the Freemasons, despite his interest and the wide-open door.

Therese, who was baptized at an earlier age than normal in the Protestant community of her youth, believed her desire for baptism and her awareness of God at such a young age protected her on many occasions later in life when she was in the occult. In one instance Therese, like John, had been chosen to be "crowned" in a ceremony, which would have led to a demon possessing her. At that very moment, when she could feel that some entity was trying to enter her and "ride" her, as it is called, she was internally prompted to say, forcibly, "No, this is not okay." She said she had an instinctive reaction, at the moment she sensed an entity descending upon her, to push it away and refuse to consent. She made this sudden refusal despite her having prepared for a week, through fasting and separation from the world, as well as paying several thousand dollars for the ceremony. It was no small action to refuse to consent at this stage, particularly since she was deep into this specific ritual already, and in a trance-like state at the moment she refused to go further. Therese described her refusal as "involuntary." In trying to understand this, she credited the graces she received when very young, during a phase where she had a great interest in Christianity and was baptized. She felt this protection manifest many other times as she drifted through the occult: allowing her to go deep in the evil but halting her before she went into an extreme commitment.

Important to note: John and Therese both stated that they wondered whether, had they not been protected in those moments, they would ever have converted.

Work of the Angels

In spiritual warfare, as we know, the angelic world is very active. It is not simply our guardian angels who are at work defending us from the infernal powers and obtaining for us protections and God's abundant blessings. Exorcists note that angels from the higher choirs are particularly active within exorcisms. Practicing occultists, too, often note that angels often appear in their lives, seeking to oppose what the occultist is doing as well as obtain more time for them to convert. Fr. Fortea stated, "The work of the angels and the prayers of Christians can impede the plans of darkness. This is why prayer and sacrifice are so important; they are a bulwark against the powers of hell in this world and a source of abundant blessings."[19] Angelic activity can be seen as part of God's counter measures against demons, for, as St. Thomas said, "the demons are held off by the good angels, lest they hurt as much as they would."[20]

The concept of angels assisting against demons is first revealed in Sacred Scripture, such as in the Book of Tobit where we see that St. Raphael, an archangel, has the power not only to heal Tobit but also to bind the demon, Asmodeus. Fr. Fortea said, "Demons of the highest rank, though they also suffer terribly during an exorcism, refuse to leave unless an angel comes to cast them out. At a certain point during the deprecatory prayer,[21] God sends an angel to free the person. Toward the end of the exorcism, an invisible fight between the angel and the demon occurs. The possessed person looks at a specific place and tries to scratch and hit those present. It is then that the worst convulsions and screams take place. Even though the exorcist may be quiet, the angel is present and the possessed is freed by means of his intervention."[22]

---

[19] Fortea. *Interview*, 39.
[20] Summa 1, Q. 113, A 4
[21] The prayers that ask God to act against the demon, compared to the imprecatory prayers, by which the exorcist commands the demon directly, in the Name of Jesus.
[22] Fortea, *Interview*, 110.

Msgr. Rossetti also wrote about the presence of angels in the work of exorcism. He said, "We have been given the special grace to know that at least one high-ranking angel from the rank of powers is always present."[23] He added, "A mystic told me that at every exorcism there is at least one angel from the rank of powers present and helping. At more difficult exorcisms, we have had as many as eight in the room with us."[24] Italian exorcist, Fr. Benigno, told the story of a possession in which the demon admitted to the presence of an angel assisting him. The demon said, "Get lost, priest. You again. Why do I always have to deal with you? I can't stand you. You have an angel close to you who protects you."[25]

What Angels Can do

The abilities of angels, and the things they can do to help us in our journey to Heaven, are vast and impossible to enumerate in a book – thanks be to God. Some examples from my research illustrate many encouraging things that angels are capable of doing. For instance, in the diary of St. Gemma Galgani, she recorded a special, and likely very rare, action of her guardian angel. After a night of specifically difficult demonic attacks, she was greeted by her guardian angel, who also presented to her a morning cup of coffee.[26] While quite extraordinary, this highlights the tenderness with which the angels are motivated, who help us daily in more ordinary and invisible ways.

Angels are secretly at work on other occasions, watching over and protecting us in many ways. Fr. Alphonsus shared a story of the apparition of an angel, captured in a photograph, which was then confirmed by a seer who works with his exorcist team. Father was at a large bonfire gathering with Catholic youth and others. At one point, when the fire had an impressively tall flame, someone took a picture of it. When the lady who took the picture got a chance to look at the image, she was shocked at what she saw and sent it to the seer whom Father knows. The photograph revealed a clear form in

---

[23] Rossetti, *Diary*, 175.
[24] Ibid 65
[25] Fr. Benigno Palilla, *Rescued from Satan*, Fr. Cliff Ermatinger trans. (Padre Pio Press, 2018), 122.
[26] As mentioned in Rossetti, *Diary*, 115.

the flames, standing about six feet tall, with what looked like two wings, a head, and a body leaning forward, positioned like it was walking in a specific direction. The complete shape of the figure was veiled within the fire, but the wings and head were clear in the overall dimensions. When the seer saw the image she said, "That's a real angel." To the people who saw the picture, it simply *looked* like an angel. To her, she could see that the angel was actually present. "I see it differently from what you see," she explained. "I see it with eyes that see the spiritual realities."

John said that he saw his life, when he was in the last years of his occult practice, in the following way: "I was the fig tree in Our Lord's parable: 'One more year and it is gone!' But my guardian angel begged for one more year to be given." John was referring to the following account in the Gospel:

> And he told this parable: "A man had a fig tree planted in his vineyard; and he came seeking fruit on it and found none. And he said to the vinedresser, 'Lo, these three years I have come seeking fruit on this fig tree, and I find none. Cut it down; why should it use up the ground?' And he answered him, 'Let it alone, sir, this year also, till I dig about it and put on manure. And if it bears fruit next year, well and good; but if not, you can cut it down'.[27]

"By the grace of God," John added, "I am here and out of that world."

Angelic vs Demonic activity

In our spiritual lives, angels and demons are both active, but their approach, tactics, techniques, and manner of interacting with us is very different. Sacred Scripture speaks of this reality of heavenly and preternatural interference in our daily activities. For instance, the Acts of the Apostles depicts variously Satan, angels, and the Holy Spirit blocking or adjusting the travels of the Apostles at different points. St. Peter was freed from prison and directed on his

---

[27] Luke 13:6-9

way by an angel.[28] St. Paul stated, "We wanted to come to you – I, Paul, again and again – but Satan hindered us."[29] The Holy Spirit is stated to clearly do the same, but to also inspire the Apostles to travel to certain areas. In the Acts of the Apostles, we read,

> And they went through the region of Phrygia and Galatia, having been *forbidden by the Holy Spirit* to speak the word in Asia. And when they had come opposite Mysia, they attempted to go into Bithynia, *but the Spirit of Jesus did not allow them*; so, passing by Mysia, they went down to Troas. And *a vision appeared to Paul in the night*: a man of Macedo'nia was standing beseeching him and saying, 'Come over to Macedonia and help us.' And when he had seen the vision, immediately we sought to go on into Macedonia, *concluding that God had called us to preach the gospel to them*."[30]

Fr. Sebastian pointed out that the real battle is not demons against angels but demons against human beings. "In this war," he said, "both angels and demons are willing to work with people, but in very different ways. The demons try to pervert any natural or spiritual gifts a person might have and use those toward evil ends. Demons tend to 'push the envelope' while angels do not." The angel, as Msgr. Rossetti wrote, is seeking to help and to guard the person but the demon is seeking to harm, manipulate, and take possession of the person.[31] "The demons," Fr. Sebastian added, "do not respect our free will and will seek to push us to consent to them, while the angel does the opposite, waiting for you to ask him for help."

Msgr. Rossetti discussed the difference in the actions of angels and demons. One of the key distinctions is the issue of freedom. "Angels," he said, "do not try to possess or dominate. They are instruments of God's love, and thus they enhance our freedom." Demons, on the other hand, "are out to possess, to control, to

---

[28] Acts 12: 6–15
[29] 1 Thess 2:18
[30] Acts 16:6–7. *Emphases* mine.
[31] Rossetti, *Diary*, 34.

dominate, and ultimately to destroy."[32] Former occultists, in describing their experiences, have revealed that these distinctions are very accurate.

John said that it is primarily in looking back that he can see that angels were often around when he was deep into the occult. "When demons were present, it was easy," he explained. "They would show up and would be happy to help, that is, fuel our vices and depravity." At times, though, the process was difficult and it seemed that angels were likely interfering, frustrating his efforts and turning them into "a comedy of errors and missteps." This is more easily believed because, at that specific time, he was looking into "Christian healing" which utilized a certain amount of Christian language and may have opened him up to God's actions in his soul. He noticed many other instances as well, saying, "Things would happen such as not being able to light candles, the sudden appearance of a storm, car problems preventing people from showing up, all through natural means. Demons, though," he added, "do not want to stop you from your occult rituals. There is no prudence or restraint; they encourage you to do everything, 'go for it.' They revel in human sin and excess, the lack of reason, and animal passions." When it began to appear to him that an angel might be present, he discerned this was possibly the case because he would also be hit with the thought, "Should I do this? Is this a good thing?" When this happens in the life of a person whose conscience has become blinded to good and evil, it is a very noteworthy incident.

Therese agreed with this observation. She stated that, in the occult, "Good becomes bad and bad becomes good. If a neo-pagan would report that something 'horrible' had happened – that would be an angel.[33] The demon, on the other hand, would appear quickly and say, 'You rang!?'" She added, "Demons try to get you to keep going by making things happen the way you want. Then, when it looks like it is going well, it all crashes." That is the demonic technique. However, she has had strange experiences with interruptions that don't match the demon's personality. At important rituals, people

---

[32] Ibid

[33] Meaning, the "horrible" thing would be an interference with the occult ritual and desired outcome and, thus, a frustration of the person's effort to dabble with diabolical forces. This interference, Therese is stating, would be the work of an angel, whereas the work of the demon would be to give the occultist the evil they wanted.

would run late or not show up, supplies would go missing, and key components would be forgotten about, completely impeding the rituals from moving along. Several of these interruptions prevented her from participating in rituals that would have likely taken her into a major negative spiritual reality.

One three-week ritual she did, with a focus on wealth, involved summoning and communicating with four demons and Satan himself. At that point, Therese was very deep into the occult and was not hiding behind the mystical veneer of Wicca. At the key moments when the diabolical communication was supposed to happen, there was something like a physical wall established between her and the demons, blocking all communication. She said, "It was like a safety foam was surrounding us." Her sense was that an angel had set up the barrier to stop the process from occurring, saying, "No, no, this is too much. You are not going to be doing this! I will petition for a storm or a car accident[34] to stop you." Again, contrary to the demons, when the angel would be interfering, there was never a dramatic entrance or attention drawn to the angel's presence. It is only in looking back that she could understand he was there.

Exorcist Fr. Benigno presented the story of Josie which highlights this battle between angels and demons. Josie, who recently returned to the Faith, witnessed the assistance of the angels when battling with a diabolical attack on her daughter. The demon, with whom Josie had made a pact, attacked her daughter and inflicted a mysterious illness upon her. Josie, having recently decided to return to God, began praying for her daughter at this point. This provoked a diabolical manifestation in which the door to the bedroom slammed shut and her cell phone turned off. At this moment, panicking, she began to use the techniques she had learned in the occult in order to heal her daughter.[35] This failed and she remembered her friend's counsel to invoke the Blood of Jesus to combat the devil. That worked and the result was an extraordinary manifestation from Heaven. She said, "The entire room was lit up with a comforting light and I saw a sword of light cut the darkness, and angels floating in the air with swords of fire. The cries of terror

---

[34] In this sense, any minor accident that would simply slow down their plans, not with harm to someone.

[35] This is one of the damages the occult does to people, ingraining within them the impulse to have recourse to occult ritual, which instinctively kicks in at difficult moments.

were halted by the voice of my son Ivan,[36] almost laughing: 'Stupid demons, don't you know that angels are stronger?'"[37]

By the power of God, man can resist all forms of demonic attacks. By the power of God, man is also capable of being freed from all forms of demonic tyranny and oppression. Further, this power of God is that of the all-good Trinity, whose desire for man's salvation was such that the Father sent His only-begotten Son, Our Lord Jesus Christ, to become man for our salvation. He did not simply become man but He allowed Himself to be killed by the men who, inspired by the all-pervasive "spirit of the world," conspired together to bring about His end. It was here that all who had been blind could finally see how glorious was His victory over sin, for, by the power of His own divine nature, He rose from the realm of death. It is this very power of God which is wielded against the diabolical and wielded in favor of those who are trapped in Satan's kingdom of death. Therefore, no one trapped in the occult today should fear for their salvation if they can simply muster the courage and the humility to surrender their lives to the power of the Crucified and Risen Lord.

---

[36] Her other child, sleeping in the same room where she was with her daughter.
[37] Palilla, *Rescued from Satan*, 225.

Chapter Seventeen

The Church is the Great Liberator

It is through the Church that souls will find the liberation that Our Lord Jesus Christ has brought to the world. The Church, "the household of God, is the "pillar and bulwark of truth,"[1] "built upon the foundation of the apostles and prophets, Christ Jesus Himself being the cornerstone."[2] To these Apostles was given "authority over unclean spirits, to cast them out, and to heal every disease and every infirmity."[3] Christ Our Lord, to whom "all authority in heaven and on earth has been given,"[4] gave further authority to the Apostles, beginning with St. Peter, to whom He entrusted "the keys of the kingdom of heaven."[5] This authority, in which they became "stewards of the mysteries,"[6] that is, "of the Sacraments,"[7] included the power to forgive the sins of men[8] and to call down the Holy Spirit through the laying on of their hands.[9] Our Lord promised that these Apostles, the foundations of His Church, and the conduits of the grace of salvation to the nations, will join Him when He is enthroned in glory in the "new world," and, as the "twelve foundations" of the New Jerusalem, will sit on their own thrones of glory.[10]

As members of His Mystical Body, the Church, the Apostles and their successors dispense the graces, the "power [that] came forth from Him,"[11] to generation after generation, from the days of the

---

[1] 1 Tim 3:15
[2] Eph 2:20
[3] Matt 10:1
[4] Matt 28:18
[5] Matt 16:19
[6] 1 Cor 4:1
[7] CCC 1115
[8] John 20:23
[9] Acts 8:18
[10] Matt 19:28 and Rev 21:14
[11] Luke 6:19

early Church down to our own. Entrusted with this authority, the Apostles "freely give"[12] in the same manner as all has been freely given to them. By faith and right living, the Sacraments of salvation, namely Baptism, Confirmation, and Confession, will bring the soul out of the darkness of perdition and into the light of Redemption.[13] As Christ administered healing and the Sacraments of salvation, so the Church, through this Apostolic foundation, administers the grace of divine adoption, freedom from sin and death, and restoration of body and soul.

To encounter this healing and transformative love of Christ, we must come to Him, and welcome Him when He comes to us, humbly presenting ourselves to His representatives in the Church. His priests, as coworkers with the Bishops,[14] who are themselves the successors of the Apostles, are the first ones a man will encounter when seeking the help of Christ. These priests possess the same Apostolic and sacramental authority as the Bishops, though to a slightly lesser degree.[15] For those fleeing the occult, recourse to the Church and to the power granted to the clergy is absolutely necessary in order to break free from occultic grips, recover spiritual strength, and begin the process of growing in grace and holiness. This may include simply going to Confession and having the priest pray a prayer of deliverance over the individual, but it may also require deliverance prayer sessions, often repeated, or a customized prayer routine, even going so far as to necessitate the Rite of Exorcism. The amount and kind of extraordinary ecclesial intervention depends on the level of involvement in which the person was engaged while in this evil realm.

In order to purge the occult from one's life, it is essential that the person learn the art of spiritual warfare, which the Church has the wisdom, power, and experience to teach. Not only are demons

---

[12] Matt 10:8 DR

[13] Ongoing repentance and conversion of the heart is necessary to block and more deeply remove all wickedness from the heart that remains after Baptism, lest we return to the "bond of iniquity," as seen in St. Peter's condemnation of Simon Magus in Acts 8:19-24.

[14] CCC 1562

[15] Priests cannot ordain new priests. Further, though they have the power to do the following, they need permission from the Bishop to administer the Sacrament of Confirmation (in the Roman Rite) and to perform exorcisms.

legalistic, as exorcists are quick to point out,[16] but Our Lord places demands on us, requiring us to work with Him in the effort to destroy the hold of evil, make reparation for our sins, be received back into His grace, and allow the abundance of grace to flow into our lives. Our Lord's demands, while requiring perseverance and patience, are ultimately simple: surrender to His love. However, that surrender is often difficult for us, as weak as we are, so Our Lord, through His Church, has given us many steps and approaches and techniques for progressing in the spiritual life. These, accompanied by love and surrender to God, will destroy the reign of evil in the hearts of occultists and bring them peace.

The first step in receiving deliverance from evil affiliations is for the occultist to humbly present himself to the Church. This humility essentially guarantees the transmission of God's love and power to the soul of the occultist, fracturing if not annihilating any holds the demons have on the person. As with all cases of diabolical harassment, liberation is a process and takes time. It depends on many factors for its full realization.

Fr. Alphonsus, in commenting on humility, gave an example illustrating how priests must also be humble when dealing with these issues of deliverance. Father told a story in which he, and a few others on his deliverance team, did not fill themselves with this key virtue. He said, when they once went to a residence that had been determined to be filled with demons, "We thought this would be easy. We'll go in, do these prayers – easy," he said, admitting, "We were almost treating it like magic." Once they started doing the exorcism prayers over the place, "The Lord let us really know," he said. "The demons were noisy, things were happening, the seer was really beaten up. We realized we came in there with a lot of pride; that is what [the demons] feed off." He said they learned many things in that moment. They were reminded of how important it is to maintain great humility and virtue and love for God and for His people. They must also recognize that "in the demonic realm, and the spiritual realm as a whole, there is so much more than we will ever fully understand." On that last point, Fr. Ermatinger agreed, stating, "In this field, there seem to be more unknowns than knowns."[17] As a

---

[16] Legalistic: they strictly follow, and even obey, laws of governance as established by God, in particular those which either allow or forbid them from having influence over man.

[17] Palilla, *Rescued from Satan*, 13.

result, humility and obedience to what Christ has revealed and instructed through His Church is essential for both the clergy and the laity.

To humility must be joined a willingness to change. Without this, not only is the grace of God blocked from reaching the person, but the person himself is unwilling to let go of and renounce the very diabolical associations that are causing his misery. When the person is unwilling to do so, it blocks the Church's ability to bring the person to Christ. In the case of the Monroes, an exorcist they spoke to told them that he was willing to do an exorcism for their daughter and assess her spiritual situation, but the girl would need to be willing to go to Confession first. She has so far refused to do that so the exorcist is simply unable to assist.[18] However, when humility and repentance *are* truly present, grace will flow freely and bring real help. Adelaide was led through one of the programs in her diocese, in which priests are trained to assist individuals who come to them for help. This program is the *Liber Christo* program, put together by Fr. Ripperger and his associates.[19] When she went through the program, she said, "I had to rearrange everything I thought about forgiveness and self-absorption." She realized that she had a lot of disordered thinking on the issue. The Church, through the program, "helped me bring that into order and look at it in a correct and true light."

The Importance of Fighting

It is important to learn how to pray well and fight well against diabolical attacks. Fr. Cyprian said that *Liber Christo* helps individuals do just that: pray well and fight. "The person needs to take authority over his life and order it toward God," he said. "That brings healing." *Liber Christo,* he said, focuses on getting the person to establish a holiness of life first before deliverance is carried out. This strengthens the person to fight the demon from within, makes the body hostile to the demons, and makes it more difficult for the demons to get further into the person. This will often lead to the demons begging to be released from the possession because the person has become so holy through the process. However, Our Lord

---

[18] Despite possession, or other diabolical activity, the person still has the power to choose.
[19] More details at *LiberChristo.org*

still requires the demons to remain for the exorcism, which is a real punishment for the demons, inflicting real suffering on them.

This program, and others like it which a parish priest or exorcist will use, depends on the involvement of and the support given by priests. They are our spiritual fathers, endowed by God with many spiritual abilities and gifts, flowing from the Heart of Christ, which will bring healing, strength, and spiritual renewal. Sadly, given the state of the world and the Church, not everyone can find a good and faithful priest who is able to assist them in their spiritual warfare needs. This is a great tragedy but, nonetheless, a reality. Philomena, thanks be to God, had a supportive priest who listened and, after hearing her whole story and situation, said, simply and supportively, "We will go from here." A lot of priests were dismissive of her and her past in the occult. Many former occultists have encountered this same dismissiveness, with priests treating the occult as a joke that has no real impact on a person's life. Ultimately, it comes down to ignorance. As with many spiritual warfare issues, most priests today are not being properly trained. As a result, faithful Catholics, as well as modern pagans who seek the help of the Church, are being left without the good shepherds they need. Philomena said, on this issue of dismissing former occultists, "They must not! [The occult] is like a scar – it does not leave you." Of the former occultists that I interviewed, who have had to approach the Church for some form of exorcism or deliverance prayer, they have all praised the power of Our Lord to bring substantial change to their lives through His Church's intervention.

Andrew's Story

When Andrew and his wife were preparing to enter the Church, they had the help and direction of a local priest who took them through a session of deliverance prayers. Though not an exorcism, these prayers were particularly powerful, and need to be utilized by more priests, who all have the authority to pray them over people. Andrew said, "Immediately after reciting those prayers, I felt like a new man entirely." Since that time, he has kept up with deliverance prayers, and focused on fortifying his soul through a devout reception of the Sacraments.[20] "You can never defend yourself from the Enemy enough," he added.

Andrew described the powerful effect brought about by the prayers of the priest. He said, "It was as if a weight was lifted off my shoulders." They did prayers to break both generational spirits and occult attachments. The priest did a preliminary evaluation of his spiritual association with the occult, gathering, in the process, the names of specific entities that he had contacted. The priest "wanted specifics," he added. "It was like a general gathering intel together in order to form a battle plan for a frontal assault against the enemy – and then he carried it out!" The priest emphasized the importance of being faithful to prayer as required by the process and, if they faltered, to start over again and be more focused the next time.

In meeting with the priest, Andrew and his wife prayed a prayer called the "Invocation of the Entire Heavenly Court."[21] Recalling the moment, he said he had a very memorable experience during this prayer: "I remember seeing, within my mind, clouds opening up and bright angelic beings with swords bursting out of the sky, and darkness being driven away. I felt lighter, like a weight had lifted off me."[22] During the prayers to remove the Freemasonic curse,[23] which involved the symbolic removing of garments associated with oaths and curses invoked by practitioners of various levels of Freemasonry, Andrew experienced a particular sensation, as if these things were truly happening to him, leaving him again feeling lighter. "I left the Church that day feeling like a new man," he said. "Such an insane experience, I don't know how to explain it."

Gabriel's Story

The people Gabriel came to know in the local parish Church as he neared his conversion at the Easter Vigil, and who were aware of his history with the New Age movement, told him to get in touch

[20] Prayers such as those in the book, *Deliverance Prayers for Use by the Laity*.
[21] A prayer found both in the Auxilium Christianorum prayers and Deliverance Prayers for Use by the Laity.
[22] His vision sounds similar to visions experienced by the possessed during the process of liberation.
[23] The Freemasonic curse, as an example of something similar to a generational curse, is not a teaching of the Church. On this matter, some priests and exorcists believe in generational curses while others reject the idea.

with a priest for deliverance. After being directed to the diocese for assistance, he was instructed to begin a particular prayer routine to help alleviate the symptoms and/or reveal whether there was a diabolical presence involved. A few weeks after he began these prayers, he experienced what amounted to a full deliverance from a diabolical affliction while praying the Rosary.

One night, with a Rosary in his hand, Gabriel was listening to a video of Gregorian chant on the computer, part of a video with sacred images. While he was praying the Rosary in this manner, looking at an image of Mary, he began to fall asleep. As a result of the fatigue, he decided to stop and go to bed, first saying the nightly prayers that were part of the assigned spiritual routine. Suddenly, when saying the routine Our Father prayers, he began to apparently speak in tongues.[24] He began to repeat, "Thank you, Jesus," over and over again until it became a jumbled mess. "It was the craziest thing I've ever been through," he said. Then he began to go through these strange motions and, while conscious of what was happening, he was not sure why he was doing it. He felt like he had no choice but to move in a very specific manner: kneeling, praying, lifting his arms, etc. He eventually thought his hands were about to be pierced and he became quite disturbed by what he was experiencing.

Looking over at the screen, he saw an image of Mary. "All of a sudden," he said, "It was just like, 'I don't wanna see Mary, I don't want anything to do with Mary.' And I look at the Cross, 'Ah, no, the Cross! No, no, no,' and it was almost like I was trying to run away from it." The repetitive statements then changed to "Let him go!" and "No, I'm burning!" and "No, I don't want to go," and "Get out! Get out!" and "Leave him alone!" All of this lasted for approximately thirty to forty minutes. After this had all stopped, he felt like he had been freed from something. He explained, "In my head, I was like, 'Was I just delivered by God Himself? Did He just do it *for* me? What just happened here?' So, then, I go to sleep, and I sleep the whole night. I didn't wake up." For a long time, since first renouncing the occult, Gabriel had experienced diabolical attacks routinely in the middle of the night. Sleeping soundly was a clear indicator that a spiritual change had occurred. In the morning, his

---

[24] Speaking in tongues is a gift of the Holy Spirit and is typically given alongside the gift, in another person, of interpreting the language. In this case, it might not have been this gift but simply that Gabriel did not know what else to call this strange phenomenon.

house felt all clear again, just as it did many months before, when he had first prayed and surrendered his life to Our Lord, before the diabolical retaliations had begun.

"Just Make it to Easter" – Lucy's Story

Though Lucy's liberation truly began when she received certain extraordinary graces from Our Lord while in the mental health facility, the full process of her liberation would be a battle. With the help of her exorcist, those battles became more intense just before Easter, impacting her ability to think, compelling her to remain in her bed, and striking her with confusion when driving in her car, so much that she could not make it to a nearby friend's house. "I would drive around and around in confusion, trying to visit a friend only a few minutes away. There were times," she added, "when I switched back and forth between being myself and being heavily influenced by evil. I wore a cross necklace around my neck, but the next minute I couldn't wait to rip it off, I detested it so much. Sometimes I could pray the Rosary; other times the only words I could form in my mind were a very short song about how Jesus' love was bubbling over."

"I nearly did not make it to the Easter Vigil," she said. It was clear to her that Satan was trying to block her conversion. She suffered attacks of suicidal ideation so strong and constant that she feared she would end up back in the hospital. Eventually, she met the diocesan exorcist and her parish priest. With permission from the Bishop, they performed either a major or a minor exorcism over her, though she was not certain which. Describing the experience, she said, "I remember feeling very scared and kept saying that I don't think I wanted it anymore. In hindsight, it was probably not me that was scared!" During this time, Our Lord assured her with these words, "Just make it to Easter, and you will be saved." Describing this, she said, "I still don't understand exactly what happened. It was as if the words were heard by my heart. I've never figured out a way to explain it. It was like words were spoken to my soul, and I heard them, but not with my ears." Nonetheless, with the help of the Church, and a generous pastor who let her begin RCIA just a few weeks before its completion at Easter, she received her liberation at Easter.

The Power of the Presence of an Exorcist

Fr. Velinde, recounting the time when he realized the evil of the energy practices with which he had associated himself after first leaving Hinduism, stated that, after his initial conversion, and during his naïve association with a Christian esoteric group, he thought he had sincerely embraced Christ and was doing these healings with a mind that was inspired by evangelical charity. He was also going to Mass and Adoration and praying the Rosary. Gradually, he noticed a subtle alienation when working with the "entities," the spirits involved in this energy practice. One day, as he stated, they revealed themselves.

When doing a "magnetic collective" ritual with his group, he began to hear his name being called. He responded to it, as if someone in the room had spoken to him, but no one had said anything. It happened repeatedly and it was clearly not an interior voice. He spoke to one of the leaders who then smiled and told him that no one is able to have that much power without the help of certain "spirits" called *healing angels*. They referred him to the Book of Tobit as a way to justify their recourse to these entities, and this temporarily reassured him. The truth, as he was about to discover, was that these "healing angels" were demons in disguise.

At a Mass soon after this, at the elevation of the Host, "Through Him, with Him…", he heard these same *healing angels* shouting blasphemies against Christ present in the Blessed Sacrament. He was terrified and knew that he had been completely wrong. After Mass, he told the priest the whole story. The priest said, "It doesn't surprise me. I am the exorcist for the diocese." Fr. Velinde then realized that, all along the way, at Mass, the spirits had hidden themselves. But, in the presence of this priest, who had such authority, they were forced to reveal themselves. The deliverance from these spirits came eventually after intense prayers and a long period of convalescence. He then became a priest himself, after ten years of study, and waited twenty years more before he shared his story.

Deliverance Prayers Work

The Church teaches that deliverance from the activity of the diabolical can occur on multiple levels: by the direct extraordinary action of Christ, through the Church's immediate intervention through the Rite of Exorcism, through deliverance prayers (minor exorcisms) prayed by the priest, and through the laity praying on their own behalf, or on behalf of those under their authority. The individuals who shared their experiences for this book benefitted from all these avenues of God's grace.

The Becketts benefitted from both the prayers of a priest and the prayers that the laity can say on their own. This was related to a strange neighbor who moved in next door shortly before Catherine, their daughter who fell into the occult, went off to college. After he moved in, his presence became a disruption to the whole house. The parents speculated about whether he had exerted some sort of influence on Catherine's decision to explore the occult. The father mentioned that, as they work to bring her back to safety and to the Faith, they are beginning to see many different angles of the spiritual problems their daughter has been facing and trying to make sense of it. Though the neighbor was supposedly Catholic, he was mean, cowardly, and would even growl at them. He would occasionally harass them and was generally a negative presence. A priest friend of theirs once came to visit their home. He led them in a Rosary around the house and blessed the house and the outside property. Without knowing of the problematic neighbor, he stopped at the fence, gave that area an extra blessing, and later said that there was something bad over there in the neighbor's property. When the Becketts started doing the perimeter prayers[25] after the visit from the priest, they noticed that the neighbor calmed down. "He is still a mess to this day," the father said, "but the spiritual warfare prayers continue to help."

Like the Becketts, Elizabeth benefitted from both the prayers of the priest as well as those of her husband. Though it has been many years since escaping from Damien, Elizabeth is still dealing with diabolical oppression and working with priests to finally be liberated. After she got married, years after leaving Damien, she would wake

---

[25] From Fr. Ripperger's book, *Deliverance Prayers for Use by the Laity*

up being choked by an invisible entity. She was not able to get much sleep. This oppression left her almost unable to pray at all, except when in the presence of the Blessed Sacrament. She would also often suffer from flashbacks to her time with Damien. She had moments of disassociation and out of body experiences. When her husband, exercising his spiritual authority which comes through their marriage, would say the appropriate deliverance prayers over her, she would shake. When the priest prayed those same prayers over her, she said it felt like she was going to vomit. Her house, though, was not suffering from any diabolical manifestations. They moved at one point and, in the process of packing, she found a necklace charm that Damien had given her. She refused to touch it and had nightmares and flashbacks after being around it. She gave it to the priest who was helping her and he said the appropriate prayers over it and destroyed it.

Seek and Ye Shall Find

As the toll of the occult is different for each former occultist, so the things they seek through the Church's intervention are also different and specific to their needs. Many who are emerging from the occult are dealing with ongoing diabolical manifestations which continue to try to tear their lives apart. Others have a notable absence of peace in their homes as a result of the damage done by the presence of the occult. Still others are seeking to break bad habits of sin, or break evil associations they made in the occult, both of which are slowing their progress in grace and holiness. In the end, they are all seeking healing from the damage the occult has brought.

Making the Manifestations Stop

When Adelaide became dedicated and focused in spiritual warfare, her goal was to make the diabolical manifestations stop. It was a "save me!" attitude, she said. Once they were properly educated in the Faith and in spiritual warfare by tradition-minded priests, the war, at first, got really bad, so much so that she was afraid for her kids. Adelaide said that, after they had moved to their third house and she realized that *she* was the cause of these diabolical manifestations, the local priests, trained in exorcism and deliverance ministry, did an exorcism over the house and prayed deliverance prayers over the family. This, she said, finally brought a little relief. However, though some manifestations remained, they did not give into fear but held fast to the counsel of the priests. The battle with these diabolical manifestations eventually came to a near complete halt. From there, they felt fully equipped to handle the "few and far between" manifestations without difficulty.

After she first returned to the Faith, Clare turned to the deliverance prayers that the laity can safely use, including the prayer to break generational curses. She sought this out not because of the influence she feared that her occultic father had brought, which she was still unclear about, but due to the ongoing diabolical manifestations in her home. She was also going to Mass and Confession, seeking to close all the doors the demons could be using to gain entry, but the attacks persisted. As a result, she began to conclude that the cause was generational and something in her family line. "I had thought only houses were haunted," she said, "but then I realized *I* was haunted."

The deliverance prayers did help the experience of the children but not her own. Clare had done all she could think to do. At that point, her husband was still very lukewarm about the Faith, only attending Mass because she wanted him to give the kids a good example. When Clare turned to the deliverance prayers, she did not understand anything about the occult except for the fact that you could open doors to the diabolical through a Ouija board or mortal sin. When Clare was young, her mother had also instructed her to invoke the Holy Name of Jesus when she saw something diabolical in the house or elsewhere. She said, "I used it all the time as a kid and it worked every time!" When her husband eventually stepped up his practice of the Faith and became a real spiritual leader, they called in a priest to bless the home and Clare stopped experiencing any manifestations. She saw this play out in a progressive manner. She said, "The more my husband became a spiritual leader, the less these things happened. The holier he got, the less I experienced."

The Need to Break old Habits

Once Andrew set his mind and heart on becoming Catholic, he set aside the practice of the occult as he had known it for years, but his heart lagged behind. He admitted to an emotional attachment which lingered even after he stopped the practice. "I think that is the hardest thing to shake," he said, "You do it for so long and it's very convincing; you have seeming evidence of the preternatural and the supernatural existing right in front of you." He stated that Fr. Ripperger's teachings on spiritual warfare gave him all the means he needed to understand these attachments and the explanations about how he needed to remove them. "Yes, the preternatural does exist," he said, regarding what he learned through his occult practice, "but the evidence I had was not the right evidence. It's like having a loaded gun in my hand as evidence that death exists – that's what this was like."

John said that, when he feels he is being spiritually attacked now, he often slips back into reciting mantras automatically. He was trained so deeply in them that he starts to do that and then has to stop himself. This is one of the dangers of the occult. Others I spoke to mentioned a lingering strong inclination to cast a spell as a solution to an issue. As with Andrew, spiritual warfare is needed to break these old habits and form new and holy ones.

The Need to Break Occult Affiliations

Many former occultists cling to the practices and teachings of spiritual warfare in order to completely break and sever any ties they have to the demons with whom they were once associated. Therese said she feels like she has a spiritual responsibility to do *all* the prayers from the *Deliverance Prayers for the Laity* book as a result of the deals and connections that still remain from her time in the occult.

While many occultists struggle to leave behind all the attachments from their time in close association with the diabolical, many also comment that they fear they will never be fully free of it. Fr. Augustine said that, while the demons are eager and attempting to return to these individuals, as we know from Our Lord's teaching,[26] Christ's healing power can indeed be definitive. What is important here is that the person focuses on making full reparation

---

[26] Matt 12:43–45

for their sins. The issue of justice is very important in deliverance ministry, he added.

Adelaide, following Fr. Ripperger's advice, developed a devotion to Our Lady of Sorrows as part of her spiritual warfare plan, in order to discern the true nature of her ongoing spiritual issues. After two days of doing a novena, the word "Freemason" began to repeatedly come to mind. She was unsure if she was simply suggesting the word herself but, by the end of the novena, she was reminded of an odd symbol she had seen in a relative's house as a kid. She then looked into what that symbol meant and realized it was connected to the Blue Lodge of Freemasonry. Some exorcists have noted respiratory illnesses connected with the Freemasonic curse and she found it to be interesting to note that there have been a lot of respiratory diseases on that side of her family.[27]

Later, after going through the *Liber Christo* program, Adelaide was able to reconcile with her mother after a two year estrangement. In the conversations that followed, she asked her mother about Freemasonry in the life of that relative. Her mother replied, "Oh, yes, he and his brother and both parents were in it." Adelaide herself would eventually suffer from respiratory issues requiring medical therapy when, following an apparent attack by a diabolical entity in her house, she began to suffer from a sudden onset of asthma.

Feeling the weight of guilt from the harm Adelaide once caused by casting curses against people, she said she was also eager to learn how to undo these curses, thereby helping to break, hopefully, any associations with demons that she may have brought into the lives of others. The closest answer she found on how to do that was at one point in the *Liber Christo* training module for laity.[28] In that training, they discussed making deep renunciations of grave evils you have committed in your life. This involves breaking what are called 'soul ties' with people which arise through committing mortal sins, such as fornication or occult rituals, with that person. These sins have a binding effect on the souls involved. The verbiage given for making these renunciations is, as she said, the closest thing she had found to

---

[27] Fraune, *Slaying Dragons*, 104. Not all respiratory illnesses have a connection to Freemasonry. Some priests reject the idea that such a "curse" could afflict one's health.

[28] A four-stage protocol.

undoing a curse or a binding spell.[29] It instructs the person to say, "I take back anything I gave, and I give back anything I took." She specifically remembered the curse she issued against her mother and used this renunciation formula for that. It was after renouncing these curses that her mother came back into her life and they reestablished a connection. She fully credits the Church's spiritual warfare wisdom, as presented in the *Liber Christo* program, for this reconciliation.

In seeking to help break Ava free from her occult entanglements, the Monroes were always on the lookout for signs of any explicit evil associations. On one occasion, they found some tarot cards which belonged to Ava. Familiar with how to properly dispose of cursed items,[30] they were a bit crafty and employed the extra help of blessed candles. They put the cards in a container[31] with the blessed candles and burned them all together, as the mother said, "So the cards would burn and burn and burn!" Then, they tossed the ashes into a stream.

Seeking Peace

When the positive changes began to appear in Lucy's mind, the wisdom she was gaining from the Church's intervention helped her begin to understand the way in which the devil had been operating against her for so long, and what he was actually capable of doing. "I wasn't aware that Satan could insert thoughts into people's minds," she said, "but he can, especially when you partake in activities that purposely have you empty your mind and open it up to other 'sources'." It was at this point that Lucy understood the importance of spiritual warfare wisdom when it comes to mental health. "I then realized that the thoughts weren't all mine, they were being put into my mind," she said. Further, she began to understand that there were ways to protect her mind from these attacks and prevent the

---

[29] Since curses are issued with malice, renouncing them is key to healing the will and increasing the souls ability to grow in charity.

[30] Handling cursed items directly is not recommended, as any curse on the item can affect the individual who holds it. This is addressed further in *Slaying Dragons* and the companion book *Slaying Dragons – Prepare for Battle* (Slaying Dragons Press).

[31] Though it is best to avoid directly touching cursed items, not all occult items are cursed. For example, if the tarot cards were purchased from a popular mainstream store, they were likely not yet cursed (or "blessed," as witches would describe it) as would be the case if purchased from an occult store.

thoughts from harassing her. "You can reject thoughts," she said, "but I never knew this. Just because something is in your mind, does not make it true, nor do you have to continue with the thoughts. I learned a lot of 'tools' to help the thoughts leave. For example, saying 'Satan, get behind me!', or calling on the Name of Jesus, or even thinking hard about more positive thoughts. Custody of the mind is something I'd never heard of. It's so important, yet rarely every discussed."[32]

Lucy added, "I learned to turn my mind away from all the horrible thoughts in my head, from the confusion, from the lies, and to focus on Bible verses, Christian music, to good things, to holy things, to Jesus. *'Whatever is true, whatever is honorable, whatever is just, whatever is pure, whatever is lovely ... think about these things'* (Philippians 4:8). I knew that when I felt that my mind was starting to be overcome again, I could think about Godly things or say words such as, 'Get behind me Satan,' and the attack on my mind would cease." Every time Lucy would invoke the Holy Name of Jesus, the evil voices and thoughts would slightly recede. This struck her clearly as a supernatural occurrence, which was a special grace of understanding that Our Lord had imparted.

After the Becketts, following the counsel of the Church, removed all the items associated with their daughter's witchcraft, and the daughter moved out, and they started blessing the home regularly, the whole family noticed that an oppressive spirit noticeably cleared. The remaining teenagers in the home, one by one, stated that they could feel a positive difference in the home. It was like the roof had been taken off the house and the whole place had aired out. In the daughter's bedroom, there had even been a horrible odor that would not resolve by any cleaning method. After the house was blessed by a priest, the odor also finally departed. Every time the daughter visited, once she had left, the father would bless the house and pray deliverance prayers over everyone.

In consultation with a Catholic with an approved spiritual gift (a seer), alongside the counsel of an exorcist, the Monroes discerned that they may have been suffering from a curse. As a result of this

---

[32] Here, "positive thinking" refers to what is often called "self-talk" within cognitive behavioral therapy, as well as "custody of the mind." These are practices that encourage us to govern the thoughts we allow in our minds. This is a rational and Christian thing to do. St. Paul also advises to think about "positive" things. (Phil 4:8).

discernment, they began doing binding prayers and the *Auxilium Christianorum* prayers.[33] Within a few weeks, the family was flooded with an abundance of positive changes: their career and financial concerns cleared up, one child returned to the Faith, another child set his course toward the seminary, and Ava reached a potential pivot point in her struggles with the occult. As a result of these great graces, they decided to never stop praying the *Auxilium Christianorum* prayers. "We can see the power of protection it places over the family," they said. One thing they noticed, as a result of these prayers, was that the full extent of the evils and problems into which Ava had become entangled reached a point where they were sharply manifesting. They thought this was a turning point, seeing that the daughter had bottomed out and the parents were in deep spiritual warfare at the time. After bottoming out, Ava then began to make an apparent recovery. "It was as if everything came to a head and then began to turn around," they said.

Healing the Wounds from the Occult

Those who leave the occult and enter the embrace of Christ through His Church often experience deep and profound, or at least tangible, healings as Our Lord continues to break them free from these diabolical entanglements. Gabriel, for example, said that all his relationships, which had been hindered and damaged by the anger that filled him as a practitioner of the occult, greatly improved after he left the New Age movement. Timothy's wife commented on the changes she noticed in Timothy after his conversion. She said, "I saw the Holy Spirit watching over the whole family through him. He became a real spiritual leader; it was amazing." As a pagan father, he realized he did not know what he was doing in his paternal role. He was not being the spiritual teacher which Christianity held up as the model. The spiritual teaching he had been looking for, and the ultimate father figure that he was looking for, was Jesus Christ and the priestly model of Jesus Christ. Christ gave guidance to people in the way he was called to give to his children. Now, within the

---

[33] A short series of daily prayers put together by a few exorcists which brings an individual into a spiritual community praying for exorcists and those in need of deliverance or protection.

Church, Timothy was able to more easily and completely seek to imitate this fatherly love.

An Example of Healing – Lucy's Story

Our Lord worked many healings in Lucy's life as well, which deserve to be told here in full. She no longer suffered from OCD, bursts of anger, a desire to control her life, or a slavish attitude toward work. Instead, she had become lighthearted, more connected with her loved ones, and filled with a peace "which I never knew existed." One spiritual, even mystical, experience that Lucy had during this time was the literal sensation, after receiving Our Lord in Holy Communion, of God knitting her mind back together from the diabolical confusion which had torn it apart. She spoke about this, saying, "It was at times like this that I wish I could see the spiritual world, so I could see what was truly happening. However, I'd learned the hard way, that trying to get a glimpse into what should be the unknown is not wise. If God wanted me to see anything, He would show me."

This transformation from being "plugged in" to diabolic harassment to receiving the gift of peace was a bit jarring for Lucy in the beginning. "When my mind started to quiet down, I would wake up and my head would be a bit quieter. It was a little scary for a while," she admitted. She gave a description of how the evil and horrid thoughts which had accompanied her previous state of diabolical possession began to fade away as she utilized the new spiritual warfare techniques she was learning. She said, "But slowly, the [racing demonic] thoughts would disappear. They would first feel as if they were far in the back of my mind, and only if I tried to connect with them would they come to the forefront. Over months, I learned to not connect with the thoughts, and then they would disappear."

As part of converting, Lucy went to Confession, where she received absolution for "sins that were very grave, ones that I now realized were completely against God. They were mortal sins. It was no wonder that Satan was so prominent in my life! I had opened many doors and let him in," she said. The healing process was gradual but evident, beginning on the first day she became Catholic. Every day after, her mind was changing as if a barrier had literally been removed. "Every morning, it felt like a layer of understanding had been added to my mind, and I felt more and more separated from the evil thoughts and words that had been plaguing me."

The healing took the form of God *knitting her back together*, as is said in the Psalms, "You knit me together in my mother's womb,"[34] providing another example of the power of the Church, our Mother,[35] to bring us into a new and supernatural life in Christ. When, at times, the voices would return or evil thoughts arose, it was as if they were coming from far away, trying to break into Lucy's mind, but were easily ignored. This feeling of the evil thoughts being further and further away increased each day. It was more pronounced for her because she had grown accustomed to her mind being perpetually confused and burdened with many thoughts running through it at the same time. At this point, her mind had become calm and she enjoyed "true peace."

As Lucy said, "I was not the angry, stubborn, impatient woman that I had been for so long. I had a peace that was beyond my understanding. I now understand this: 'I will give you a new heart and a new mind. I will take away your stubborn heart of stone and give you an obedient heart'."[36] The healing God accomplished within Lucy appeared to be complete. In the nine years that have passed since her conversion, she feels that she has been released by God from all the negative effects of her dabblings. She feels like God has broken all connections to the occult and has liberated her completely, leaving no connections to the diabolical associations she had made during those years.

All who associate themselves with sin, whether through the occult or not, experience the bondage to sin, Satan, and death which Our Lord came to destroy. Through His Church, and through our incorporation into her, we will experience the liberation He came to bring.

---

[34] Psalm 139:13
[35] Eph 5:22f. The Church is the bride of Christ and thus our Mother.
[36] Ezek 36:26

Chapter Eighteen

What Priests Need To Know

In the light of everything that has been presented thus far in this book, it is clear that the Church is facing a situation which calls upon her to muster all her resources in order to give a thorough response. The responsibility for this effort will primarily be placed on the individual priests who are at the frontlines of this spiritual crisis. With them are their Bishops, whose responsibility it is that their priests have all the resources and training that they need to be fully equipped to go into battle. Nonetheless, as is sadly clear, many Bishops are of no help in this war. Thus, it falls on the local parish priest to study, get prepared, and do everything he can to save the souls in his parish boundaries that are being ravaged by the diabolical.[1]

It is here that the priest must rest on Our Lord's admonition to His Apostles, "Behold, I send you out as sheep in the midst of wolves; so be wise as serpents and innocent as doves," adding, "Beware of men."[2] St. Thomas[3] said that Our Lord advised them in such a way in order to make it clear to them that there are dangers in this mission, but also to counsel them on how to navigate it properly. Going out as sheep, the supernatural success of their mission will reveal that it is the message of the Gospel itself, rather than violence and the force of arms, which is the power by which the Apostles have converted the nations. In counseling them to "be wise...and innocent," Our Lord advised them to defend the Faith well, to focus on living as the "new creatures" they have become in Christ, and to preach according to the way in which man has fallen through the serpent's lies, all the

---

[1] The parish priest is spiritually responsible not simply for those who attend his Church but for all who reside within the territorial boundaries established for his parish. This includes Catholics and non-Catholics, Christians and pagans.

[2] Matt 10:16-17a

[3] Commentary on the Gospel of Matthew, Ch. 10, Lecture 2

while ensuring there is no anger that resides within their own hearts. With this, as priests, like the Apostles, go out into this fallen world in order to draw it toward Christ, they will encounter men who have become, through sin, as wolves and beasts in their affections, and stubborn in the darkness of their intellects. Many will resist the message of the Gospel until the power of grace can break into their hearts. The eloquence of the preaching of the priests, whether through holy preparation[4] or through spontaneous inspiration,[5] will, by the gift of God, enable many to "believe in Him of whom they have never heard"[6] and thereby obtain their salvation.

The Occult is Here, in Your Own Town

Many priests today are becoming aware of the situation regarding the rise of the occult by coming face to face with it in ways they did not expect. Fr. Stephen said that, in just one year, he and his pastor had two people approach them seeking help to leave the occult, deliverance prayers, and entrance into the Church through their parish. He highlighted the fact that this is happening in a highly Catholic area. These two cases made Father think, "Wow, it [the occult] is *here*! It was very eye-opening." He added, "I take it seriously that it is in the area. It is startling for the pastor and me, in our little old town. You don't think that it's here. 'That's Chicago, that's New York,' you say. It is, and that's opened our eyes in a certain way."

Not only is the occult in most towns in the US now, but one exorcist, who has studied these issues extensively, painted a very grim picture of how widespread, established, aggressive, and confident the occultic world has become in our day. The impression he gave is that the world is ripe for a spiritual battle with the occult, a sentiment shared by many former occultists. Thus, every priest *must* be trained and aware of the situation and how to handle it, for it is bound to emerge in his priestly ministry at some point and to some extent.

---

[4] 1 Peter 3:15
[5] Matt 10:20
[6] Rom 10:14

Fr. Dominic said the parish priest needs to be ready for these issues because he is the one who gets called in first when things start going wrong in a person's life. This is where Fr. Dominic's own experiences first occurred. People came to him, confused and/or desperate, many of them being non-Catholics. Fr. Dominic explained, "I have encountered people who had used Ouija boards, did tarot readings, used crystals and 'energy' rituals, did pagan rituals (usually 'Nordic'), had curses put on them, attempted to offer their soul to Satan, received a cursed rosary (once), or had people in their sphere of influence who did/used these things and may have gotten sucked into these sorts of things. In the aftermath of these activities, once obsession or infestation came into play, people often consulted with 'spiritualists' and had them do sage-cleansings etc., which of course only exacerbated what was going on."

Two things often stir a person to get out of the occult and seek the help of the Church. "They turn a corner suddenly," Fr. Dominic said, "and realize by the grace of God (and sometimes from the repercussions of their occult practices) that something needs to change. This is the moment of truth, because they have no 'tools' available: they don't know what to do, they don't know where to turn. When they turn to the priest, things can get better." Though, he said, while it is not a case of "everyone everywhere" being involved in the occult today, nonetheless, he explained, "This stuff is happening in many different lives, and we priests typically only see it when something has gone wrong, as it always will if someone persists in it long enough."

The Church has the evangelical responsibility now of reaching out to former occultists and, as one exorcist insisted, even active occultists. Former occultists agree. These people are exiting what might be referred to as a newly discovered spiritual disease which is either not yet on the radar of most of the Church hierarchy, or they simply don't realize there is a treatment available. The majority of the medicines needed, Philomena argued, reside in the Traditions of the Church which are being buried in the current era of unbelief and horizontal novelties.[7] This evangelical responsibility rests upon the fact that all souls are the responsibility of the Church and that all souls within a parish are the responsibility of the local pastor.

---

[7] "Horizontal" as in focused on man alone vs. "vertical" which implies a focus on God.

Therefore, dear priests who read this book, if the occult is in your town, it is your responsibility to do what you can to convert them to the One True Faith. The reality is that, yes, indeed, the occult, today, is truly in your midst.

Trial by Fire – Welcome to Deliverance Ministry

Despite the necessity of being prepared both spiritually and intellectually before entering this ministry, priests are often pulled into deliverance work without a *proper* invitation from the Bishop. Many priests are learning about spiritual warfare, possession, deliverance ministry, and the presence and dangers of the occult by literally being thrown into these experiences. The issues of diabolical harassment are *so* present in the culture, and the number of priests who are trained and knowledgeable about how to deal with it is *so* low, that often the two meet and the priest gets his training in a *trial by fire.*

Fr. Augustine told me that, in the first few years of his priesthood, he saw a decent number of cases of people with diabolical issues, "like one every week or two." Thankfully, he was at a parish where the pastor was a trained exorcist, so he had all the help he needed. Fr. Dominic said that, in the first six months of his priesthood, he was doing several house blessings, and destroying Ouija boards and Satanic books – every week. This "crash course" is helpful to a lot of priests who harbor doubts. Fr. Louis told me that he used to be skeptical about the occult and the diabolical but after two or three experiences, he knew it was real.

One case of *trial by fire* concerns a priest who was given a copy of my book, *Slaying Dragons,* early after its publication, when there were still very few reviews for it and word had not spread very far. He thanked me for the book and simply put it on his bookshelf and forgot about it. About ten months later, he was helping someone who had come to him and suddenly found himself in the middle of a diabolical manifestation. Totally untrained and unprepared, he ran back to his office after the incident, grabbed *Slaying Dragons,* and read it in two days. He sent me an email a week later apologizing for dismissing the book when he received it. He admitted that priests are not trained in this field at all in seminary and he was clueless about the realities. My book, he said, (thanks be to God) taught him what he needed to know. As a result, he was, with the additional help of local priests trained in exorcism, able to handle the case that came to him. The Bishop then realized that the priest was gifted in this field and he now assists his diocese in exorcism and deliverance ministry.

Fr. Anselm told me the story of his first involvement with deliverance. After agreeing to meet a family at the Church to help a college-aged boy who had serious spiritual issues, and apparent diabolical manifestations, he quickly realized that he was not prepared for what was happening. "I had no idea what I was doing," he said, "We are completely ill-prepared as priests. I was a believer but I was never prepared for anything like that." After bringing the boy into the Church, he quickly realized he was dealing with a full-blown case of possession, in which, at one point, Father was almost lifted off the ground by the boy and, at another point, the boy was slithering across the floor like a snake. Though he knew about traditional holy water and blessed salt, he had nothing on hand and knew it would take about ten or more minutes for him to get that prepared. Thankfully, God provided a devout family and a parishioner who was experienced in deliverance work to assist him.

Fr. Anselm said the night of his first encounter with the diabolical left him restless and sleepless. Afterward, he began to buy every book on the topic that he could find in order to understand better what it was that he just went through. He also started to attend conferences on exorcism, deliverance, and spiritual healing. "I had the theology," he said, "but no praxis, no practical experiences."

Fr. Stephen and many other priests of his diocese appealed to their Bishop to appoint an exorcist after they all noted the clear rise in the number of cases of occultists seeking the Church's help and experiencing diabolical harassment in general. Though the Bishop did not appoint an exorcist, he made it clear to the priests that they had the authority to perform minor exorcisms. In working with the Satanists who came to his parish, Fr. Stephen did these prayers with them and their Confirmation sponsors. He noted the battle they were in during the process, saying, "You can see where the Evil One is trying to cast doubt, make them doubt the Church, make them angry at us, create division. It has taught me a lot."

Fr. Stephen and his pastor agreed that they need to do something for these people, to the extent they can without an exorcist. He said, "We need to do this to learn how to better minister to folks in these situations because it seems like," he then paused for emphasis, "they keep coming." He added that he has been actively working on learning everything he needs to know for this work of deliverance. He said, "I have been pursuing my own contacts, trying to figure things out, whether it's talking to exorcists, like, 'give me a crash course, not in exorcism but in deliverance ministry,' what are the things to watch out for, and all that."

People Need the Priests to Believe

As the Becketts sought to help their daughter, and their whole family, the most important thing, they said, which really helped, was having a priest that really believed in spiritual warfare. However, when they first sought out a knowledgeable priest to help their daughter, it was not easy to acquire one. When speaking to the best priest the area had to offer, he was dismissive about people needing special prayers after leaving the occult. Eventually, they stopped asking local priests for help because it was clear they did not understand. Eventually, they were connected to a traditionally minded priest who came over and blessed and exorcised their house. After that, they noticed a big change and an increase in peace which the whole family felt, especially the younger sibling who had been severely affected by the occultic sister.

A priest's spiritual readiness and holiness are critical in his pastoral ministry in today's culture. However, sadly, the criticism of many is that both of these are lacking in many priests. In a discussion with Fr. Ambrose on whether every priest should be instructed to pray deliverance prayers over people more freely, he expressed a severe hesitation. Even though he has observed that positive reactions come from doing spontaneous or "just in case" deliverance prayers with people with whom he interacts, he does not think a Bishop will instruct his entire presbyterate to start doing that. The reason is not that the Bishop is unbelieving but that the priests are ill-equipped. "The reason," he said, "is that not all priests are living a lifestyle that would make them strong enough and prepared for this approach." He then cited the example of the sons of Sceva from the Acts of the Apostles.[8] "If you are not in a state of

---

[8] Acts 19:11f

grace," he added, "you can get beaten up if you take on a demon. The Bishop," he continued, "has to be careful whom he chooses to do deliverance and exorcisms. They need to go to Adoration every day, be deep in prayer, receive and offer the Sacraments with great reverence, and fast regularly."

In his book, Msgr. Rossetti wrote about how he explains the need for holiness in priests who engage in spiritual warfare. He wrote, "I was recently giving a training session for new exorcists. A few were a little skittish, fearing demonic retaliation. I assured them the ministry was safe. God would protect them. But I did add, 'You need to up your game.' I explained. Being an exorcist is like flying an airplane (I used to be in the Air Force). It is very safe…but mistakes can be deadly."[9] Fr. Ambrose has also observed the fear in other priests to confront the realities of evil and sin. He has many pastors, whose parishioners are seeing him for an exorcism, "who won't even come to the exorcism of their parishioner because they are terrified of it. They won't be very helpful handling the rest of the issues either."

Know Why People Choose the Occult

Priests need to understand why people are attracted to the occult, Helena said. Most people are not drawn to it for the evil purposes of destroying the Church and spreading evil in the world. "They are people," she stated, "ones often hurt by abuse or other things, that want to have a part of their life that they have a say in, and to feel like they belong to something."

Therese believes that occultists are looking for a regimented prayer life, something the Church provides. However, she observed that the more the Church has removed the structure and ritual in the Mass, the more individuals are trying the best they can to replace it with other religions, including the occult. From the beginning of her practice in the occult, she wanted a liturgical rhythm to her life, with daily rituals and spiritual routines. The more the Church neglects this in her modern practice, the more witches and occultists will pick it up from outside the Church.

---

[9] Rossetti, *Diary*, 27

John, for example, was once in the Hermetic Order of the Golden Dawn. During this time, he had an incredibly structured spiritual life. He would wake up with certain practices and perform the sun salutations throughout the day. He had a daily liturgical spiritual life. When he converted after RCIA, he was given nothing like that in the Church. He felt like he had to hunt it all down himself. He had to learn the Rosary and the Liturgy of the Hours himself, all the while also enduring the scoffing of other Catholics who thought those were outdated devotions. John said these things are what give former occultists the spiritual protection they need on a daily basis. It is a must-have for people with a background in the occult. They need these weapons against the attacks and retaliations and to heal the wounds they carry. Referring to the fact that he feels he will never be free of diabolical affliction because the demons he fraternized with are not going to forget about him, he said former occultists need the entire Church to be on the same page about saying "NO!" to the occult and "YES!" to the devotions from the Church's great traditions.

Don't Be Dismissive

Far too often, former occultists report that the priests they have spoken to were quickly dismissive of their spiritual concerns about their occult baggage. Some believe, erroneously, that simply stopping the activities and joining the Church ends any spiritual battle from the previous life. Others dismiss their concerns as being purely psychological issues. Still others dismiss it because they either don't believe, have not been trained, or are afraid to get involved.

Lucy had very frank words for priests who are dismissive of the issues related to the occult. She said, "Catholic Priests and Bishops should be ashamed of how poorly they are teaching their flock about the dangers of the occult. I'm constantly horrified and disappointed at the lack of care factor about occult practices – it's as if most people don't know, or don't care, that they exist." John agreed that priests are too dismissive of the occult. He said some will give a few deliverance prayers to the person and think that is all you need. It seems like priests either don't believe in the occult's existence or don't know anything about it.

As a result of being in the occult, Therese said she has become very much aware of when a demon is present or causing something to occur. When they seek out the help of priests in the process of suffering from retaliation, they often get comments of dismissal and doubt about this involvement of demons. Priests seem to want to dismiss it as if she is simply having a "bad day" but she, with her experience, knows what is really happening.

Lucy added that priests need to also make it less difficult for people to join the Church. "They should not dismiss spiritual baggage and burdens as a 'mental health issue'," she said, "but, instead, realize they have authority in this arena and Christ calls them to use it. They need to speak more plainly and boldly about the Truth. When this comes from the Shepherds, it carries a special weight with it. The faithful are in dire need of strong, vocal, and faithful priests but, around the world, they cannot find them. Priests need to know," she continued, "that without them stepping up, speaking boldly and declaring the truth, they are contributing towards many souls being led to Hell."

The tendency to dismiss these concerns can be a very grave issue on the part of the priest. The priest needs to ask himself where the hesitation is coming from. Does it flow from a lack of faith, a rejection of a doctrine, a fear of the devil, or a personal habitual sin? The belief that those who involved themselves in the occult *do not* suffer in some extraordinary way and *do not* need special spiritual assistance could reveal that the priest does not understand, or rejects, the teachings on progression in grace, the power of vice and virtue, the need for reparation for sin, the power of the will to make a choice of evil, the fact that sin begets sin, the need for penance in order to break free from sinful attachments, among many other critical doctrines of Christianity.

Not the Normal RCIA

From his experience, John said too many priests don't understand that former occultists need more than simply RCIA.[10]

---

[10] The *Rite of Christian Initiation for Adults*, which has become the modern standard for permitting entry into the Church. It usually entails a program spanning about nine months, in which the candidate for admission into the Church receives education and passes through various rites to slowly prepare the individual for Baptism, when entering

The latter need spiritual direction from the very moment that they show up at the Church and are ready to convert. Sometimes, a priest will dismiss their experiences as merely silly experimentation, or they dismiss the problems as being psychological only. John agrees that there will be psychological issues in former occultists but that is a result of how the demons have harmed the person on both the level of the intellect and the will. Occultists are all vulnerable to psychological problems, he added. Priests need to understand that diabolical issues and psychological issues are not mutually exclusive but can exist together in the same person.

Fr. Anselm agreed that people leaving the occult do need to be handled differently than everyone else. "Most priests," he added, "don't know how to handle these things; they are not trained." That being said, "the Church needs to meet people where they are. A 'one size fits all' mentality does not work. Not everyone needs the RCIA structure or timetable. The needs of each person need to be assessed and then a plan can be developed. That being said," he continued, "you also don't want to rush the process. People coming from the occult have a variety of backgrounds, experience with evil, and need for healing. Some convert with powerful experiences of grace, others are wounded and dragging along and need extra support. Some have no clue how to pray or meditate like a Christian while others have picked it up quite quickly. Some have a deep craving for the Eucharist and believe only with the Sacraments will they begin to find true healing. Others need a lot of coaching and prayer, even deliverance or exorcisms, before being ready to approach the Sacraments."

On this last important note, Fr. Anselm added, "The greater portion of healing can only happen through the Sacraments. To get them to a place where they can receive the Sacraments takes time, but it doesn't have to take a year." The priest who is bringing the person into the Church needs to assess what the person knows and then supply for the catechesis they are lacking. This may be quick or it may take quite a while. As Our Lord said in the Gospel, converting a person is a matter of both teaching *and* Baptism. Our Lord declared, "Going therefore, *teach* ye all nations; *baptizing* them in the

---

the Church as a non-Christian, or for reception into the Church, when coming from a Protestant background.

name of the Father, and of the Son, and of the Holy Ghost. Teaching them to observe all things whatsoever I have commanded you."[11] These two must go together for many reasons, Fr. Anselm added. "The person needs the catechesis in order to have understanding which, in turn, illuminates and bolsters faith, a condition for full openness to the workings of grace poured into the soul through the Sacraments. Further, if the person is not properly prepared, and enters the Church too early, there may still be lingering issues with diabolical attachments. The Evil One, still having a hold on the person, may incline the person to sacrilege or retaliate against the person with some sort of diabolical manifestation. The devil may also take advantage of the situation and seek to thwart the person's faith just as it is trying to flower."

Fr. Anselm's advice is extensive and can serve to help former occultists, parents, friends, and priests understand the situation a bit better. Every person's experience and needs are different and a properly trained priest can help the former occultist navigate the process of responding to God's grace and entering the Church. It is important for former occultists to be able to track down a knowledgeable priest and, thankfully, networks are slowly emerging which make this less difficult.

A final note in relation to Fr. Anselm's advice is on the issue of potential sacrilege in relation to the use of sacramentals as spiritual aids, which many of the faithful freely offer those who are straying from the Church, with the hope that these spiritual aids will help steer them back to the Church. One concern about the use of sacramentals by former occultists was raised by Fr. Athanasius, who said, "The occult person needs a deep conversion first so they don't approach the sacramentals with a magical mentality." That conversion will order the person first toward God and then toward created things as God intends for them to be used. Sacramentals, at that point, would be understood as the vehicles, chosen by God and His Church, through which He desires to give us certain graces according to His own desire, and not something that we can use to cause spiritual effects to occur in a manner divorced from Him or in a manner that controls Him.

---

[11] Matt 28:19-20 DR. The Greek says, "make disciples" but the Latin says "teach."

Similar to the concerns about a protracted RCIA process, Margaret mentioned to me criticisms that she had heard about some spiritual programs priests use to help people leave the occult behind and find healing. Some of these systems entail a long and extensive regimen of prayer and penance in order to teach the diabolically afflicted person how to do the work of liberation themselves, and thus achieve peace in a manner that flows from within their own will, from their new love and desire for God, rather than relying so much on the external work of the exorcist or the parish priest. While these have proven to be effective for many people, these also cannot be a 'one size fits all' approach, like Fr. Anselm stated. "They just throw these people into this routine and bypass the priest," Margaret explained. Her big concern appeared to be people like her own kids, who would not go through this program if they ever got to the point of wanting to get out of all these evils. "A program like this takes dedication and focus. What about my son!? He is ravaged by it. What do *they* do, when they are spiritually sick and dying? They can't do a program." This is one of the areas that the Church needs to think better about: the occult has harmed people in a myriad of ways; the Church needs a myriad of ways to heal them.

It seems like Fr. Ambrose would agree with Margaret's concerns. He said that those who have left the occult essentially need a guardian angel in human form. They need to be teamed up with someone strong in the Faith who can effectively hold them accountable, making sure they are okay and moving forward. They may need to meet as frequently as weekly, perhaps over a meal. They also need a spiritual director because, as he said, "The devil is going to harass them and confuse them and push them to despair and to give up." This should be done for about a year, after which the extra efforts could be scaled back. "No," he said, "they are *not* like everyone else." Lucy agreed that ex-occultists need a different program. "Having to wait a *year* to enter the life of grace in the Church for a person who had lived in Satan's dungeon?" she said, adding, "My healing began the moment I was *part* of the Church." People seeking to enter the Church need to be welcomed and addressed quickly and urgently. Lucy was permitted to join RCIA with just three weeks remaining until Easter. It ended up being a *very* good decision by the priest.

Exorcists are quite clear that, as a result of these dabblings in *extraordinary* evils, the solutions must involve the special rites of the Church. "The Church has her normal spiritual helps," Fr. Sebastian said, "but she also has her extraordinary helps, such as the Rite of Exorcism. Something that was brought in with extraordinary effect will not be sufficiently dealt with by the Church's normal spiritual assistance." Therefore, priests need to be trained in what these extraordinary means of spiritual assistance look like and how to properly make use of them.

What Priests Can Really Do

Fr. Blaise said that priests need to understand the power of their priesthood when seeking to help those who are trying to leave the occult. They need not fear to pray with people, for example. Often, he said, priests shy away from this, but it is perfectly Catholic and priestly to pray and bestow a blessing on someone. Avoiding this irrational hesitation can put the priest in a position where he could make a huge difference in the life of someone who could literally be on the verge of despair and suicide.

One of the sources of the hesitation Fr. Blaise mentioned is, of course, a lack of preparation. I asked Fr. Alphonsus whether priests are prepared to deal with people in these situations. He said that, while certain seminaries are trying to do a better job preparing people, "Most priests are not prepared; they know very little," he said, adding, "which is why they call me, because they feel they are out of their depths to discern if it is real and how to handle it. Some are willing to ask lots of questions and then go for it; others say, 'This is so completely out of my realm, can you handle it?'"

However, priests truly are capable of doing a lot, much more than they realize. They just need to know this and find the courage to proceed. Further, there are things they can do which are less in the realm of "deliverance" and perhaps less intimidating. As Fr. Blaise said, one focus that the priest should have is to help the individual make a good and complete Confession. This would require a conversation on the nature of Confession, the nature of sin, the gravity of the occult, and the importance of contrition and penance. Further, the person will benefit from being guided through a thorough examination of conscience where they can fully understand all their sins and come to a personal rejection of them in favor of God's love, forgiveness, and grace.[12]

A lot of people coming from the occult today are gravitating to the Traditional Latin Mass for a variety of reasons, Fr. Blaise added. One reason is the clear sense of ritual and structure. As a result, the priest could consider inviting such individuals to a Holy Hour as part of the process of renouncing the occult and more deeply encountering the beauty of divine worship. In this context, the individual would experience the beauty of sacred chant, vestments, ritual gestures, incense, and candles, and would have an opportunity to behold Our Lord and petition His mercy for an extended period of silent Adoration. This time, coupled with a Gospel reading and exhortation from the priest, will deeply affect the person and greatly aid their will in renouncing evil and choosing Christ more definitively.

Deliverance Prayers by Any Priest

Once priests are comfortable using the full power of their priesthood to help liberate souls and remove spiritual obstacles that are blocking the flow of grace, there are many deliverance prayers that they can do without special permission from the Bishop and without being an exorcist. Deliverance prayers and minor exorcisms can be done by any priest, Fr. Ambrose said. If you have your Bishop's permission, it is even better, as you are then more protected when doing so. The best prayer is the Leo XIII prayer found in the Roman Ritual after the Rite of Exorcism.[13] Deliverance prayers, he added, are just that, *prayers,* and some can be spontaneous, whereas a major exorcism is a fixed Rite. Prayers of supplication are calling on God to do the deliverance (deprecatory prayers), but exorcisms and some deliverance prayers involve commanding the demon to depart (imprecatory prayers).

---

[12] The "Interior Healing Process," crafted by a group of exorcists, is helpful for this process. It is in my other book, *Slaying Dragons – Prepare for Battle.* The individual can also ask their pastor to guide them through making a good Confession. This will require a scheduled time with the priest, rather than simply getting in line for Confession at the regular times. Priests are happy to do this.

[13] Found in the *Roman Ritual,* Vol. II, called "Exorcism Against Satan and the Fallen Angels"

The prayers that Fr. Cyprian uses to help people, since he is not an exorcist but only an assistant, are normal deliverance prayers which any parish priest can use. The diocese and the exorcist, or the exorcist team, can guide parish priests on what these prayers are.[14] They can also give further instructions on important things to keep in mind, such as always being in a state of grace when using these prayers. While working with someone, the average priest will be able to handle the "lesser things"[15] in the person's spiritual life, even driving away the lower demons that are harassing them. If there are stronger demons remaining, or it is determined that the person is possessed, then the priest can simply send the person on to the diocesan exorcist.[16] The parish priest can do quite a bit of good himself and move forward without fear, knowing that the diocese is there to support him, and that, through his priesthood, Our Lord has entrusted to him real spiritual power and authority.

Fr. Alphonsus said that he finds that, as a pastor, he is using deliverance prayers and healing prayers with people much more than he imagined he would. "It is having such a powerful effect on people dealing with obsession and with fear," he said. "Then, they will experience a radical change in terms of the temptation." He admitted that, before these experiences, he very often dismissed these as primarily psychological issues. "Now I am seeing that, no, it is the demonic," he added. He was aided in this discernment and realization by the help of one of the other exorcists who is well-trained in psychology.

Priests Must Preach

"What is not preached from the pulpit is not heard in the confessional."

Fr. Ambrose said that the preaching of the pastor can have a huge impact on the parish as a whole, in particular with regard to rooting out the occult from the lives of parishioners. He said, "If he preaches about this stuff, he can then gauge from the confessional

---

[14] If a priest's diocese is not knowledgeable or supportive, they should reach out to those exorcists who are teaching publicly and counseling priests on this subject.
[15] This refers to the typical spiritual issues, which are very important. For former occultists, though, these do not always resolve their problems.
[16] There needs to be one in every diocese.

what needs to be addressed. For example, if he preaches on tarot cards and people come and confess it, he needs to keep preaching on that issue and weed it out of the parish. Pastors don't need personal experience with demons," he added. "Just flip through a book by an exorcist and pull stories into your homilies." On one occasion, Father preached about an exorcism that he had once performed and tied it to the readings. Afterward, people came up to him and said, "Thank you! That was so enlightening."

In Fr. Louis' home country in Africa, where there was more adventuring into the occult, he said he preached on the occult more than he does in the U.S. After speaking to me in our interview, he began to realize that he should be preaching more on it here in the States as well. "We need to talk about it more; it is happening," he said, adding, "but they are not coming to us. I have had very few cases. Maybe it is because people don't hear about it and don't know they can come forward. Maybe they are dealing with it in their own way or dying from it in silence. Until you tell them they can come to the priest and lay the problem before the priest, they won't come."

Fr. Louis then gave the example of preaching about abortion and LGBT issues. Priests, he said, will say it is delicate to preach about these issues; that is how he was taught in seminary, adding that he was also taught that he was bound to preach from the readings in the Mass of the day. One day, desiring to preach on the issue of marriage, he realized that the readings also spoke about marriage and he saw his opportunity. The following week, after preaching on marriage that Sunday, he had several people come to see him and ask for help with serious marital problems. He reflected on the fact that, had he not said anything, the individuals could have been dying in silence. Likewise, he reflected, if the priest preaches on the occult, and a young person is listening, they may come quickly to see the priest and get the help they need before going too deeply into it. The healing is easier if the damage is less, he added.

Fr. Blaise said priests need to preach on the New Age and the occult in some manner. There are likely youth and adults sitting in the pews who are dabbling in the occult and still others who have practically abandoned the Faith and have embraced the occult. There will be parents sitting there who are silently suffering the impact of the occult on their family. All this needs to be taken into account when the priest looks out over his flock. Not only homilies but also bulletin catechesis is a great way to teach the people what they need to know about the occult. Further, if this is not already done, the St. Michael the Archangel prayer needs to return to its place just after the close of the Mass. "It was added for a good reason and was taken away without one," Fr. Blaise added.

Fr. Anselm told the story of how, at one RCIA class, he was speaking about the evil of seeking out a medium to communicate with the dead. In the audience was a couple who had lost a young child and, many years ago, had sought out a medium to try to contact the child. The couple had completely forgotten about this sin and had been practicing the Faith for years without ever addressing it. After hearing Father preach the truth about this issue, they were able to bring it to Confession, find healing, and close the spiritual door which the devil could have easily been using against them.

Priests need to understand that, if they would preach on these things, people, especially the youth, would listen. Fr. Gregory said that the youth are truly interested in these topics and really desire to hear the truth about them. With his background as a high school chaplain, he said, "I can guarantee I will have their complete attention when I give my 'Angels and Demons' talk." During his talk, "I have their full attention and full silence," he said. When I myself was teaching on the high school level, and actively researching for what would become *Slaying Dragons*, one of the more devout students told me, "Mr. Fraune, when you're talking about theology, most of the time, they're not interested. But when you start talking about demons, everyone's looking at you. They're listening."

Failure to Preach

Fr. Ambrose said the pastor can have a detrimental impact on his flock if he fails in being protective and solicitous for his parishioners. "Pastors who talk about sunshine and rainbows," he added, "won't talk about any of this stuff and there is probably quite a bit of it in those parishes." The number of Catholics in a given parish who dabble in occultic things will vary accordingly. "It depends on where you are," he added. "In a parish that focuses on the Traditional Latin Mass, you won't see much of it. If you have a devout pastor, Marian devotion, and Adoration, you won't see a lot of it. The pastor sets the tone for the parish," he added.

Fr. Ambrose said that he was placed in a parish where the priests who had been pastors for decades before him taught that there was no such thing as the devil or Hell and, as a result, no need for Confession. So, Fr. Ambrose started preaching the Truth and a lot of people hated him for it. Some even said to him, as he remarked with exasperation, that the St. Michael the Archangel prayer frightened their children. He made it clear to them that anyone who was properly catechized would have no fear of that prayer. He told them, "The only ones who shake with that prayer are Satan and the demons."

Fr. Ermatinger recounted the story of a man who embraced the occult out of ignorance of its sinfulness, even though he was a practicing Catholic. The man turned to a tarot card reader for help with the suffering that had become overwhelming in his life. The man stated, "I went to Sunday Mass and confessed my sins from time to time, and never thought that going to an occult practitioner was a sin, so I never confessed it. Further, I never heard a priest preach on the dangers of occult practices, so I did not know that it was offensive in the eyes of our Lord."[17]

Fr. Ermatinger shared a similar story of a woman who, after beginning to practice the occult because she was convinced she could remove curses from people who were suffering under the evil eye, soon spiraled down into palm reading, tarot card reading, and necromancy. With this, she said, she never felt at peace and was beginning to have doubts about what she was doing. She was directed by some friends to a priest who could help her. The priest ended up being an exorcist and was able to tell her that, "even though I had good intentions and sought to help people, I was actually [doing] the work of the devil." The woman then stated, "If every priest was able to explain this to the faithful, how many people would be spared falling into traps as I had fallen, saved from certain disaster?"[18]

---

[17] Ermatinger, *The Trouble with Magic*, 28.
[18] Ibid 102.

Spiritual Warfare and the Diocese

First and foremost, the diocese itself needs to be ready with resources for priests. As is now commonly known, priests generally leave seminary without the knowledge necessary to handle these situations. However, if the priest's diocese is knowledgeable and has the resources, and a sufficient number of trained clergy, every priest in that diocese could easily learn what to do should a case emerge in his parish, which will most likely happen before long.

"More than anything, priests need to be aware and believe and know what resources the diocese has," Fr. Alphonsus said. "It's not that every priest should deal with these things, because they're just not ready. Still, there is a certain natural charism, since in the old days we would all be exorcists by the office. If they know the resources and who the priest is to have people see, to know what's going on. I don't think everyone needs to be trained because that's not everyone's call, but they need to have the courage and confidence in the Lord, because that is huge." The diocese could take a good lead, as some have done, and train more priests in exorcism and deliverance work. They can then, in turn, train more deacons and laity so more people have the tools and know-how to assist. Fr. Blaise added that it is important for pastors to be updated and trained by the diocese on what to do. The diocesan exorcist is the primary resource for this.

Fr. Ambrose said that books on deliverance prayer are often difficult to find. The Dominicans in the Philippines have a good one, but it is not easy to get a copy of one. He also recommended prayers written by St. Basil, St. Gregory of Nazianzus, St. Cyprian, and others, as well as Eastern Catholic prayers to break the power of magic and additional diabolical influences. The St. Michael Center for Spiritual Renewal is another excellent resource. It has prayers for exorcists, parish priests, and the laity, in addition to recommendations for books on the subject. Fr. Chad Ripperger has a wealth of knowledge and has published many books on the topic, including a book of minor exorcisms for priests. The organization he helped establish, *Liber Christo*, is also very helpful. Finally, the Pope Leo XIII Institute, which offers resources and conferences for priests, is an excellent resource.

Welcoming the Converting Occultist

It is important for parishes to be ready to receive calls or visits from people leaving the occult. They will be seeking help but will not be sure what to expect. Once the parish does respond to these individuals, it is important that they take their situation seriously and provide what the converting occultist really needs. As was already addressed, they cannot simply be thrown into the standard RCIA program. Fr. Stephen told me that the former Satanist who reached out to his parish said he had reached out to another parish a few years ago but got no response. "He was over the moon that we responded to him, let alone took him seriously," he said. The man was still experiencing what he called "blowback" from his time in Satanism, even though he was now an Evangelical Protestant.

John said that, when he entered the Church, he was not taught how to pray or how to embrace a Catholic spiritual life. He saw Catholic spirituality as an absolute antidote and counter to what he experienced in the occult and to the ongoing affliction he endured, and he desperately wanted, and needed, to be trained in it. It would help him heal from the occult, atone for those sins, and give him the strength he needed to go through that whole transition, especially if it lasted for the rest of his life, as he feared it might. Depending on the background of the person, it will be more or less difficult to build these Christian prayer habits.

Fr. Blaise said he questions <u>all</u> RCIA candidates about the occult as a routine thing. He also sends out guidelines to the RCIA team regarding things that they need to be looking into when they help people who are entering the program. He said he has not seen a lot of people coming into the Church from the occult through RCIA, perhaps one every two years or so. In addition to screening all RCIA candidates about the occult, exorcists recommend that all dioceses also screen their new seminarians about any history in the occult. These diabolical ties must be resolved before the seminarian can receive Holy Orders.

Protecting Against the Occult

There are many threats from the occult of which priests need to be aware. In addition to those already discussed in this book, exorcists have also warned that witches will seek to infiltrate prayer groups and even deliverance ministry groups, based on the claim that they possess spiritual gifts that will be of benefit to the group. The latter groups are likely those led by laymen. Exorcists warn that priests need to be very careful about this. Witches, it has also been reported, have been known to attempt to curse the priests who attend exorcism conferences.

Fr. Stephen, after dealing with someone stealing the Eucharist, said that the pastor of his parish decided they needed to address this with the whole parish. They began leading prayers of reparation before Masses and establishing people to carefully watch everyone during Communion. The Bishop, while refusing to appoint or train an exorcist, despite it being a heavily Catholic area, was supportive of their initiative, to the surprise of the pastor. The Bishop's seriousness on the issue, despite his history of laxity on spiritual warfare concerns, was edifying to the priests. The Bishop also permitted them to disallow Communion in the hand if they felt the need, but they said that the attention they had given to the matter, the support of parishioners, and ongoing education, appeared to be sufficient.

Fr. Athanasius told me of an approach that he took, with his Bishop, to protect the diocese as a whole from further diabolical issues tied to the occult. He said that he and the Bishop went around the entire archdiocese and prayed minor exorcisms around the whole area. In one instance, there was a parish that was apparently suffering from a diabolical attack, since there was evidence of entry into the Church and of an occult ritual having taken place. As a solution to that, he advised the priest to bury blocks of blessed salt in the four corners of the property. In addition, they did a procession around the property praying for the conversion of the Satanist who had done the ritual, followed by an "exorcism of a place" in the sanctuary of the Church. Further, if there are problematic priests in the diocese, or other things similar to that, the exorcist can, with the Bishop and a priest at each corner of the diocese, pray the Chapter Three prayers in the Ritual, from Pope Leo XIII. Fr. Athanasius saw this employed for the reason just stated, and the problems with two priests were quickly resolved. For the protection of a parish, Fr. Athanasius recommended praying the Pope Leo XIII exorcism prayers privately (which does not require permission from the

Bishop) and driving the perimeter of the parish while praying the Pope Leo XIII exorcism prayers and sprinkling blessed salt. Further, if there are tarot card readers in the parish boundaries, he recommended installing blessed bells in the parish.

Be Aware of Occultic Rites and Presence

The occult world follows a calendar with certain times of the year dedicated to specific celebrations. Occultists will experience an increased presence of the diabolical at these times because they have opened themselves up to these "spirits" and the spirits indeed come. As a result, they are likely to be employing the help of demons to a greater degree at these points in the year. This could cause an increase in diabolical activity in the life of the occultists, as well as potential evil influences in the lives of their friends and family and the culture around them as a whole. With the number of occultists rising rapidly, priests need to learn the basics about these celebrations and the times when they are happening so they can be ready for any potential negative effects. Given the fact that some occult rituals involve attacking a Church in some manner, Catholics might need more protection and prayer as a defense and as a remedy. Further, occultists may be more in need of deliverance or priestly assistance around these times and might be more willing to reach out to a priest as a result.

The chief event of the occultic calendar is Halloween, also known as Samhain in the occult world. Though there is a big debate in the Catholic world about what to do with Halloween, since it truly is a sacred time in the Church's calendar, it must be known that it is also a day of summoning evil in the expanding occultic world. Msgr. Rossetti discussed Halloween and said that he and his team spend that evening in Adoration, keeping vigil for the Feast of All Saints. At the same time, they are on alert for increased spiritual attacks, which not only they but the people they are assisting, tend to endure that day.[19]

In addition to being aware of the occultic calendar, one exorcist recommended mapping where occultic shops and covens and other groups are within a given diocese, as well as where occult activity

---

[19] Rossetti, *Diary*, 250.

has been reported or is active. He said the biggest groups in the US are Santeria and Wicca, but he encouraged each priest to find out what the biggest groups are in the areas where he lives. Once this is known, the priest can be more aware and prepared and can also go out to those specific areas to pray.

Evangelize the Occultists

This brings up a very important, and likely uncomfortable, point: the priest must go out and try to convert the occultists located within his parish. Those occultists are his parishioners and he is spiritually responsible for them. They, like everyone else in the parish boundaries, is under his spiritual care and authority. One exorcist brought up this issue, retorting, "How does a Bishop evangelize these communities and Satanists?" Giving his own answer, he added, "He has to! The Gospel must go out to the darkest areas of the world. Priests need to know how to confront the issue, offer alternatives, and reach out to them." John, from his experience, agreed with this exorcist and said that priests need to be equipped; they need to go out to convert the occultists and help those who are leaving it. There needs to be a full apostolate for this, like *Auxilium Christianorum* but more focused on helping the laity, John said, adding, "The occult is everywhere and booming; we are saturated in it." When I mentioned the idea of someone starting a religious order dedicated to evangelizing those who are in the occult, his answer was a very firm, "Yes!"

One thing that is important to realize is that occultists are searching for what the Church has to offer, they just don't realize the connection yet. For example, witches create something called a *sacred circle* when doing their rituals. One witchcraft website stated, "Creating a circle in a Wiccan ritual or ceremony is performed in order to delineate the sacred space from the mundane world." In this we can see something very important: witches are seeking sacredness and are, in this post-Christian world, left to their own devices to do so. The evangelization of a witchy world should include the creation of more Catholic sacred spaces. We owe it to the world to create more sacred spaces within the reach of all: truly magnificent structures that will draw in the masses, and lift up their souls, and sanctify them before the majesty of God; as well as

319

wayside shrines and wall niches where images of Our Lord and Our Lady are more frequently presented to the eye. Remembering that a possessed girl was liberated merely by entering into the presence of St. John Bosco in a Church, and that many people become aware of a demonic presence within them simply by visiting a dedicated Catholic shrine or place of pilgrimage,[20] imagine the liberating effect that these grand Catholic sacred spaces, and these more common Catholic shrines, could have on the curious occultist who would eventually wander in or pass by.

---

[20] Fraune, *Slaying Dragons*, 130.

Chapter Nineteen

How Catholics Can Help

Pope Pius XII, in his encyclical *Mystici Corporis Christi*, explained the important role that the Church and every member of the faithful have in Our Lord's work of salvation. Contrary to many heretical beliefs that are prominent in the world, the good deeds of individual Christians do have a connection to the fruitfulness of Our Lord's efforts to save as many men as possible. As we know, Our Lord "desires all men to be saved and to come to the knowledge of the truth,"[1] but, as St. Paul reveals, Christ depends on us to continue this work as members of His Mystical Body. St. Paul said, "Now I rejoice in my sufferings for your sake, and in my flesh I complete what is lacking in Christ's afflictions for the sake of His Body, that is, the Church."[2] The sufferings of Christ on the Cross are infinitely valuable and redemptive but Christ willed that we should become members of His own Body and suffer with Him, so that the fruits of His suffering and death may continue and may be applied to the world throughout all generations.[3]

Pope Pius XII explained this, saying, after "He won for us, His brethren, an ineffable flow of graces," though "it was possible for Him of Himself to impart these graces to mankind directly," nonetheless, Christ "willed to do so only through a visible Church made up of men." This allows us to "cooperate with Him in dispensing the graces of Redemption."[4] This utilization of men in His redemptive work mirrors His decision to utilize our human nature for the original accomplishment of our salvation when He suffered

---

[1] 1 Tim 2:4
[2] Col 1:24
[3] See also, John14:12, "Truly, truly, I say to you, he who believes in me will also do the works that I do; and greater works than these will he do, because I go to the Father."
[4] *Mystici Corporis Christi* (MCC) #12

and died on the Cross as a man. After that, "throughout the centuries He makes use of the Church that the work begun might endure."[5]

Since Our Lord is clearly the Head of His Mystical Body, it logically follows that Our Lord "require[s] the help of the Body."[6] St. Paul explains this, saying, "The Head cannot say to the feet: I have no need of you."[7] Pius XII explains that, while it is obvious that the faithful need the help of the Divine Redeemer, without Whom we can do nothing, "Yet this, also, must be held, marvelous though it may seem: Christ has need of His members."[8] This, of course, is the will of God who, out of a generous love, *chose* to incorporate us and our works and sufferings into His work of redemption. This cooperation must be fully understood and appreciated for it impacts the eternal destiny of countless souls. Pius XII said that, after Our Lord imparted grace to the Church in "the immense treasury of the Redemption,…when those graces come to be distributed, not only does He share this work of sanctification with His Church, but He wills that in some way it be due to her action."[9]

Pope Pius XII admitted in his encyclical that this is indeed a "deep mystery" and an "inexhaustible subject of meditation."[10] The depth and mystery of this profound association with Christ must not incline us to shy away from hearing and believing in this solemn teaching of the Church and acting accordingly. Summing up the teaching, Pius XII stated solemnly, "The salvation of many depends on the prayers and voluntary penances which the members of the Mystical Body of Jesus Christ offer for this intention and on the cooperation of pastors of souls and of the faithful, especially of fathers and mothers of families, a cooperation which they must offer to our Divine Savior as though they were His associates."[11]

---

[5] MCC #12. Remember that Our Lord told Saul that Saul's persecution of individual Christians was actually a persecution of Christ Himself (Acts 9:4–5).

[6] MCC #14

[7] 1 Cor 12:21

[8] MCC #14

[9] MCC #44

[10] MCC #44

[11] MCC #44

Catholics – Be Ready to Help

With the rising number of people entering the occult, there is also a great number of occultists who are becoming disenchanted, discouraged, scared, and damaged by the occult and are trying to get out. Leaving the occult is no easy task. For those who successfully extract themselves from the occult, with God's help and that of His Holy Church, there are many things that they need in order to safely navigate the rough waters of that conversion process. Catholics need to be ready to help because there may be a moment when you are suddenly presented with the situation and need to understand what to do. The first step is understanding the power of being united to Christ through His Holy Church and then seeking to deepen that union and allow it to bear the fruit that Christ needs for it to bear. After that, there are many things that Catholics can do to reach out to and assist occultists in seeing the dangers of this dark realm, the beauty of the Faith, and how to break free from evil.

Andrew's case is a perfect example of this. While observing an online debate between a Norse pagan, a Mormon, and a Catholic, the Catholic debater pointed Andrew in the direction of a Catholic forum full of other debates where he could look around. Staying there for months, and researching on other Catholic catechetical websites, he eventually posted a comment in the forum asking if someone would be willing to hear his story in a private message. A man with the username "Deus Vult and Chill" sent him a message.[12] Andrew and this man spoke for an hour on the phone, during which Andrew told him his whole story. The man admonished him for his involvement in the occult, something Andrew had never experienced before, and he was filled with an overwhelming sense of guilt. The man sent him videos to continue his Catholic education and learn about Confession, among other necessary things. He told Andrew to seek out a parish with a Traditional Latin Mass and leave behind the life of sin. "That conversation, and his admonishments," Andrew explained, "led me and my wife and child into the Catholic Church and specifically to the Traditional Latin Mass. He completely turned our lives around and led us to Christ."

---

[12] I include this detail here especially because Andrew told me, "*Deus Vult and Chill* left the server eventually, and I have never been able to find him. Hopefully he sees or hears about this, because I would like to thank him."

Lucy happened to have several close Catholic friends at the time of her conversion who understood the dangers of the occult and offered their help. They counseled her, prayed for her, taught her the Rosary, and kept up with her. For the first time ever, she started to read the Bible, listen to Christian music, and pray. This helped her focus on the good and ignore the bad, which still attacked her mind. She had the support not only of her friends but also of her husband, children, and mother. Helena, likewise, also had supportive friends, and said that another element that helped her was that a good Catholic friend encouraged her to watch "The Passion" early on in her process of converting.

Fr. Sebastian said that life often brings a moment that opens a door for grace to flow into the occultist's life. These are moments when Catholics need to be ready to guide them. "Sometimes the person's child or a family member is praying for them, or there is a tragedy in his life like the death of a loved one," he said. "God can use these things to bring him back; he wants to see his loved one again. It could be this light that turns things around."

Giving Advice to Current Occultists

When speaking to someone who is in the occult, Philomena said to remember that the diabolical operates on pride and pride will be apparent in the person with whom you are speaking. You should start by trying to have a conversation with them, asking, "Tell me how things are going. How's your mental health. Understand," she added, "There is a lot of pride present." She said of herself, when she was in the occult and aware of how dark it was getting, that her attitude was, "I made this bed, I'm going to lie in it." It is important to get them talking so they open up about their life as it is at the moment. "This might help them recognize the despair, anger, emptiness, and the façade of having control," she added. You should be honest, "don't sugar-coat it," she said, adding, "Tell them, 'You are under the influence of the demonic and need to fix it – here's how'. If they are willing to have a conversation, it will take a few."

When the opportunity arises, Catholics need to have the courage to tell an occultist that what he is doing is evil and he needs to leave it in the past and quickly enter, or return to, the Church. "You have to convince the person," Fr. Sebastian said, "that what they are doing is bad. The original thing that started it all and pushed them in that direction – they have to realize that this thing was only an apparent good, and was, in actuality, evil. Once they see this, and no longer go along with it blindly, the battle begins."

Andrew said, "Do not be afraid to tell people straight to their face that the life they are living is one that is evil and that Hell is a real danger. Many may laugh at you, mock you, attack you. But you may end up getting someone like me, who needed to hear that admonishment. It's what led me to Christ's Church." He continued, adding, "Also, don't throw pearls before swine. Figure out how to discern when it's fruitful to converse and convert, and when you should reserve yourself to praying for conversion and leaving it in Heaven's hands."

A bold approach to reaching out to occultists was taken by Bl. Bartolo Longo. After the restoration of his soul, he was filled with such gratitude and he decided that he must seek to save the souls of his friends who were still lost in the occult. Bravely, he attended one more séance in order to renounce the occult in the presence of his old friends. He stood up in the middle of the ritual, renounced those occult practices as a "maze of error and falsehood," and held up a medal of Our Lady for all to behold. From that point forward, he dedicated himself to prayer, in particular to a devotion to the Rosary and Our Lady.[13]

From my research, there is much to give us hope that, if they will listen, see the joy that Christians possess, and have a few examples of holy Christians, occultists will admit to the fact that they lack that peace and joy and happiness which they originally hoped they would find in the occult. From there, the turn to the Church can be initiated.

Spiritually Assisting

Camilla said that it is very difficult to talk people out of the occult. What works is prayer. "Intercessory prayer is the most powerful weapon against the deceptions of the New Age," she said, adding that "they work wonders." She also recommended Catholic devotions, like to the Infant of Prague and the Holy Face of Jesus,

---

[13] Mary's Dowry, Bl. Bartolo Longo documentary, YouTube

that have proven to be great helps. Christopher said that his own return to the practice of the Faith made no sense apart from considering the impact that a supernatural influence was having in his life. He credited the prayers of his devout grandmother, who had already died by the time of his reversion, with bringing about his conversion from the occult. One thing that Andrew emphasized was to pray the Rosary every day for a person you know who is in the occult, and to take seriously the promises Our Lady made to those who do so. One promise that he focused on is that everything we ask of her through the Rosary will be granted. Our Lady promised, *"By the recitation of the Rosary you shall obtain all that you ask of me."*

Andrew added that, motivated by a mind and will that take the occult very seriously, Catholics should offer prayer and reparation every day, in particular through the Rosary, "that these diabolical organizations would be routed and all those within them would be rescued." The damage, and the likelihood of enslavement to the devil's deceptions, are so severe that those involved in these practices might not ever emerge from them without the powerful intercession of the Church and her members. Acts of penance, he said, are also necessary to atone for the countless blasphemies and sacrileges committed daily by members of the occult throughout the world. He recommended the traditional and highly neglected practice of acquiring indulgences for the Poor Souls in Purgatory. These indulgences aid the purification of those Christians who died in a state of grace but were not yet sufficiently pure to enter Heaven. Once they make their entrance into the Presence of God, they are then equipped to intercede for those who still make their way through this vale of tears, including those lost in the occult. "We should flood Heaven," he added, "with as many souls as possible to get as many more Saints as possible praying for us and for the whole world."

Community

"One has to be careful," Fr. Alphonsus said, "and realize there are wounds connected with that person, because that is often the doorway. They especially need community. We need to build a Christian and Catholic community, otherwise it is easy for the demons to come back when the person is lonely and say, 'Hey, let us back in; let us be with you'." Father said he has served as the spiritual director to a number of people like this because they need to build a relationship with Our Lord and a relationship with the Church. While the RCIA is critical for them to learn the basics of the Faith, "They need a more one-on-one approach, which RCIA cannot give them."

Since leaving the occult, John said he is very isolated. When he left, he lost a lot of family and friends. There are few other people that he has known who, having gone as deep into the occult as he did, were able to get out. From his experiences, there just aren't many people who understand, or are willing to, even priests. Helena said it is critical to have a support system, whether comprised of family or fellow parishioners, who can help keep you on the right path. It may also be necessary to seek out a Christian counselor to help resolve many of the issues which pushed the person into the occult or which are a result of having spent time there.

The conversion of Satanist Riaan Swiegelaar provides a great example of the power of community and the love shared by Christians. With great emotion, Riaan said, "I've never known unconditional love in my whole life and up to today [the day he met the Christian woman], there's only four Christians in my whole life that have shown me what unconditional love is. I want to thank those four people. Words cannot express what you have done for me," he said. While the individual Christian at the center of his conversion, with the pseudonym of Amy, did not understand and said it was just such a simple thing she did, showing him love, he said, "To show someone love is everything – it's not just a simple thing. It's everything. You've shown me the love of Christ. I've seen it in you." He said that Amy loved him at a time when he was a monster, an ugly person, and when he did not respect Christians like her. Catholics, thus, can be ready to reach out not just to those who are struggling to rid themselves of the occult, but to those who have not yet turned away from it. Christ's love can reach out to those in both situations.

As Bl. Bartolo Longo's family watched his decline, they made efforts to convince him to abandon Satanism and the occult and return to the Church. Surprisingly, that simple intervention, combined with two other experiences, made him open to the Faith again. This openness was also prompted by an experience where his deceased father apparently appeared to him. Despite being a Satanist at the time, Bartolo arranged to have a Mass offered for him. A professor, who was a friend of the family, also reached out to him and, in their conversations, told him that the path of the occult would destroy him, sending him either to an insane asylum or to the grave. That conversation, and others with the same professor that would follow, woke him up and he began to distance himself from Satanism completely. With these positive signs occurring, his family and many others, whom the professor had called upon, began praying for him to completely convert.[14]

Sacramentals to Help Former Occultists?

Sacramentals are a powerful gift from God through His Holy Church. They are used by the Church in all her Rites, they fill the Churches themselves, and they sanctify the many aspects of the daily lives, dwellings, and vocations of the faithful. In this age of the world, they are not sufficiently appreciated or understood, but the spreading knowledge of spiritual warfare in the Church is remedying this ignorance and neglect of such powerful aids.

The Rite of Exorcism itself is filled with sacramentals. As Msgr. Rossetti pointed out, "The entire Rite of Exorcism is a powerful sacramental, and we regularly use a crucifix, holy water, exorcised oil, relics of the saints, and other holy objects. Time and again, we witness the effect that these instruments of God's holiness have over the demons."[15] He added an important detail, saying, "When [a demon is] manifesting, the demons may complain that these blessed objects burn them." Here, he is referring to St. Benedict medals placed in the hands of the possessed at the beginning of the session.[16]

For former occultists, sacramentals can prove to be of great benefit. Former occultists long for ritual and the use of sacred objects in worship. The Church supplies an abundance of sanctified elements, many of which resemble the counterfeit ritual elements used in the occult. As a result, former occultists are naturally drawn to these sacramentals. This is a great good and can assist them in

---

[14] Mary's Dowry, Bl. Bartolo Longo documentary, YouTube
[15] Rossetti, *Diary,* 277-278.
[16] Ibid 77

developing a deep Catholic spiritual life. When I asked Adelaide about sacramentals, she said, "Yes, I very much believe in the power of sacramentals." As soon as she learned about them after her conversion, she was drawn to them. She burns incense when she prays, carries holy water in her purse, and uses blessed salt in her food.

There are certain concerns that need to be addressed, though, to prevent former occultists from using sacramentals with a "magical mentality" that might linger from their previous life. Fr. Blaise addressed many aspects of this question, including whether it would be possible or prudent to give a *practicing* occultist, especially someone who makes use of trinkets or talismans or altars, a sacramental or blessed item from the Church, such as a blessed medal, holy water, or blessed candle. Fr. Blaise, expressing hesitation, emphasized that the occultist would need to first get rid of all occult and magical items. Everything related to the occult would need to be expunged and the house would need to be blessed. At that point, of course, the entry of sacramentals into the home would not be a worrisome thing.

The question remains, Fr. Blaise added: "Is it prudent or helpful to give a sacramental item to an occultist knowing that it might end up on their altar?" Questions then come to mind, such as, "Would it not be a 'battle of the G/gods' at that moment?" We have seen historically that the power of a blessed medal can effectively reach those who are not truly open to it, as in the case of the Miraculous Medal. That famous case, of Alphonse Ratisbonne, a Freemason and atheist of Jewish descent, involved an individual who was at least slightly open, though reluctantly, to the idea and "tested out" the promises of the sacred Medal. Similarly, then, it might not be a bad thing to give a practicing occultist a blessed medal, so long as it is accompanied by some essential catechesis. If they are even slightly open to the promises of the sacramental, that could be the door by which salvation comes to them eventually.[17] They will not fully be healed, of course, until they have left behind the evils of their past dealings with the occult and entered the Church.

---

[17] We should also remember the warning, from the stories in Chapter 12, that some occultists will defile sacramentals if they acquire them.

When considering giving sacramentals to current or even former occultists who have entered the Church, Fr. Alphonsus warned that a true faith must be present first in order to avoid a magical or superstitious mentality that could easily emerge. "They might use them as just another source of power, as a superstition or magic, and not as a gift received from the Lord, of His love," he said. Fr. Alphonsus has even seen poorly catechized Catholics use them in a very superstitious way. I said to him, summarizing his thoughts, that they need to go through a time of deepening their faith first. "Exactly," he replied, "so they can tell the difference between a sacramental and a good luck charm."

Sacramentals rely on the action of Our Lord to impart a grace through their use. A proper use of these items entails humbly allowing Our Lord to make the decision of how and whether He will give a grace to us through their use; the sacramentals do not function by a power that naturally resides within them, but by the action of God through the item which accompanies the one who uses it with true faith and surrender to Him. A magical mentality would treat the sacramental item as if it contained a power that could be accessed by the one who used it regardless of that person's disposition toward God. Sacramentals are aids to the faithful not mystical trinkets possessing a magical energy.

Brotherly Love for Souls

Pope Pius XII said that the "infinite treasure of graces" which our Savior merited for His Church was not willed by Him to be distributed to us all at once. "The greater or lesser abundance [of these graces] will depend in no small part on our own good works, which draw down on the souls of men a rain of heavenly gifts freely bestowed by God."[18] These heavenly gifts "will surely flow more abundantly" if we participate deeply in the life of prayer as taught and provided through the Church. Our fervent prayers, in particular by a frequent participation in the Eucharistic Sacrifice, and our relief of the "distress of the needy and of the sick by works of Christian charity," are some of the means to fulfill this. Even more will this be brought about if, Pope Pius XII continues, "We also set our hearts

---

[18] MCC #106

on the good things of eternity rather than on the passing things of this world; if we restrain this mortal body by voluntary mortification, denying it what is forbidden, and by forcing it to do what is hard and distasteful; and finally, if we humbly accept as from God's hands the burdens and sorrows of this present life."[19] By these, as St. Paul teaches, "we shall fill up those things that are wanting of the sufferings of Christ in our flesh for His Body, which is the Church,"[20] meriting, in Christ, for those who are in need, the graces necessary to obtain their salvation.

---

[19] MCC #106
[20] MCC #106, Col. 1:24

Chapter Twenty

The Church Fulfills What Occultists Truly Desire

"Upon this Rock I will build My Church, and the gates of Hell shall not prevail against it."[1] These are the words of Our Lord to describe the power and authority which His Holy Church will bring and wield in our world. Founded on St. Peter, to whom Our Lord gave the "keys of the Kingdom of Heaven,"[2] Our Lord Jesus Christ endowed the Church with the supernatural power necessary to continue His own work of ransacking the Kingdom of Satan.[3] Not only does the Church have the power to tear down the structures of evil which the fallen angels had brought about on this earth, but she possesses supernatural gifts which she presents to all the world in order to draw them out of darkness and into the light of faith. It is this draw and this beauty which occultists are seeing in the Church when the Church is allowed to shine in all the glory and power that God intended. The infinite riches and blessings and wisdom of God are within the Church whose mission it is to make them flow freely into all the world. When occultists, like all fallen men, begin to catch a glimpse of this divine Light shining through the Church, they are irresistibly drawn to her and to Christ Our King who will receive them to Himself as they enter within her embrace.

The Holiness of a Church

Helena said, "When I walked into a Catholic Church, it was a completely different feeling than any protestant church I have ever been in. An overpowering feeling of holiness that made me want to be reverent and to worship. It was a very visceral feeling." One of the "tipping points" in her decision to become Catholic was the fact that,

[1] Matt 16:18 DR
[2] Matt 16:19
[3] Matt 12:29, 1 John 3:8

only when she was in a Catholic Church, and not in any Protestant community sanctuary, she was able to clearly recognize the Real Presence of Our Lord in the Eucharist. I asked her how she would describe this and she said, "Well, it really was more of a sixth sense. I was immediately struck with a feeling of holiness and peace around me when I was in a Catholic Church. It was unlike anything that I had felt in a protestant church, or anywhere else for that matter, and I knew it was the Real Presence."

Lucy was brought into an encounter with the Church as a result of deciding to send her oldest child, who was approaching school age at the time, to a Catholic school. Though she had been brought up in public schools, her husband had been through Catholic schools, so she left it to her husband to educate the kids on religion, since she did not believe in anything herself. What she noticed about the school, even as a non-Christian, was the care and nurture they provided, "quite different from what I had known," she said. The school encouraged the students to help others, something Lucy and her own parents had had a strong inclination toward already. It seemed, though, that the school went beyond the basic care for others that Lucy knew by teaching the students a unique and deep love for others. Without understanding that the morals and values were coming from the teachings of Christ, she found them appealing. Occasionally, after joining the kids for a school Mass, she would stay in the Church and weep; she was not sure why, but she found it all very moving.

When Therese was entering the Church, at the first Mass she attended, before she was confirmed, she said, "I felt like weights were lifted, that I was free. I cried because it was like chains had been lifted and I could breathe again. There was finally space for my mind and soul to expand." After initially dropping Wicca, Adelaide decided she should return to Christianity. The Church appealed to her more than Protestantism did, in part because of her father, who had already returned to the Church, and also because the "smells and bells" were attractive on a spiritual level.

The Church Reaches Out

After Mass one Sunday, Timothy and his wife spoke to the pastor. Timothy's wife was now very engaged in the process of returning to the Faith. The priest asked Timothy if he would be open to learning more about the Church as his wife worked on coming back to the Sacraments. He told the priest, yes, he would. Then the priest asked him if he would be willing to raise the kids Catholic, to which he also replied, "Yes." Then the priest said to him, "Mothers tell the kids what they believe and fathers show them." It was at this moment, in his wife's mind, that she knew he would convert. This was only the beginning of the priest's support for his journey. From there, he started going to Mass and realized he needed to do that every Sunday, as well as become active with the kids in learning the Faith.

The teachings in the Twelve Step program that Timothy had so enjoyed for many years ultimately, he realized, brought no benefits to his family. Protestantism, with its deep focus on Sacred Scripture yet its inability to interpret it, was also lacking so much. In the Church, with her thousands of years of focus on Scripture, he found real moral guidance. It was the clear, specific, and long-standing moral teaching that drew him into the Church. This clarity was exactly what he was looking for.

Having not been raised Christian, Alex Frank was first exposed to Christians while in the Army. From his observations of them, he said, "Christians seemed to have a natural way of doing" what he had spent so much time researching and trying to learn from personal growth gurus. This was very attractive and planted many seeds that later led to his conversion.

Drawn to the Church by Study, Mary, and the Eucharist

What instigated Philomena's journey back to the Church was a Christmas Eve service at her husband's non-denominational community where the speaker gravely de-emphasized Mary. This hit her hard and did not make sense to her. As a result of always having a sense of Mary's presence in her life, when the Protestants demoted her like that, it stung and became a big problem. So, she told her husband she needed to take a break from attending that Protestant community for a while. Then, she did a deep dive into the matter. "I want to worship as apostolically as possible, though I don't know what that looks like," she said. She had grown tired of the "song and dance" worship style of the Protestant community she was a part of at that point.

Thankfully, Philomena's husband supported her intellectual endeavor, though he was vocally convinced that she would eventually realize *he* was correct in *his* beliefs. She began with all the major Protestant teachers and worked backwards, eventually researching the *Didache*, the "Teaching of the Twelve," which is a first century document believed to have been written by the Apostles or their close collaborators. The obvious Catholic nature of the *Didache* was unnerving because she now had to admit she was wrong to practice Protestantism. After reading the *Didache*, her Kindle app began to suggest all the great ancient and modern Catholic writers and theologians and "everything began to click into place," she said. She said she was making notes in her Protestant KJV Bible and saw the Truth of the Catholic Faith all throughout it. Once she worked her way through John Chapter 6 and was clearly convinced about the Eucharist, she told her husband, "I have to become Catholic." This stirred a division between them which they both detected contained a demonic quality. As she entered the Church, various diabolical attacks tried to slow her down, but she pushed through. Her husband, in an effort to prove her wrong, studied John Chapter 6 as well, and eventually realized for himself that the Catholic Church was indeed the true Church. He converted a year later.

It was Helena's daughter's request for Baptism, having entered a Protestant school and hearing all the kids talking about it, that set her on the intellectual path toward the Church. Seeing her daughter's desire as a reasonable request, Helena began considering how to proceed since she was still not comfortable with Presbyterianism. As a result, she decided to do a lot of research on Christianity. After a year of study, "I became more and more convinced that the Catholic Church was the original Church started by Jesus Christ. And if I had come to believe that, it didn't make any sense for her to be baptized as anything but a Catholic." Her non-practicing Catholic husband was fine with it – surprised but fine. "At this point," she said, "I began to be drawn to the Church myself."

Surrendering and Seeing the Power

As Gabriel was converting, he began to see clearly both the inadequacy of the New Age and the real power of Christ. "You try to do all this to heal yourself but nothing is changing," he said. It felt like something was holding him down. "I was desperately trying to get to this point where I felt whole and complete inside," he added. This did not happen until he accepted Christ and invited Him into his life. When he did that, everything felt different. "The day I did that, all of a sudden, my house felt clear, my whole being felt clear, things just felt different. I just thought that I was crazy because I was doing all this New Age nonsense, thinking that it's going to help me. You're doing it but you never really feel like you're being helped at all," he explained.

As a result of watching a video about the Warrens, and other factors, Gabriel quickly began to move in the direction of the Church which, he said, was drawing him in through its history, its great traditions, and all that richness. After speaking to some Catholic friends, they invited him to their parish and told him about the RCIA process and some well-educated parishioners who could help guide him. He entered the RCIA soon after and never looked back.

At one point in Helena's research on Catholicism, it was October and, having already learned that this month is dedicated to the Holy Rosary, "I decided," she said, "that I would pray it every day for the month of October and see what happened. There was a tremendous difference in my thoughts and emotions. The peace I felt and the changes in me helped to solidify my decision to become Catholic."

The Traditional Latin Mass

In my conversations with former occultists, the Traditional Latin Mass loomed large. Every person with whom I spoke expressed to me that the Traditional Latin Mass had a strong pull, had a huge impact on them, and has the potential to be a powerful cure and antidote for the occult. The priests and exorcists with whom I spoke agreed about this power of the Traditional Liturgy and sacramentals. They either had personal experiences that demonstrated it or they saw that the logic by which former occultists explained its importance made perfect sense to them, given what they themselves understand about the nature and structure of the Traditional Liturgy, especially when compared to that of the modern version.

Helena, for example, when she was becoming Catholic, said there was no question for her whether the Traditional Latin Mass or the modern Mass was more attractive. From the very beginning, she has been completely drawn to the Traditional Latin Mass. When I asked her which one appealed to her more, her immediate answer was emphatically, "Traditional, traditional, and traditional!" Similarly, Adelaide told me that the Traditional Latin Mass had a significantly greater appeal to her than the modern Mass, and she completely agreed that making the Traditional Latin Mass widely available would greatly aid those fleeing the occult. Agreeing with another former occultist, she said she believed she never would have gone into the occult in the first place if she had been brought up with the Traditional Latin Mass and the traditional sacramentals.

Reasons for the Appeal of Tradition

The great philosopher Josef Pieper, in his book *An Anthology*, when speaking about the importance and power of the Catholic Mass, offered a helpful image. He said, "What happens in the liturgical celebration of the Eucharist is something for which *all religions of mankind have expressed longing*, dimly sensed was coming, and as a rule even prefigured – the physical presence of the divine Logos made man, in the presence of his sacrificial death, in the midst of the congregation celebrating the mysteries."[4] Andrew wholeheartedly agrees with this image, having come to see that the most important prayer is the Traditional Latin Mass. "This is what I was looking for," he said, "not just mystery, which a reverent modern Mass could offer, but ritual, mystery, and ceremony. This," he added, "is what I wanted in my life and what I looked for in the occult first, not realizing it was in the Traditional Latin Mass."

When commenting on the power of the Traditional Mass, when Andrew first experienced it, he added a very important insight, shared by many other former occultists, regarding what the Mass meant in relation to his occult interests and practices. He said, "I

---

[4] As quoted in Ermatinger, *The Trouble with Magic*, 110. *Emphasis* mine.

knew that all the magickal ceremonies and rituals I had ever performed myself, or participated in, were merely a shadow of a shadow of what was happening in front of me [at the Traditional Latin Mass]. I had the tangible feeling that this was precisely what my soul had been seeking the entire time, and I never even knew it existed at all. It was very emotional and overwhelming."

Since Andrew was already acclimated to the ceremonial aspects of religion, when he attended this Mass, he immediately noticed that they were doing the same kinds of things that he had been doing for years. The smells of incense, the vestments, the priest facing toward God instead of toward the people, and the silent Latin prayers, all struck him as familiar and enticing. With a good bit of Catholic knowledge already in his mind from some of his internet explorations in recent months, he became aware this was indeed a very powerful ritual, especially at the moment of the elevation of the Host. As he said, "I knew, absolutely, that something *very* powerful was happening at that altar." When he saw the priest elevate the Host, as Andrew explained, he knew "*This* is the center of everything we are doing. I noticed all these things that I was familiar with: the use of incense and vestments and chanting, specifically in a dead language, and these [chant] tones, and everybody is doing these postures, bowing during the Gloria and kneeling during the Credo – I started to think, 'Everything I have been doing is pretty much just a *rip-off* of this'." He explained that it was like the occult was the generic, vastly inferior, and even poisonous version of a famous name brand product. He had been eating the unsatisfying and poisonous generic version for a long time, all the while desiring the extraordinary name brand product that he did not even know existed.

"From my personal experience, and from my observations of others who are still in that life," Andrew added, "a large part of what they are seeking is ceremonial beauty and mystery. The Tridentine Mass made me immediately realize what it is I really was seeking all those years."

Adelaide agreed. She said she realized that, in her embrace of rituals with music and incense and other things the Church also used, she was truly desiring the Faith but, as she said, "I was just focused on the wrong things." As a result, the presence of so much beautiful and sacred ritual in the Church's traditional liturgy made it easier for her to move from the occult to Catholicism.

The power of the ancient traditions of our Faith pulled Adelaide deeper into the Church and into a more complete conversion. Shortly after entering the Church through the very modern parish she first attended, Adelaide noticed someone she knew receive Holy Communion kneeling and on the tongue, which no one else in the parish was doing. She had never seen this before but thought, "Well, if it really is Jesus, as the RCIA class taught, why wouldn't you?" This really got her thinking. When the priest at the same parish later refused to bless her son or help him after his exposure to a Ouija board, what went through her mind, she said, was, "This is not the real thing. I am not getting the real thing. I need *movie* Catholics. I need 'movie Catholicism': priests wearing cassocks, Gregorian chant, confessionals, and somebody that knows how to wield a Crucifix! I need movie Catholicism. What I was not able to articulate yet was, 'We're gonna need an exorcism and these people can't do it'."

John pointed out something very interesting which resonates with Adelaide's longing for "movie Catholicism." "When you see the Mass depicted in movies," John said, "it is always the Traditional Latin Mass, not the modern Mass." There is a reason for this, he explained. The modern Mass does not have the same sense of order and uniformity in its nature as the Traditional Latin Mass does. There are many examples for this. In a given city, for instance, he said, there are a wide variety of different modern Mass experiences, all within the allowance of the rules of the modern reformed Rite. In one parish, it will be very traditional; in another, you will have a Church structured "in the round"; in another, it will be very politically motivated; in another, it will be very modern and "happy clappy." Some will hold hands, some won't; some have Communion rails, some don't; some have altar *girls*, some don't; some have Gregorian chant, some have guitars and drums. The Traditional Latin Mass, on the contrary, is very structured, intentionally crafted in that way by centuries and millennia of Christian worship and devotion. If you go to a Traditional Latin Mass in one part of the city, it will be the exact same as a Traditional Latin Mass in another part of the city, and the exact same as a Traditional Latin Mass in another part of the country and even the world. We all desire this structured and reliable presentation of the mystery of God's love for mankind and the Church's traditions provide it.

Priests Comment on the Traditional Liturgy and Sacramentals

Fr. Ambrose said it makes perfect sense to him that former occultists would be attracted to the Traditional Latin Mass. "Those in the occult are dealing with the supernatural and the preternatural. Now they are looking for the transcendent on the *good* side. The mystery is much more evident in the Traditional Latin Mass than the Novus Ordo. It is easier to enter into the fullness of the mystery at the Traditional Latin Mass. There is also the risk that a Novus Ordo Mass is easy to find presented in an irreverent manner, and it is repulsive. Ex-occultists," he added, "are looking for the rituals more deeply, not cut back to near nothing." Fr. Sebastian agreed. He sees this mysterious appeal and power in the Latin language itself. "There is something about Latin that is more powerful on a spiritual level," he said, adding, "The same thing is true for the Traditional Latin Mass."

Fr. Alphonsus said, "Especially with the Rite of Exorcism, exorcists across the board state that prayers prayed in Latin [from the traditional Roman Ritual] have more force against the demonic." Msgr. Rossetti agreed, saying, "The 1614 Rite of Exorcism in Latin remains the general favorite of exorcists."[5] Fr. Alphonsus added, "A lot of the traditional prayers and exorcisms have such a powerful punch to them. Formerly possessed people have also talked about how the Latin prayers were powerful. Objects blessed in the traditional rites, when they are used with possessed people, also have a great power." Circling back to the issues we see today, which raise many red flags about just who is orchestrating the internal attack on the Church which is, unfortunately, manifesting worldwide, Fr. Alphonsus said, "Then you look at the weakness of the 'Book of Blessings,'[6] how it doesn't really bless the object, but only those who

---

[5] Rossetti, *Diary*, 106.
[6] The "Book of Blessings" is the modern version of the traditional Roman Ritual. The prayers are very different in their style and in the force of command that they possess. Every priest I have spoken to speaks dismissively of the Book of Blessings, favoring instead, without hesitation, the traditional Roman Ritual.

use the object. Exorcisms are *gone* from the Book of Blessings. There is definitely something going on here."[7]

Former occultists notice the help of these traditional blessings. In the process of moving multiple times to escape the mysterious source of her spiritual issues, Adelaide and her family landed at a parish that offered the Traditional Latin Mass. After meeting the pastor, and explaining her situation, he assigned her a new, and very traditional, priest to assist her and her family. The young priest started to teach her and her family a great many things they did not know about the Faith and the spiritual issues they were dealing with. Further, these priests knew how to deal with the occult and the diabolical, unlike the previous priest she consulted. Adelaide, for instance, still had a chest with all her witchcraft items in it and these traditional priests knew what to do with it. "The priests came in with gloves on and took the stuff out," she said. "With the Traditional Latin Mass and the real learning of the Faith, the true fighting really began at this point."

Helena spoke about her lingering attachment to the emphasis which her occult practices placed on nature. She said the traditional Catholic Faith provides a remedy for, and a fulfillment of, this attraction to the beauty of nature. "Studying Catholicism," she said, "especially traditional Catholicism, showed me how it does some of the same things. Being a true steward of the earth, old prayers for harvest, the ember days, etc., helped me understand that there is a way to honor the beauties that God has given us, without nature itself becoming a god." These traditions include the blessing of items which many occultists are drawn to, such as water, candles, incense, salt, and medals. Further, the Church supplies blessings for just about everything we use in our lives, such as eggs, bread, oil, cheese, beer, wells, vines, crops, seeds, farms, animals, and even bees.

Advice to Occultists

To those who are just now leaving the occult, Lucy said, "Trust in the power of the Name of Jesus, His desire to save you from this

[7] In the traditional Roman Ritual, many of the numerous sacramental blessings contain an exorcism of the item that is receiving the blessing. This has vanished in the reformed "Book of Blessings" published in 1988.

darkness, His ability to bring healing and to liberate you from diabolical entanglements. Yes, you may 'lose' a lot of what you currently have and enjoy by cutting ties with the Kingdom of Satan and binding yourself to Christ, but you will gain immeasurably more and better in this life and, particularly, in the next." She added, "The losses are worth it. Having a relationship with Jesus is beyond any 'wonderful life' you could ever imagine."

Helena said that, since the occult impacts the person on more levels that just the state of their soul, breaking free from the occult successfully, and sustaining it, will also require work on many levels. A former occultist needs a strong prayer life with regular reception of the Sacraments. "I think many are attracted to the more mystical aspects of the occult," she said. "This is tied into our deep desire for worship and the mysteries of God. The Catholic Faith has an incredible well to pull from; there are so many beautiful traditions and teachings that many are not aware of. I think people need to be aware of the beauty of the Church and focus on the Real Presence."

To this collection of advice, John added, "Go to Mass as much as possible. Stay in a state of grace. Don't be intimidated by the temptations and retaliations you experience." Andrew said that the Holy Rosary, the Chaplet of St. Michael, the consecration to St. Michael, and the Scapular of St. Michael have all been of great benefit to him. Andrew, for whom the occult entailed a great deal of contemplation, meditation, and prayer, found that he was able to remove the demonic and pagan concepts and practices and integrate the Catholic concepts and practices. Everything, of course, is substantially different and actually efficacious as a Catholic. In addition, he said that, with prayer and spiritual direction, the surrender to Divine Providence, which his focus on *self-worship* for many years had made very difficult, has gotten easier.

Christianity Stands out as the Sweet Gift of God

When Therese converted, she said that everything she had ever wanted, and was looking for her entire life in the occult, was right here in the Catholic Church the whole time. John agreed, saying, "Everything I was looking for in the occult, and had longed for my whole life, was waiting for me in the Catholic Church." In the Church, John saw the beauty and order that God brings to everything. "He causes uniformity and structure," he said, "where nothing is boring and all has beauty." Having descended into dark occult rituals, one thing stood out to him: how "peaceful and painless the rituals of the Church are, in comparison to these occult groups." The beliefs of the Church are also inspiring, such as the teaching that we go to Heaven and that the body will come later to be reunited with the soul. "This teaching," he pointed out, "is foreign to other religions."

Andrew observed that God's activity in creation and redemption shows that the Christian God is the most intimate of all deities, making and saving the world for all of us, and for each individual one of us. "We are *cosmically* small," he said, "but God created it this way so we could come to know Him and then be exalted, made *large,* in His eyes." Catholics are very privileged, in a good way, he added, with the abundance of Sacred Tradition and Magisterial guidance to understand Sacred Scripture.

The intimacy of the Christian God was also felt by Therese through the tradition of taking a new name at her Confirmation. Though, at her liberal Novus Ordo parish, she was discouraged from taking the name of a Saint at her Confirmation, she decided to do so anyway. This new name, for her, fulfilled the role it did also for the early Christians, who often took a new name at Baptism: it represents the beginning of a whole new life founded on the grace of Jesus Christ which brought her into the family of God. She uses this name all the time now and experiences a great consolation every time she sees it. It is a reminder for her that everything is a gift from God.[8]

As with other occultists, Christopher loves hearing stories with a theme of redemption in them. "Redemption stories," he said, "are like catnip. If someone says, 'Hey! We're gonna tell a redemption story,' I am there!" In the movie *For Greater Glory*, for example, he said, "I know it was mainly about the boy who became a Saint, but I was there for the general and his redemption.[9] I was glued to his

---

[8] This is something that former occultists should be encouraged to consider doing, for they are truly leaving behind an old life and embracing a new one.

[9] This movie focused a lot on St. José Sánchez del Río, the fourteen-year-old martyr of the Mexican Cristero War. However, it also featured the journey of faith of the general who led an army of Cristeros. For Christopher, the story of this man's redemption had the most appeal.

story. When he cried, I cried." Of course, it is not just this story, Christopher said, but the whole category of redemption that grabs his soul. "Absolutely, the redemption stories," he added, explaining with great excitement how satisfying they are, "I will cross the Atlantic with only my *hands and feet* to get me there – it's not even *funny!*" In response to that, in our conversation, I replied, "I have heard that from lots of people – it is THE BEST story: redemption." He responded, "Especially for anyone coming out of something like the occult, you absolutely see it – it is very visceral."

Conclusion

While the spiritual situation today is, in many ways, quite dire, there is still hope. The same hope that entered our world at the Annunciation, which manifested to the nations at the Nativity, and which was presented in the saving Truth of the Gospel in the Life, Death, and Resurrection of Our Lord Jesus Christ, is the hope that still abides in our world today. The Most Blessed Trinity, the God of love and grace, while permitting our age to be rife with sin, lawlessness, tyranny, death, faithlessness, and the rise of the occult, has not abandoned us. This is not the first time our world has suffered from the consequences of sin. Holy Mother Church, the Bride of Christ, continues to comfort us with the treasury of grace entrusted to her by Christ through the Apostles. From there, a lot of the work, with the help of God, rests on us. Do we pull from this treasury by the means revealed to us by God through His Holy Church? Do we trust Our Lord and turn to Him every day? Do we seek to impart the Truth to our neighbors that they too might find salvation in Christ?

When the reign of sin embraces the world, or one nation in particular, the citizens and individuals who confront this great burden of temptation are given a choice: turn to God or turn away from Him. God is always ready to intervene in our lives and in the specific concrete situations in which we face grave or minor, moral or spiritual dilemmas. He is always calling out to us, beckoning us, not from some far-off mountain top from which His voice only faintly reaches our ears: He calls to us from Heaven, with the glory of eternal life promised in His words; He calls to us through the Church, offering the means of acquiring the graces we need to be strong, joyful, and holy in this life; He calls to us in the quiet whisper in our souls, telling us of His love, and seeking to show us the Way

347

to the Father. He is always at our side, and we can take His sacred Hand in ours whenever we desire.

In this age, to hear His Voice we must listen and discern; the voice of the Shepherd is intentionally obscured by the hackles of the wolves, whose viciousness is on full display for those who have eyes to see and ears to hear. We must discern the voice of the Shepherd not just to ensure the salvation of our own souls, but also the souls of those who fall into the occult, who are becoming legion today. Occultists have either run out of, or away from, the sheepfold of Christ, lured by the flashy promises of the beasts, not knowing that the flashes and glimmers they beheld were merely the points of the fangs of their new masters. But this allure can be shattered. The coming of Christ as a man, Origen said, stole away the power which the demons had over those who dabbled in the dark arts: "the evil spirits…became feeble, and lost their strength, the falsity of their sorcery being manifested, and their power broken."[1] Like the Magi, who were enticed by a distant and supernatural Light to seek out Christ whom they did not yet know, and who were gifted, by their new faith in Him, with the comforting guidance of an angel, occultists today can meet Him as well and be set free from their blindness.

We who are coming to see the horror of the present situation must pray for these occultists. Many are simply seeking meaning in their lives, spiritual adventures, the ability to help others, an experience of the sacred and supernatural, and a welcoming spiritual home. However, they have been taken into Satan's counterfeit religion, seduced by the illusion of the sacred within the disordered rituals of the occult. Christians must show the world the beauty of the true Sacred Rites and rituals of the One, Holy, Catholic, and Apostolic Church, those that draw us near to Him who is always drawing near to us through His Son, Our Lord Jesus Christ. By this, those who are suffering beneath the lies of the occult will see the true Light shining from faithful Christians and may, God willing, reach out to them and find true peace.

---

[1] Origen, *Contra Celsum*, Book I, Ch. 60.

Conclusion

O Lord Jesus Christ,
reach out, we beseech Thee,
with Thine Eternal Love and Mercy,
through the tenderness of Thy Most Sacred Heart,
willingly pierced for our salvation,
and let Thy Precious Blood pour out
onto those unworthy to receive it,
us, Thine ungrateful children,
and the poor souls who have fallen for the Enemy's lies and entered
his false religion.
Let Thy voice, which ever resounds on the earth,
pierce the suffocating shadows of this valley of tears.
Let Thy praises, from Thy Holy Church,
both on earth and in Heaven,
echo throughout all the lands,
that those who have strayed from Thee,
or who have never known Thee,
or who have embraced the idolatry of false gods and self-worship,
may behold the Truth and the Beauty of Thy Holy Name
and, set free from their captivity in sin,
may join us in praising Thee in the company of the angels and the
saints.
Amen.

Afterword

The intent behind writing this book was to provide insight and understanding on the devastating plague of the occult. Many who read this book have friends or family who are either becoming curious about the occult or have already become trapped in its web. Further, some who read this book may be reminded that they themselves, at some point in the past, dabbled in some form of occult practice, but have never spiritually resolved this issue. Additionally, some readers may only now understand that certain spiritual practices they have adopted are actually occultic and spiritually dangerous.

For those in these situations, it is import to remember:
-   Occult involvement is a grave matter and will constitute a mortal sin if done willingly and with knowledge of its gravity.
-   The Sacrament of Confession is the first step in breaking free of diabolical influences that may have come from occult practices. After this, a life of prayer, centered on the Eucharist and Our Lady's intercession, will sustain the soul in grace.
-   Be sure to confess the specific occult practices in which you were involved so the priest can counsel you appropriately.
-   Renounce, in prayer, all occult practices and destroy (see Ch. 18) any occult items you may have in your possession.
-   Do not be discouraged if your priest is not knowledgeable about these matters. Ask around and see if there is a priest who knows how to address your concerns.
-   Non-Catholics who desire to enter the Church should look for a Church in their area and make an appointment to speak to a priest. Since not all priests are knowledgeable on this issue, do not give up if you experience anything discouraging in the beginning. Pray to Our Lord and Our Lady to guide you.

References

Amorth, Fr. Gabriele. *An Exorcist Explains the Demonic,* Manchester: Sophia Institute Press, 2016.

Damian, St. Peter. *Book of Gomorrah: An Eleventh Century Treatise Against Clerical Homosexual Practices,* Pierre J. Payer, trans. Waterloo, Ont., Wilfrid Laurier University Press, 1982.

De Montfort, St. Louis. *True Devotion to the Blessed Virgin Mary.* New York: Montfort Publications, 1996.

De Sales, St. Francis. *Introduction to the Devout Life.* CCEL. ccel.org/ccel/desales/devout_life.pdf

Ermatinger, Fr. Cliff. *The Trouble with Magic.* Padre Pio Press, 2021.

Fortea, Fr. Jose Antonio. *Interview with an Exorcist.* Ascension Press, West Chester, 2006.

Gallagher, Dr. Richard. *Demonic Foes.* New York: Harper One, 2020.

Kalvelage FI, Br. Francis Mary. *Kolbe: Saint of the Immaculata.* Ignatius Press, 2014.

Liguori, St. Alphonsus. *Preparation for Death.* Ascetical Works, Vol. I, Grimm Ed., Brooklyn: Redemptorist Fathers, 1926.

Liguori, St. Alphonsus. *The True Spouse of Christ.* Ascetical Works, Vol. X, Grimm Ed., New York: Benziger Brothers, 1888. Accessed via https://archive.org.

Palilla, Fr. Benigno, *Rescued from Satan*, Fr. Cliff Ermatinger trans. Padre Pio Press, 2018.

Pratt, Sr. Antoinette Marie, A.M. *The Attitude of the Catholic Church Towards Witchcraft and the Allied Practices of Sorcery and Magic.* Washington: National Capital Press, 1915.

Rossetti, Fr. Stephen. *Diary of an American Exorcist,* Manchester: Sophia Institute Press, 2021.

Sarah, Robert Cardinal. *The Day is Now Far Spent.* San Francisco: Ignatius Press, 2019.

Documentaries and Features

BBC News. "The Three Witches of Instagram – BBC News." *YoutTube,* 10 February 2019, youtube.com/watch?v=XuX6yxOP7xY

CBNNews.com, July 6, 2022, "A Warlock Got Him Hooked on the Occult - Then He Was Hounded by Demons Until the Power of Jesus Set Him Free."

CheminNeuf NetforGod. "A Guru or Jesus Father Joseph-Marie Verlinde." *YouTube,* 20 June 2017, youtube.com/watch?v=kHoKWxp8Imo

Dr. Taylor Marshall. "Why are Exorcisms Taking Much Longer Today? | Dr Taylor Marshall and Fr Chad Ripperger." *YouTube,* 5 August 2022, youtube.com/watch?v=covnJgIK5Tc

EWTN. "EWTN on Location - 2019-10-26 - Allure and Truth About Wicca and Witchcraft (The)." *YouTube,* 26 October 2019, youtube.com/watch?v=FCf7JJ4w0dc

Jesus 911. "06 May 2020 The Most Evil Woman in the World." *YouTube,* 7 May 2020, youtube.com/watch?v=krLGDzFdbR4

Larson video #1 – Occult Demon Cassette. "The First Family of Satanism [VHS]." *YouTube*, 24 June 2014. youtube.com/watch?v=uRf-FyDfRY0

Larson video #2 – Satania. "Showdown with Satanism - Bob Larson Interviews Zeena Lavey and Nikolas Schreck." *YouTube*, 14 March 2020. youtube.com/watch?v=jfk9NZ5pgRw

Marysdowry. "Bartolo Longo, NEW FULL FILM, biography, power of the Rosary, Mary's Dowry Productions." *YouTube*, 30 May 2018, youtube.com/watch?v=3OQLRndbHIM (see also youtube.com/watch?v=NdR4bn2Bl-E)

Riaan Swiegelaar video #1, Facebook, July 4th, 2022. Accessed July 20, 2021. Video was taken down in the months following this research. Similar video here: youtube.com/watch?v=3g81MbTEw_Q&t=1630s

Saint Joseph Studios. ""Former Satanist Becomes Catholic", Betty Brennan." *YouTube*, 10 April 2013. youtube.com/watch?v=-hudedR2iPM

TFP Student Action. "Satanic Temple Event Hits Big Wall of Prayer." *YouTube*, 20 February 2022, youtube.com/watch?v=9R1vg5y4HDg

7NEWS Spotlight. "'SATANISTS NEXT DOOR' | Our cameras capture a secret ritual as a 'curse' is cast | 7NEWS Documentary." *YouTube*, 27 February 2021. youtube.com/watch?v=Wqa5F6vWWXM

Additional Resources

Summa Theologiae of St. Thomas
http://www.newadvent.org/summa/index.html

Catena Aurea and Gospel Commentaries of St. Thomas
https://aquinas.cc

About the Author

Charles D. Fraune is the founding Theology teacher of Christ the King Catholic High School in Huntersville, NC and was a Theology teacher there for ten years. He left teaching on the high school level to found the *Slaying Dragons Apostolate* and *Slaying Dragons Press*, as a result of the response to his best-selling spiritual warfare book, *Slaying Dragons: What Exorcists See & What We Should Know*. This Apostolate is dedicated to sharing the wisdom of spiritual warfare from the counsel of modern public exorcists in the context of the Church's two-thousand-year history of authoritative teaching on the subject.

In addition to the above, he has taught nearly every grade level, from second grade to adult, including on the college and diocesan level. He spent three semesters in seminary with the Diocese of Raleigh at St. Charles Borromeo Seminary in Pennsylvania. This completed a nine-year discernment of the priesthood and religious life after which he discerned that Our Lord was not calling him to the priesthood. He has a Master of Arts in Theology from the Christendom College Graduate School, as well as an Advanced Apostolic Catechetical Diploma. His enjoyment of writing began over twenty years ago and culminated in his first completed book, *Come Away By Yourselves*, a guide to prayer for busy Catholics. He has also written a spiritual warfare manual for youth and their parents, called *Swords and Shadows: Navigating Youth Amidst the Wiles of Satan*, and a companion book to *Slaying Dragons*, which serves as a workbook, study guide, and spiritual warfare manual, called *Slaying Dragons – Prepare for Battle: Applying the Wisdom of Exorcists to Your Spiritual Warfare*.

Find him at:
SlayingDragonsPress.com

Slaying Dragons Press

Slaying Dragons Press, founded in 2021, is the fruit of a spiritual work begun in 2016 which sought to find new ways to bring people the joy and beauty of the Catholic Faith. By God's Providence, what began under the name *The Retreat Box* has grown into *The Slaying Dragons Apostolate* and *Slaying Dragons Press.*

This work is a grassroots apostolate which thrives on support and endorsements from those who enjoy these books. As a result, fans of the books and supporters of the mission help increase the reach of *Slaying Dragons Press* by telling friends, family, priests, religious, and Bishops about these books.

Please consider supporting this work in any way that you can. While *Slaying Dragons Press* is *not* a non-profit, financial support is always welcome. Please visit SlayingDragonsPress.com for ways to support this apostolate. If you do not have a copy of the other celebrated books we have published, get one today!

*Support this work on **Patreon!**
~patreon.com/**theslayingdragonsapostolate**

***Subscribe to the author's website for discounts and news!**
~SlayingDragonsPress.com/pages/**Subscribe**

Popular Titles

Slaying Dragons: What Exorcists See & What We Should Know
(also in Spanish – *Matando Dragones*)

Slaying Dragons - Prepare for Battle: Applying the Wisdom of Exorcists to Your Spiritual Warfare

Swords and Shadows: Navigating Youth Amidst the Wiles of Satan

Come Away By Yourselves: A Guide to Prayer for Busy Catholics

و